McCall's Best Recipes

1990

Oxmoor House®

Library of Congress Catalog Number: 88-43142
ISBN: 0-8487-1005-3

Manufactured in the United States of America
First printing 1990

Published by arrangement with Oxmoor House, Inc.
Book Division of Southern Progress Corporation
P.O. Box 2463, Birmingham, AL 35201

McCall's
Editor-in-Chief: Anne Mollegen Smith
Executive Editor: Lisel Eisenheimer
Managing Editor: Leslie Smith

Food Editor: Marianne Langan
Senior Associate Food Editor: Mary B. Johnson
Test-Kitchen Supervisor: Holly Sheppard
Associate Food Editors: Pamela Berger, Joanne Borkoski, Lynne Giviskos, Donna Meadow, Karen Sethre White
Assistant Food Editors: Carmen McLeod, Mennie Nelson
Executive-Dining Room Chef: Melva Victorino
Photographer: Victor Scocozza

Oxmoor House, Inc.
Executive Editor: Ann H. Harvey
Production Manager: Jerry Higdon
Associate Production Manager: Rick Litton
Art Director: Bob Nance

McCall's Best Recipes 1990

Senior Editor: Olivia Kindig Wells
Copy Editor: Melinda E. West
Editorial Assistant: Leigh Anne Roberts
Senior Designer: Cynthia R. Cooper
Production Assistant: Theresa Beste

Cover: *Antipasto Buffet, page 54.*

Back cover: *(Clockwise from top right) Molded Salmon Mousse, page 196; Perfect Chocolate Cake, page 156; Chicken Fajitas, page 89; Crimson Pears, page 34.*

Contents

McCall's Annual Collection 4

January **6**

Company's Coming Cookbook 12
Quick & Easy: Last-Minute Gifts 19
Hurry-Up One-Dish Dinners 20
Lite Eating: Elegant Duck Dinner 24
Micro-Way: Festive First-Course Soups 26

February **28**

Dessert Lovers' Cookbook 34
Quick & Easy: Sweet Treats for Kids 42
Micro-Way: Chocolate Desserts 44

March **48**

Best Ever Italian Cookbook 54
Quick & Easy: Breads Italian Style 60
Lite Eating: Pizzas With Pizzazz 62
Micro-Way: Pasta Main Dishes 64

April **66**

Home-Style Chicken Cookbook 72
Lite Eating: Perfect Puddings 78
Micro-Way: Tasty Chicken Sandwiches 80

May **82**

30-Minute Menu Cookbook 88
Lite Eating: Pronto Pasta 94
Micro-Way: Quick-As-Can-Be Dinners 96

June **100**

Backyard Barbecue Cookbook 106
Quick & Easy: Breads on the Barbecue . . . 112
Micro-Way: Easy-on-Dad Barbecue 114

July **116**

Fruit Cookbook 122
Lite Eating: Savory Grilled Vegetables 129
Micro-Way: Summer Snacks for Kids 130

August **132**

Summer Salads Cookbook 138
Easy, Extra-Special Birthday Cakes 143
Kid-Pleasing Treats 145
Lite Eating: Summery Desserts 147
Micro-Way: Super-Easy Barbecue 148

September **150**

Best of *McCall's* Cookbook 156
Quick & Easy: Light Chicken 'n' Rice Dishes 164
Lite Eating: Late-Summer Salads 166
Micro-Way: Super Savory Soups 168

October **170**

Great Side Dishes Cookbook 176
Lite Eating: Terrific Halloween Treats 182
Micro-Way: Quick Chicken Suppers 184

November **186**

Thanksgiving Cookbook 192
Easy Party Appetizers 198
Spirited Drinks Without Spirits 199
Deluxe Holiday Desserts 200
Special Breakfast Section:
Weekend Brunch 202
How to Get Kids to Love Breakfast 203
Lite Eating: A Savory Holiday Feast 204
Micro-Way: Festive First Courses 206

December **208**

Old-fashioned Christmas Cookbook 214
Fabulous Fruitcake Finale 221
A World of Christmas Cookies 224
Santa's Dream House 232
Over the River and Through the Woods . . .235
Holiday Centerpieces to Savor 248
Micro-Way: Holiday Party Drinks 250

Cake and Cookie Patterns 252

General Recipe Index 262

Recipe Title Index 270

McCall's
Annual Collection

McCall's *food staff includes (back row, left to right) Melva Victorino, Executive-Dining Room Chef; Pamela Berger, Associate Food Editor; Mary B. Johnson, Senior Associate Food Editor; Lynne Giviskos, Associate Food Editor; Carmen McLeod, Assistant Food Editor; (front, left to right) Donna Meadow, Associate Food Editor; Joanne Borkoski, Associate Food Editor; Marianne Langan, Food Editor; Holly Sheppard, Test-Kitchen Supervisor. Not pictured, Karen Sethre White, Associate Food Editor; Mennie Nelson, Assistant Food Editor.*

Welcome to our second annual edition of recipes from the food pages of *McCall's*. Our staff is deservedly proud of our work and we hope this edition will join the first as a valuable entry to your cookbook collection.

Each year we are impressed by the number of letters we receive from readers. I hope each of you, in turn, has been pleased with our efficient response to your many requests. We welcome hearing from our readers; it gives us insight into your needs and desires and helps us in planning our future stories. We like to think our pages offer something for everyone, using products that are readily available and giving implicit and clear directions in our recipe writing style. We hope that with our help you can recreate the beautiful recipes as we have photographed them.

The presentation of food is important. I have always believed we are a nation that eats with our eyes and that even mistakes in flavoring or less than perfect cooking techniques will often be overlooked when the dish presented is pretty. That's one of the reasons we are so particular in showing as many innovative garnishes as possible.

Our staff is responsible for the development of every recipe on our pages. Each month we select appropriate recipe ideas, and each member of the staff picks the recipes she would like to develop. Next, she researches these recipes, looking for new and unusual flavor combinations as well as easy methods for preparations. She then moves into the kitchen and starts cooking. An average day means tasting between 20 and 25 dishes and giving an objective and critical review of each. (And some of us actually go home and cook for our families.) Each recipe is tested over four times before it is published. And each recipe is rechecked by someone on the staff who did not do the intitial development.

Once we have selected the recipes we like best and have made them taste and look the way we think they should, they are all presented to our management for photography selection. Often this is a difficult decision because each recipe is worthy of a photograph.

The recipes are prepared once again for the photograph. And yes, it is the real food and yours should look just as attractive—if you follow our directions.

As you can tell from our pictures, we like beautiful food placed in appropriate and appetizing environments. Food to me is beautiful, and it deserves careful attention. As a result, each photograph contains ideas for you to apply to your own food presentation.

Our staff works very hard in keeping abreast of the latest trends and procedures in both cooking and eating. We travel as much as possible and read constantly to expose ourselves to many new ideas from all over the world. We then try to adapt these to your life style. We are aware of your many diverse interests in food; we all love desserts—everyone deserves rewards—but we also like casseroles. Because everyone's time is being stretched, you will see many recipes made in shorter time with ease of preparation, but don't be fooled—they are still special enough to be served to your most particular guests.

We hope you are pleased with our efforts and will enjoy reaching for this collection many times in the coming year.

Marianne Langan

Marianne Langan, Food Editor

January

Celebrate the New Year with a party. Whether it's brunch or buffet, dinner or dessert, you're sure to impress your guests with the simply spectacular recipes from this chapter's offerings. The desserts pictured at right are followed by a holiday brunch and a buffet.

Della Robbia Pound Cake

Perfect Chocolate Mousse

Pumpkin-Apricot Chiffon Pie

Bloody Mary Slushes   Eggs in a Cloud

Seafood-Filled Dutch Babies

Champagne-Glazed Canadian Bacon

Omelets on Demand

Warm Apricot-Cheese Strudel

Pepper-Baked Brie   Zippy Cheddar Crisps

Appetizer Ribs With Two Sauces

Chicken Pesto   Warm Cucumber Toss

Pear-Stuffed Roast Pork

Chocolate Temptation Cake

Company's Coming Cookbook

Start the year off right with a fabulous brunch, a festive buffet, or an impressive dessert party.

Della Robbia Pound Cake

(pictured, page 7)

1 cup butter, softened
½ cup shortening
1 package (1 pound) brown sugar
½ cup granulated sugar
5 large eggs
2 teaspoons vanilla extract
3 cups unsifted all-purpose flour
½ teaspoon baking powder
1 cup milk
1 cup chopped pecans
White Icing Glaze (recipe follows)
Dried-Fruit Compote (recipe follows), drained

1. Preheat oven to 350° F. Grease 10-inch tube pan; set aside.

2. In large bowl of electric mixer, at high speed, beat butter with shortening until fluffy. Gradually add sugars, beating until light and fluffy, about 5 minutes. Add eggs, one at a time, beating well after each addition. Mix in vanilla.

3. On sheet of waxed paper, combine flour with baking powder. Add to butter mixture alternately with milk, beginning and ending with flour and beating at medium speed just until blended. Stir in pecans.

4. Pour batter into prepared pan; bake 1 hour and 10 minutes, or until cake tester comes out clean. Cool cake in pan 10 minutes. Invert onto wire rack; cool completely. Top with White Icing Glaze; using photograph as a guide, decorate with Dried-Fruit Compote.

Makes 16 servings.

Page 7: (Clockwise from top) Della Robbia Pound Cake, Perfect Chocolate Mousse, Pumpkin-Apricot Chiffon Pie.

Pages 8 and 9: (Clockwise from top left) Eggs in a Cloud, Seafood-Filled Dutch Babies, Caviar-Crème Fraîche Omelet Filling, Double-Cheese Omelet Filling, Warm Apricot-Cheese Strudel, Champagne-Glazed Canadian Bacon, Omelets on Demand With Chicken-Liver Filling, Bloody Mary Slushes.

Pages 10 and 11: (Clockwise from top) Chocolate Temptation Cake, Pepper-Baked Brie, Zippy Cheddar Crisps, Appetizer Ribs With Two Sauces, Chicken Pesto, Warm Cucumber Toss, Pear-Stuffed Roast Pork.

White Icing Glaze

4 cups confectioners' sugar
⅓ to ½ cup milk

In small bowl, blend sugar with just enough milk to make a spoonable consistency.

Makes 2 cups.

Dried-Fruit Compote

2 cups assorted dried fruit (apricots, raisins, figs, pears, peaches and apple slices)
¼ cup citrus-fruit-peel strips
2 cups cold water
1 cup firmly packed light-brown sugar
1 cup granulated sugar
1½ cups apple cider or apple juice
¼ cup brandy
2 (2-inch) cinnamon sticks
4 whole allspice
2 whole cloves
½ cup cranberries

1. In 3-quart saucepan, combine dried fruit (except apple slices, if using) and peel strips with water. Bring to boiling; simmer, covered, 5 minutes, or until fruit softens. Add apple slices at the last minute. Drain fruit in colander.

2. In same saucepan, combine sugars, cider and brandy. Tie spices in cheesecloth square; add spice bag

to saucepan. Bring to boiling, stirring until sugar dissolves. Return dried fruit and peel strips to saucepan; simmer, covered, stirring occasionally, 10 minutes, or until fruit is almost plump. Add cranberries; cook 5 minutes. Remove and discard spice bag.

3. Ladle fruit and syrup into 1-quart jar. Cover; cool completely. Store mixture in refrigerator at least a week before using to allow flavors to blend.

Makes 1 quart.

Perfect Chocolate Mousse

(pictured, page 7)

4 squares (1 ounce each) unsweetened chocolate
¾ cup sugar
¼ cup water
4 large eggs, separated
2 tablespoons dark rum
1 cup coarsely chopped walnuts
1 cup heavy cream
2 tablespoons sugar
¼ teaspoon vanilla extract
8 chocolate curls

1. In top of double boiler, combine chocolate, ¾ cup sugar and the water. Over hot, not boiling, water, heat, stirring, until chocolate is melted. Stir in egg yolks, one at a time, beating vigorously after each addition.

2. Remove top of double boiler from over water; set aside until cool. Stir in rum.

3. In large bowl of electric mixer, at high speed, beat egg whites until stiff peaks form. With rubber spatula, fold into chocolate mixture just until no white streaks remain. Fold in walnuts. Spoon into 8 glasses, dividing evenly. Refrigerate 3 hours or overnight.

4. Before serving: In small bowl of electric mixer, beat cream with 2 tablespoons sugar and the vanilla until stiff peaks form. Place whipped cream in pastry bag fitted with ½-inch star tip; pipe some cream onto top of each serving of mousse, dividing evenly. Garnish each with a chocolate curl.

Makes 8 servings.

Pumpkin-Apricot Chiffon Pie

(pictured, page 7)

½ can (8-ounce size) almond paste
1 cup vanilla-wafer crumbs
½ cup unsifted all-purpose flour
¼ cup butter or margarine
1 large egg white
2 envelopes unflavored gelatine
⅓ cup apricot-flavored brandy
1 can (6 ounces) apricot nectar
2 cups heavy cream
½ cup granulated sugar
2 large eggs, separated
1 can (1 pound) pumpkin
¼ cup confectioners' sugar

1. Generously grease 9-inch pie plate. In food processor or electric mixer, blend almond paste, wafer crumbs, flour, butter and 1 egg white until smooth. Place dough between 2 sheets of waxed paper; roll to a 12-inch round. Remove top sheet of paper; carefully invert dough over prepared plate. Remove waxed paper; pressing gently, fit dough in plate. Fold edge of crust over ½ inch; decoratively crimp or flute. Place in freezer 10 minutes.

2. In small bowl, sprinkle gelatine over brandy; let stand 1 minute to soften. In medium saucepan, bring nectar, ½ cup cream and ¼ cup granulated sugar to boiling. In small bowl, beat egg yolks with fork. Add 2 tablespoons hot apricot liquid; return to saucepan. Add softened gelatine; simmer, stirring constantly, until gelatine is dissolved, about 1 minute. Remove from heat; stir in pumpkin.

3. Preheat oven to 325°F. Transfer pumpkin mixture to medium bowl; set in large bowl of ice water, stirring every 5 minutes, until mixture mounds slightly and is cooled, about 20 minutes.

4. Meanwhile, bake piecrust until lightly golden, about 20 minutes. Cool on wire rack.

5. In small bowl with electric mixer, beat 2 egg whites until foamy. Gradually beat in remaining ¼ cup granulated sugar, 1 tablespoon at a time, until stiff, moist peaks form. With same beaters, in large bowl, beat remaining 1½ cups cream and the confectioners' sugar until stiff peaks form. Set aside 1 cup whipped cream for garnish.

6. Fold beaten egg whites and remaining whipped cream into pumpkin mixture until no white streaks remain. Spoon into prepared piecrust; refrigerate until firm, 1 hour or overnight. Garnish with reserved whipped cream and, if desired, whole unblanched almonds and an apricot- or orange-peel rose.

Makes 8 servings.

■ Don't fret if an elegant soufflé deflates before you serve it. Simply spoon it into pretty stemmed glasses and top with sauce or fruit and whipped cream.

Eggs in a Cloud
(pictured, page 8)

10 (1/8-inch) slices salami
8 (3/4-inch) slices Italian bread, toasted and buttered
1/4 pound sliced Jarlsberg cheese
8 large eggs
1 teaspoon salt
1/2 teaspoon dry mustard
1/4 teaspoon pepper
1/4 teaspoon paprika

1. Preheat oven to 400°F. Lightly grease a 13-by-9-by-2-inch baking dish.

2. Cut salami in half; arrange, cut side down, around edge of prepared dish. Arrange bread over bottom of dish; place cheese slices over bread.

3. Separate eggs, placing each egg yolk in a shell half; place in egg-carton compartments until ready to use. Place egg whites in large bowl of electric mixer; at high speed, beat with 1/2 teaspoon salt and the mustard until stiff, moist peaks form.

4. Lightly spread egg-white mixture over bread in pan. With back of spoon, make 8 depressions; carefully place 1 yolk in each depression. Sprinkle with 1/2 teaspoon salt, the pepper and paprika. Bake 10 minutes, or just until yolks are set.

Makes 8 servings.

Omelets on Demand
(pictured, pages 8 and 9)

10 large eggs
1/3 cup light cream
1 1/2 teaspoons salt
Dash pepper
1/4 cup capers, drained
5 tablespoons butter or margarine
Filling (recipes follow)

1. Make omelet: In large bowl, with mixer on low speed or with rotary beater, beat eggs with cream, salt and pepper. Stir in capers. (If desired, refrigerate until ready to cook omelets.)

2. Over medium heat, slowly heat 6-inch nonstick skillet. Add 1 tablespoon butter; heat until sizzling (do not brown).

3. Ladle about 1/2 cup egg mixture into skillet; as egg sets, run plastic spatula around edge to loosen omelet. Tilt skillet to let uncooked portion run underneath. Continue to loosen omelet and tilt skillet until omelet is almost dry on top and golden-brown underneath, about 4 minutes.

4. Place filling of your choice on half of omelet away from handle of skillet. Fold other half over; slide omelet out of skillet onto heated serving plate. Repeat procedure with remaining egg mixture.

Makes 5 omelets.

Chicken-Liver Filling
(pictured, page 8)

1 pound chicken livers, rinsed and patted dry
1/4 cup butter or margarine
1 tablespoon all-purpose flour
1 can (3 ounces) sliced mushrooms
1/2 cup sour cream
1/4 cup brandy
1 teaspoon salt

1. Cut livers in half. In medium skillet, over medium-high heat, melt butter. Add livers to skillet; sauté until browned on the outside but pink inside, about 5 minutes. With slotted spoon, remove to bowl.

2. Add flour to skillet, stirring to make smooth paste. Remove skillet from heat. Drain mushrooms; reserve liquid. Slowly whisk in mushroom liquid, sour cream, brandy and salt. Bring to boiling, stirring constantly. Simmer 1 minute, until thickened and smooth. Add liver and mushrooms to skillet; heat through.

Makes about 2 cups, enough for 6 omelets.

Double-Cheese Omelet Filling
(pictured, page 9)

1/4 cup crumbled Stilton cheese
2 cups (8 ounces) shredded Jarlsberg cheese
2 tablespoons all-purpose flour
1/2 teaspoon dried tarragon leaves
1/3 cup light cream or half-and-half

In heavy 1-quart saucepan, over very low heat, combine ingredients. Heat, stirring, until cheeses melt and mixture is blended. Simmer 1 minute (mixture will not be smooth).

Makes 1 cup, enough filling for 5 omelets.

Caviar-Crème Fraîche Omelet Filling
(pictured, page 9)

1 jar (4 ounces) black caviar
1 container (8 ounces) crème fraîche or sour cream

Place ingredients in small bowls; spoon off excess liquid from caviar. While omelet is in skillet, spread 3 tablespoons crème fraîche over entire top. Fold omelet in half; slide onto serving plate. Top with a dollop of crème fraîche and spoonful of caviar. Serve at once.

Makes enough for 4 or 5 omelets.

Smoked-Oyster Filling

2 tablespoons butter or margarine
1 large shallot, chopped
1/4 cup unsifted all-purpose flour
1 1/4 cups milk
1/2 teaspoon salt
1/4 teaspoon pepper
2 cans (8 ounces each) smoked oysters, drained
2 whole pimientos, cut in strips

In medium saucepan, over medium-high heat, melt butter. Add shallot; sauté 2 minutes. With wooden spoon, blend in flour. Cook until bubbly, about 1 minute. Remove from heat; gradually whisk in milk, salt and pepper. Bring to boiling, stirring constantly; simmer 1 minute, until thickened and smooth. Stir in oysters and pimientos; heat through.

Makes 1¾ cups, enough for 6 omelets.

Seafood-Filled Dutch Babies

(pictured, page 9)

Dutch Babies

1 cup unsifted all-purpose flour
1 cup milk, at room temperature
4 large eggs, at room temperature
3 tablespoons hot melted butter or margarine

Filling

4 tablespoons butter or margarine
¼ cup thinly sliced green onions
1 medium tomato, seeded and chopped
½ pound shrimp, shelled and deveined
3 tablespoons all-purpose flour
⅛ teaspoon ground red pepper
1 cup milk
½ pound surimi (fish and crab blend)
½ cup sour cream
2 tablespoons dry sherry
½ teaspoon salt

1. Preheat oven to 450°F.

2. Make Dutch Babies: In bowl, whisk flour with milk, eggs and melted butter until smooth. Generously grease six 11-ounce soufflé dishes or straight-sided custard cups. Pour ⅓ cup batter into each dish; place dishes in center of oven. Bake 30 minutes, or until puffy and golden-brown.

3. Meanwhile, make filling: In 2-quart saucepan, over medium heat, melt 2 tablespoons butter. Add onions and tomato; sauté 3 minutes, or until onions are tender. Add shrimp; cook 5 minutes, or until pink and slightly curled. With slotted spoon, remove mixture to bowl; set aside.

4. In same saucepan, over low heat, melt remaining 2 tablespoons butter. Blend in 3 tablespoons flour and the pepper. Remove pan from heat; gradually whisk in 1 cup milk. Return pan to heat; bring to boiling. Cook 2 minutes, or until thick and bubbly. Remove pan from heat; stir in shrimp mixture, surimi, sour cream, sherry and salt until blended. Cover; set aside.

5. Spoon ½ cup filling into each Dutch Baby. Serve immediately.

Makes 6 servings.

Warm Apricot-Cheese Strudel

(pictured, pages 8 and 9)

1 package (8 ounces) cream cheese, softened
1 large egg yolk
⅓ cup granulated sugar
½ cup dried apricots, coarsely chopped
10 leaves phyllo pastry, at room temperature
½ cup unsalted butter, melted
½ cup ground blanched almonds
Confectioners' sugar

1. In large bowl of electric mixer, at medium speed, beat cream cheese, egg yolk and sugar until smooth. Stir in apricots; set aside.

2. Preheat oven to 400°F. Grease large baking sheet; set aside. On large kitchen towel, place 1 sheet phyllo. Brush phyllo lightly with some butter; sprinkle with some almonds. Cover with another sheet; repeat, making layers with remaining butter, almonds and phyllo, reserving a little butter for top.

3. With long side of pastry facing you, and starting at short side of pastry rectangle, spread cheese mixture evenly over three-fourths of pastry; leave 1-inch border on sides. Fold up border; starting from filled short end, roll up strudel, jelly-roll fashion, using towel to roll and guide it.

4. Place strudel on prepared baking sheet, seam side down. Brush with remaining butter. With wooden pick, make small holes in side of strudel for air vents. Bake 10 minutes; reduce heat to 350°F. Bake 30 minutes longer, or until golden-brown. Sprinkle with confectioners' sugar; serve warm.

Makes 6 to 8 servings.

Champagne-Glazed Canadian Bacon

(pictured, pages 8 and 9)

2 tablespoons butter or margarine
1½ pounds Canadian bacon, sliced ¼-inch thick (12 slices)
½ cup champagne or dry white wine
½ cup apple jelly

1. In large skillet, over medium-high heat, melt butter. Sauté half of bacon until lightly browned on each side; remove to plate. In butter in skillet, sauté remaining bacon.

2. Return bacon to skillet; add champagne. Simmer, uncovered, 10 minutes, or until liquid is reduced to ½ cup. With tongs, remove bacon to serving platter; cover and keep warm. Add jelly to skillet; stir until melted. Spoon glaze over bacon. Serve immediately.

Makes 6 servings.

Bloody Mary Slushes

(pictured, page 8)

1 medium onion, quartered
1 can (46 ounces) vegetable juice
3 tablespoons white-wine Worcestershire sauce
1 tablespoon lemon juice
2 cups pepper-flavored vodka
Lime slices

1. The night before serving, make slush mixture: In food processor or electric blender, combine onion, half the vegetable juice and all the Worcestershire and lemon juice; process until smooth. Pour mixture into shallow nonaluminum baking pan. Stir in remaining vegetable juice. Cover; freeze.

2. One hour before serving, remove pan of frozen juice mixture. Let stand at room temperature 30 minutes. With fork, break mixture into small chunks; place half the pieces in food processor or electric blender. Add 1 cup vodka; process until smooth. Spoon into 4 large stemmed glasses. Repeat with remaining chunks and vodka. Garnish each glass with a lime slice.

Makes 8 servings.

Chocolate Temptation Cake

(pictured, pages 10 and 11)

Ganache
1 cup heavy cream
4 squares (1 ounce each) semisweet chocolate, finely chopped

Cake
1 box (about 18 ounces) chocolate cake mix
1 cup water
2 large eggs, at room temperature
½ cup salad oil
½ cup dark rum

Filling
1 package (3.5 ounces) chocolate-flavored pudding-and-pie-filling mix
½ cup half-and-half
3 tablespoons dark rum
¼ cup crème fraîche or sour cream

Garnish
½ cup heavy cream
2 tablespoons confectioners' sugar
Candied violets

1. Make ganache: In heavy 2-quart saucepan, heat 1 cup cream over medium-high heat, until simmering. Remove from heat; add chocolate. Whisk until chocolate melts and mixture is smooth. Pour into small bowl of electric mixer; refrigerate at least 2 hours.

2. Meanwhile, make cake: Preheat oven to 350°F. Grease and flour two 8- or 9-inch round or hexagonal-sided cake pans. In large bowl of electric mixer, mix as package label directs, using water, eggs, oil and ½ cup rum. Pour batter into prepared pans; bake as package label directs. Cool layers on wire racks 1 hour.

3. Make filling: In 1½-quart saucepan, over medium heat, combine pudding mix, half-and-half and 3 tablespoons rum. Bring to boiling, stirring constantly; simmer 1 minute, or until thick. Cool to room temperature; whisk in crème fraîche. Refrigerate 1 hour, or until mixture is cool.

4. With electric mixer at medium-high speed, beat ganache 5 minutes, or until it is thick enough to spread. Refrigerate.

5. Make garnish: In small bowl of electric mixer, combine heavy cream and confectioners' sugar. At high speed, beat until stiff peaks form. Place mixture in pastry bag fitted with ½-inch star tip. Cover tip with plastic wrap; refrigerate until ready to use.

6. Assemble cake: Invert one cake layer onto serving plate; spread with filling. Top with second cake layer. With broad spatula, spread ganache over top and sides of cake. Pipe whipped cream on cake, using photograph as a guide. Decorate with candied violets.

Makes 10 servings.

Appetizer Ribs With Two Sauces

(pictured, page 11)

2 packages (2 pounds each) cooked barbecued spareribs

Roasted Red-Pepper Dipping Sauce
¼ cup loosely packed cilantro (fresh coriander) or parsley
2 jars (7 ounces each) roasted red peppers, drained
3 large celery stalks, cut in 1-inch pieces
2 tablespoons lime juice
1 tablespoon honey
½ teaspoon salt

Oriental Dipping Sauce
½ cup honey
2 teaspoons ginger root, pared and minced
1 cup low-sodium soy sauce
1 cup orange juice

1. Preheat oven to 375°F. Line jelly-roll pan with aluminum foil. Remove racks of ribs from packages, reserving sauce. With sharp knife, separate ribs; place on prepared pan. Cook, uncovered, 40 minutes, basting occasionally with sauce.

2. Meanwhile, make Roasted Red-Pepper Dipping Sauce: Place cilantro in food processor; process until finely chopped. Add drained peppers, celery pieces, lime juice, honey and salt. Process until finely chopped. Cover; refrigerate.

3. Make Oriental Dipping Sauce: In saucepan, mix all ingredients. Bring to boiling; simmer 5 minutes. Keep warm.

4. Arrange ribs on platter; if desired, garnish with additional cilantro. Serve with prepared sauces. If desired, use any remaining sauce from packages of ribs as a sauce.

Makes 8 servings, about 3 ribs each serving.

Chicken Pesto

(pictured, page 10)

1 cup fresh basil (see *Note*)
½ cup parsley
3 medium cloves garlic, peeled
1 teaspoon grated lemon peel
¼ cup grated Parmesan cheese
¼ cup olive oil
6 tablespoons butter or margarine
2 pounds boneless chicken breasts, skinned and cut in ½-inch-wide strips
1 large onion, sliced
½ pound medium mushrooms, quartered
½ red pepper, cut in strips
½ yellow pepper, cut in strips
2 tablespoons lemon juice
½ teaspoon salt
¼ teaspoon pepper
2 tablespoons toasted pine nuts
1 pound fusilli, cooked as package label directs

1. In food processor, puree basil, parsley, garlic and lemon peel. Add Parmesan; process until blended. With processor running, add olive oil; set aside.

2. In 12-inch skillet or large wok, over medium-high heat, melt 3 tablespoons butter. Add half the chicken; sauté until brown and firm, about 4 minutes. With slotted spoon, remove chicken to bowl; in drippings in pan, sauté remaining chicken. When browned, remove chicken to bowl.

3. In same skillet, melt remaining butter. Add onion, mushrooms and pepper strips; sauté until tender-crisp, about 4 minutes. Return chicken to skillet; stir in reserved pesto, the lemon juice, salt and pepper. Cook, stirring, until mixture is heated through. Stir in toasted pine nuts. Serve with hot fusilli.

Makes 4 to 6 servings.

Note: One cup parsley leaves plus 4 teaspoons dried basil leaves may be substituted for fresh basil.

Pepper-Baked Brie

(pictured, page 11)

8-inch (2 pounds) Brie cheese
¾ cup blanched whole almonds
3 tablespoons unsalted butter, softened
½ small green pepper, chopped
½ small red pepper, chopped
⅓ cup toasted sliced almonds
Assorted crackers or sliced French bread
Red and green grapes, rinsed and cut in small bunches

1. Preheat oven to 350°F. Place Brie on baking sheet. With sharp knife, cut out and discard center piece of rind from top of Brie, leaving 1 inch of rind around top edge of cheese. Set aside.

2. In food processor, blend whole almonds with butter until mixture is a thick paste; spread over exposed portion of Brie. Place chopped peppers in center.

3. Bake 15 minutes, or until puffed and melted inside. Quickly decorate edges with almond slices. Serve immediately with crackers or French bread and grapes.

Makes 12 appetizer servings.

■ If a recipe requires softened butter, but you forgot to take it out of the refrigerator, it will be easier to cream if you shred it first with a vegetable parer.

Warm Cucumber Toss

(pictured, page 10)

1 (14-inch) cucumber
2 tablespoons salad oil
1 large red pepper, coarsely chopped
1 small onion, sliced
1 package (6 ounces) frozen snow pea pods, thawed
½ cup white-wine vinegar
2 teaspoons sugar
1 teaspoon salt
1 teaspoon dried chervil leaves

1. Cut cucumber lengthwise in half; with a spoon, scoop out and discard seeds. Cut cucumber halves crosswise into ⅛-inch slices.

2. In skillet, heat oil. Add pepper and onion; sauté until tender-crisp, about 3 minutes. Add cucumber and pea pods; sauté 1 minute. Add remaining ingredients; heat.

Makes 6 servings.

Zippy Cheddar Crisps

(pictured, page 11)

1 cup yellow cornmeal
2 tablespoons butter or margarine
1 tablespoon sugar
½ teaspoon salt
1 cup boiling water
¾ cup (3 ounces) shredded Cheddar cheese
3 green onions, minced
1 to 2 jalapeño peppers, seeded and minced
1 tablespoon chopped pimiento

1. Preheat oven to 400°F. Generously grease 2 large baking sheets.

2. Combine first 4 ingredients. Add water, mixing until blended. Stir in remaining ingredients.

3. Drop level teaspoonfuls batter, 1 inch apart, onto sheets. With spatula, flatten into 2-inch rounds. Bake 18 minutes, or until golden and slightly brown around edges.

Makes 6 dozen.

Pear-Stuffed Roast Pork
(pictured, page 10)

5-pound center-cut pork roast (do not cut backbone)
2 large onions, cut in wedges
1 package (5 ounces) brown-and-wild-rice mix with mushrooms
2 pears, pared, cored and chopped
½ cup raisins
½ cup chopped pecans
2 teaspoons butter or margarine
2 tablespoons salad oil
1 large clove garlic, peeled
1 teaspoon rosemary leaves
1 teaspoon fennel seeds
1 teaspoon salt
½ teaspoon black peppercorns
1 can (about 14 ounces) chicken broth
Water
2 tablespoons cornstarch
2 tablespoons water

1. With sharp knife, cut deep pockets between bones of the pork roast, almost through to backbone. Place fat side up on rack in roasting pan. Scatter onions around bottom of roast. Preheat oven to 325°F.

2. Cook rice mix as package label directs for firmer rice. Stir in pears, raisins and pecans. Spoon some mixture into each pocket, dividing evenly; place extra mixture in greased 1-quart casserole. Dot with butter; cover with aluminum foil, and set aside.

3. In electric blender, blend oil with garlic, rosemary, fennel, salt and peppercorns; rub over pork.

4. Cook pork 1½ hours; pour chicken broth over onions. Return roast to oven, placing foil-covered rice casserole beside pan with pork. Cook 30 minutes longer, or until meat thermometer inserted in end of roast registers 170°F. Remove meat to heated platter. Cover loosely with foil while making gravy.

5. Pour liquid in pan into 2-cup glass measure (leave onions in pan); skim off fat. Add enough water to make 2 cups; pour into roasting pan. In custard cup, dissolve cornstarch in 2 tablespoons water. Add to broth in pan. Place pan on range burner; over medium-high heat, bring to boiling, stirring constantly. Simmer, stirring 2 minutes, or until gravy thickens.

6. Slice meat sections of roast pork to include a pocket of stuffing for each serving. Pass additional stuffing and gravy.

Makes 8 servings.

Holiday Cassata

¾ cup orange marmalade
⅓ cup golden rum
2 (1 pound each) pound cakes

Fillings
1 pound ricotta cheese
½ cup confectioners' sugar
1 tablespoon golden rum
2 tablespoons semisweet-chocolate minipieces, melted
½ cup semisweet-chocolate minipieces
1 container (4 ounces) mixed candied fruit, finely chopped

⅓ cup seedless strawberry jam
1½ cups heavy cream
2 tablespoons confectioners' sugar
5 red candied cherries, halved
5 green candied cherries, halved

1. In small bowl, combine marmalade and ⅓ cup rum; set aside. Slice each pound cake horizontally into 4 layers. Trim and discard crust from long sides of each cake. Set cake layers aside.

2. Make fillings: In medium bowl, combine ricotta and ½ cup confectioners' sugar. With portable electric mixer, beat until blended. Stir in 1 tablespoon rum. Remove 1 cup cheese mixture to small bowl; stir in melted chocolate until blended. Set aside. To remaining filling, add chocolate minipieces and candied fruit. Cover fillings; refrigerate.

3. Assemble cassata, using the 8 cake layers to make 4 layers: Place 2 cake layers, long sides together, on serving plate. Drizzle with 3 tablespoons of the marmalade mixture; spread with half the candied-fruit-and-cheese filling. Spread one side of a remaining cake layer with half the strawberry jam. Place cake, jam side down, over cheese layer. Drizzle with 3 tablespoons marmalade mixture. Spread with the melted-chocolate-and-cheese filling. Top with another cake layer, long sides together; drizzle with 3 tablespoons marmalade mixture. Spread with remaining candied-fruit-and-cheese filling. Spread remaining jam over one side of remaining cake layer. Place cake, jam side down, over cheese mixture; drizzle with remaining marmalade mixture.

4. In small bowl of electric mixer, at high speed, beat cream with confectioners' sugar until stiff peaks form; with spatula, spread over top and sides of cassata. Garnish with candied cherries. Refrigerate. Cut into 2-inch squares.

Makes 16 servings.

■ For a quick dress-up for dessert, swirl thick fudge sauce or partially thawed frozen fruits or chopped candies into softened ice cream; refreeze and scoop into pretty dishes. For a special touch, add a fancy cookie and a sprig of mint.

■ Here's a ready-in-an-instant dessert recipe. Just melt ¼ cup preserves or jam in a small saucepan; then stir in one tablespoon almond- or orange-flavored liqueur. Drizzle over ice cream, and serve with thin toasted pound cake strips.

Quick & Easy: Last-Minute Gifts

Macadamia Brittle

2 jars (7 ounces each) macadamia nuts
2 cups sugar
½ cup light corn syrup
½ cup water
2 tablespoons butter
½ teaspoon baking soda

1. Butter large baking sheet; set aside on wire rack. Cut nuts in half; set aside. In 10-inch nonstick skillet, combine sugar with corn syrup and water. Over medium-high heat, cook, stirring occasionally, until golden-brown.

2. Stir in nuts; cook, stirring constantly, until medium brown (do not burn mixture). Remove from heat; quickly stir in butter and baking soda. Pour onto prepared baking sheet; cool. Break into pieces.

Makes about 4½ cups.

Pear Kuchen

1 package (23.5 ounces) bakery-style blueberry-muffin mix
1 teaspoon ground ginger
1 large egg
¾ cup water
1 large pear, pared, cored and sliced lengthwise into 16 pieces
1 teaspoon grated lemon peel

1. Preheat oven to 400°F. Grease 8-inch round pan; set aside. In large bowl, combine muffin mix with ginger (reserve berries). Add egg and water; stir until blended. Drain and rinse berries; fold into batter. Pour into prepared pan; arrange pear slices on top.

2. In small bowl, combine contents of muffin-mix-topping package with peel; sprinkle over pears. Bake 35 minutes. Cool 10 minutes; remove from pan.

Makes 6 servings.

Coffee Liqueur

3 cups sugar
¼ cup dark roast instant coffee crystals
2 cups water
1 teaspoon vanilla extract
1 quart vodka

In medium saucepan, combine sugar and coffee with water. Bring to boiling. Cool; stir in vanilla. Pour into 2-quart container; stir in vodka. With spoon, skim off foam. Cover liqueur tightly; let stand 48 hours. Pour into decanters or bottles.

Makes 7½ cups.

Clockwise from top: Pear Kuchen, Coffee Liqueur, Holiday Citrus Cookies, Macadamia Brittle.

Holiday Citrus Cookies

½ cup butter
1¼ cups unsifted all-purpose flour
¼ cup confectioners' sugar
1 cup granulated sugar
¼ teaspoon baking powder
1 tablespoon grated lime peel
2 large eggs, beaten
2 tablespoons lime juice
2 drops green food color
Additional confectioners' sugar
Candied lime- or lemon-peel twists

1. Preheat oven to 350°F. Line 8-inch square pan with aluminum foil; grease lightly. In bowl, with pastry blender or two knives, cut butter into 1 cup flour and the confectioners' sugar until mixture resembles coarse crumbs. Press into pan. Bake 15 minutes.

2. Combine granulated sugar with remaining flour, the baking powder, lime peel, eggs and lime juice; stir in food color. Pour over mixture; bake 25 minutes longer.

3. Sprinkle warm cookies with confectioners' sugar. Grasp corners of foil; lift cookies from pan. Cut into 16 squares; top with peel twists.

Makes 16 cookies.

Hurry-Up One-Dish Dinners

The holiday hustle and bustle leaves little time for cooking, but you can still treat your family with a little help from our no-fuss meals.

Sweet 'n' Sour Shrimp

2 tablespoons sesame seeds
1 pound large shrimp
2 tablespoons salad oil
1 large red pepper, seeded and cut in strips
½ cup sweet-and-sour sauce or duck sauce
1 can (16 ounces) pineapple chunks, drained
1 can (8 ounces) water chestnuts, drained
1 bunch green onions, trimmed and cut in 2-inch lengths
½ teaspoon salt
4 cups hot cooked white rice

1. Preheat oven to 350°F. Place sesame seeds on baking sheet; bake 10 minutes, or until golden-brown.
2. Remove and discard shell from shrimp, leaving tail section intact; devein. In large skillet, heat oil over medium-high heat. Add shrimp and pepper strips; sauté 2 minutes, or until shrimp turns pink. Stir in sweet-and-sour sauce, pineapple, water chestnuts, onions, salt and sesame seeds; heat. Serve over rice.

Makes 4 to 6 servings.

Clockwise from top left: Upside-Down Pizza, Sweet 'n' Sour Shrimp, Beef Dinner in a Bag, Never-Fail Seafood Soufflé, Glazed Ham-and-Squash Bake.

Never-Fail Seafood Soufflé

1 teaspoon curry powder
1 tablespoon lemon juice
4 large eggs, separated, at room temperature
½ cup mayonnaise
⅓ cup unsifted all-purpose flour
½ teaspoon salt
¼ teaspoon pepper
¼ cup sour cream
1 pound surimi (fish and lobster blend), finely chopped
1 package (10 ounces) frozen chopped broccoli, thawed and drained

1. Preheat oven to 350°F. Generously butter 1½-quart soufflé dish or straight-sided casserole.
2. In large bowl, blend curry powder with lemon juice; whisk in egg yolks, mayonnaise, flour, salt and pepper. Gradually whisk in sour cream. Stir in surimi; set aside.
3. Place egg whites in large bowl of electric mixer; at high speed, beat until stiff peaks form. With rubber spatula, fold whites into curry mixture until no white streaks remain.
4. Place broccoli in bottom of prepared dish. Gently spread egg-white mixture over broccoli. Bake 55 minutes, or until puffed and golden-brown. Serve immediately.

Makes 6 servings.

Upside-Down Pizza

(pictured, page 21)

1 pound sweet Italian sausage, thinly sliced
1 medium onion, sliced
1 jar (14 ounces) pizza sauce
½ cup pitted ripe olives, halved
½ pound Jarlsberg cheese, sliced

Crust
2 large eggs, beaten
1 cup unsifted all-purpose flour
⅓ cup grated Parmesan cheese
¼ teaspoon salt
1 cup milk
1 tablespoon salad oil

1. In 10-inch skillet with oven-safe handle, over high heat, sauté sausage 5 minutes. Add onion; sauté 8 minutes longer, until sausage is well browned.

2. Preheat oven to 425°F. Pour off all but 1 tablespoon fat from skillet. Stir in pizza sauce and olives. Bring to boiling; arrange cheese slices on top of sauce.

3. Make crust: In food processor or medium bowl, combine eggs with flour, Parmesan, salt, milk and oil. Evenly spread mixture over sausage mixture. Bake, uncovered, 30 minutes, or until crust is golden-brown. Cut pizza in wedges; serve immediately from skillet. Or let stand 10 minutes; invert onto serving platter. If desired, sprinkle top side of crust with additional shredded Jarlsberg cheese.

Makes 8 servings.

Glazed Ham-and-Squash Bake

(pictured, pages 20 and 21)

1½-pound ham, sliced into six ¼-inch slices
1½-pound acorn squash

Stuffing
1 can (16 ounces) apricot halves
½ package (8-ounce size) cornbread-stuffing mix
½ cup butter or margarine
⅓ cup water
½ cup pecan halves

¼ cup apricot preserves, melted

1. Preheat oven to 400°F. Cut each slice of ham crosswise in half. Cut squash in half; scoop out and discard seeds. Cut each half crosswise into ¼-inch-thick slices. In 2-quart shallow baking dish, alternately arrange slices of ham and squash in two lengthwise rows, leaving middle of dish clear; set aside.

2. Make stuffing: Drain apricots, reserving ¼ cup juice; coarsely chop. Make cornbread stuffing as package label directs, using ⅓ cup each butter and water; stir in chopped apricots and the pecans. Spoon stuffing mixture over center of baking dish.

3. In small saucepan, melt remaining butter; stir in reserved apricot juice. Spoon sauce over ham and squash slices. Cover pan tightly with aluminum foil. Bake 30 minutes, or until fork easily pierces squash. Remove foil; brush ham and squash with preserves; bake 5 minutes longer.

Makes 6 servings.

Beef Dinner in a Bag

(pictured, page 21)

1 package (1 ounce) pepper-sauce-with-green-peppercorns mix
1 tablespoon all-purpose flour
2-pound sirloin steak, about 1½ inches thick, well trimmed
12 small new red potatoes, quartered
½ package (20-ounce size) round baby carrots, partially thawed
1 package (10 ounces) frozen whole green beans, partially thawed
½ pound whole mushrooms, washed and stems trimmed
¼ cup white-wine Worcestershire sauce

1. Preheat oven to 400°F. In small bowl, combine pepper-sauce mix and flour. Spoon half the mixture into regular-size oven cooking bag; shake to coat inside.

2. Place steak in bag; place bag in 13-by-9-by-2-inch baking pan. Arrange potatoes in bag around steak. Place carrots and green beans on top of meat; top with mushrooms.

3. Blend Worcestershire with remaining flour mixture; pour over mushrooms in bag. Close bag with nylon tie. With small knife, make six ½-inch slits in top of bag.

4. Bake 50 minutes, or until potatoes are easily pierced with fork. To serve, cut or slit top of bag carefully, avoiding steam; remove contents to serving platter.

Makes 6 servings.

■ Give a family-style supper a touch of country charm. Set the mood by using tattersall dish towels as place mats and napkins. A textured tablecloth and chunky candles complete the effect.

■ Overcooked veggies? Puree and serve as a fancy side dish (no one has to know it wasn't what you had in mind from the beginning!); or use the puree as a base for a cream soup.

Cottage Supper Bake

1 package (24 ounces) frozen Southern-style hash-brown potatoes with butter sauce and onions
1 pound ground beef
1 medium onion, chopped
1 can (10¾ ounces) golden cream-of-mushroom soup
1 cup sour cream
1 package (10 ounces) frozen Italian-style vegetables with green beans, red peppers and ripe olives, slightly thawed
½ cup French-fried onions

1. Preheat oven to 475°F. In 9-inch square baking dish, arrange hash-brown potatoes over bottom and sides; cover tightly with aluminum foil. Bake 15 minutes.

2. Meanwhile, in large skillet, over medium-high heat, sauté beef and onion until meat is lightly browned, about 10 minutes. Stir in soup, sour cream and vegetables.

3. Remove dish from oven; discard foil. With back of spoon, press over bottom and sides of dish to within ½ inch of top. Pour meat mixture into center, leaving a 1-inch potato border. Bake 15 minutes. Sprinkle with French-fried onions.

Makes 4 to 5 servings.

Quick Lasagna

1 package (8 ounces) wide egg noodles
1 tablespoon salad oil
1½ pounds ground beef
1 jar (about 16 ounces) spaghetti sauce
⅓ cup chopped green onions
1 cup small-curd cottage cheese, drained
1 package (8 ounces) cream cheese
¼ cup sour cream
1 package (8 ounces) shredded mozzarella cheese

1. Generously grease 2½-quart baking dish. Cook noodles as label directs for *al dente*; drain. Toss with oil. Preheat oven to 350°F.

2. Meanwhile, in large skillet, over high heat, brown beef, stirring to break into small pieces. Stir in spaghetti sauce and onions. Remove skillet from heat.

3. In bowl, mix cottage cheese with cream cheese and sour cream. Arrange half the noodles in dish; spread with half the cheese mixture. Repeat with remaining noodles and cheese mixture. Spread meat mixture over top; sprinkle with mozzarella. Bake 35 minutes, or until bubbling around edges.

Makes 6 servings.

Quick Chicken Casserole With Rice and Vegetables

1 package (4.5 ounces) chicken-flavored rice-and-pasta mix
1⅓ cups water
6 whole chicken legs (3½ pounds)
1 large zucchini, sliced
1 yellow squash, sliced
1 tablespoon dried tarragon leaves
1¼ teaspoons salt
1 teaspoon garlic powder
¼ teaspoon pepper

1. Preheat oven to 475°F. Sprinkle rice mix in 3-quart shallow baking dish; stir in water. Place chicken over rice mixture; arrange zucchini and squash around chicken. Combine seasonings; sprinkle over chicken and vegetables.

2. Cover tightly with aluminum foil. Bake 45 minutes; remove foil. Bake 10 minutes longer, or until chicken is lightly browned.

Makes 5 to 6 servings.

Fruited Chicken and Stuffing

6 slices bacon
6 boneless chicken-breast halves
½ cup butter or margarine
1 jar (16 ounces) applesauce
1 cup water
2 packages (6 ounces each) vegetable-and-almond top-of-stove stuffing mix
⅓ cup raisins
1 medium red apple, cored and thinly sliced

1. Preheat oven to 450°F. In large skillet, sauté bacon until crisp; drain on paper towels and reserve. Add chicken breasts to drippings in skillet; over high heat, sauté 10 minutes, until browned, turning once. Remove to plate. In same skillet, melt butter; stir in applesauce and water. Bring to boiling; stir in contents of seasoning packet and stuffing mix until blended. Stir in raisins. Remove from heat.

2. Lightly grease 3-quart shallow baking dish. Spoon stuffing mixture over bottom of dish; place chicken breasts on top. Arrange apple slices around edge of dish. Cover tightly with aluminum foil. Bake 15 minutes, or until stuffing is steaming. Arrange reserved bacon slices on top of chicken.

Makes 6 servings.

■ Extra salad needn't be tossed away. Instead, use it to make this interesting chilled soup for the next day's dinner: Puree the salad, dressing and all, and add chicken or vegetable broth; chill well. Serve with a dab of sour cream or yogurt and a sprinkling of chives. Your family will be amazed!

Lite Eating: Elegant Duck Dinner

ROASTED DUCK
WITH ORANGE-BERRY RELISH
LEEK-AND-ASPARAGUS PLATTER
PINEAPPLE-BANANA TORTE
CEYLON TEA WITH LIME

Roasted Duck With Orange-Berry Relish

4½-pound duck, quartered
2 large onions, sliced
1¼ cups water
2 teaspoons dried rosemary leaves, crushed
2 teaspoons salt
½ teaspoon pepper
½ cup orange juice
½ package (1-pound size) cranberries
1 can (11 ounces) mandarin-orange segments, drained
Low-calorie sweetener
1 tablespoon grated orange peel
2 packages (8 ounces each) frozen sugar snap peas, cooked

1. Preheat oven to 350°F. Remove excess fat from duck; with knife, score skin in crisscross fashion. In large skillet, over medium-high heat, sauté duck on both sides until crisp, 5 minutes in all. Drain on paper towels.

2. In roasting pan, place onions and ½ cup water. Sprinkle duck with rosemary, salt and pepper; place skin side up over onions. Bake 50 minutes.

3. Meanwhile, in saucepan, bring ¾ cup water and the orange juice to boiling; stir in cranberries. Simmer 5 minutes, until skins pop.

4. For relish, pour half of cranberry mixture into medium bowl. Stir in oranges; sweeten to taste. Set aside. Pour remaining cranberry mixture into blender; puree. Place puree in saucepan; stir in orange peel. Over low heat, cook, stirring, until thickened, about 5 minutes. Drain water and fat from roasting pan. Brush duck with puree; bake 10 minutes longer. Place duck and onions on platter; surround with hot peas. Pass relish separately.

Makes 4 servings, 290 calories each.

Left: (Clockwise from top) Leek-and-Asparagus Platter, Pineapple-Banana Torte, Roasted Duck With Orange-Berry Relish.

Leek-and-Asparagus Platter

2 large leeks, trimmed
1 package (10 ounces) frozen asparagus spears

Dressing
1 tablespoon minced parsley
¼ cup white-wine Worcestershire sauce
1 tablespoon white-wine vinegar

8 leaves lettuce
4 radishes, julienned
1 hard-cooked egg yolk

1. Wash leeks and slice crosswise into ½-inch rounds. In 10-inch skillet, in boiling, salted water, cook leeks until tender. Drain; place in shallow bowl. Cook asparagus as package label directs; add to leeks.

2. In bowl, combine dressing ingredients; pour over leeks and asparagus. Cover; refrigerate 30 minutes.

3. Line platter with lettuce; top with asparagus and leeks, reserving dressing. Sprinkle with radishes; over salad, push yolk through sieve. Spoon dressing over all.

Makes 4 servings, 96 calories each.

Pineapple-Banana Torte

1 envelope unflavored gelatine
½ cup water
1½ cups cold lowfat milk
1 package (1.1 ounces) sugar-free vanilla-flavored instant pudding mix
2 small bananas
2 cups nondairy whipped topping
1 can (5¼ ounces) pineapple chunks
½ package (3-ounce size) ladyfingers

1. With plastic wrap, line 1½-quart bowl; set aside. In small cup, sprinkle gelatine over water; set aside 5 minutes, until softened.

2. Using lowfat milk, prepare pudding mix as package label directs. In microwave, dissolve gelatine on HIGH 1 minute. Stir into pudding. Refrigerate 5 minutes. Chop one banana; fold banana and whipped topping into pudding.

3. Spoon ¾ cup pudding into prepared bowl. Drain pineapple, reserving 2 tablespoons juice. Split ladyfingers; brush with reserved pineapple juice. Arrange ladyfingers, rounded side out, around bowl; spoon remaining pudding in center. Cover; refrigerate 4 hours or until firm. Invert bowl over plate; remove bowl and plastic wrap. Slice remaining banana; arrange over pudding. Top with pineapple.

Makes 8 servings, 103 calories each.

Micro-Way: Festive First-Course Soups

Squash Bisque

¼ cup butter or margarine
3 leeks, white part only, sliced
2 Bartlett pears, pared, cored and chopped
1½-pound butternut squash, pared, seeded and chopped
¼ teaspoon dried thyme leaves
¼ teaspoon salt
⅛ teaspoon pepper
3 cups chicken broth
1 cup heavy cream

1. In 3-quart microwave-safe casserole, combine butter, leeks and pears. Cover with plastic wrap and fold back over corner to vent; cook on HIGH 5 to 7 minutes, or until leeks are tender, stirring once. Stir in squash, thyme, salt, pepper and broth. Cover and vent; cook on HIGH 8 minutes, or until squash is tender.

2. With slotted spoon, remove leeks, pears and squash. Place in food processor; puree. Stir into broth mixture in casserole; stir in cream. Cook on HIGH 2 minutes, or until heated through. If desired, garnish with pear slices and chives.

Makes 6 servings.

■ Store leftover soup conveniently by dishing it into microwave-safe, single-serving containers. All you have to do is reheat—and eat! (Stir soup several times while cooking to distribute heat evenly.)

Cod-and-Crab-Creole

2 medium carrots, diagonally sliced
2 medium celery stalks, sliced
1 large onion, chopped
1 small green pepper, chopped
1 small red pepper, chopped
2 medium cloves garlic, crushed
3 tablespoons salad oil
3 cups chicken broth
1 can (28 ounces) crushed tomatoes
½ teaspoon dried basil leaves
½ teaspoon dried thyme leaves
½ teaspoon ground turmeric
1 bay leaf
⅛ to ¼ teaspoon ground red pepper
1 pound cod fillets, cut in 1-inch pieces
½ pound surimi (fish and crab blend)
2 tablespoons dry sherry
2 tablespoons chopped parsley

1. In 4-quart microwave-safe casserole, combine carrots, celery, onion, peppers, garlic and oil. Cover with plastic wrap and turn back to vent; cook on HIGH 4 minutes, stirring once. Add broth, tomatoes and their juice, basil, thyme, turmeric, bay leaf and ground red pepper. Cover and vent; cook on HIGH 5 minutes, stirring several times during cooking.

2. Stir in cod. Cover and vent; cook on HIGH 3 minutes, or until fish flakes easily with fork. Add surimi and sherry; cook on HIGH 1 minute, or until heated through. Remove and discard bay leaf; stir in parsley.

Makes 10 servings.

February

You'll lose your heart to our sweet sensations. For starters, try the elegant, easy-to-do Double-Sauced Coeur à la Crème, Crimson Pears or Pistachio Baklava pictured here, or turn the pages and select from other festive finales in this chapter.

Crimson Pears

Double-Sauced Coeur à la Crème,

Pistachio Baklava   Triple-Chocolate Cake

Praline Cream-Puff Ring   Hazelnut Triangle Treat

Pecan Meringue Torte   Mango Mousse Pie

Viennese Pouf   Pineapple Bombe

Orange Mousse With Chocolate Wraparound

Floating Heart Ritz

Berry-Topped Apricot Soufflé

Elephant Ears (Palmiers)

Almond Twists   Jam Packets

Dessert Lovers' Cookbook

Our romantic Valentine's Day collection of recipes is filled with delicious delicacies to please dessert lovers everywhere.

Crimson Pears

(pictured, page 29)

1 package (10 ounces) frozen raspberries in light syrup, thawed
1 cup sugar
4 cups water
¼ cup lemon juice
2 (3-inch) cinnamon sticks
6 Bartlett pears, pared
2 tablespoons cornstarch
¼ cup pear-flavored liqueur

1. Drain raspberries, placing juice in saucepan; reserve berries. To juice, add sugar, water, lemon juice and cinnamon sticks. Bring to boiling, stirring until sugar dissolves. Add pears. Return to boiling; simmer, covered, 45 minutes, basting occasionally with poaching liquid.
2. Remove pan from heat. Cool pears in liquid. With slotted spoon, remove pears to serving dish.
3. Return poaching liquid to boiling; cook, uncovered, until reduced to 2 cups. Discard cinnamon sticks. In 1-cup glass measure, blend cornstarch with liqueur; stir into hot poaching liquid. Bring to boiling; simmer, stirring, 1 minute, until thickened. Stir in berries; pour sauce over pears. Serve warm or cold. If desired, place a mint leaf at stem end of each pear.

Makes 6 servings.

Pistachio Baklava

(pictured, page 29)

1 package (1 pound) phyllo pastry, at room temperature
1½ cups butter or margarine, melted
4 cups finely chopped pistachios
½ cup sugar

Syrup
1 cup sugar
1 cup honey
2 (3-inch) cinnamon sticks
Juice of 1 orange
Juice of 1 lemon
¾ cup water

1. Preheat oven to 325°F. On 15½-by-10½-by-2-inch jelly-roll pan, place 2 sheets phyllo, overlapping. Generously brush top sheet with some of the butter; repeat with 12 more sheets phyllo, buttering every other sheet. (Cover remaining phyllo with damp kitchen towel.)
2. In bowl, mix nuts with ½ cup sugar; sprinkle buttered top sheet with 1½ cups mixture. Top with 6 more sheets, buttering every other sheet. Sprinkle 1½ cups nut mixture over top sheet; top with 6 more sheets, buttering every other sheet. Continue with remaining mixture, phyllo and butter.
3. Bake 1 hour. Turn off oven; leave baklava in oven 1 hour.
4. Meanwhile, in saucepan, mix syrup ingredients. Bring to boiling, stirring until sugar dissolves. Simmer, uncovered, 20 minutes. Discard cinnamon sticks.
5. Remove baklava from oven; quickly and gently cut into diamond shapes, cutting down through all layers into crosswise, diagonal rows 1½ inches apart. Repeat, cutting crosswise rows at opposite angle. Pour hot syrup over baklava. If desired, sprinkle with additional chopped pistachios.
6. Cool in pan on wire rack at least 2 hours. Cover with aluminum foil; let stand overnight. Store at room temperature or refrigerate.

Makes about 40 servings.

Page 29: (From top) Crimson Pears, Double-Sauced Coeur à la Crème, Pistachio Baklava.

Pages 30 and 31: (Clockwise from top left) Triple-Chocolate Cake, Praline Cream-Puff Ring, Hazelnut Triangle Treat.

Pages 32 and 33: (Clockwise from right) Pecan Meringue Torte, Mango Mousse Pie, Viennese Pouf, Pineapple Bombe, Orange Mousse With Chocolate Wraparound.

Double-Sauced Coeur à la Crème

(pictured, page 29)

½ vanilla bean
1 package (8 ounces) cream cheese, at room temperature
½ cup confectioners' sugar
1 cup heavy cream, whipped to soft peaks

Apricot Sauce
1 teaspoon cornstarch
2 tablespoons Cognac
⅔ cup apricot jam
¼ cup water

Raspberry Sauce
1 teaspoon cornstarch
2 tablespoons raspberry-flavored liqueur
1 package (10 ounces) frozen raspberries in light syrup, thawed

1 cup sliced blanched almonds, lightly toasted

1. Line 6½-inch coeur à la crème mold with dampened, folded 1½-foot length of cheesecloth. Set aside.

2. Split vanilla bean; scrape seeds into medium bowl. Add cream cheese and confectioners' sugar; with wooden spoon, beat until mixture is light and fluffy. With rubber spatula, gently fold in whipped cream. Spoon mixture into prepared mold. Cover with plastic wrap; place on dinner plate to drain. Refrigerate 8 hours or overnight.

3. Make Apricot Sauce: In small saucepan, blend 1 teaspoon cornstarch with Cognac. Add jam and water; stir until smooth. Bring to boiling, stirring; simmer 5 minutes, until thickened. Set aside to cool.

4. Make Raspberry Sauce: In small saucepan, blend 1 teaspoon cornstarch with liqueur; set aside. Place raspberries in food processor or blender; puree. Pour through sieve into cornstarch mixture; stir until smooth. Bring to boiling, stirring; simmer 5 minutes, until thickened.

5. To serve: Unmold coeur à la crème onto large serving plate. Remove and discard cheesecloth. Decorate sides of heart with almonds. Pour enough Apricot Sauce onto plate to surround one half of heart; pour enough Raspberry Sauce onto plate to surround other half. Pass remaining sauces. If desired, place a rosebud on top of heart.

Makes 6 servings.

Note: To make coeur à la crème without a heart-shape mold, spoon mixture into footed dessert dishes; chill until ready to serve. Top with apricot and raspberry sauces, or serve sauces on the side.

Praline Cream-Puff Ring

(pictured, page 31)

½ cup butter or margarine
¾ cup water
¼ teaspoon salt
1 cup unsifted all-purpose flour
5 large eggs

Praline Cream
1 package (3 ounces) French-vanilla-flavored pudding mix
1⅓ cups half-and-half
2 tablespoons butter or margarine
1 teaspoon vanilla extract
1 cup heavy cream, whipped
1 cup crushed peanut brittle

1 tablespoon confectioners' sugar
Unhulled strawberries

1. In medium saucepan, heat ½ cup butter, the water and salt until butter melts and mixture boils. Remove pan from heat. Immediately add flour; with wooden spoon, beat dough until smooth. Return pan to heat. Over medium heat, beat in eggs, one at a time, until blended into dough.

2. Preheat oven to 400°F. Line large baking sheet with aluminum foil. With blunt point, mark 7-inch circle in center of foil; mark 3-inch circle in center of first circle. Place dough in pastry bag fitted with ½-inch star tip; pipe ¾-inch-high, concentric rings of dough between outlined circles. Pipe 8 large rosettes of remaining dough over rings. Bake 50 minutes, until ring is firm and deep golden-brown. Turn off oven; leave ring in oven 30 minutes. Cool on wire rack.

3. Meanwhile, make Praline Cream: Prepare pudding as package label directs, using half-and-half. While pudding is hot, stir in 2 tablespoons butter and the vanilla. Let pudding cool to room temperature. With rubber spatula, fold ¼ cup whipped cream into pudding mixture to lighten. Fold in remaining whipped cream and the peanut brittle. Place mixture in pastry bag fitted with large star tip.

4. Place cream-puff ring on large serving plate. With serrated knife, cut ring in half horizontally. Pipe Praline Cream into bottom half; cover with top of ring. Place confectioners' sugar in sieve; sprinkle over top of ring. Arrange unhulled strawberries in center.

Makes 10 servings.

■ Use only real vanilla and other extracts when preparing baked goods that will be frozen.

Triple-Chocolate Cake

(pictured, page 30)

1 package (about 18 ounces) chocolate cake mix
3 large eggs
½ cup butter or margarine, softened
2 squares (1 ounce each) semisweet chocolate, melted and cooled

Frosting
3 large egg whites, at room temperature
2¼ cups firmly packed light-brown sugar
2 tablespoons light corn syrup
½ cup water
2 teaspoons vanilla extract

1 bar (16 ounces) milk chocolate
2 teaspoons confectioners' sugar
1 teaspoon unsweetened cocoa powder

1. Preheat oven to 350°F. Grease and flour two 9-inch round cake pans; set aside. Prepare cake as package label directs, except add eggs, butter and melted chocolate to dry mix. Cool layers on wire rack.

2. Make frosting: In top of 2-quart double boiler, combine egg whites, brown sugar, syrup and water. Cook over boiling water, beating constantly with portable electric mixer at medium speed 7 minutes, or until soft peaks form. Remove top from over water; beat vanilla into frosting. Beat 4 more minutes, until frosting is thick enough to spread.

3. Invert 1 cake layer onto serving plate; spread with 1 cup frosting. Top with second cake layer. Cover cake with remaining frosting.

4. Place chocolate bar on warm stove top or other warm place until slightly softened. Draw vegetable parer or cheese plane over length of chocolate bar, removing thick curls; arrange over top of cake. In small sieve, combine confectioners' sugar and cocoa powder; sprinkle mixture over cake.

Makes 12 servings.

Hazelnut Triangle Treat

(pictured, pages 30 and 31)

Cake
1½ cups unsifted all-purpose flour
1 cup toasted hazelnuts, skins removed
1½ teaspoons baking powder
¼ cup milk
¼ cup hazelnut-flavored liqueur
½ cup butter or margarine, softened
1 cup sugar
2 large eggs, separated

Buttercream
1 cup sugar
½ cup water
5 large egg yolks
1¼ cups butter, softened (do not use margarine)
2 tablespoons hazelnut-flavored liqueur
1¼ cups semisweet-chocolate pieces, melted and cooled

12 assorted small leaves, rinsed and patted dry
Additional toasted hazelnuts

1. Make cake: Preheat oven to 325°F. Grease and flour 10-inch square cake pan; set aside. In food processor or electric blender, place 2 tablespoons flour and 1 cup hazelnuts. Process until nuts are finely chopped; set aside. Place remaining flour on sheet of waxed paper. Stir in baking powder; set aside. In small glass measure, mix milk with ¼ cup liqueur; set aside.

2. In large bowl of electric mixer, at high speed, cream ½ cup butter with 1 cup sugar and 2 egg yolks until light and fluffy, about 5 minutes. At medium speed, alternately blend flour and milk mixtures into butter mixture, beginning and ending with flour mixture. Set aside. In another bowl, with clean beaters, beat egg whites at high speed until stiff peaks form. With rubber spatula, fold beaten whites and hazelnut mixture into batter until no white streaks remain.

3. Spread batter in prepared pan. Bake 40 minutes, or until wooden pick inserted in center comes out clean. Invert onto wire rack; cool.

4. Make buttercream: In small saucepan, combine 1 cup sugar and the water. Bring to boiling, stirring until sugar dissolves; cook over medium heat until syrup registers 234°F on candy thermometer. In large bowl of electric mixer, at medium speed, beat egg yolks until pale yellow. With mixer at high speed, pour in hot syrup in thin stream; beat 5 minutes, or until mixture is cooled. Gradually beat in butter. Add liqueur; beat until smooth. Remove 1 cup buttercream; reserve. To remainder, add ¾ cup melted chocolate; stir until blended.

5. Assemble cake: With serrated knife, cut cake in half diagonally. Place one half on serving plate. Place 2 tablespoons chocolate buttercream in pastry bag fitted with small writing tip; set aside. Spread remaining chocolate buttercream over top of first cake layer. Cover with remaining cake layer; spread plain buttercream over top and sides of cake. With chocolate buttercream in pastry bag, using photograph as a guide, pipe pinstripes on top and sides of cake; pipe dots of frosting on stripes at edges of cake.

6. With small brush, coat backs of leaves with some remaining melted chocolate; set aside. When chocolate has hardened, peel away leaf. Arrange chocolate leaves and hazelnuts on top of cake. Refrigerate.

Makes 16 servings.

Pineapple Bombe

(pictured, page 32)

1 pint chocolate chocolate-chip ice cream, slightly softened
1 pint vanilla ice cream, slightly softened
¼ cup ginger preserves
½ to 1 pint strawberry ice cream, slightly softened

Crème Anglaise
⅓ cup sugar
1 tablespoon cornstarch
4 large egg yolks
1¾ cups milk
1 teaspoon vanilla extract

1 bottle (7.25 ounces) chocolate shell coating
1 pineapple

1. Place halves of 1-quart pineapple mold on baking sheet, or line 1-quart bowl with plastic wrap, extending plastic wrap 1-inch past edge of bowl. With spoon, spread chocolate ice cream over inside of mold halves; freeze 1 hour.

2. In medium bowl, mix vanilla ice cream with preserves until blended; spread over chocolate ice cream in mold. Freeze 1 hour.

3. Spoon strawberry ice cream over vanilla ice cream in center of mold. Fasten sides of mold together; stand mold upright. Freeze 8 hours, or overnight.

4. Make Crème Anglaise: In small bowl, mix sugar with cornstarch. Beat in egg yolks until blended. In small saucepan, bring milk to boiling. Whisk a little hot milk into egg-yolk mixture; whisk into pan of hot milk. Cook over medium heat, stirring constantly, 5 minutes, or until sauce coats back of a spoon. Remove from heat; stir in vanilla. Pour into small bowl. Cover with plastic wrap placed directly on sauce; chill.

5. Cut a round of cardboard the size of pineapple-mold bottom. Place a cloth dipped in hot water over mold; unfasten mold and release ice cream. (If using bowl, hold down edges of plastic wrap and remove bowl. Peel off plastic wrap.) Place on cardboard round; place on wire rack over waxed paper. Shake and squeeze bottle of chocolate shell coating to blend. Squeeze coating evenly over ice cream, scraping excess from waxed paper and reapplying to mold if necessary to cover. Freeze ice cream mold on large platter while preparing pineapple.

6. Cut off frond from pineapple in one piece; insert long bamboo skewer far enough into base of frond to support leaves. Set aside. Cut pineapple crosswise in ¼-inch-thick slices. Cut each slice in quarters.

7. Remove mold and serving plate from freezer. Insert skewer into mold so frond sits on top of ice cream pineapple. Pour some of the Crème Anglaise around the mold; arrange pineapple slices on plate. Pass remaining Crème Anglaise.

Makes 8 to 10 servings; 1½ cups sauce.

Pecan Meringue Torte

(pictured, page 33)

Meringue
1⅓ cups toasted pecans
1¼ cups granulated sugar
6 large egg whites
¼ teaspoon cream of tartar

Praline
1 cup granulated sugar
¼ cup water
½ cup pecan halves

3 cups heavy cream
½ cup confectioners' sugar
2 tablespoons almond-flavored liqueur

1. Preheat oven to 375°F. Grease and flour three 8-inch round cake pans. Cut out three 8-inch rounds from waxed paper; place 1 in each prepared pan. Grease and flour paper. Set aside.

2. Make meringue: In food processor, combine pecans with ¼ cup granulated sugar; process until nuts are finely ground. Set aside. In large bowl of electric mixer, at high speed, beat egg whites with cream of tartar until foamy. Gradually beat in remaining 1 cup granulated sugar, 2 tablespoons at a time, beating until stiff, glossy peaks form. With rubber spatula, fold in ground-pecan mixture just until blended. Spread meringue in prepared pans, dividing evenly. Bake 30 minutes. Cool in pans on wire rack. Invert onto rack; remove paper rounds.

3. Make praline: Grease medium baking sheet; set aside. In small saucepan, over medium heat, combine granulated sugar with water, stirring until sugar dissolves. Bring to boiling; cook sugar until amber colored, swirling pan to brown sugar evenly. Remove pan from heat; swirl in pecans, coating with syrup. Pour mixture onto baking sheet, and let cool. Break into several large pieces; finely chop remainder in food processor.

4. Assemble cake: In large bowl of electric mixer, at high speed, beat cream with confectioners' sugar and liqueur until stiff peaks form. Place in pastry bag fitted with star tip. Place one meringue layer on serving plate; cover with some whipped cream. Repeat with remaining meringue and cream, ending with cream. Stand large praline pieces on top; gently press ground praline into whipped cream on side. Refrigerate 2 hours, or until serving.

Makes 10 servings.

■ To roast nuts, place in a microwave-safe bowl with a dollop of butter. Cook on HIGH 2 minutes; let stand for 1 minute. Stir mixture well; then cook 2 minutes more on HIGH.

Orange Mousse With Chocolate Wraparound

(pictured, pages 32 and 33)

Mousse

2 envelopes unflavored gelatine
1 container (5 ounces) frozen orange-juice concentrate, thawed
½ cup butter or margarine
1 pound white chocolate or vanilla-flavored candy melting wafers
8 large eggs, separated, at room temperature
¼ cup unsweetened cocoa powder
½ teaspoon cream of tartar
⅓ cup sugar

Chocolate Wraparound

1 package (12 ounces) semisweet-chocolate pieces

Sugared Orange Peel (recipe follows)

1. With salad oil, lightly grease 9-inch springform pan. Set aside. In small bowl, sprinkle gelatine over orange-juice concentrate; let soften 5 minutes.

2. In heavy medium saucepan, over low heat, slowly melt butter and white chocolate, stirring frequently, until mixture is smooth. Remove from heat; stir in gelatine mixture. Heat 5 minutes longer, stirring until gelatine dissolves. Whisk in egg yolks until blended.

3. Place about one-third of mixture in medium bowl. Transfer remaining mixture to large bowl; whisk in cocoa. Place each bowl of mixture in a larger bowl of ice and water. Stir frequently until mixtures thicken to consistency of unbeaten egg white.

4. Meanwhile, in large bowl of electric mixer, at high speed, beat egg whites with cream of tartar until soft peaks form. Beat in sugar until stiff peaks form.

5. With rubber spatula, fold one-third of beaten whites into orange mixture until no white streaks remain. Fold remaining whites into chocolate mixture.

6. Pour half of chocolate mixture into pan. Carefully spread orange mixture on top to avoid blending mixtures. Cover with remaining chocolate mixture. Refrigerate 8 hours or overnight.

7. Prepare chocolate wraparound: From waxed paper, cut 2 sheets, 1 each 30-by-3-inch and 28-by-1½-inch lengths. Place each on long tray. In top of double boiler, over hot, not boiling, water, melt chocolate, stirring until smooth. Remove from heat; with spatula, spread a thin layer of melted chocolate over each length of waxed paper to within 1 inch of one end of each length. Let stand 1 hour, until chocolate is firm. (Do not let chocolate harden.) With small biscuit cutter, cut out chocolate rounds from one long side of wider strip to make scalloped edge.

8. Release side of springform pan; remove mousse. Place on serving plate. With waxed paper attached, wrap chocolate wraparound, scalloped side up, around side of mousse, pressing gently to attach. Chocolate should meet at ends but not overlap; band will be higher than top of mousse. Refrigerate.

9. With kitchen shears, cut remaining chocolate strip into 7 equal lengths. With waxed paper attached, fold 5 strips into loops, paper on outside. Pinch ends together; place on tray. Refrigerate 15 minutes, until hardened. Trim a *V* from one end of each remaining strip.

10. Peel off waxed paper from all chocolate strips. With short wooden picks, attach untrimmed end of each flat chocolate strip to chocolate wrap for bow ends; over untrimmed ends, with more picks, attach each loop to make bow. Refrigerate to harden chocolate, about 30 minutes. Garnish top of mousse with Sugared Orange Peel.

Makes 16 servings.

Sugared Orange Peel

1 large orange
1 large egg white, slightly beaten
⅓ cup sugar

1. With sharp paring knife, remove narrow strips of peel from orange. Scrape off any white pith on peel. Place egg white in small bowl; add peel. Toss to coat. Drain peel on waxed paper.

2. Place sugar on another sheet of waxed paper. Roll peel strips in sugar; place on baking sheet. Let stand 30 minutes, or until peel strips are dry.

Mango Mousse Pie

(pictured, page 33)

Crust

1 jar (7 ounces) macadamia nuts, finely chopped
½ cup unsifted all-purpose flour
¼ cup firmly packed brown sugar
¼ cup cold butter or margarine, cut in small pieces
1 large egg yolk

Mousse

1 mango, pared and seeded
2 envelopes unflavored gelatine
1 can (20 ounces) pineapple chunks, drained; reserve 1 cup juice
¼ cup rum
2 tablespoons lime juice
¼ cup cornstarch
1 can (15 ounces) cream of coconut
1 can (7 ounces) flaked sweetened coconut
1 cup heavy cream, whipped until stiff

5 or 6 mango slices
Fresh coconut curls (see *Note*)

1. Prepare crust: In bowl, with fork, mix all crust ingredients until blended. With back of fork, evenly press into 9-inch pie plate. Crimp edge decoratively. Refrigerate 30 minutes. Preheat oven to 375°F; bake crust 20 minutes, or until golden, covering edge with strip of aluminum foil to prevent over-browning. Cool on wire rack.

2. Meanwhile, prepare mousse: Place mango in food processor or blender. Puree; set aside. In medium saucepan, sprinkle gelatine over reserved pineapple juice. Let stand 3 minutes, until softened. In custard cup, mix rum, lime juice and cornstarch until smooth; pour into gelatine mixture. Stir in cream of coconut until blended. Bring mixture to boiling, stirring constantly. Cook 1 minute, until slightly thickened. Transfer to medium bowl; stir in mango puree. Place bowl in larger bowl of ice and water; let stand, stirring occasionally, until mixture is chilled and thickened.

3. Place half of mousse in large bowl; stir in pineapple chunks and flaked coconut until blended. Spread mixture in prepared crust. With rubber spatula, fold whipped cream into remaining mousse; spread over pineapple mixture, swirling decoratively. Arrange mango slices and coconut curls on top. Refrigerate until chilled, at least 4 hours.

Makes 8 servings.

Note: To make coconut curls, crack and remove hard outer shell of coconut, leaving brown skin on coconut meat. Drain off juice. Cut coconut in large pieces. With vegetable parer, remove long, wide strips from broken edges of pieces, removing some of brown skin with meat.

Viennese Pouf

(pictured, pages 32 and 33)

½ package (10¾-ounce size) frozen pound cake, thawed
¼ cup butter or margarine, softened
½ cup apple juice
⅓ cup blackberry preserves
4 large egg whites, at room temperature
¼ teaspoon cream of tartar
1 cup granulated sugar
1 large egg yolk
1 tablespoon all-purpose flour
3 tablespoons confectioners' sugar

Blackberries Flambé
1 can (16 ounces) blackberries
1 tablespoon cornstarch
2 tablespoons brandy

1. Cut cake crosswise into ½-inch-thick slices. Spread both sides of slices with some of the butter. Place on baking sheet; broil on both sides, 8 inches from heat, until golden. Arrange slices over bottom of 2-quart oval casserole.

2. Preheat oven to 350°F. Sprinkle apple juice evenly over cake slices; spread with preserves, dividing evenly. Set aside.

3. In large bowl of electric mixer, at high speed, beat egg whites with cream of tartar until foamy. Beat in granulated sugar, 2 tablespoons at a time, until stiff peaks form. In custard cup, with fork, beat egg yolk until smooth; pour egg yolk into egg-white mixture. Sift flour over egg-white mixture; with whisk, fold flour and egg yolk into whites until blended. Do not overfold. Cover cake slices with egg-white mixture; sprinkle top with confectioners' sugar. Bake 25 minutes, or until crisp on outer edges but slightly soft in center.

4. Meanwhile, make Blackberries Flambé: Drain blackberries; reserve juice. In medium saucepan, mix reserved juice from berries with cornstarch until blended. Bring to boiling, stirring constantly; cook 1 minute, until thickened. Garnish top of pouf with a few blackberries; stir remainder into sauce. Heat thoroughly; pour sauce into serving bowl. Just before serving, place brandy in small saucepan. Heat over medium heat, until vapors rise; pour over sauce, and carefully ignite. Serve immediately with pouf.

Makes 8 servings.

■ You probably know how to bake an unfilled piecrust, but how do you handle small, unfilled tart pastry? Follow the same procedure, but just substitute a paper muffin cup liner for the usual disposable pan. Place it over the uncooked crust, fill it with dried beans or rice and remove halfway through baking time.

Almond Twists

(pictured, page 41)

1 cup ground almonds
About ½ cup sugar
1 teaspoon ground cinnamon
Quick Puff Pastry (page 40)
1 large egg, beaten

1. Preheat oven to 400°F. Line large baking sheet with aluminum foil; generously grease foil.

2. In small bowl, combine almonds, ⅓ cup sugar and the cinnamon; set aside. On surface sprinkled with half the remaining sugar, roll 1 piece pastry into 12-inch square. Brush with beaten egg. Sprinkle with half the nut mixture; with rolling pin, press mixture into pastry. With long, sharp knife, cut pastry square in 1-inch-wide strips; cut strips crosswise in half. Twist each strip 2 or 3 times. Place twists 1 inch apart on prepared baking sheet. Repeat with remaining pastry, sugar and nut mixture. Bake 15 minutes, or until golden. Cool on baking sheet; peel away foil.

Makes 4 dozen.

Elephant Ears (Palmiers)

(pictured, page 41)

About 3/4 cup sugar
1 teaspoon ground cinnamon
Quick Puff Pastry (next column)

1. In small bowl, combine 1/2 cup sugar with the cinnamon. On surface sprinkled with half the remaining sugar, roll 1 piece pastry into a 12-inch square. Sprinkle evenly with half the cinnamon-sugar mixture.

2. Fold 2 opposite sides of square until sides meet in center of square. Fold one half lengthwise over the other to make 3-by-12-inch roll. Wrap in plastic wrap; refrigerate. Repeat with remaining pastry, sugar and cinnamon-sugar mixture. Refrigerate 1 hour, until firm.

3. Preheat oven to 400°F. Line large baking sheet with aluminum foil; generously grease foil. Cut each piece of prepared pastry crosswise in 1/4-inch-thick slices; place 1 inch apart on baking sheet. Bake 15 minutes, or until golden. Cool on baking sheet; peel away foil.

Makes 8 dozen.

Jam Packets

(pictured, page 41)

About 1/4 cup sugar
Quick Puff Pastry (recipe follows)
3/4 cup jam

1. Preheat oven to 400°F. Line large baking sheet with aluminum foil; generously grease foil. Sprinkle half of sugar on foil. On heavily sugared surface, roll 1 piece pastry into 12-inch square.

2. With long, sharp knife, cut in 2-inch squares. With small spatula, spread 1/2 teaspoon jam over each square. With water, dampen corners of each square. Bring opposite ends of each square to center; press to seal. With fork, crimp edges decoratively. Place on prepared baking sheet. Repeat with remaining sugar, pastry and jam. Bake 15 minutes, or until golden. Cool on baking sheet; peel away foil.

Makes 6 dozen.

Quick Puff Pastry

1 cup butter
2 cups unsifted all-purpose flour
1/2 cup sour cream

In large bowl, with pastry blender or two knives, cut butter into flour until mixture resembles coarse crumbs. With fork, stir in sour cream until blended. Turn out onto lightly floured surface; knead briefly until smooth. Pat pastry into two 1/2-inch-thick squares; wrap in plastic wrap. Refrigerate 2 hours.

Berry-Topped Apricot Soufflé

(pictured, page 41)

3 cans (1 pound each) apricot halves
2 envelopes unflavored gelatine
4 large eggs, separated
1/4 cup apricot-flavored brandy
1 tablespoon lemon juice
1/2 cup sugar
1 1/2 cups heavy cream
1/2 pint raspberries

1. Fold 26-inch length of aluminum foil in half lengthwise; fold again. Wrap strip around outside of 1-quart soufflé dish so collar stands 2 inches above rim. Secure with string. Set aside.

2. Drain apricots, reserving 1 cup syrup. In food processor, puree apricots; set aside.

3. In small saucepan, sprinkle gelatine over 1/2 cup reserved apricot syrup. Set aside 1 minute, until gelatine softens. In small bowl, beat egg yolks with remaining 1/2 cup apricot syrup; add to gelatine mixture. Over medium heat, dissolve gelatine, stirring constantly, 3 minutes, or until mixture is smooth. Pour into large bowl; stir in apricot puree, brandy and lemon juice. Place bowl in larger bowl of ice and water. Chill, stirring mixture occasionally, until consistency of unbeaten egg white, about 20 minutes.

4. In large bowl of electric mixer, at high speed, beat egg whites until soft peaks form. Gradually beat in sugar, 2 tablespoons at a time, until stiff peaks form; set aside. In small bowl of electric mixer, at high speed, beat 1 cup heavy cream until stiff peaks form. With rubber spatula, fold beaten whites and whipped cream into gelatine mixture until no white streaks remain. Pour into prepared soufflé dish; refrigerate 3 hours, or until firm.

5. To serve: Remove paper collar. Whip remaining cream until stiff. Place in pastry bag fitted with star tip; decorate top edge of soufflé. Sprinkle raspberries over center.

Makes 12 to 16 servings.

Floating Heart Ritz

(pictured, page 41)

3/4 cup sugar
1/3 cup water
3 large egg yolks
1/4 teaspoon salt
1 cup crushed bittersweet almond-flavored Italian cookies
2 cups heavy cream
2 teaspoons vanilla extract
8 ladyfingers
2 tablespoons almond-flavored liqueur
1 package (10 ounces) frozen raspberries in syrup, thawed
Mint sprig

1. Line 5-cup heart-shape cake pan with aluminum foil. Set aside.

Clockwise from left: Floating Heart Ritz, Berry-Topped Apricot Soufflé, Elephant Ears (Palmiers), Almond Twists, Jam Packets.

2. In small saucepan, combine sugar with water. Bring to boiling, stirring until sugar dissolves. Boil, without stirring, until syrup reaches 230°F on candy thermometer.

3. Meanwhile, in large bowl of electric mixer, at high speed, beat egg yolks with salt until pale yellow. Beat in syrup in a thin stream, until mixture is cool. Stir in cookies until blended. Refrigerate 30 minutes.

4. In another large bowl of electric mixer, at high speed, beat 1½ cups heavy cream with vanilla until stiff peaks form; with rubber spatula, fold into egg-yolk mixture. Pour half of mixture into prepared pan. Split ladyfingers lengthwise in half; arrange, cut side up, over mixture in pan. Sprinkle ladyfingers with liqueur; cover with remaining cream mixture. Freeze 4 hours, or until firm. Invert onto chilled serving plate; remove foil.

5. In food processor or blender, puree raspberries with syrup. Pass pureed mixture through sieve; discard seeds. Pour sauce around heart. In small bowl of electric mixer, at high speed, whip remaining cream until stiff peaks form; place in pastry bag fitted with star tip. Pipe cream around top edge of heart. Garnish with mint sprig.

Makes 8 to 10 servings.

Quick & Easy: Sweet Treats for Kids

Party Popcorn Cake

1 package (8 ounces) candy-coated fruit-flavored candies
½ cup butter or margarine
1 jar (7½ ounces) marshmallow creme
16 cups popped corn
Assorted candy decorations

1. Grease 9-inch tube pan. Reserve ¼ cup candies; coarsely chop remaining candies. Set aside.

2. In 8-quart stockpot or Dutch oven, over low heat, melt butter and marshmallow creme, stirring constantly until blended. Remove pan from heat; stir in popped corn and chopped candies. With large spoon, lightly pack in prepared pan. Refrigerate 15 minutes, until cool.

3. Invert cake onto serving plate. Garnish with reserved whole candies and candy decorations.

Makes 12 servings.

Strawberry Parfaits

½ pint strawberries
1 package (3 ounces) strawberry-flavored gelatin
1 cup boiling water
1 pint vanilla ice cream, slightly softened
½ cup graham-cracker crumbs
¼ cup frozen nondairy whipped topping, thawed

1. Reserve 6 whole strawberries for garnish; hull and thinly slice remaining berries. Set aside.

2. In bowl, dissolve gelatin in water. With whisk, blend ice cream into mixture until smooth.

3. Spoon ¼ cup gelatin mixture into each of six parfait glasses. Top with a few strawberry slices; sprinkle with ½ tablespoon graham-cracker crumbs. Repeat layers; spoon a third layer of gelatin mixture over all, dividing evenly. Sprinkle top with remaining crumbs, dividing evenly.

4. Place whipped topping in pastry bag fitted with star tip; pipe a rosette of topping onto each parfait. Slice each reserved whole strawberry lengthwise into a fan, keeping slices attached at hull. Place 1 berry fan on each rosette of topping.

Makes 6 servings.

Three-Fruit Crisp

3 medium cooking apples
3 medium pears
1 can (8 ounces) pineapple chunks, drained
¾ cup uncooked rolled oats
½ cup butter or margarine, softened
⅓ cup unsifted all-purpose flour
⅓ cup firmly packed light-brown sugar
¾ teaspoon ground cinnamon

1. Preheat oven to 400°F. Pare, core and thinly slice apples and pears. Place with pineapple in 1½-quart baking dish. Set aside.

2. In bowl, with fork, mix remaining ingredients until blended. Sprinkle over fruit mixture. Bake 35 minutes, or until fruit is tender.

Makes 6 servings.

Banana Cone-Cake Kids

1 package (14 ounces) banana-bread mix
3/4 cup peanut-butter-flavored morsels
14 (3-inch high) flat-bottomed ice cream cones
1 can (16 ounces) cream-cheese- or vanilla-flavored frosting
Assorted candies and decorations, such as string licorice, jelly beans, candy hearts and silver dragées
1 tube (.68 ounce) colored gel icing

1. Preheat oven to 350°F. Prepare banana bread as package label directs, except add peanut butter morsels to batter. Spoon batter into ice cream cones, dividing evenly. Place cones on jelly-roll pan. Bake 25 minutes, or until wooden pick inserted in center comes out clean. Cool completely on wire racks.

2. With spatula, spread frosting on cake tops. Decorate as doll faces, using candies for facial features and gel icing and licorice for hair. If desired, tie ribbon around each cup for bow tie or necktie.

Makes 14 servings.

Clockwise from top: Party Popcorn Cake, Banana Cone-Cake Kids, Strawberry Parfaits, Three-Fruit Crisp.

Micro-Way: Chocolate Desserts

Brandy Alexander Pie

6 tablespoons butter or margarine
1½ cups chocolate-wafer cookie crumbs
34 large marshmallows
½ cup milk
½ cup semisweet-chocolate pieces
¼ cup brandy
1 teaspoon vanilla extract
2 containers (8 ounces each) frozen nondairy whipped topping, thawed
Foil-covered heart candies and chocolate pastilles
Additional chocolate-wafer cookie crumbs

1. In 9-inch glass pie plate, melt butter on HIGH 30 seconds. Blend in 1½ cups crumbs. Press evenly over inside of plate; cook on HIGH 1 minute, rotating once.

2. In glass bowl, heat marshmallows and milk on HIGH 3 minutes, stirring after 2 minutes, until smooth. Remove ½ cup mixture to another medium glass bowl; add chocolate. Heat on MEDIUM 2 minutes; stir until melted and smooth. Stir in 2 tablespoons brandy.

3. To remaining mixture, add remaining brandy and the vanilla. Refrigerate both mixtures 20 minutes, until thickened. Fold 2 cups whipped topping into each mixture. Spoon chocolate mixture into pie shell; top with plain mixture. Chill 2 hours, or until firm. Spread with remaining topping. Garnish with candies and additional crumbs.

Makes 8 to 10 servings.

Sacher Torte

6 tablespoons unsifted all-purpose flour
6 tablespoons unsweetened cocoa powder
¼ teaspoon baking soda
6 tablespoons butter or margarine
⅔ cup sugar
1 teaspoon vanilla extract
4 large eggs, separated
¼ teaspoon cream of tartar
½ cup heavy cream
½ cup semisweet-chocolate pieces
¼ cup seedless raspberry jam
¾ cup chopped almonds or hazelnuts

1. Grease 2 8-inch round microwave-safe baking dishes. Line each with 2 waxed-paper rounds. Mix flour, cocoa and baking soda.

2. In bowl, cream butter with ⅓ cup sugar and the vanilla. Blend in yolks, 1 at a time, and flour mixture. In another bowl, beat egg whites with cream of tartar until stiff. Gradually beat in sugar, 2 tablespoons at a time, until stiff peaks form. Fold into yolk mixture until no white streaks remain. Spread in prepared dishes. Cook, 1 at a time, on inverted microwave-safe bowl, on MEDIUM 6 minutes, rotating dish a quarter turn every 2 minutes. Top may be moist; let stand 5 minutes.

3. In glass bowl, heat cream and chocolate on MEDIUM 3 minutes; stir until blended. Cool.

4. Invert cakes onto racks over baking sheet. Discard paper rounds. Spread top of 1 layer with jam; cover with second layer. Pour glaze over cake. Pat nuts around side. Refrigerate, if necessary, to set glaze. With excess glaze, pipe the word *Sacher* over cake.

Makes 8 to 10 servings.

Espresso Cheesecake

⅓ cup butter or margarine
¾ cup graham-cracker crumbs
½ cup ground almonds
1 cup sugar
2 packages (8 ounces each) cream cheese, softened
¼ cup unsweetened cocoa powder
1 tablespoon all-purpose flour
1½ teaspoons instant espresso-coffee powder
2 large eggs
1 cup sour cream
¼ cup milk
1 teaspoon vanilla extract
Whipped cream
Chocolate-covered coffee beans

1. In medium glass bowl, melt butter on HIGH 40 seconds. Stir in crumbs, almonds and ¼ cup sugar until blended. With back of spoon, press over inside of 10-inch microwave-safe quiche pan with removable bottom. Cook on HIGH 2 minutes, rotating dish once.

2. In large bowl of electric mixer, at medium speed, blend cream cheese with remaining sugar, the cocoa, flour and coffee powder. At medium-high speed, blend in eggs and next 3 ingredients. Pour into glass bowl; cook on HIGH 6 minutes; stir every 2 minutes.

3. Pour into prepared crust. Cook on MEDIUM 6 minutes, rotating every 2 minutes, or until almost set in center. Let stand 30 minutes; refrigerate until chilled. Garnish with whipped cream and chocolate-covered coffee beans.

Makes 12 to 16 servings.

■ Store chocolate tightly wrapped or covered in a cool, dry place or in the refrigerator.

Layered Chocolate-Mint Mousse

1 package (10¾ ounces) frozen pound cake, thawed
1 envelope unflavored gelatine
½ cup milk
1 package (8 ounces) cream cheese, softened
½ cup sugar
½ teaspoon peppermint extract
8 drops green food color
1½ cups heavy cream, whipped
1 cup semisweet-chocolate pieces
Additional heavy cream, whipped
Chocolate pastilles

1. Line 9-by-5-by-3-inch loaf pan with foil. Cut cake crosswise into sixteen ¼-inch-thick slices. Arrange 4 slices, short end down, along each side of pan; arrange remainder over bottom.

2. In glass cup, sprinkle gelatine over milk; soften 1 minute. Heat on HIGH 2 minutes; stir until dissolved. In large bowl of electric mixer, at medium speed, beat cream cheese with sugar 1 minute. At low speed, blend in gelatine mixture. Remove ½ cup mixture to bowl; blend in mint extract and food color. Fold in 1 cup whipped cream. Set aside.

3. In small glass bowl, melt chocolate on MEDIUM 2 minutes. Beat into remaining cream-cheese mixture; fold in remaining whipped cream. Spoon half of chocolate mixture over cake in bottom of pan. Top with mint mixture; cover with remaining chocolate mixture. Trim off any excess cake from sides.

4. Refrigerate 3 hours or until firm. Invert onto platter; discard foil. Garnish with additional cream and pastilles.

Makes 12 servings.

March

Savory and satisfying—that's Italian cooking! Our superb collection of classic and new dishes shown in the next few pages is sure to tempt your appetite. Here, an antipasto array of tangy cheeses, zesty meats and garden-fresh vegetables.

Antipasto Buffet

Braciòla Torino

Fruit Medley With Zabaglione

Herb-Crusted Leg of Lamb

Gnocchi With Hazelnut Butter

Linguine Verdi Alfredo   Biscotti

Tortellini in Brodo

Tirami Su

Chicken Parmigiana

Zucchini With Veal-and-Cheese Filling

Parmesan Knots and Rings

Cioppino With Garlic-Cheese Bread

Best Ever Italian Cookbook

Serve up our tortellini soup piping hot and paired with melt-in-your-mouth Parmesan rolls. Or star an old favorite—Chicken Parmigiana—in your next dinner menu.

In March of 1967, *McCall's* compiled a memorable collection of traditional Italian recipes. This extensive treasury inspired our latest collection of favorites that reflect the warmth and hospitality of the Italian coutryside. Even today readers constantly write to have us replace their treasured recipes worn with time. Here we've updated many of the most requested and added a few new tempting ideas.

Our fettuccine Alfredo, for instance, boasts a new twist—we used spinach linguine and added pine nuts for crunch. Other variations on our classic recipes would transform an ordinary meal into an Italian feast—1990 style.

Page 49: Antipasto Buffet featuring Lamb-Stuffed Artichokes and Tomato-Basil Toasts.

Pages 50 and 51: (Clockwise from left) Braciòla Torino, Fruit Medley With Zabaglione, Herb-Crusted Leg of Lamb, Gnocchi With Hazelnut Butter, Linguine Verdi Alfredo, Biscotti. (Inset) Cioppino With Garlic-Cheese Bread.

Pages 52 and 53: (Clockwise from left) Tortellini in Brodo, Parmesan Knots and Rings, Tirami Su, Chicken Parmigiana, Zucchini With Veal-and-Cheese Filling.

Antipasto Buffet

(pictured, page 49)

Antipasto Dressing, Lamb-Stuffed Artichokes, Tomato-Basil Toasts (recipes follow)
¾ pound red-leaf lettuce, washed and crisped
½ pound Romaine lettuce, washed and crisped
1 small head radicchio, separated
½ pound Genoa salami, thinly sliced
¼ pound mortadella, thinly sliced
½ pound small balls marinated mozzarella cheese
½ pound Gorgonzola cheese
½ pound Parmesan cheese
1 pound fresh figs
1 small bunch broccoli, separated into flowerets
1 small fennel bulb, cut in wedges
½ pound green beans, blanched
1 pint cherry tomatoes
1 each green and yellow pepper, cut in wedges
1 can (10½ ounces) chickpeas, drained
1 jar (9 ounces) pickled Tuscan peppers, drained
1 jar (7 ounces) roasted red peppers, drained
1 jar (6 ounces) marinated artichoke hearts, drained
¼ cup stuffed green olives
¼ cup pitted ripe olives
Italian breadsticks; bread rings

1. Make Antipasto Dressing, Lamb-Stuffed Artichokes and Tomato-Basil Toasts; set aside.

2. Line large silver platter or shallow basket with plastic wrap; cover with lettuce leaves. Arrange radicchio-leaf "cups" over platter. Roll salami and mortadella into cornucopias; place point side down in a group on platter. Arrange Lamb-Stuffed Artichokes, Tomato-Basil Toasts and all remaining ingredients except breadsticks and bread rings in groups on platter, using radicchio cups to hold chickpeas and olives. Pass dressing and breads separately.

Makes 8 servings.

Antipasto Dressing

1 medium clove garlic, crushed
1 tablespoon chopped parsley
1 teaspoon salt
½ teaspoon sugar
½ teaspoon dried Italian-herb seasoning, crushed
⅛ teaspoon pepper
½ cup olive oil
⅓ cup tarragon vinegar
1 small tomato, peeled, seeded and chopped

In medium bowl, whisk all ingredients except tomato until blended. Whisk in tomato.

Makes 1¼ cups.

■ For a quick salad, slice ½ cucumber and ¼ red onion; mix with greens and dressing.

Lamb-Stuffed Artichokes
(pictured, page 49)

1 pound ground lamb
1 small onion, chopped
1 medium clove garlic, crushed
1 cup bulgur (medium cracked wheat)
1 can (16 ounces) whole tomatoes
1½ cups water
1 teaspoon dried basil leaves, crushed
1 teaspoon salt
¾ teaspoon grated lemon peel
⅛ teaspoon pepper
6 large artichokes
1 small lemon

Lemon Butter
½ cup butter or margarine
1 tablespoon chopped parsley
½ teaspoon salt
¼ teaspoon garlic powder
⅛ teaspoon ground red pepper
¼ cup lemon juice
2 tablespoons water

1. In large skillet, over medium-high heat, sauté lamb until browned, about 5 minutes. Stir in onion and garlic; sauté 3 minutes longer. Add bulgur; sauté until golden, about 5 minutes. Add tomatoes and their liquid, 1½ cups water, the basil, 1 teaspoon salt, the lemon peel and pepper. With wooden spoon, break up tomatoes; bring mixture to boiling. Simmer, covered, 20 minutes, or until liquid is absorbed.

2. Meanwhile, prepare artichokes: With stainless-steel kitchen shears, trim ends of leaves; cut off stem and 1 inch from top of each artichoke. With grapefruit spoon, remove fuzzy choke. Rinse artichokes well under cold water; drain. Cut lemon in half; rub cut ends of artichokes with lemon.

3. Spoon some lamb mixture into center of each artichoke. Spread apart leaves; spoon remaining lamb mixture between leaves, dividing evenly.

4. Place artichokes in 8-quart Dutch oven; add 1 inch water and the lemon halves. Bring to boiling; simmer, covered, 35 minutes, or until filling is hot and a leaf can be pulled off easily.

5. Meanwhile, make Lemon Butter: In small saucepan, melt butter. Add all remaining ingredients. Heat through.

Makes 6 servings, ⅔ cup Lemon Butter.

Tomato-Basil Toasts
(pictured, page 49)

2 small plum tomatoes, chopped
3 tablespoons olive or salad oil
2 tablespoons balsamic vinegar
2 tablespoons sliced pitted ripe olives
1 tablespoon chopped fresh basil leaves
1 tablespoon chopped Italian parsley
1 loaf whole-wheat Italian bread

1. In small bowl, combine all ingredients except bread. Cover mixture and let stand 10 minutes to blend flavors.

2. Cut bread crosswise into eight 1-inch-thick diagonal slices; reserve any remaining bread for other use. Place bread slices on baking sheet; broil on both sides until lightly toasted. Set aside.

3. Spoon tomato mixture over whole-wheat toasts, dividing evenly.

Makes 8 servings.

Fruit Medley With Zabaglione
(pictured, page 51)

Zabaglione
4 large egg yolks
1 cup confectioners' sugar
¼ cup almond-flavored liqueur

1 package (20 ounces) frozen unsweetened peach slices, partially thawed
1 pint strawberries, washed, hulled and halved
1 package (12 ounces) frozen unsweetened blueberries, partially thawed
½ cup red or green seedless grapes
¼ cup almond-flavored liqueur
¾ cup heavy cream
Mint sprig

1. Make Zabaglione: In top of double boiler, over simmering water, combine egg yolks, sugar and ¼ cup liqueur. With portable electric mixer, at high speed, beat 10 minutes, or until mixture is warm and has tripled in volume. Pour into large bowl; refrigerate several hours (will settle and thicken).

2. Meanwhile, in serving bowl, toss fruits with ¼ cup liqueur.

3. In chilled small bowl of electric mixer, with chilled beaters, whip cream until stiff. With rubber spatula, fold whipped cream into egg-yolk mixture. Pour over fruit mixture; garnish with mint sprig. Serve immediately.

Makes 8 servings, 2 cups sauce.

■ Need to slice a pizza but can't find the cutter? Let clean scissors snip through the crust and topping for a neat job of cutting.

Braciòla Torino

(pictured, pages 50 and 51)

4 thin slices round steak, each pounded to 12-by-8 inches
½ pound thinly sliced prosciutto
1½ pounds ground round
2 large eggs, slightly beaten
1 cup fresh bread crumbs
¾ cup freshly grated Parmesan cheese
½ cup raisins
¼ cup chopped parsley
1 teaspoon salt
¾ teaspoon dried basil leaves, crushed
¼ teaspoon coarsely ground black pepper
4 large hard-cooked eggs
2 tablespoons salad oil
1 jar (28 ounces) spaghetti sauce
¾ cup water
2 cups sliced Italian frying peppers
½ teaspoon sugar

1. On large sheet of waxed paper, arrange steaks, slightly overlapping, to form a long rectangle. Cover steaks with overlapping slices of prosciutto. Set aside.

2. In large bowl, combine ground round with beaten eggs, bread crumbs, Parmesan, raisins, parsley, salt, ½ teaspoon basil and the black pepper until well mixed. Evenly spread mixture over prosciutto. Arrange hard-cooked eggs lengthwise over center of mixture; using waxed paper, lift and roll up steak, jelly-roll fashion, over eggs. With kitchen string, tie up roll at 1-inch intervals.

3. In large Dutch oven, over medium heat, in hot oil, brown braciòla on all sides. Add spaghetti sauce and water. Cover; simmer 1 hour, stirring occasionally. Add sliced peppers, remaining ¼ teaspoon basil and the sugar. Cook 15 minutes longer, or until beef and peppers are tender. If desired, serve with hot cooked pasta.

Makes 12 servings.

Herb-Crusted Leg of Lamb

(pictured, pages 50 and 51)

6- to 7-pound leg of lamb
1 teaspoon salt
¼ teaspoon pepper
1 cup coarsely chopped onion
1 cup dry white wine
2 cups fresh white-bread crumbs
½ cup chopped parsley
4 large cloves garlic, crushed
2 tablespoons dried oregano leaves, crushed
¾ cup butter or margarine, melted
¼ cup Dijon-style mustard

1. Preheat oven to 350°F. Line large roasting pan with aluminum foil. Set aside. With sharp knife, remove and discard fell and fat from leg of lamb. Sprinkle lamb with salt and pepper; place on rack in prepared pan. Place onion around lamb in pan; pour in wine. Roast 1 hour, basting occasionally with pan juices.

2. In medium bowl, with fork, toss bread crumbs with parsley, garlic, oregano and butter. Remove lamb from oven; let stand 15 minutes. With knife, coat lamb with mustard. Evenly and firmly pat bread-crumb mixture into mustard. Lightly cover lamb with sheet of aluminum foil; bake 30 minutes. Remove foil; bake 30 minutes longer, or until internal temperature of lamb reaches 140°F for medium-rare, 160°F for medium or 180°F for well done. Place lamb on heated platter. For easier carving, let lamb set, loosely covered with aluminum foil, 15 minutes.

Makes 10 servings.

■ To add extra flavor to just about any dish, chop parsley and onion in a food processor; then freeze the mixture in a small plastic container. It's ready to use whenever you need it.

Gnocchi With Hazelnut Butter

(pictured, pages 50 and 51)

2 pounds potatoes, pared and quartered
2½ teaspoons salt
2 large eggs, lightly beaten
¼ teaspoon ground white pepper
⅛ teaspoon ground nutmeg
2¼ cups unsifted all-purpose flour

Hazelnut Butter
½ cup butter or margarine
⅓ cup finely chopped hazelnuts
¼ teaspoon salt
⅛ teaspoon ground white pepper

1. In medium saucepan, cover potatoes with water; sprinkle with 1 teaspoon salt. Cover; bring to boiling. Cook 20 minutes, or until tender. Drain through colander; return to pan. Over low heat, dry potatoes 3 minutes, shaking pan frequently.

2. Place potatoes in large bowl of electric mixer. At medium-high speed, beat until smooth. Add eggs, 1½ teaspoons salt, ¼ teaspoon white pepper and the nutmeg; beat until blended. Add 1½ cups flour; with wooden spoon, stir until blended. Turn out dough onto floured board; with floured hands, knead in remaining flour, a little at a time, until dough is no longer sticky.

3. Divide dough into 8 pieces; on floured surface, gently shape each into a 10-by-¾-inch rope. With floured knife, cut each rope crosswise into ½-inch-wide pieces. With floured thumb, gently press each gnocchi on the floured side (not the cut side) to make indentation.

4. In large saucepan of boiling, salted water, add gnocchi, a few at a time. When gnocchi rise to surface, boil 1 minute. With slotted spoon,

remove to colander. Drain well; keep warm while cooking remaining gnocchi.

5. Make Hazelnut Butter: Drain cooking water from saucepan; add butter. Over medium-high heat, melt butter; add hazelnuts, salt and white pepper. Cook, stirring, until hazelnuts are lightly toasted. Add gnocchi; cook, stirring gently, until lightly browned.

Makes 8 to 10 servings.

Biscotti

(pictured, page 50)

3½ cups unsifted all-purpose flour
½ cup hazelnuts, toasted, skinned and finely chopped
¼ teaspoon baking soda
¼ teaspoon salt
3 large eggs
1½ cups sugar
½ cup butter or margarine, melted
½ teaspoon anise extract

1. Preheat oven to 350°F. Grease large baking sheet; set aside.

2. In medium bowl, combine flour with hazelnuts, baking soda and salt; set aside. In large bowl of electric mixer, at medium speed, beat eggs with sugar, butter and anise extract 5 minutes, or until well blended. With wooden spoon, gradually stir in the flour mixture, kneading with hands, if necessary, until the mixture forms a stiff dough.

3. Divide dough in half. With floured hands, shape each piece into a 12-by-1¼-inch roll; place 5 inches apart on prepared baking sheet. Bake 30 minutes, or until rolls are firm and very lightly browned.

4. With long spatula, transfer rolls to cutting board. With serrated knife, cut each crosswise, and at a diagonal, into ¾-inch slices. Place slices, cut side down, on baking sheet. Bake 30 minutes, turning once, until firm and crisp on both sides. Cool on wire racks.

Makes 2 dozen.

Linguine Verdi Alfredo

(pictured, page 50)

1 package (9 ounces) refrigerated spinach linguine
1 tablespoon salad oil

Alfredo Sauce
½ cup butter or margarine
1 cup heavy cream
1 cup grated Parmesan cheese
1 large egg yolk, beaten
1 tablespoon lemon juice
¼ teaspoon pepper
1 tablespoon water

1 jar (3 ounces) pine nuts

1. In large saucepan, cook linguine as package label directs. Drain; toss with salad oil. Keep warm in serving bowl.

2. Make Alfredo Sauce: In medium saucepan, heat butter and cream until butter is melted. Whisk in Parmesan, egg yolk, lemon juice and pepper. Bring almost to boiling, whisking constantly; simmer, whisking, 3 minutes. Whisk water into sauce until blended. Pour over linguine; sprinkle with pine nuts. Serve immediately.

Makes 6 servings.

■ To hold cooked pasta for later, drain and run under cold water in colander. Toss with 1 tablespoon salad oil and place in plastic bag; seal and refrigerate. For use in a recipe, measure and proceed. To serve, run pasta under very hot tap water in colander.

Cioppino With Garlic-Cheese Bread

(pictured, page 51, inset)

1 dozen littleneck clams
2 tablespoons olive oil
1 medium onion, chopped
1 large green pepper, chopped
1 large clove garlic, crushed
1 can (28 ounces) crushed tomatoes in puree
⅔ cup dry red wine
⅓ cup chopped parsley
1½ teaspoons salt
½ teaspoon dried oregano leaves, crushed
½ teaspoon dried basil leaves, crushed
⅛ teaspoon pepper
1 pound cod or scrod fillet, cut in 1½-inch chunks
1 pound large shrimp, peeled and deveined
¾ pound sea scallops, cut in half horizontally

Garlic-Cheese Bread (page 58)

1. Scrub clams well to remove sand; place in large saucepan. Add 1 inch water; bring to boiling. Cover; simmer 5 minutes, or until clam shells open. Discard any clams that do not open. With slotted spoon, remove clams from pan; remove and discard empty half of shell. Reserve 1½ cups of cooking liquid; strain through fine sieve to remove any sand. Set aside.

2. In same saucepan, heat oil over medium-high heat until hot. Add onion, pepper and garlic; sauté 3 minutes, or until softened. Add reserved cooking liquid, the tomatoes and puree, wine, parsley, salt, oregano, basil and pepper. Bring to boiling; simmer, covered, 30 minutes. Add cod, shrimp and scallops; bring to boiling. Simmer 3 minutes, stirring gently, until fish flakes easily when tested with fork, shrimp are pink and scallops are opaque. Add clams and heat through. Serve with Garlic-Cheese Bread.

Makes 8 servings.

Garlic-Cheese Bread

1 loaf (10 ounces) Italian bread
1 package (8 ounces) mozzarella cheese
¼ cup butter or margarine
½ teaspoon garlic powder
½ teaspoon dried oregano leaves, crushed
⅛ teaspoon ground red pepper
16 small Italian parsley leaves

1. With serrated knife, cut bread crosswise into 16 slices. Place cut side down on large baking sheet. Broil on each side until golden-brown; set aside. Cut cheese crosswise into 8 slices; cut each slice in half lengthwise. Set aside.

2. Preheat oven to 400°F. In small saucepan, melt butter. Stir in garlic powder, oregano and ground red pepper. Brush top side of each bread slice with some butter mixture, dividing evenly. Top each bread slice with a slice of mozzarella; gently press 1 parsley leaf into center of mozzarella slice. Bake 5 minutes, or until mozzarella melts. Serve immediately with Cioppino.

Makes 8 servings.

Parmesan Knots and Rings

(pictured, pages 52 and 53)

1 package (16 ounces) hot-roll mix
½ cup grated Parmesan cheese
1¼ cups hot water
3 tablespoons olive oil

1. Preheat oven to 375°F. Lightly grease 2 large baking sheets; set aside. Prepare hot roll mix as label directs, except add Parmesan, hot water and olive oil to dough.

2. Divide dough in half. Roll each piece of dough into an 11-inch rope. Cut each rope crosswise into ½-inch-thick pieces. On lightly floured surface, roll each piece of dough to a 6-inch rope; tie half the ropes into knots and shape the other half into rings, pinching ends together. Place on prepared baking sheets. Bake 15 minutes, or until knots and rings become golden-brown.

Makes 44 breads.

Tortellini in Brodo

(pictured, page 52)

⅓ cup olive oil
3 large leeks, white part only, cleaned and thinly sliced
3 large carrots, pared and diced
3 large celery stalks, diced
1 can (28 ounces) whole plum tomatoes
8 cups water
3 extralarge beef-flavored bouillon cubes
1 package (10 ounces) garlic-and-herb or cheese tortellini
1 can (19 ounces) cannellini beans, drained and rinsed
1 package (10 ounces) frozen Italian green beans, partially thawed
½ cup Italian parsley leaves, minced
1 teaspoon dried basil leaves, crushed
¼ teaspoon seasoned pepper
Grated Parmesan cheese

1. In large stockpot, heat oil over medium-high heat until hot. Add leeks; sauté 5 minutes. Add carrots and celery. Cover; cook 5 minutes, stirring occasionally, until vegetables are tender-crisp. Add plum tomatoes and their liquid; simmer 10 minutes.

2. Meanwhile, in large saucepan, bring water to boiling. Stir in bouillon cubes until dissolved. Add tortellini; cook 6 minutes, or until tender. To mixture in stockpot, add tortellini and their cooking liquid, cannellini beans, green beans, parsley, basil and seasoned pepper; simmer 5 minutes, or until soup is heated through. Pour into soup bowls; sprinkle each with some grated Parmesan cheese.

Makes 12 servings.

Tirami Su

(pictured, page 53)

3 large eggs, separated
½ cup sugar
½ pound mascarpone cheese (see *Note*)
2 tablespoons rum
1 bar (3 ounces) sweet cooking chocolate
1 package (3 ounces) ladyfingers
½ cup triple-strength espresso coffee

Sugared Rosebuds
1 large egg white
3 rosebuds
About ¼ cup sugar

½ cup heavy cream
¼ teaspoon vanilla extract

1. In large bowl, combine egg yolks and ½ cup sugar. With wire whisk, beat 2 minutes, or until light. Add mascarpone and rum; mix until smooth.

2. In large bowl of electric mixer, at high speed, beat 3 egg whites until stiff but not dry. With rubber spatula, gently fold whites, one-third at a time, into mascarpone mixture. Cover bowl with plastic wrap and refrigerate.

3. On sheet of waxed paper, shred chocolate bar on coarse side of metal grater or with vegetable parer. Set aside.

4. Split ladyfingers; place on baking sheet. Brush all sides with coffee. Arrange half the ladyfingers over the bottom of a 1½-quart dish. Spread half the mascarpone mixture over the ladyfingers; sprinkle with half the shredded chocolate. Repeat, making another layer each of split

ladyfingers, mascarpone mixture and shredded chocolate. Cover; refrigerate 1 hour, or overnight.

5. Make Sugared Rosebuds: In small bowl, beat egg white until frothy. Brush each petal of rosebuds with beaten white. Over waxed paper, sprinkle with sugar. Place on wire rack until white hardens.

6. When ready to serve, in small bowl of electric mixer, at high speed, beat heavy cream with vanilla until stiff. Place in pastry bag fitted with star tip; pipe over shredded chocolate. Garnish dessert with Sugared Rosebuds.

Makes 6 to 8 servings.

Note: Or substitute 1 cup ricotta cheese pureed in food processor or blender with ⅓ cup heavy cream.

Chicken Parmigiana

(pictured, pages 52 and 53)

3 whole chicken breasts (1 pound each)
½ cup fine dry seasoned bread crumbs
½ cup grated Parmesan cheese
1 large egg, beaten
About ¼ cup olive oil
1 jar (16 ounces) spaghetti sauce
1 large clove garlic, crushed
1 teaspoon dried oregano leaves, crushed
1 package (8 ounces) mozzarella cheese, cut in 6 slices
3 cups hot cooked pasta
1 tablespoon salad oil
2 tablespoons minced parsley

1. Preheat oven to 350°F. Remove skin from each chicken breast; cut each breast in half. In shallow bowl, combine bread crumbs with ¼ cup Parmesan; place egg in another shallow bowl. Dip chicken pieces first into egg and then into crumb mixture until coated.

2. In skillet, heat olive oil over medium-high heat until hot. Add half the chicken pieces; sauté 5 minutes on each side, turning once, until golden-brown. Remove to plate; repeat with remaining chicken, adding oil if needed.

3. In small bowl, combine spaghetti sauce with garlic and oregano until mixed. Pour into 13-by-9-by-1¾-inch baking dish. Arrange chicken pieces over sauce mixture. Cover loosely with sheet of aluminum foil; bake 40 minutes. Remove foil; top each piece of chicken with a slice of mozzarella. Sprinkle with remaining Parmesan. Bake 10 minutes longer, or until mozzarella is lightly browned and sauce is bubbly. Toss pasta with salad oil and parsley. Serve with chicken.

Makes 6 servings.

Zucchini With Veal-and-Cheese Filling

(pictured, page 52)

8 medium zucchini
1 pound ground veal
½ cup ricotta cheese
½ cup finely chopped mozzarella cheese
¼ cup grated Parmesan cheese
1 cup fine dry bread crumbs
¼ cup grated onion
1 medium clove garlic, crushed
1 large egg
1 tablespoon chopped fresh basil leaves
1½ teaspoons salt
¼ teaspoon pepper
3 tablespoons olive oil
2 cups prepared spaghetti sauce
3 tablespoons toasted pine nuts
Italian parsley leaves
2 cherry tomatoes, halved

1. Rinse zucchini; pat dry. Trim ends; with apple corer, hollow out center, leaving a shell no wider than ¼ inch. Finely chop enough zucchini pulp to make 1 cup; reserve remainder for another use. With fork, score zucchini lengthwise. Set zucchini aside.

2. Preheat oven to 375°F. In medium bowl, combine 1 cup chopped zucchini with veal, cheeses, bread crumbs, onion, garlic, egg, basil, salt and pepper until well blended. Spoon mixture into pastry bag fitted with large plain tip. Pipe mixture into prepared zucchini shells.

3. In 12-inch skillet, heat olive oil over medium heat until hot. Add filled zucchini; sauté 5 minutes, or until lightly browned on all sides. Place zucchini in 13-by-9-by-2-inch baking dish; spoon drippings from skillet over zucchini. Bake 30 minutes, or until tender.

4. In medium saucepan, heat spaghetti sauce until hot. Place zucchini on serving plate; spoon sauce over center. Sprinkle with pine nuts; garnish with parsley and tomatoes.

Makes 8 servings.

Sautéed Escarole and Beans

1½ pounds escarole
¼ cup salad oil
2 large cloves garlic, crushed
1 can (19 ounces) cannellini beans
¾ teaspoon sugar
1 teaspoon salt
¼ teaspoon pepper

1. Separate leaves of escarole; wash thoroughly under cold running water. Drain well; tear each leaf crosswise in half. Pat leaves dry with paper towels.

2. In 8-quart Dutch oven, heat salad oil over medium-high heat. Add escarole and garlic; sauté until escarole is tender-crisp, about 3 minutes. Add beans and their liquid, sugar, salt and pepper. Bring to boiling; simmer, covered, 10 minutes, or until flavors are blended.

Makes 6 servings.

Quick & Easy: Breads Italian Style

Mozzarella Bread

8½-inch round loaf Italian bread
¼ cup bottled Italian dressing
1 package (8 ounces) mozzarella cheese, shredded
1 jar (7 ounces) roasted red peppers, drained and cut in ½-inch strips

1. Preheat oven to 400°F. Line baking sheet or pie plate with aluminum foil. Set aside. With serrated knife, cut bread into 12 wedges, being careful not to cut all the way through bottom crust. Place loaf on prepared baking sheet.

2. Brush cut side of wedges with Italian dressing. Place cheese and peppers between slices, dividing evenly. Bake 10 minutes, or until cheese melts.

Makes 12 servings.

Anchovy Crisps

1 loaf (about 15 by 2½ inches) Italian bread
6 tablespoons butter or margarine, softened
2 tablespoons chopped parsley
1 tablespoon anchovy paste
2 teaspoons lemon juice
2 tablespoons capers

1. Cut bread crosswise into ¾-inch-thick slices; arrange on ungreased baking sheet. Broil slices on each side until lightly toasted.

2. Preheat oven to 400°F. In small bowl, combine butter with parsley, anchovy paste and lemon juice until smooth. Spread mixture on one side of each bread slice; place coated side up on baking sheet. Bake 10 minutes, or until lightly browned. Before serving, sprinkle a few capers over anchovy mixture on each slice of bread.

Makes 8 servings.

Seasoned Breadsticks

1 can (11 ounces) refrigerated soft breadsticks
1 large egg white, lightly beaten
3 tablespoons instant minced onion
1¼ teaspoons dried rosemary leaves, crushed
½ teaspoon seasoned pepper

1. Preheat oven to 350°F. Unroll breadstick dough; separate into 8 strips. Twist strips and place 1 inch apart on ungreased baking sheet. Brush with beaten egg white.

2. In small bowl, combine onion, rosemary and seasoned pepper; sprinkle over breadsticks. Bake 15 minutes, or until lightly browned.

Makes 8 servings.

■ Leftover bread makes great fresh bread crumbs—just crumble and grind for several seconds in a food processor or electric blender. When used to coat cutlets for frying, fresh crumbs absorb less oil than do dried ones.

Deluxe Focaccia

2 tablespoons butter or margarine
1 small red onion, thinly sliced
1 cup sliced mushrooms
¼ cup chopped prosciutto
¼ cup chopped sun-dried tomatoes in oil, drained
½ teaspoon dried Italian-herb seasoning, crushed
1 package (8.46 ounces) refrigerated focaccia (Italian flatbread)
¼ cup crumbled Gorgonzola cheese

1. Preheat oven to 400°F. In medium skillet, melt butter over medium-high heat. Add onion slices, sliced mushrooms, prosciutto, chopped tomatoes and Italian seasoning to melted butter in skillet. Sauté 3 minutes, or until vegetables are tender-crisp.

2. Place focaccia on baking sheet. Spread vegetable mixture over top; sprinkle with cheese. Bake 6 minutes, or until vegetable mixture is heated through.

Makes 8 servings.

Clockwise from left: Mozzarella Bread, Anchovy Crisps, Deluxe Focaccia, Seasoned Breadsticks.

Lite Eating: Pizzas With Pizzazz

Roasted-Pepper Mini-Pizzas

4 medium cloves garlic, unpeeled
$\frac{1}{2}$ package (8-ounce size) part-skim-milk mozzarella cheese, cubed
1 each medium green, red and yellow pepper
$\frac{1}{2}$ package (9-ounce size) frozen artichoke hearts, thawed and halved lengthwise
1 tablespoon balsamic vinegar
Nonstick cooking spray
Cornmeal
$\frac{1}{3}$ recipe Quick and Thin Pizza Dough (third column)
1 teaspoon dried oregano leaves, crushed

1. Rinse garlic under running water until skins are slightly softened. Enclose in plastic wrap, leaving a small opening. Cook in microwave oven on HIGH 3 minutes. Let stand until cool. Cut off and discard root ends; pinch uncut ends to squeeze out garlic pulp. Place in food processor with cheese; process until cheese is finely chopped.

2. Broil peppers, 5 inches from heat, turning with tongs, 10 minutes in all, or until blackened on all sides. Place in plastic bag; let steam 5 minutes. With paring knife, remove peel, seeds, ribs and core from peppers. Slice into $\frac{1}{4}$-inch-wide strips. In small bowl, toss artichoke hearts with vinegar.

3. Preheat oven to 450°F. Grease 3 baking sheets with nonstick cooking spray; sprinkle with cornmeal.

4. Cut pizza dough into 8 equal pieces; on well-floured surface, roll each piece to a 6-inch round. Arrange on prepared baking sheets. Sprinkle half of cheese mixture over rounds, dividing evenly. Sprinkle peppers, artichoke hearts, remaining cheese mixture and the oregano on top, dividing evenly. Bake 8 minutes, or until crisp.

Makes 8 servings, 120 calories each.

Clockwise from left: Roasted-Pepper Mini-Pizzas, Three-Cheese Broccoli Pizza, Ratatouille Pizza.

Three-Cheese Broccoli Pizza

Nonstick cooking spray
Cornmeal
$\frac{1}{3}$ recipe Quick and Thin Pizza Dough (next column)
$\frac{1}{3}$ cup part-skim-milk ricotta cheese
2 tablespoons grated Parmesan cheese
$1\frac{1}{2}$ cups broccoli flowerets, blanched
2 tablespoons sliced black olives
1 cup shredded Italian fontina cheese
1 teaspoon dried Italian-herb seasoning, crushed

1. Preheat oven to 450°F. Grease 12-inch pizza pan with nonstick cooking spray; sprinkle pan with cornmeal.

2. On floured surface, roll out dough to a 13-inch round. Place in prepared pan; fold edge under $\frac{1}{2}$ inch and crimp. Evenly spread with ricotta; sprinkle with half the Parmesan and all the broccoli, olives and fontina. Sprinkle with remaining Parmesan and the Italian seasoning. Bake 15 minutes, or until crisp.

Makes 8 servings, 144 calories each.

Ratatouille Pizza

$\frac{3}{4}$ cup diced eggplant
1 tablespoon salt
1 teaspoon olive oil
1 medium clove garlic, minced
$\frac{1}{2}$ cup diced green or red pepper
$\frac{1}{2}$ small zucchini, diced
$\frac{1}{4}$ cup prepared tomato sauce
$\frac{1}{4}$ teaspoon dried basil leaves, crushed
Nonstick cooking spray
Cornmeal
$\frac{1}{3}$ recipe Quick and Thin Pizza Dough (recipe follows)
$\frac{1}{2}$ package (8-ounce size) part-skim-milk mozzarella cheese, finely shredded

1. Toss eggplant with salt. Let stand 10 minutes. In 3 cups boiling water, cook eggplant 3 minutes. Drain; pat dry. Heat oil over medium heat. Add garlic and pepper; sauté 4 minutes. Add eggplant and zucchini; sauté 4 minutes. Stir in sauce and basil. Simmer 8 minutes.

2. Preheat oven to 450°F. Grease 12-inch pizza pan with spray; sprinkle with cornmeal. On floured surface, roll dough to a 13-inch round. Place in pan; fold edge under $\frac{1}{2}$ inch and crimp. Sprinkle with one-third of cheese; spread with ratatouille. Top with remaining cheese. Bake 15 minutes, or until crisp.

Makes 8 servings, 134 calories each.

Quick and Thin Pizza Dough

1 package (16 ounces) hot-roll mix
2 tablespoons olive oil

Prepare mix as label directs for pizza dough, using olive oil. Divide dough into 3 equal pieces.

Micro-Way: Pasta Main Dishes

Ham-and-Peppers Fettuccine

2 tablespoons butter or margarine
1 large onion, cut in ¼-inch wedges
1 medium red pepper, cut in 2-by-¼-inch strips
1 medium yellow pepper, cut in 2-by-¼-inch strips
2 medium cloves garlic, crushed
½ teaspoon dried rosemary leaves
3 tablespoons all-purpose flour
2 cups half-and-half
¼ pound boiled ham, cut in 2-by-¼-inch strips
½ package (9-ounce size) frozen peas, thawed (1 cup)
½ cup grated Parmesan cheese
⅛ teaspoon pepper
1 package (12 ounces) fettuccine, cooked

1. In large glass bowl, combine butter with onion, pepper strips, garlic and rosemary. Cover with plastic wrap; turn back one corner to vent. Cook on HIGH 5 minutes, stirring once.

2. Stir in flour until blended. Gradually add half-and-half, stirring until smooth. Add ham, peas, Parmesan and pepper; mix well. Cook, uncovered, on HIGH 8 minutes, stirring occasionally, until boiling and slightly thickened.

3. Add fettuccine; toss to coat with sauce. Cook on MEDIUM 2 minutes, or until heated through.

Makes 4 to 6 servings.

Pasta Timbales

¼ cup butter or margarine, softened
1 package (10 ounces) frozen leaf spinach, thawed
1 small onion, chopped
1 medium clove garlic, crushed
1 cup half-and-half
3 large eggs, beaten
½ pound ditalini pasta, cooked
1 cup (4 ounces) Italian fontina cheese, shredded
¼ cup grated Parmesan cheese
½ teaspoon salt
¼ teaspoon pepper
⅛ teaspoon ground nutmeg
1 jar (about 16 ounces) marinara sauce

1. With 1 tablespoon butter, grease six 6-ounce custard cups. In glass bowl, mix remaining butter with next three ingredients. Cover with plastic wrap; vent. Cook on HIGH 5 minutes, stirring once. In food processor, puree with 2 tablespoons half-and-half; return to bowl.

2. Add remaining half-and-half and next 7 ingredients; mix well. Spoon into prepared custard cups.

3. Arrange cups, 1 inch apart, in ring in oven; cook, uncovered, on MEDIUM 20 minutes, rotating every 4 minutes. Cook on HIGH 1 minute; let stand on counter 5 minutes. Meanwhile, remove lid from sauce; heat sauce in jar on HIGH 4 minutes, stirring twice, until boiling. Pour onto platter to cover. Run knife around timbales to loosen; invert onto platter. Pass remaining sauce.

Makes 6 servings.

Three-Cheese Lasagna

1 tablespoon olive oil
1 large onion, chopped
½ pound mushrooms, sliced
½ pound zucchini or yellow squash, sliced
1 medium clove garlic, crushed
½ teaspoon dried rosemary leaves, crushed
½ teaspoon dried oregano leaves, crushed
½ teaspoon salt
⅛ teaspoon pepper
1 jar (40 ounces) spaghetti sauce
½ pound uncooked lasagna noodles
1 container (15 ounces) ricotta cheese
2 cups (8 ounces) shredded mozzarella cheese
¾ cup grated Parmesan cheese

1. In glass bowl, combine oil, onion, mushrooms, zucchini, garlic, rosemary, oregano, salt and pepper. Cover with plastic wrap; turn back one corner to vent. Cook on HIGH 6 minutes, stirring once.

2. In shallow 2½-quart microwave-safe baking dish, spread 1 cup sauce. Cover with 3 noodles; spread with half the ricotta. Drain vegetable mixture; arrange half the mixture over ricotta. Sprinkle with half the mozzarella and ¼ cup Parmesan; spoon 1 cup sauce over cheeses. Repeat with remaining ingredients, ending with 3 noodles spread with 1 cup sauce; sprinkle with remaining Parmesan.

3. Cover baking dish; vent. Cook on MEDIUM 35 to 40 minutes, rotating dish every 10 minutes, until noodles are tender. Let stand, covered, 5 minutes.

Makes 8 servings.

Spaghetti Pie

¾ pound zucchini, shredded (1½ cups)
1 large onion, chopped
1 large clove garlic, crushed
½ teaspoon dried basil leaves, crushed
1 cup half-and-half
3 large eggs, beaten
1 package (8 ounces) spaghetti, cooked
¼ pound sliced prosciutto or Virginia ham, cut in strips
½ cup shredded mozzarella cheese
¼ cup grated Romano cheese
1 jar (4 ounces) roasted red peppers, chopped
½ teaspoon salt
⅛ teaspoon pepper

1. In 10-inch microwave-safe quiche dish, combine zucchini, onion, garlic and basil. Cover with plastic wrap; turn back one corner to vent. Cook on HIGH 3 minutes. Add half-and-half, eggs, spaghetti, prosciutto, the cheeses, chopped peppers, salt and pepper; mix well. Evenly spread mixture in dish.

2. Cook, uncovered, on HIGH 6 minutes, rotating dish every 2 minutes, and, with fork, stirring cooked egg around side of dish with mixture in center. Cook on MEDIUM 12 minutes, or until just set in center. Let stand on counter 5 minutes before serving.

Makes 8 servings.

April

Stuffed, sautéed, roasted or fried—chicken is a family favorite. Our golden selection begins with glazed Cornish hens and rice-stuffed capon and continues with two mouth-watering feasts of fabulous chicken.

Roast Capon With Fruited Rice

Honey-Roasted Cornish Hens

Beer-Batter Chicken and Onions With Fennel Slaw

Cinnamon Chicken With Couscous

Chicken Stir-Fry With Pilaf

Lemon Chicken in a Basket

Chicken Bisque

Coq au Vin Blanc

Chicken Ratatouille Nests

Coconut Bites

Chicken Pinwheels

Lime Chicken

Red-Glazed Chicken

Warm Chicken Salad

PEPPER

HO
SWE
HO

HOME
SWEET
HOME
CLOVES
PEPPER

Home-Style Chicken Cookbook

Just for openers, sample our country-style chicken soup and our tempting chicken appetizers—easy to fix, even easier to eat!

Roast Capon With Fruited Rice

(pictured, page 67)

8-pound capon
½ cup butter or margarine
2 medium onions, chopped
1½ cups uncooked long-grain rice
2 cups chicken broth
1 teaspoon salt
¼ teaspoon pepper
1 McIntosh apple, cored and chopped
1 pear, cored and chopped
1 cup shredded carrots
1 cup (4 ounces) chopped dried dates
1 cup coarsely chopped walnuts, toasted
1 large egg, lightly beaten
1 tablespoon minced fresh thyme or 1 teaspoon dried thyme leaves, crushed
Dash salt and pepper
Mâche (lamb's lettuce), lady apples and fresh apricots

1. Wash capon inside and out with cold water; pat dry with paper towels. Remove and discard excess fat from neck and body cavity. Set capon aside.

2. In medium saucepan, over medium-high heat, melt ¼ cup butter. Add onions; sauté 3 minutes, or until tender. Add rice, broth, salt and pepper. Bring to boiling; simmer, covered, 20 minutes, or until rice is tender and all liquid is absorbed. Spoon into large bowl; stir in apple, pear, carrots, dates, walnuts, egg and thyme until well mixed.

3. Preheat oven to 425°F. Loosely pack neck and body cavity of capon with stuffing. Pull excess skin over opening; secure with poultry pins. With kitchen string, tie legs together. Place remaining stuffing in greased small casserole; bake during last 30 minutes of cooking capon. Place capon on rack in roasting pan; rub outside with remaining butter. Sprinkle with dash each salt and pepper; roast 15 minutes. Reduce oven temperature to 350°F. Roast 1½ hours longer, basting with drippings every 30 minutes, or until internal temperature of thigh registers 180°F. Place on serving platter; garnish with mâche, lady apples and apricots. If desired, let stand, covered loosely with aluminum foil, while making gravy (see *Note*).

Makes 8 servings, 5 cups stuffing.

Note: To make gravy, drain off all fat from roasting pan. Add 3 cups chicken broth. Bring to boiling. In small bowl, combine ¼ cup unsifted all-purpose flour and ½ cup cold water until blended; whisk into broth, scraping up browned bits from bottom of roasting pan. Simmer 5 minutes, or until thickened. Stir in ½ teaspoon salt and dash pepper. Makes about 3 cups.

Page 67: Roast Capon With Fruited Rice, Honey-Roasted Cornish Hens.

Pages 68 and 69: (Clockwise from top right) Beer-Batter Chicken and Onions With Fennel Slaw, Cinnamon Chicken With Couscous, Chicken Stir-Fry With Pilaf, Lemon Chicken in a Basket; (Inset) Warm Chicken Salad.

Pages 70 and 71: (Clockwise from top left) Chicken Bisque, Coq au Vin Blanc, Chicken Ratatouille Nests, Coconut Bites, Chicken Pinwheels, Lime Chicken.

■ Liven up your cooking with the taste of fresh herbs. Fresh ginger, for instance, is more popular—and more available—than ever. It's wonderful on fish and chicken dishes. Buy ginger in the produce section of your supermarket, refrigerate in a paper bag and use within a week. If you need to store the ginger longer, freeze it in a plastic bag; or pare the ginger, and store it in a jar of dry sherry in the refrigerator.

Honey-Roasted Cornish Hens

(pictured, page 67)

½ cup butter or margarine, softened
6 tablespoons lemon juice
¼ cup minced parsley
Pepper
Salt
4 Cornish hens (1¼ pounds each)
½ cup honey
2 quarts water
1 package (12 ounces) baby carrots, pared
8 small new potatoes, halved
1 package (10 ounces) pearl onions
1 small bulb fennel, thinly sliced crosswise (8 ounces)

1. In small bowl, with wooden spoon, beat butter with 2 tablespoons lemon juice until blended. Stir in 2 tablespoons parsley and ½ teaspoon pepper. Set aside.

2. Sprinkle body cavity of each hen with 1 teaspoon salt and ¼ teaspoon pepper. For each hen, using two fingers, loosen skin from breast, being careful not to tear skin; spread breast under skin with one-fourth of the butter mixture. With kitchen string, tie legs together. Place hens in large roasting pan. In small bowl, mix honey with remaining lemon juice until blended. Brush hens with half of honey mixture.

3. Preheat oven to 375°F. In large saucepan, combine water, carrots, potatoes, onions and 2 teaspoons salt. Cover; bring to boiling. Simmer 5 minutes; drain. When onions are cool enough to handle, remove skins. Toss vegetables with fennel and ½ teaspoon pepper; place around hens in roasting pan. Bake 40 minutes.

4. Brush hens with remaining honey mixture; bake 15 minutes longer, or until hens and vegetables are tender. If necessary, broil hens, 6 inches from heat, 3 minutes, or until skin is evenly browned. Transfer hens to serving platter; remove string. Strain pan juices into glass measure; strain off fat. In roasting pan, toss vegetables with remaining parsley; place around hens. Serve with pan juices. If desired, garnish platter with fresh herbs.

Makes 4 servings.

Beer-Batter Chicken and Onions With Fennel Slaw

(pictured, pages 68 and 69)

4 pounds chicken parts
2 teaspoons salt
½ teaspoon pepper
1 large Bermuda onion (1 pound)

Beer Batter
2 cups buttermilk baking mix
1 teaspoon garlic powder
1 teaspoon onion powder
1 large egg, at room temperature, separated
1 can (12 ounces) beer
Salad oil

Fennel Slaw (recipe follows)

1. Sprinkle chicken with salt and pepper; set aside. Peel onion; cut crosswise into ¼-inch slices. Separate into rings; set aside.

2. Make batter: In large bowl, mix baking mix with garlic and onion powders. Stir in egg yolk and beer until blended. In small bowl of electric mixer, at high speed, beat egg white until stiff peaks form; fold into batter.

3. In 5-quart Dutch oven, heat 2 inches salad oil over medium-high heat until it reaches 375°F on deep-fat thermometer. Preheat oven to 350°F.

4. Dip several chicken pieces into batter; shake off excess. Fry 10 minutes, turning once, until chicken is deep golden-brown. Remove to wire rack set on large baking sheet. Keep warm in oven while coating and frying remaining chicken.

5. Place onion rings in remaining batter; toss well to coat. With long fork, lift out a few. Drain off excess. Fry 6 minutes, turning once, until deep golden-brown. With slotted spoon, remove to paper-towel-lined wire rack set on large baking sheet; keep warm in oven while frying remaining rings. Serve with slaw.

Makes 6 servings.

Fennel Slaw

1 large bulb fennel (1 pound)
8 radishes, cut in wedges
1 medium onion, thinly sliced

Dressing
¾ cup olive oil
2 tablespoons lemon juice
2 tablespoons white-wine vinegar
2 teaspoons sugar
1 teaspoon celery seeds
½ teaspoon salt

1. Remove fern from fennel; finely chop enough to make about ¼ cup. Set aside. In food processor or with knife, finely shred bulb and stalks; place in large bowl. Add radishes and onion. Set aside.

2. Make dressing: In jar with tight-fitting lid, combine dressing ingredients; shake vigorously. Add to slaw mixture; toss to coat. Sprinkle with chopped fennel fern. Cover; refrigerate until serving.

Makes 6 servings.

Cinnamon Chicken With Couscous

(pictured, page 69)

1 tablespoon butter or margarine
1 tablespoon salad oil
4 pounds chicken parts
8 small yellow onions
2 cups chopped onion
2 navel oranges, peeled and coarsely chopped
2 large cloves garlic, crushed
3 cinnamon sticks
2 teaspoons salt
¼ teaspoon pepper
1 can (about 14 ounces) chicken broth
⅓ cup tomato paste
2 cups couscous
½ cup water
½ cup golden raisins
1 jar (3 ounces) pine nuts
2 large tomatoes, quartered and seeded
1 large yellow pepper, julienned

1. In 6-quart Dutch oven, over medium-high heat, melt butter in oil. Add half the chicken pieces; brown on both sides, about 5 minutes in all. Remove to plate. In drippings in pan, brown remaining chicken; remove to plate. Remove fat from pan; discard. To pan, add yellow onions, chopped onion, oranges, garlic, cinnamon sticks, 1 teaspoon salt, the pepper, chicken broth and tomato paste; mix well. Return chicken to pan. Cover; bring mixture to boiling.

2. In large bowl, mix couscous with 1 teaspoon salt. Stir in water, a little at a time, until couscous is crumbly and damp. Stir in the raisins and pine nuts. Place in colander or strainer. Set colander over chicken in pan. Completely cover colander and top of pan with heavy-duty aluminum foil. Simmer stew 40 minutes, or until chicken is tender.

3. Spoon couscous onto heated serving platter; top with chicken. In sauce in pan, heat tomatoes and yellow pepper until pepper is tender-crisp. Spoon sauce over chicken.

Makes 6 to 8 servings.

Chicken Stir-Fry With Pilaf

(pictured, pages 68 and 69)

1 large egg white
2 boneless chicken breasts, skinned and cut in ¾-inch-wide strips (1¼ pounds)
1½ teaspoons brown sugar
¼ cup soy sauce
1 tablespoon rice vinegar
1 package (7 ounces) rice-pilaf mix
1 package (10 ounces) frozen peas, thawed
2 tablespoons salad oil
1 large carrot, pared and cut diagonally in ¼-inch-thick slices
1 can (6 ounces) mushroom caps, drained
2 green onions, chopped
2 teaspoons grated ginger root
1 tablespoon cornstarch
1 cup chicken broth
¼ cup dry roasted peanuts

1. In small bowl, whisk egg white until frothy. Add chicken; toss to coat. Set aside. In another small bowl, combine brown sugar, soy sauce and vinegar; set aside.

2. Prepare rice mix as package label directs; place in large bowl. Stir in peas. Keep warm.

3. In large skillet, heat oil over medium-high heat. Add chicken; sauté 1 minute, stirring. Add carrot, mushrooms, green onions and ginger; cook, stirring, 2 minutes, or until onions are tender-crisp.

4. In bowl, mix cornstarch with ¼ cup broth until blended. Stir in remaining broth; add to chicken. Bring to boiling, stirring; boil 2 minutes. Stir in rice; sprinkle with nuts.

Makes 6 servings.

Lemon Chicken in a Basket

(pictured, page 68)

Fried Noodle Basket (recipe follows)

Lemon Chicken
2 boneless chicken breasts, skinned and cut in ¼-inch-wide strips
2 tablespoons cornstarch
1 teaspoon salt
¼ teaspoon pepper
1 lemon
2 teaspoons sugar
½ cup chicken broth
¼ cup dry sherry
2 tablespoons soy sauce
¼ cup salad oil
6 medium fresh Chinese mushrooms, sliced
1 medium red pepper, julienned
1 teaspoon grated ginger root
6 green onions, cut in ½-inch diagonal slices

1. Make Fried Noodle Basket.

2. Make Lemon Chicken: In medium bowl, toss chicken with cornstarch, salt and pepper. Set aside.

3. With vegetable parer, remove peel from lemon in strips; thinly slice into ⅛-inch-wide strips. Set aside. Into small bowl, squeeze 3 tablespoons juice from lemon; stir in sugar, broth, sherry and soy sauce until blended. Set aside.

4. In wok or large, heavy skillet, heat oil over medium-high heat. Add chicken; stir-fry 4 minutes, or until golden-brown. Remove from wok; keep warm. To wok, add mushrooms, red pepper and ginger; stir-fry 1 minute. Add lemon-peel strips and green onions; stir-fry 1 minute. Return chicken to wok. Mix lemon-juice mixture until blended; stir into chicken. Cook, stirring, until boiling. Cook 2 minutes, stirring, until liquid thickens and coats chicken.

5. Place noodle basket on serving platter; fill with chicken. If desired, garnish with green-onion flowers.

To serve, break off some of noodle basket and serve with chicken.

Makes 6 servings.

Fried Noodle Basket

½ pound spaghetti
2 tablespoons cornstarch
Salad oil

1. Cook spaghetti as package label directs; drain. In bowl, with fork, toss spaghetti with cornstarch.
2. Pour 3 to 4 inches salad oil into 10- to 12-quart Dutch oven or saucepan. Be sure pan is deep enough to hold a 7½-inch-diameter strainer used as the noodle-basket mold. The oil will bubble as the noodles begin to cook, so be sure to fill pan to no more than one-third its depth. To find out how much oil to use, place strainer (see step 3) in pan (this will grease strainer); pour in enough oil to reach just below edge of strainer. Heat oil to 375°F.
3. Use a 7½-inch wire mesh strainer, preferably with a wood-and-metal handle that may be bent up to fit inside saucepan. Place greased strainer in shallow bowl to stand upright. Drape 5 or 6 strands of spaghetti around edge of strainer, forming a 2-inch-wide loop; let loops hang 1½ inches over edge, with ends falling into strainer. Continue to form loops around top edge of strainer, overlapping loops.
4. Arrange ends of spaghetti and any leftover spaghetti to cover bottom and side of strainer in an even layer. Lightly press a second, smaller, greased strainer (about 7 inches) into spaghetti to keep basket in place. Holding the two strainers, with potholders if necessary, lower into hot oil. (It will bubble but will then settle back down.) When oil stops bubbling vigorously, it may not cover basket; therefore, with spoon or ladle, occasionally spoon hot oil around edge of basket. Or tilt basket in oil to fry top edge evenly. Fry basket for 15 minutes, or until light golden-brown.
5. Place strainers on paper towels to drain. Carefully lift off smaller strainer. Loosen spaghetti basket from large strainer; drain on paper towels. Set basket in shallow serving dish; place dish on large serving plate. (Basket may be fried up to two hours before serving.) Before serving, place basket on baking sheet; heat through in warm oven.

Chicken Bisque
(pictured, pages 70 and 71)

3-pound broiler-fryer
6 cups water
½ pound asparagus
4 slices bacon
2 medium carrots, thinly sliced
1 medium onion, chopped
⅓ cup unsifted all-purpose flour
1 pound potatoes, pared and cut in ½-inch cubes
2¼ teaspoons salt
¾ teaspoon dried thyme leaves, crushed
¼ teaspoon pepper
1½ cups half-and-half
2 tablespoons chopped parsley

1. Place chicken, breast side down, in 5-quart Dutch oven or saucepan. Add water. Cover; bring to boiling. Simmer until chicken is tender, about 30 minutes.
2. Meanwhile, trim and discard tough ends from asparagus; cut stalks diagonally into ½-inch pieces.
3. Remove chicken from broth; cool. Remove and discard bones and skin; cut meat into thin strips. Place broth in large bowl.
4. With paper towels, wipe out pan. Over medium-high heat, cook bacon in pan until crisp. Remove from pan; set aside. Discard all but 2 tablespoons bacon drippings from pan; add asparagus, carrots and onion; over medium-high heat, cook, stirring, until tender-crisp. Stir in flour; cook 1 minute. Gradually stir in reserved broth. Heat to boiling, stirring. Add potatoes, salt, thyme and pepper; return to boiling. Cover; simmer until potatoes are tender, about 20 minutes.
5. Stir in half-and-half, chicken and parsley. Heat through. Crumble bacon; sprinkle over soup.

Makes 6 to 8 servings.

Coq au Vin Blanc
(pictured, pages 70 and 71)

2 tablespoons butter or margarine
3- to 3½-pound chicken, quartered
18 small white onions
2 medium cloves garlic, crushed
2 tablespoons brandy
2 cups dry white wine
4 small carrots, pared and cut diagonally in 1-inch-thick pieces
1 tablespoon minced parsley
1 bay leaf
1 teaspoon salt
¼ teaspoon ground white pepper
¼ teaspoon dried thyme leaves, crushed
⅛ teaspoon ground cloves
1 package (8 ounces) frozen sugar snap peas

1. In skillet, melt butter. Over medium-high heat, brown chicken; transfer to baking dish.
2. Preheat oven to 350°F. To drippings in pan, add onions and garlic; sauté until lightly browned. Add brandy; holding skillet handle with potholder, carefully ignite. When flames subside, add wine, carrots, parsley, bay leaf, salt, white pepper, thyme and cloves. Heat until boiling; add to chicken.
3. Cover; bake 30 minutes. Add sugar snap peas. Cover; bake 30 minutes longer, or until chicken and vegetables are tender.

Makes 6 to 8 servings.

Chicken Ratatouille Nests

(pictured, page 71)

12 phyllo-pastry leaves, thawed if frozen
⅓ cup melted butter

Ratatouille
3 tablespoons olive or salad oil
6 boneless chicken thighs, skinned and cut in ¾-inch cubes (1½ pounds)
1 small onion, chopped
1 small green onion, chopped
1 large clove garlic, crushed
1 small eggplant, cut in ½-inch cubes (½ pound)
2 large tomatoes, chopped
1 small zucchini, chopped
1 teaspoon salt
1 teaspoon sugar
½ teaspoon dried oregano leaves, crushed
⅛ teaspoon pepper
¾ cup chicken broth
3 tablespoons water
2 tablespoons cornstarch
Fresh oregano sprigs

1. Preheat oven to 375°F. Grease six 10-ounce glass custard cups. Brush 1 phyllo leaf with some of the melted butter; fold crosswise in half. Brush with more butter; fold crosswise in half. Brush with butter; carefully fit into prepared custard cup, allowing edges to hang over outside of cup. Repeat with another phyllo leaf and more butter; arrange over sheet in cup so that corners do not overlap. Repeat with remaining phyllo, butter and custard cups.

2. Place prepared cups on baking sheet. Bake 15 minutes, or until golden-brown. Remove from oven; cool on wire rack 5 minutes. Carefully remove phyllo from cups; cool on wire rack.

3. Prepare ratatouille: In large skillet, heat oil over medium-high heat. Add chicken; cook until lightly browned and tender, about 5 minutes. Remove to plate. To drippings in skillet, add onion, green onion and garlic; cook until onions are golden, about 3 minutes. Add eggplant, tomatoes, zucchini, salt, sugar, oregano, pepper and broth; bring to boiling. Cover; simmer 10 minutes, stirring occasionally, until vegetables are tender.

4. In small bowl, mix water with cornstarch until blended. Stir into vegetable mixture; cook, stirring, until boiling. Add reserved chicken. Simmer 1 minute, until mixture is thickened and clear. Spoon mixture into phyllo nests; garnish with oregano sprigs.

Makes 6 servings.

Coconut Bites

(pictured, page 70)

1¼ cups flaked coconut
¾ cup sieved apricot jam
2 tablespoons lemon juice
1 pound chicken cutlets
1 teaspoon salt
¼ teaspoon pepper

1. Preheat oven to 350°F. Spread coconut over baking sheet; toast 7 minutes, stirring occasionally, or until golden-brown. Set aside.

2. In saucepan, combine jam and lemon juice. Over low heat, melt jam; stir until blended. Set aside.

3. Place chicken between sheets of waxed paper; with meat mallet, lightly flatten to ¼-inch thickness. Remove waxed paper; cut chicken lengthwise into ½-inch-wide strips. Sprinkle strips with salt and pepper. Thread each strip in an *S*-shape onto wooden skewer or pick; place on large baking sheet. Bake 7 minutes, or until lightly browned.

4. Remove chicken from oven; turn oven to 400°F. Pat chicken dry with paper towels; dip into jam mixture, coating completely. Place on baking sheet; bake 3 minutes, or until jam bubbles. Remove chicken from oven; roll in coconut, coating completely. Serve immediately.

Makes about 3 dozen.

Chicken Pinwheels

(pictured, page 70)

1 pound chicken cutlets
½ cup bottled Italian dressing
1 large clove garlic, crushed
¼ pound thinly sliced boiled ham
½ cup butter or margarine
1 tablespoon salad oil

Chutney Dipping Sauce (recipe follows)

1. Place chicken between sheets of waxed paper; with meat mallet, pound to ¼-inch thickness. Remove waxed paper; cut chicken lengthwise into ½-inch-wide strips. Place in medium bowl; toss with Italian dressing and garlic. Cover; refrigerate 1 hour.

2. Cut ham lengthwise into ½-inch-wide strips; set aside. Drain chicken; place on large baking sheet. Place 1 ham strip over each chicken strip; roll up, pinwheel fashion. Insert wooden skewer or pick into end and through center of pinwheels. Set aside.

3. In large skillet, melt butter in oil. Over medium-high heat, sauté pinwheels 3 minutes, or until lightly browned, turning once. Serve with Chutney Dipping Sauce.

Makes about 4½ dozen.

Chutney Dipping Sauce

1 jar (15½ ounces) chutney
½ cup dry white wine

In blender or food processor, combine chutney and wine; puree. Serve with Chicken Pinwheels.

Makes 1¼ cups.

■ When cooking chicken, as well as other meats, it is usually best to add salt near the end of cooking time. Salt draws moisture from the meat.

Lime Chicken

(pictured, page 70)

Marinade
1 tablespoon paprika
1 teaspoon garlic powder
1 teaspoon onion powder
1 teaspoon salt
½ teaspoon dry mustard
1 tablespoon salad oil
2 tablespoons bottled sweetened lime juice
Dash hot-red-pepper sauce

1 pound chicken cutlets, cut in 1-inch squares
Salad oil
Peanut Sauce (recipe follows)

1. In large bowl, combine the marinade ingredients. Add chicken and toss to coat. Marinate at room temperature 15 minutes.

2. Preheat oven to 250°F. Line baking sheet with paper towels; set aside. In skillet, heat 2 tablespoons oil over medium-high heat. Add half the chicken; sauté, stirring until browned, about 3 minutes. Drain on prepared baking sheet. Keep warm in oven. In drippings, sauté remaining chicken, adding oil if necessary. Arrange on platter; serve hot or warm with Peanut Sauce. If desired, garnish with lime wedges.

Makes about 3 dozen.

Peanut Sauce

1 jar (4 ounces) whole pimientos, drained
⅓ cup chopped cilantro (fresh coriander) leaves
¼ cup chunk-style peanut butter
1 large clove garlic
2 tablespoons bottled sweetened lime juice
2 tablespoons soy sauce
2 tablespoons water

In blender or food processor, combine all ingredients; puree. Serve with Lime Chicken.

Makes 1 cup.

Red-Glazed Chicken

5-pound roasting chicken

Stuffing
1 package (7 ounces) cornbread-stuffing mix
½ cup sliced pitted black olives
½ cup pecan halves
⅓ cup minced onion
¼ cup chopped parsley

Red Glaze
1 bottle (14 ounces) ketchup
1 cup ginger ale

6 medium onions, peeled and cut crosswise in half

1. Remove and discard excess fat from chicken; set aside. Preheat oven to 325°F.

2. Make stuffing: In large bowl, prepare stuffing mix as package label directs, except add ½ cup additional water. Stir in olives, pecans, onion and parsley. Loosely pack chicken with stuffing mixture. Pull excess skin over opening; secure with poultry pins. With kitchen string, tie legs together. Place remaining stuffing in greased 1-quart casserole; cover with aluminum foil. Bake during last 30 minutes of cooking chicken.

3. Place a 36-inch sheet of heavy-duty aluminum foil crosswise in large roasting pan. Place chicken, breast side up, in center of foil. Fold the 2 short ends of foil over chicken; fold sides together to seal completely. Bake 1 hour.

4. Meanwhile, make Red Glaze: In medium bowl, whisk ketchup with ginger ale until blended.

5. Open foil package containing chicken; roll back edges to fully expose chicken. Pour ½ cup glaze over chicken. Add onions; bake 1½ hours longer, basting with additional glaze every 15 minutes. If chicken browns too quickly, cover loosely with aluminum foil.

6. Place chicken on heated serving platter; surround with roasted onions. Discard foil from pan, scraping glaze into pan. Place pan on range top; skim off excess fat from glaze. Bring glaze to boiling; simmer 5 minutes, or until thickened. Pass glaze separately.

Makes 6 servings.

Warm Chicken Salad

(pictured, page 69, inset)

1 pound boneless chicken cutlets, cut in ¼-inch-wide strips
2 tablespoons cornstarch
2 tablespoons salad oil
1 small red onion, thinly sliced
1 cup snow pea pods
½ red pepper, cut in ¼-inch-wide strips
4 large mushrooms, thinly sliced
¼ cup water
2 tablespoons soy sauce
2 tablespoons balsamic vinegar
1 teaspoon salt
¼ teaspoon pepper
1 medium tomato, cut in wedges and seeds removed
2 cups spinach leaves, washed
2 small heads Bibb lettuce, leaves separated and washed
1 tablespoon pine nuts

1. In medium bowl, toss chicken with cornstarch until coated. In large skillet, heat oil over medium-high heat. Add half the chicken; sauté until golden-brown, about 5 minutes. Remove to bowl. Repeat with remaining chicken.

2. To drippings in skillet, add onion, pea pods, red pepper and mushrooms; sauté 2 minutes. Return chicken to pan; add water, soy sauce, vinegar, salt and pepper. Bring to boiling; cook, stirring, 1 minute. Add tomato; heat through. On serving dish, arrange spinach and lettuce; spoon chicken mixture on top. Sprinkle with nuts.

Makes 4 servings.

Lite Eating: Perfect Puddings

Bread Pudding With Orange Sauce

Nonstick cooking spray
3 large eggs
3 cups skim milk
½ cup reduced-calorie pancake syrup
2 teaspoons grated orange peel
¼ teaspoon salt
11 slices reduced-calorie bread
½ cup currants
Boiling water

Orange Sauce
1 tablespoon cornstarch
2 envelopes low-calorie sweetener
½ cup orange juice
½ cup water
1 orange, peeled and chopped

1. Preheat oven to 325°F. Grease shallow 2-quart casserole with nonstick cooking spray; set aside.
2. In large bowl, whisk eggs until frothy. Whisk in milk, syrup, orange peel and salt. Set aside.
3. Quarter 3 slices bread; cut remainder into 1-inch cubes. Dip bread quarters into milk mixture; arrange, points up, around side of casserole. Soak bread cubes and currants in milk mixture 5 minutes. Pour bread cubes, currants and any milk mixture into casserole.
4. Place in roasting pan in middle of oven. Pour boiling water into pan to halfway up side of casserole. Bake 1 hour and 10 minutes, until knife inserted in center comes out clean.
5. Make sauce: In saucepan, combine cornstarch and sweetener. Blend in juice and water. Bring to boiling, stirring. Cook 1 minute. Cool slightly; stir in orange.
6. Serve pudding warm with Orange Sauce. If desired, garnish with lemon-peel rose and mint sprig.

Makes 8 servings (1½ cups sauce), 178 calories each.

Strawberry-Pineapple Bavarian

1 package (.03 ounce) sugar-free strawberry-flavored gelatin
Water
1 can (8 ounces) crushed pineapple in natural juices, undrained
½ package (2.6-ounce size) dessert-topping mix (1 envelope)
½ cup skim milk

1. In 1-quart glass measure, dissolve gelatin in 1 cup boiling water. Stir in ½ cup cold water and the pineapple with its juice. Refrigerate mixture 30 minutes, or until slightly thickened.
2. In large bowl, prepare topping mix as package label directs, using

Clockwise from top left: Strawberry-Pineapple Bavarian, Black 'n' White Parfaits, Bread Pudding With Orange Sauce.

skim milk. Fold thickened gelatin mixture into topping. Pour into 1-quart mold. Refrigerate 3 hours, or until firm.

3. To serve: Dip mold into bowl of warm water. Pat mold dry; invert Bavarian onto serving platter. If desired, garnish with unhulled strawberries and fresh pineapple wedges.

Makes 8 servings, 51 calories each.

Black 'n' White Parfaits

⅓ cup raisins
2 tablespoons dark rum
1 package (1.3 ounces) sugar-free cook-and-serve chocolate pudding
1 quart skim milk
1 package (0.8 ounce) sugar-free cook-and-serve vanilla pudding
1 medium banana

1. In custard cup, soak raisins in rum 15 minutes. Prepare chocolate pudding as package label directs, using 2 cups skim milk. Stir in raisins and rum; cover and refrigerate 2 hours, or until thoroughly chilled.

2. Prepare vanilla pudding as package label directs, using remaining 2 cups milk. Cut banana crosswise in thin slices; stir into vanilla pudding. Cover; refrigerate 2 hours, until chilled.

3. Assemble parfaits: Stir each pudding mixture; spoon ¼ cup chocolate mixture into each of 8 parfait glasses. Spoon ¼ cup vanilla mixture over chocolate mixture in each glass. Repeat layering with remaining mixtures.

Makes 8 servings, 108 calories each.

Micro-Way: Tasty Chicken Sandwiches

Grilled Chicken 'n' Cheese

2 whole boneless chicken breasts, skinned and split
1/3 cup butter or margarine
8 slices country-style white bread
8 slices Jarlsberg cheese
1/4 cup bottled chutney
1 small Red Delicious apple, cored and thinly sliced

1. In glass pie plate, arrange chicken with thicker portions toward outside. Cover with plastic wrap; turn back one corner to vent. Cook on HIGH 6 minutes; turn chicken over after 4 minutes. Let stand 5 minutes.

2. Melt butter on HIGH about 30 seconds; brush some onto both sides of bread. Top each with cheese slice. Slice each chicken breast horizontally in half; arrange chicken over each slice of cheese. Spread chutney over chicken; cover each with some apple slices. Top with a slice of remaining bread.

3. Preheat hinged or flat microwave sandwich grill as manufacturer directs. If using hinged grill, place cover on upper hinge for a thick sandwich. Place one sandwich on bottom half of grill; close cover or place 2 sandwiches on flat grill. Cook on HIGH 45 seconds for hinged grill or 25 seconds for flat grill. Remove sandwich; clean and preheat grill before repeating procedure with other side of sandwich for flat grill or remaining sandwiches for hinged grill.

Makes 4 servings.

Tarragon Chicken-Salad Loaf

2 pounds boneless chicken breasts, skinned and split
1 pound asparagus, cut diagonally in ½-inch pieces
½ cup water
1 cup mayonnaise
2 tablespoons lemon juice
1 tablespoon minced fresh tarragon or 1½ teaspoons dried tarragon leaves, crushed
¼ teaspoon salt
⅛ teaspoon pepper
1 large carrot, shredded
1 small red pepper, chopped
3 green onions, minced
1 pound oval loaf egg bread, unsliced

1. In 13-by-9-by-2-inch microwave-safe baking dish, arrange chicken breasts with thicker portions toward outside. Cover with plastic wrap; turn back one corner to vent. Cook on HIGH 10 minutes, turning chicken over after 5 minutes. Let cool in dish.

2. In medium glass bowl, combine asparagus and water. Cover; vent. Cook on HIGH 3 minutes; drain. Rinse with cold water; drain. Set aside.

3. In bowl, whisk mayonnaise with lemon juice, tarragon, salt and pepper until blended. Stir in asparagus, carrot, red pepper and onions. Cut chicken into 1-inch pieces; stir into mayonnaise mixture.

4. With serrated knife, cut off a thin slice from top of bread; remove inside (reserve for other use), leaving a ½-inch shell. Spoon salad into bread shell, mounding slightly. If desired, garnish with fresh tarragon. To serve, cut into wedges.

Makes 8 to 10 servings.

■ To dry fresh herbs in a quick, easy way, line a microwave-safe plate with 2 paper towels, one on top of the other. Evenly spread 2 cups of clean, dry leaves or sprigs on towels. Cook herbs on HIGH 4 minutes, turning at least once. Store the dried herbs in a tightly covered container.

May

Presenting our easy-on-Mom collection of meals that take just minutes to make. Starting here, a spring lamb dinner, followed by six other quick-to-fix menus, all listed below by entrée.

Cheese-Topped Lamb Chops

Chicken Fajitas

All-American Chili Dogs

Wrapped Grilled Shrimp

Basil Fillet Pinwheels

Veal Piccata

Pork Satay With Spicy Peanut Dipping Sauce

30
30

30-Minute Menu Cookbook

Surprise Mom with one of our effortless entrées, complete with accompaniments and even mouth-watering desserts.

*CHEESE-TOPPED LAMB CHOPS
FRESH VEGETABLE MÉLANGE
*TANGY SPINACH SALAD
*STRAWBERRIES EN CHEMISE

■ Make dessert; refrigerate. Prepare salad and dressing; keep dressing warm. While chops cook, prepare vegetables.

Cheese-Topped Lamb Chops

(pictured, page 83)

4 (6 ounces each) loin lamb chops, about 2 inches thick
Salt
Pepper
1 package (5 ounces) garlic-and-herb cheese spread
1 jar (2 ounces) chopped pimientos, drained

1. Place chops on rack in broiler pan; sprinkle with salt and pepper. Broil 6 inches from heat 8 minutes. Turn chops; broil 5 minutes.
2. In small bowl, mix cheese with pimientos; spoon on top of lamb chops, dividing evenly. Broil 3 minutes longer. Serve immediately.

Makes 4 servings.

Tangy Spinach Salad

(pictured, page 83)

½ pound spinach leaves, washed
3 cups sliced mushrooms
6 slices bacon
2 tablespoons brown sugar
2 tablespoons Dijon-style mustard
3 tablespoons lemon juice

1. Remove and discard stems from spinach; tear into bite-size pieces. Place in salad bowl. Add mushroom slices; refrigerate.
2. In medium skillet, cook bacon until crisp. Remove from pan; drain on paper towels. Crumble; set aside.
3. To bacon drippings in pan, add brown sugar, mustard and lemon juice. Cook, stirring, 1 minute. Pour into salad; toss to coat. Sprinkle with bacon. Serve immediately.

Makes 4 servings.

Strawberries en Chemise

(pictured, page 83)

1 pint unhulled strawberries, with stems
½ can (16-ounce size) ready-to-spread cream-cheese frosting
1 tablespoon orange-flavored liqueur

1. Gently rinse strawberries with cold water; pat dry with paper towels. Set aside.
2. In small glass bowl, combine frosting with liqueur until blended. Soften in microwave oven 10 seconds on MEDIUM, stirring after 5 seconds.
3. Line a baking sheet with waxed paper. Holding a strawberry by its stem, dip bottom two-thirds of berry into frosting mixture. Place on prepared baking sheet. Repeat with remaining strawberries and frosting mixture.

Makes 4 servings.

Page 83: Cheese-Topped Lamb Chops, Fresh Vegetable Mélange, Tangy Spinach Salad, Strawberries en Chemise.

Pages 84 and 85: Chicken Fajitas with toppings, Flour Tortillas, Sangría, Mexican Salad Bowl, Deluxe Caramel Sundaes; (Inset, above right) Zesty Avocado Dip, All-American Chili Dogs, "Flowerpot" Dessert; (Inset, below right) Wrapped Grilled Shrimp, Risotto With Mushrooms, Steamed Asparagus, Bread Flats, Three-Green Salad, White-Chocolate Parfaits.

Pages 86 and 87: Basil Fillet Pinwheels, Creamy Zucchini 'n' Rice, Dinner Rolls, Orange Tea, Royal Fruit Delight; (Inset, above right) Veal Piccata, Parsley Pasta, Stir-Fried Squash, Mixed Green Salad, Dry White Wine, Pear-Raspberry Tart; (Inset, below right) Pork Satay With Spicy Peanut Dipping Sauce, Cold Brown-Rice Salad, Fresh Pita Chips, Lime Tea, Sautéed Apples With Warm Custard, Cookies.

*CHICKEN FAJITAS
FLOUR TORTILLAS
*MEXICAN SALAD BOWL
*DELUXE CARAMEL SUNDAES
SANGRÍA

■ Make dressing for Mexican Salad Bowl; set aside. Arrange salad in bowl. Cover; refrigerate. Make fajitas while steaming tortillas. Pour dressing and peanuts over salad. Serve with sangría. Make sundaes just before serving.

Chicken Fajitas

(pictured, page 84)

12 flour tortillas
1 can (16 ounces) refried beans
4 tablespoons salad oil
2 medium onions, cut in ½-inch wedges
2 large jalapeño peppers, finely chopped
1 large green pepper, cut in ½-inch-wide strips
1 large red pepper, cut in ½-inch-wide strips
2 large cloves garlic, crushed
1¼ teaspoons salt
2 whole boneless chicken breasts, skinned and cut in ½-inch-wide strips (1¼ pounds)
1 teaspoon chili powder
2 tablespoons chopped cilantro (fresh coriander) leaves
¼ cup (1 ounce) shredded Monterey Jack cheese
Prepared picante sauce

1. Steam tortillas as package label directs. In small saucepan, heat refried beans; keep warm.

2. In 5-quart saucepan, heat 2 tablespoons salad oil over high heat. Add onions, peppers, garlic and ½ teaspoon salt; sauté 3 minutes, or until vegetables are tender-crisp. Remove to bowl. Add 2 tablespoons salad oil to drippings in pan. Add chicken, chili powder and ¾ teaspoon salt; sauté 5 minutes, or until chicken is tender. Return onion mixture to pan; heat through.

3. Place chicken mixture in bowl on large warm serving platter; sprinkle with cilantro. Arrange tortillas around bowl. Spoon beans into small bowl; sprinkle with cheese. Spoon picante sauce into another small bowl. Pass tortillas and fillings.

Makes 6 servings.

Mexican Salad Bowl

(pictured, pages 84 and 85)

Dressing
¼ cup white vinegar
2 tablespoons sugar
¼ teaspoon chili powder
¼ teaspoon salt

¾ pound jicama, pared
2 medium oranges
1 large red apple
1 medium banana
2 tablespoons lime juice
1 can (8 ounces) sliced beets, drained
Green-leaf lettuce leaves, washed and crisped
2 tablespoons unsalted peanuts

1. Make dressing: In small container with tight-fitting lid, combine vinegar, sugar, chili powder and salt. Shake until sugar dissolves.

2. Cut jicama crosswise in half; cut each half into thin slices. Place in large bowl. Cut off and discard peel and pith from oranges; cut crosswise into ¼-inch-thick slices. Place in bowl with jicama. Core apple; cut into ½-inch wedges. Place in bowl with jicama. Peel and thinly slice banana; add to jicama with the lime juice. Add beets; toss until pieces are coated with lime juice. Place in lettuce-lined salad bowl. Before serving, pour dressing over salad; sprinkle with peanuts.

Makes 6 servings.

Deluxe Caramel Sundaes

(pictured, page 85)

1 quart coffee ice cream
¾ cup bottled butterscotch-caramel sauce
½ cup chopped walnuts or pecans
⅓ cup toasted flaked coconut

Scoop ice cream into 6 dessert bowls; top with caramel sauce, walnuts and coconut, dividing evenly. If desired, serve with cookies.

Makes 6 servings.

■ Facing the challenge of creating a meal in less than 30 minutes? Serve soup (commercial or frozen homemade) and sandwiches, but plan ahead. You can save time by making sandwiches ahead and freezing them. For best results, use day-old bread and spread with butter or margarine to keep sandwiches from becoming soggy. Use meat, poultry, fish, cheese or peanut butter; avoid fresh vegetables, jam, hard-cooked eggs, and salad dressing or mayonnaise. Cured meats will undergo flavor changes during long-term freezing, so prepare and freeze this type of sandwich only a day ahead.

*ZESTY AVOCADO DIP *ALL-AMERICAN CHILI DOGS *"FLOWERPOT" DESSERT

■ Prepare chili; simmer. Prepare grill. Make dessert; freeze. Cut vegetables for dip and make dip; refrigerate. Cook frankfurters.

Zesty Avocado Dip

(pictured, page 85, inset)

1 medium ripe avocado
1 cup sour cream
1 package (.56 ounce) green-onion dip mix
1 tablespoon lemon juice
Carrot slices, cucumber rounds, broccoli flowerets, red- and yellow-pepper strips, green beans and radishes

In food processor, blend first 4 ingredients until smooth. Transfer to small bowl. Cover tightly with plastic wrap; refrigerate. Serve with vegetables.

Makes 4 servings, with about 2 cups dip.

All-American Chili Dogs

(pictured, page 85, inset)

½ pound ground beef
1 small onion, chopped
1 small green pepper, chopped
1 medium clove garlic, crushed
1 tablespoon chili seasoning
1 can (16 ounces) tomatoes, undrained
2 tablespoons tomato paste
1 teaspoon salt
⅛ teaspoon ground red pepper
1 package (16 ounces) frankfurters (8)
8 frankfurter rolls
½ cup (2 ounces) shredded extrasharp Cheddar cheese

1. In large skillet, over medium-high heat, sauté beef 3 minutes, or until browned. Add onion, green pepper, garlic and chili seasoning; cook, stirring, 3 minutes longer. Stir in tomatoes and their juice, tomato paste, salt and ground red pepper; bring to boiling. Reduce heat; simmer, uncovered, 10 minutes.

2. Prepare barbecue grill. With knife, score frankfurters crosswise about one-third through. Grill, 6 inches from heat and turning occasionally, 5 minutes. Place rolls on grill to toast lightly.

3. Place frankfurters in rolls. Spoon some chili onto each frankfurter; sprinkle each with cheese. If desired, serve with potato chips.

Makes 4 servings.

"Flowerpot" Dessert

(pictured, page 85, inset)

1 pint vanilla (or other flavor) ice cream
10 (2½-inch-long) pink sugar wafers
11 (2½-inch-long) vanilla sugar wafers, cut crosswise in half
1 tube (4.25 ounces) pink decorating icing, fitted with star tip
1 tube (.75 ounce) green gel icing
¼ cup chopped pistachios or peanuts
Assorted lollipops

1. Remove ice cream from container in one piece; place on cold serving plate. Working quickly, press pink sugar wafers upright around base of ice cream.

2. Sandwich 2 cut wafers together with pink icing; press sandwiches into ice cream just above pink cookies. With tiny rosettes of green gel icing, decorate between sandwiches; with a tiny rosette of pink icing, decorate outside of sandwiches. Sprinkle chopped nuts over top of ice cream.

3. With green gel icing, decorate lollipops; insert lollipop "flowers" into "flowerpot." Place in freezer until serving. To serve, cut lengthwise in wedges.

Makes 4 servings.

*WRAPPED GRILLED SHRIMP *RISOTTO WITH MUSHROOMS STEAMED ASPARAGUS BREAD FLATS THREE-GREEN SALAD *WHITE-CHOCOLATE PARFAITS

■ Begin making White-Chocolate Parfaits; do not assemble. Sauté mushrooms. While risotto cooks, prepare shrimp skewers and salad. Assemble parfaits; refrigerate. Steam asparagus; grill shrimp.

Wrapped Grilled Shrimp

(pictured, page 85, inset)

4 slices prosciutto or other ham
12 jumbo shrimp (about 1 pound), peeled and deveined
¼ cup butter or margarine
¼ cup lemon juice
2 tablespoons lime juice
½ teaspoon curry powder

1. Prepare barbecue grill. Cut each prosciutto slice lengthwise in thirds; wrap 1 piece around each shrimp. Thread 3 shrimp onto each of four 12-inch skewers.

2. In small saucepan, melt butter; stir in lemon juice, lime juice and ¼ teaspoon curry powder. Brush mixture over wrapped shrimp. Sprinkle with remaining curry powder.

3. Grill shrimp, placing skewers 4 inches from heat 2 to 3 minutes on each side, basting occasionally with butter mixture. If desired, serve

shrimp with cheesecloth-wrapped lemon half.

Makes 4 servings.

Risotto With Mushrooms

(pictured, page 85, inset)

1 tablespoon salad oil
¼ pound medium mushrooms, sliced
1 package (4.2 ounces) risotto-with-mushrooms mix

In 2-quart saucepan, heat oil over medium heat. Add mushrooms; sauté 3 minutes, or until golden-brown. In same saucepan, prepare risotto as package label directs.

Makes 4 servings.

White-Chocolate Parfaits

(pictured, page 85, inset)

6 ounces white chocolate, finely grated
1½ cups heavy cream, chilled
3 tablespoons coffee-flavored liqueur
8 chocolate sandwich cookies, crushed

1. In 2-quart glass bowl, melt chocolate in microwave oven on MEDIUM 2 minutes, stirring occasionally, or melt in top of double boiler over simmering water. Gradually add ¼ cup cream and the liqueur, stirring until blended. Chill in freezer 10 minutes.

2. In small bowl of electric mixer, at high speed, whip remaining cream until stiff. With rubber spatula, fold into chocolate mixture.

3. Spoon into 4 dessert dishes, alternating cream mixture with crushed cookies. Chill in freezer until serving time.

Makes 4 servings.

*BASIL FILLET PINWHEELS
*CREAMY ZUCCHINI 'N' RICE
DINNER ROLLS
ORANGE TEA
*ROYAL FRUIT DELIGHT

■ Prepare Creamy Zucchini 'n' Rice; while mixture bakes, cut up fruit for Royal Fruit Delight. Roll up and poach fish fillets. Make sauce for fish.

Basil Fillet Pinwheels

(pictured, pages 86 and 87)

12 fillets of sole (about 3 ounces each)
½ teaspoon dried basil leaves, crushed
¼ teaspoon pepper
1 medium clove garlic, crushed
¾ cup dry white wine
About 1¼ cups milk
1 package (1.8 ounces) white-sauce mix
2 tablespoons tomato paste

1. Cut fillets in half lengthwise. With dark side up, starting from narrow end, roll up each fillet jelly-roll fashion, secure with wooden pick. In large skillet, stand fillets on end; sprinkle with basil and pepper. Add garlic and wine to skillet. Bring to boiling; simmer, covered, 10 minutes, or until fish flakes when tested with fork.

2. With slotted spatula, remove fillets to heated serving platter. Keep warm, covered loosely with sheet of aluminum foil. Pour cooking liquid into large glass measure; add enough milk to make 2¼ cups. In same skillet, combine white-sauce mix with enough milk mixture to blend; whisk in remaining milk mixture and the tomato paste until smooth. Bring to boiling, whisking constantly; simmer 1 minute.

3. To serve: Pour some sauce onto each of 8 warm serving plates; top each with 2 or 3 rolled fillets. If desired, garnish each serving with sprig of fresh basil.

Makes 8 to 12 servings, with about 2 cups sauce.

Creamy Zucchini 'n' Rice

(pictured, pages 86 and 87)

1 package (7¼ ounces) herb-and-butter-flavor rice-and-pasta mix
3 tablespoons butter or margarine
2 pounds zucchini, shredded
1 medium onion, chopped
1 can (10¾ ounces) low-sodium cream-of-mushroom soup
⅓ cup water
½ cup (2 ounces) shredded Monterey Jack cheese

1. Preheat oven to 425°F. Remove herb packet from rice-and-pasta mix; set aside. In large skillet, melt butter. Add zucchini, onion and rice-and-pasta mix; sauté 3 minutes. Remove pan from heat.

2. In small bowl, mix soup with water; add to zucchini mixture. Stir in reserved herb packet and ¼ cup cheese. Pour into shallow 2-quart baking dish; sprinkle with remaining cheese. Bake 25 minutes, or until golden and bubbly. Let stand 5 minutes before serving. If desired, garnish with tomato-peel roses and zucchini-peel curls.

Makes 8 servings.

■ Here's a quick, refreshing summer treat to have on hand: Cook 5 cups sliced green apples with ¾ cup sugar and 1 cup water until tender, about 15 minutes. Puree in food processor; add 1 teaspoon grated lemon peel and freeze until firm. Reprocess, and freeze again. Serve this delicious concoction at a moment's notice.

Royal Fruit Delight

(pictured, page 86)

¼ cup coarsely chopped crystallized ginger root
¼ cup orange-flavored liqueur
1 ripe papaya, pared, seeded and sliced
4 cups watermelon chunks
2 cups seedless grapes
1 cup cherries, halved and pitted
½ cup raspberries
Sweetened whipped cream
Julienned orange peel

1. In large bowl, combine ginger with liqueur; let stand 5 minutes. Add fruit; toss mixture well to coat evenly. Cover; refrigerate until serving time.

2. Spoon fruit mixture into serving dish. Arrange whipped cream to one side of fruit; top cream with orange peel.

Makes 8 servings.

■ What can you do with too many guests and too little food or unexpected guests and no menu planned? Make a large bowl of pasta; toss with butter and Parmesan cheese. It's an instant party pleaser. (For a variation, if you have some heavy cream on hand, just heat and toss into the pasta with garlic powder and basil.)

■ When you need an easy dish to serve guests or to take to a get-together, make this favorite cocktail appetizer treat: Coat seedless grapes with spreadable, cold-pack cheese or a mixture of equal parts cream cheese and blue cheese; then roll in finely chopped, toasted walnuts. Freeze on tray. When they are frozen, you can put your delicious creation into a sturdy container or prechilled, widemouthed thermos container and take to neighborhood or family gatherings.

*VEAL PICCATA
PARSLEY PASTA
*STIR-FRIED SQUASH
MIXED GREEN SALAD
CRISP BREADSTICKS
DRY WHITE WINE
*PEAR-RASPBERRY TARTS

■ Prepare and bake tarts. Assemble salad. Boil water for pasta; while cooking pasta, stir-fry squash and cook veal. Toss pasta with butter and parsley.

Veal Piccata

(pictured, page 87, inset)

¼ cup unsifted all-purpose flour
½ teaspoon lemon-pepper seasoning
½ teaspoon salt
4 veal scallops or cutlets (6 ounces each)
3 tablespoons butter or margarine
3 tablespoons salad oil
3 tablespoons lemon juice
⅓ cup dry white wine
Lemon slices

1. On sheet of waxed paper, mix flour with lemon-pepper seasoning and salt. Coat veal pieces on both sides with flour mixture, shaking off excess. Set aside.

2. In 12-inch skillet, over medium heat, melt butter in oil. Add veal; sauté 2 minutes on each side. Near the end of cooking time, pour lemon juice over veal. Place 1 piece veal on each of 4 heated dinner plates; cover loosely with aluminum foil to keep warm.

3. Add wine to drippings in skillet; over medium-high heat, reduce liquid to about 3 tablespoons, stirring constantly. Pour wine mixture over veal; serve immediately with lemon slices.

Makes 4 servings.

Stir-Fried Squash

(pictured, page 87, inset)

2 tablespoons salad oil
2 medium yellow squash, sliced in wedges
2 medium zucchini, sliced in wedges
4 sun-dried-tomato halves in oil, drained and thinly sliced
1 teaspoon fresh rosemary leaves, crushed
1 teaspoon salt
½ teaspoon freshly ground pepper

1. In 12-inch skillet or wok, heat oil over medium-high heat. Add squash and zucchini; cook, stirring, 3 minutes, or until tender-crisp.

2. Add tomatoes, rosemary, salt and pepper; cook, stirring 1 minute longer.

Makes 4 servings.

Pear-Raspberry Tarts

(pictured, page 87, inset)

½ package (17½-ounce size) frozen puff-pastry sheets (1 sheet), thawed
2 ripe Bartlett pears, thinly sliced
2 tablespoons butter
2 tablespoons sugar
½ cup raspberries
¼ cup apricot preserves, warmed

1. Preheat oven to 425°F. Unroll pastry sheet; cut in half crosswise and then lengthwise to make 4 equal pieces. Cut ¼ inch from sides of each piece; moisten top edges of large pastry piece with water, and cover each edge with a pastry strip, pressing lightly to adhere strips to pastry and trimming strips if necessary. Lightly grease large baking sheet; arrange prepared pastry on baking sheet.

2. Halve and core pears; with cut side down, thinly slice each pear half, keeping slices together in half-pear shape. Arrange a pear half in center of each piece of pastry, fanning slices slightly. Dot each tart with butter and sprinkle with sugar, dividing evenly. Bake 20 to 25 minutes, until pastry is golden. Sprinkle tarts with raspberries, dividing evenly; brush fruit in each tart with some warm apricot preserves. If desired, serve tarts with sweetened whipped cream and garnish with mint sprig. Serve tarts at room temperature.

Makes 4 servings.

*PORK SATAY WITH SPICY PEANUT DIPPING SAUCE
*COLD BROWN-RICE SALAD
FRESH PITA CHIPS
LIME TEA
*SAUTÉED APPLES WITH WARM CUSTARD
COOKIES

■ Marinate pork and green onions. Make Dipping Sauce. Make custard; sauté apples. Thread pork on skewers. While satays broil, make rice salad. Assemble and garnish apple desserts just before serving.

Pork Satay With Spicy Peanut Dipping Sauce

(pictured, page 87, inset)

⅔ cup bottled Italian dressing
2 tablespoons soy sauce
⅛ teaspoon crushed red-pepper flakes
1 pound pork tenderloin, trimmed and cut in ¾-inch pieces
4 large green onions, cut in 1-inch pieces

Dipping Sauce
¼ cup chunk-style peanut butter
¼ cup sour cream
1 tablespoon brown sugar
1 medium clove garlic, crushed
2 tablespoons soy sauce
2 tablespoons water
1 tablespoon lemon juice

12 cherry tomatoes

1. In medium bowl, whisk Italian dressing with soy sauce and pepper flakes until mixed. Add pork and green-onion pieces; marinate 15 minutes.

2. Make dipping sauce: In food processor or blender, process all sauce ingredients until smooth. Pour into small serving dish. If desired, sprinkle with minced green-onion top. Cover with plastic wrap; refrigerate until serving.

3. Arrange pork, green-onion and tomatoes alternately on eight 12-inch skewers. Place on rack in broiler pan; broil 5 inches from heat 5 minutes on each side, or until pork is tender. Serve immediately with dipping sauce.

Makes 4 servings, 1 cup sauce.

Cold Brown-Rice Salad

(pictured, page 87, inset)

⅔ cup bottled Italian dressing
1 tablespoon chili powder
3 cups cooked brown rice, chilled
1 large ripe avocado, pared, pitted and cut in 1-inch pieces
1 medium red pepper, chopped
1 small red onion, chopped
1 cup (4 ounces) snow pea pods, julienned
¼ cup minced parsley
4 Romaine lettuce leaves, washed and crisped

1. In large bowl, whisk dressing with chili powder. Add rice, avocado, chopped pepper, onion, snow pea pods and parsley; toss to combine. Cover with plastic wrap; refrigerate until serving.

2. To serve: Arrange a lettuce leaf on each of 4 dinner plates. Spoon salad into center.

Makes 4 servings.

Sautéed Apples With Warm Custard

(pictured, page 87, inset)

1 package (3 ounces) egg custard mix
2 cups milk
3 large McIntosh apples, cored
2 tablespoons butter or margarine
¼ cup apple jelly
2 tablespoons apple brandy
Mint sprigs

1. Make custard as package label directs, using milk. Cover with plastic wrap, placing plastic directly on surface of custard to keep skin from forming. Set aside, unrefrigerated, whisking occasionally to keep custard smooth.

2. Slice apples crosswise into ½-inch-thick rings. In 12-inch skillet, over medium heat, melt butter. Add apples, jelly and brandy. Sauté, stirring, until apples are coated with melted jelly mixture. Simmer 5 minutes, or until apples are just tender.

3. To serve: Divide apples and their cooking syrup among 4 serving dishes. Pour custard over apples. Garnish each with mint sprig.

Makes 4 servings, 2 cups custard.

■ When storing your company-best tablecloth, fold gently to avoid setting in creases. And don't wrap in plastic bags, which won't allow the cloth to "breathe" or moisture to escape.

Lite Eating: Pronto Pasta

PASTA WITH WILD-MUSHROOM SAUCE
WARM SHRIMP SALAD
YOGURT-TOPPED FRUIT MÉLANGE

Pasta With Wild-Mushroom Sauce

Nonstick cooking spray
½ pound fresh shiitake or any other variety mushrooms, thinly sliced
2 medium cloves garlic, crushed
1 can (2 pounds, 3 ounces) whole tomatoes
¼ teaspoon salt
⅛ teaspoon pepper
½ pound pasta
1 tablespoon chopped fresh basil or ½ teaspoon dried basil leaves, crushed
2 tablespoons grated Parmesan cheese

1. Coat large skillet with nonstick cooking spray; heat skillet over medium heat. Add sliced mushrooms; sauté 3 minutes. Add crushed garlic; sauté 1 minute longer. Stir in tomatoes and their juice, salt and pepper. With wooden spoon, break up tomatoes. Bring to boiling; simmer, uncovered, 20 minutes, stirring occasionally.

2. Meanwhile, cook pasta as package label directs; drain. Remove sauce from heat; stir in basil. Spoon sauce over pasta; sprinkle with Parmesan cheese.

Makes 4 servings, 315 calories each.

Warm Shrimp Salad

Nonstick cooking spray
1 pound large shrimp, shelled, deveined and butterflied (see *Note*)
2 medium cloves garlic, crushed
½ head radicchio
½ pound spinach leaves
1 tablespoon chopped fresh dill
¼ teaspoon salt
2 tablespoons balsamic vinegar
1 tablespoon lemon juice
1 tablespoon white wine
Dash pepper

1. Coat skillet with cooking spray; heat over medium heat. Add shrimp and garlic; sauté until shrimp are cooked, about 4 minutes. Remove to bowl. Wash greens; place in skillet. Cook, covered, over medium heat, 2 minutes or until wilted; drain well.

2. Add wilted greens, dill, salt, vinegar, lemon juice, wine and pepper to shrimp; lightly toss. Arrange on individual serving plates.

Makes 4 servings, 85 calories each.

Note: To butterfly shrimp, with sharp knife, cut shrimp four-fifths through on outside curve.

Yogurt-Topped Fruit Mélange

10 ladyfingers
1 package (1 pound) frozen mixed fruit, thawed and drained
½ cup low-fat strawberry yogurt

Split ladyfingers and cut each in half crosswise; place 5 quarters in each of 4 dessert dishes. Divide fruit among dishes; top with yogurt.

Makes 4 servings, 110 calories each.

■ One way to save calories and get rid of fat at the same time is to cook meat in your oven. Remember this when your pasta sauce calls for meatballs. It's an easier method, too, because cooking meatballs on the stove requires constant attention. Instead, arrange uniformly sized meatballs (you can use a small ice cream scoop to measure) in a greased shallow baking pan. Bake at 375°F for 10 minutes—no turning necessary. Drain the meatballs on paper towels; add them to your favorite sauce and continue cooking.

■ Instead of pan-frying bacon, oven-roast it. Line a baking pan with foil; place a wire rack in the pan, and lay bacon across the rack. Since fat drips off the bacon into the pan below, the results are less greasy than those achieved with the conventional stove-top technique.

Clockwise from top left: Pasta With Wild-Mushroom Sauce, Yogurt-Topped Fruit Mélange, Warm Shrimp Salad.

Micro-Way: Quick-As-Can-Be Dinners

Turkey-Chili Potato Topper

4 large baking potatoes, scrubbed (about 3 pounds)
1 medium onion, chopped
1 medium green pepper, chopped
1 medium clove garlic, crushed
1 tablespoon salad oil
1 pound ground turkey
2 tablespoons chili powder
1 teaspoon salt
½ teaspoon dried basil leaves, crushed
½ teaspoon ground cumin
½ teaspoon dried oregano leaves, crushed
1 can (1 pound) red kidney beans, drained
1 can (1 pound) stewed tomatoes
3 tablespoons tomato paste

1. With fork, pierce potatoes; arrange on paper towel in a ring in microwave. Cook on HIGH 15 minutes, until tested done when pierced with a fork. Rotate each potato every 5 minutes. Cover potatoes tightly with aluminum foil; set aside.

2. In 3-quart microwave-safe casserole, combine onion, green pepper, garlic and oil. Cover with plastic wrap; turn back one corner to vent. Cook on HIGH 4 minutes. Add turkey; cover and vent. Cook mixture on HIGH 5 minutes, stirring after 2 minutes. Add chili powder, salt, basil, cumin and oregano; mix well. Stir in beans, tomatoes and tomato paste. Cover; vent. Cook chili

on MEDIUM 15 minutes, stirring occasionally.

3. Cut open potatoes; evenly top with chili. Place on microwave-safe plate; cook on MEDIUM 8 minutes, until heated through. If desired, pass sour cream and chives; garnish with lime wedges.

Makes 4 servings.

Salmon-Noodle Bake

½ pound asparagus, cut in 2-inch pieces
¼ cup butter or margarine
1 medium clove garlic, crushed
¼ cup unsifted all-purpose flour
1 bottle (8 ounces) clam juice
½ cup heavy cream
¼ cup white wine
1 cup (4 ounces) shredded fontina cheese
1 tablespoon chopped fresh dill
½ package (12-ounce size) wide noodles, cooked
1 can (15½ ounces) red salmon, drained and flaked
1 cup frozen peas

1. In 3-quart microwave-safe casserole, combine asparagus, butter and garlic. Cover with plastic wrap; turn back one corner to vent. Cook on HIGH 4 minutes, stirring once.

2. Stir in flour until blended. Gradually stir in clam juice, cream and wine. Cover; vent. Cook on HIGH 5 minutes, stirring once, until thickened. Stir in cheese and dill. Add noodles, salmon and peas. Spoon into shallow 1½-quart microwave-safe casserole. Cover with waxed paper; cook on MEDIUM 8 minutes, or until heated through.

Makes 6 to 8 servings.

Vegetable Lasagna

2 cups sliced zucchini
2 cups sliced mushrooms
1 large egg, beaten
1½ cups cottage cheese
1½ cups shredded mozzarella cheese
¼ cup grated Parmesan cheese
1 tablespoon minced parsley
1 jar (15¾ ounces) prepared spaghetti sauce
½ package (16-ounce size) lasagna noodles, cooked as package label directs
¼ cup seasoned bread crumbs

1. Place zucchini in 2-quart microwave-safe baking dish. Cover with plastic wrap; turn back one corner to vent. Cook on HIGH 5 minutes, or until tender-crisp. Stir in mushrooms. Cover baking dish; cook 5 minutes longer. Drain off liquid; set mixture aside.

2. In bowl, mix egg with cottage cheese, 1 cup mozzarella, the Parmesan and parsley; set aside. Spread about ½ cup spaghetti sauce over bottom of baking dish; cover with half of noodles. Sprinkle with 2 tablespoons bread crumbs. Layer with half of zucchini mixture and then half of cheese mixture. Repeat; spread remaining spaghetti sauce and mozzarella over all.

3. Loosely cover lasagna with waxed paper; cook on HIGH 15 minutes, until heated through, turning dish once.

Makes 8 servings.

■ Place fresh mushrooms in a paper bag, twisted closed, in the refrigerator for longer storage.

Wurst-and-Potato Supper

4 medium potatoes, halved
4 knockwurst
4 slices bacon, diced
1 small onion, diced
1 tablespoon all-purpose flour
1 tablespoon sugar
1 teaspoon dry mustard
1 teaspoon salt
¼ teaspoon pepper
½ cup water
¼ cup vinegar
½ teaspoon celery seeds
1 tablespoon minced parsley

1. Place potatoes, cut side down, in regular-size oven cooking bag. Leaving bag open, cook potatoes on HIGH 10 minutes, or until tender. Transfer potatoes to bowl and let cool slightly; remove skins. Slice potatoes; set aside.

2. In same bag, cook knockwurst on HIGH 1 minute. Cut each crosswise into 6 pieces; add to potatoes.

3. In large microwave-safe bowl, cook bacon and onion on HIGH 4 minutes. Stir in flour, sugar, mustard, salt and pepper. Blend in water and vinegar. Stir in celery seeds. Cook mixture on HIGH 4 minutes, stirring once. Add potatoes and knockwurst; toss to coat with hot sauce. Sprinkle with parsley.

Makes 4 servings.

■ If a stick of butter or margarine is too cold to be creamed easily, pop it in the microwave oven at low-to-medium power for 10 to 15 seconds.

■ For sweet, tender corn on the cob, try cooking it right in its husk! Place two medium ears and 2 tablespoons water in a 10-inch-square microwave-safe casserole. Pull back husks, keeping them attached to ears. Brush one tablespoon butter over each ear. Pull husks up over corn. Cover and cook 5 to 10 minutes on HIGH, turning once.

June

Summertime, and the grilling is easy! Starting here, zesty sausages, surrounded by an array of garden vegetables, are served with a Dijon sauce. More great cookout specialties are pictured, followed by recipes for those dishes and others.

Sausage-Vegetable Medley

Italian Stuffed Onions

Maple-Smoked Chicken

Roasted Corn Pudding

Creole Beef

Ice Cream Butterflies

Ham Waikiki

Warm Swordfish Salade Niçoise

Greek Lamb Kebabs

Texas-Style Ribs

Grilled Sweet-and-Sour Celery

Stuffed Chicken Turnovers

Backyard Barbecue Cookbook

Fire up the grill and get ready for a cookout. In this collection of recipes, you'll find a rich variety of meats and vegetables, and even a dessert from the grill.

Sausage-Vegetable Medley

(pictured, page 101)

1 package (.9 ounce) hollandaise-sauce mix
3 tablespoons Dijon-style mustard
2 tablespoons lemon juice
1 package (14 ounces) hot smoked-sausage links
2 large (8 ounces each) baking potatoes, cut lengthwise in 1-inch-wide slices
3 medium tomatoes, halved
1 large (12 ounces) Bermuda onion, cut crosswise in ¼-inch-wide slices
1 large green pepper, cut lengthwise in 1-inch-wide strips
1 medium yellow squash, quartered lengthwise
½ pound large mushrooms, stems trimmed even with caps
1 cup bottled Caesar-salad dressing

1. In small bowl, prepare hollandaise-sauce mix as package label directs; stir in mustard and lemon juice. Cover; keep warm.

2. Prepare outdoor grill for barbecue. On large platter, brush sausage links and vegetables with salad dressing. Using DIRECT METHOD (see page 108), over low coals, cook sausage links and potatoes 20 minutes, turning after 10 minutes; place on one side of grill, stacking if necessary. Place tomato halves, onion slices, pepper strips, squash quarters and mushrooms on grill; cook 10 minutes, turning after 5 minutes, or until well browned.

3. Remove sausage and vegetable mixture to warm serving platter. Brush lightly with any remaining salad dressing. Serve with hollandaise sauce.

Makes 6 servings.

■ The more "crowded" your grill, the longer the cooking time.

Italian Stuffed Onions

(pictured, page 101)

6 large sweet onions (2¾ pounds)
3 tablespoons butter or margarine
¼ cup fine dry Italian-style seasoned bread crumbs
¼ cup chopped pitted black olives
¼ cup chopped pepperoni

1. Prepare outdoor grill for barbecue. Peel onions; cut off and reserve a thick slice from the top of each. With spoon, scoop out and reserve center.

2. In large saucepan of boiling salted water, cook onions 10 minutes. Drain; place each onion in one cup of a disposable aluminum-foil muffin pan. Set aside.

3. Chop reserved onion tops and centers; set aside. In large skillet, over medium-high heat, melt butter. Add chopped onion; sauté until golden-brown. Stir in bread crumbs, olives and pepperoni. Spoon mixture into prepared onion shells, mounding slightly. Using INDIRECT METHOD (see page 108), over medium coals, cook onions, with grill covered, 30 minutes, or until tender.

Makes 6 servings.

Page 101: Sausage-Vegetable Medley, Italian Stuffed Onions.

Pages 102 and 103: (Clockwise from top) Maple-Smoked Chicken, Roasted Corn Pudding, Creole Beef, Ice Cream Butterflies, Ham Waikiki.

Pages 104 and 105: (Clockwise from top) Warm Swordfish Salade Niçoise, Greek Lamb Kebabs, Texas-Style Ribs, Grilled Sweet-and-Sour Celery, Stuffed Chicken Turnovers.

Maple-Smoked Chicken

(pictured, pages 102 and 103)

7- to 8-pound roasting chicken
1/4 cup coarse salt
2 tablespoons butter or margarine
1/4 cup granulated brown sugar
1 tablespoon ground cinnamon
1/4 teaspoon ground nutmeg
1/4 cup maple syrup

1. Two or three days before serving: Remove giblets and neck from chicken; reserve for stock, if desired. Wash chicken under cold running water; drain. Pat dry with paper towels. Rub coarse salt over outside and inside body cavity of chicken; place in large glass bowl. Cover with plastic wrap; refrigerate overnight.

2. Preheat oven to 350°F. Place chicken on rack in roasting pan; dot with butter. With kitchen string, tie legs together; cover loosely with aluminum foil. Cook 2½ hours, or until meat thermometer inserted in thigh registers 170°F. When cool, place chicken on plate. Cover chicken with plastic wrap; refrigerate at least 4 hours.

3. Prepare outdoor grill for barbecue. In 9-inch disposable foil cake pan, combine brown sugar, cinnamon, nutmeg and maple syrup. Place pan directly on medium coals; arrange chicken on grill rack directly over pan. Cover grill; smoke chicken 15 minutes, or until dark brown. (Avert face when lifting cover.)

4. Place chicken on plate; cool. Remove and discard kitchen string. Cover with plastic wrap; refrigerate 2 hours, or until cold. If desired, surround chicken on platter with bunches of mâche (lamb's lettuce) and carrot flowers.

Makes 8 servings.

Roasted Corn Pudding

(pictured, page 103)

5 medium ears corn, shucked
2 medium red peppers, halved, stems and seeds removed
1/3 cup butter or margarine, melted
1 medium onion, finely chopped
3 large eggs, well beaten
1/4 cup unsifted all-purpose flour
1 tablespoon sugar
1 teaspoon salt
1/4 teaspoon pepper
2 cups half-and-half

1. Prepare outdoor grill for barbecue. Using DIRECT METHOD (see page 108), place corn and peppers on grill over medium coals; brush corn with 2 tablespoons butter. Cover grill; cook 6 minutes, or until vegetables start to char. Turn vegetables; cook, covered, 6 minutes longer. Remove from grill.

2. When corn is cool enough to handle, with sharp knife, cut kernels from cobs. Set aside. Cut 3 pepper halves into ¼-inch cubes; cut remaining pepper half into ½-inch-long strips. Set aside.

3. Brush 8½-by-1½-inch disposable foil round baking pan or 9-inch cast-iron skillet with some of remaining melted butter; set aside.

4. In large bowl, combine corn, pepper cubes and onion. Add eggs; mix well. In small bowl, combine flour, sugar, salt and pepper; stir into corn mixture. Stir in remaining melted butter and the half-and-half until blended. Pour mixture into prepared pan.

5. Using INDIRECT METHOD (see page 108), with grill covered, cook corn pudding, 6 inches from medium coals, 1 hour, turning skillet a half-turn after 30 minutes. Garnish pudding with reserved roasted red-pepper strips. Serve pudding hot or warm.

Makes 8 servings.

Creole Beef

(pictured, page 102 and 103)

3 pounds boneless top-round steak, 2 inches thick
1 tablespoon Cajun- or Creole-seasoning mix (see *Note*)
½ pound baby carrots, trimmed and pared
¼ pound large mushrooms, halved lengthwise
1 small green pepper, quartered
1 small red pepper, quartered
1 small yellow pepper, quartered
2 tablespoons salad oil

1. Prepare outdoor grill for barbecue. Rub both sides of steak with seasoning mix. Cover steak with plastic wrap; let stand at room temperature 15 minutes. Using DIRECT METHOD (see page 108), cook steak 6 inches from coals, 8 minutes on each side for medium-rare; keep warm until serving.

2. In large bowl, toss vegetables with oil; place in barbecue basket. Cook 8 to 10 minutes, or until tender-crisp. Slice meat across the grain; serve with vegetables.

Makes 6 to 8 servings.

Note: Available in specialty food stores, or use a combination of 2 teaspoons paprika, 1 teaspoon each garlic and onion powder, ½ teaspoon each salt and dried thyme leaves and ¼ teaspoon pepper.

Ice Cream Butterflies

(pictured, page 102)

16 slices (¼-inch thick) pound cake
¼ cup butter or margarine
⅓ cup firmly packed light-brown sugar
3 small ripe bananas
½ pint strawberries, hulled and halved
1 tablespoon grated orange peel
¼ teaspoon ground cinnamon
¼ cup orange-flavored liqueur
1 pint vanilla ice cream

1. Prepare outdoor grill for barbecue. Using DIRECT METHOD (see instructions below), cook cake 4 inches from low coals, until toasted on both sides. Set aside.

2. In large cast-iron skillet on grill, 4 inches from coals, melt butter with sugar. Peel and halve bananas crosswise; cut halves lengthwise in half. Add to butter mixture; sauté 2 minutes, turning once. Remove pan from heat; stir in strawberries and next 3 ingredients.

3. On each of four plates, place 2 slices cake. Top each slice with a scoop of ice cream; spoon fruit mixture over ice cream. Place a cake slice on top of each scoop, tilting slices toward each other to resemble butterfly wings. If desired, sprinkle with orange-peel slivers.

Makes 4 servings.

Ham Waikiki

(pictured, page 102)

1 can (8 ounces) sliced pineapple in natural juices
2 kiwifruit, pared
1 tablespoon cornstarch
⅓ cup teriyaki sauce
2 tablespoons lime juice
1 tablespoon white-wine vinegar
2- to 2½-pound smoked-ham slice
Lettuce leaves, washed and crisped

1. Drain pineapple juice into medium saucepan; set aside. Coarsely chop 2 pineapple slices; reserve remainder. Chop 1 kiwifruit; slice and reserve remainder.

2. In saucepan, mix cornstarch with reserved pineapple juice, the teriyaki sauce, lime juice and vinegar until blended. Bring to boiling; cook, stirring, 1 minute, or until mixture is clear and thickened. Add chopped pineapple and chopped kiwifruit; set sauce aside.

3. Prepare outdoor grill for barbecue. Using DIRECT METHOD (see below), cook ham 20 minutes, turning occasionally and basting frequently with sauce. Place on serving board; spoon sauce on top. Garnish with lettuce topped with reserved pineapple and kiwifruit.

Makes 4 to 6 servings.

Barbecue Basics

■ DIRECT METHOD (ideal for searing chops, steaks and burgers): Place food over the hottest part of the fire.

■ INDIRECT METHOD (great for grilling ribs, roasts, vegetables and fish): Cover the grill or wrap foods in foil; then place food on grill, away from heat source. (If using a charcoal-type barbecue, arrange briquettes on one side, and cook on the other.)

■ TO USE WOOD CHIPS: With a charcoal-type grill, wait until coals are red-hot and covered with white ash; then spread presoaked chips evenly over the coals. With a gas grill, preheat for at least 10 minutes on high; then sprinkle on wet chips. Start to cook food on grill when the chips begin to smoke.

Warm Swordfish Salade Niçoise

(pictured, pages 104 and 105)

1 pound small (1½-inch) new red potatoes, halved
½ pound green beans, trimmed
1-pound swordfish steak
1 large red pepper, quartered lengthwise
2 tablespoons olive oil
Red-leaf or green-leaf lettuce leaves, washed and crisped
1 medium cucumber, unpared and cut crosswise in ⅛-inch-thick slices
¼ pound Greek olives
1 can (2 ounces) flat anchovies
1 tablespoon capers
1 bottle (8 ounces) Dijon-style vinaigrette dressing

1. Prepare outdoor grill for barbecue. In large skillet, in 2 inches boiling salted water, parboil potatoes and beans 10 minutes. Drain well; set aside.

2. Brush potatoes, swordfish and pepper slices on all sides with olive oil. Using DIRECT METHOD (see instruction in sidebar at left), over low coals, cook swordfish and potatoes, with grill covered, 10 minutes. Place pepper slices on grill; turn swordfish and potatoes. Cover grill; cook 10 minutes, turning pepper slices once, until potatoes and swordfish appear done when tested with a fork.

3. Cut swordfish into bite-size pieces; cut pepper slices in half crosswise. Line large platter with lettuce leaves; arrange swordfish in center of platter. Arrange red pepper slices, potato halves, beans, cucumber slices and olives around swordfish pieces. Drain anchovies; sprinkle salad with anchovies, capers and vinaigrette dressing. Serve immediately.

Makes 6 to 8 servings.

Greek Lamb Kebabs

(pictured, page 105)

1 pound small white onions, peeled
1 pound baby eggplants, trimmed and halved crosswise
8 mushrooms, ends trimmed
½ pint cherry tomatoes
1 jar (8 ounces) red-wine Italian dressing

Meatballs
1 pound lean ground lamb
½ cup fresh white bread crumbs
¼ pound feta cheese, finely crumbled
½ teaspoon cracked pepper
2 tablespoons milk

1. In large saucepan of boiling salted water, cook onions 5 minutes. Drain through colander; rinse with cold water until cool.

2. In medium bowl, mix onions, eggplant halves, mushrooms and tomatoes with dressing until well coated. Marinate 30 minutes.

3. Make meatballs: In medium bowl, mix lamb with bread crumbs, cheese, cracked pepper and milk. Form into 16 balls; set aside.

4. On each of eight 10- or 12-inch skewers, thread a meatball, a mushroom, several tomatoes, eggplant halves, onions and another meatball. Arrange kebabs in large shallow baking pan. Pour marinade from vegetables over kebabs; marinate 30 minutes at room temperature.

5. Prepare outdoor grill for barbecue. Using DIRECT METHOD (see page 108), cook kebabs over low coals, with grill covered, 20 minutes, turning once and brushing with marinade. Meanwhile, place remaining marinade in small saucepan. Bring to boiling; simmer several minutes. Serve as dipping sauce for kebabs. If desired, garnish kebabs with mint sprigs.

Makes 8 servings.

Stuffed Chicken Turnovers

(pictured, page 104)

Marinade
¼ cup rum
¼ cup low-sodium soy sauce
¼ cup salad oil
1 teaspoon grated ginger root

2 whole chicken breasts (1 pound each), skinned, split and boned
2 tablespoons butter or margarine
¼ pound green beans, trimmed and finely chopped
1 large carrot, pared and shredded
1 small onion, chopped
½ pound Monterey Jack cheese

1. In shallow bowl, combine marinade ingredients. Set aside.

2. Place boneless breast halves between two sheets of waxed paper; with meat mallet, pound to ¼-inch thickness. Set aside.

3. In medium skillet, over medium-high heat, melt butter. Add beans, carrot and onion; sauté 3 minutes, or until slightly softened. Remove pan from heat; cool. Stir in cheese. Remove top sheet of waxed paper from chicken breasts; place one-fourth of vegetable mixture over length of one-half of each, spreading to ½ inch of edge. Fold remaining half over filling; secure edges with wooden picks. Place in bowl with marinade; let stand 30 minutes, turning once.

4. Prepare outdoor grill for barbecue. Drain chicken; reserve marinade. Using DIRECT METHOD (see page 108), cook chicken, with grill covered, 20 minutes, turning and basting with reserved marinade after 10 minutes. To serve: Cut each chicken piece crosswise into 5 or 6 pieces. Place remaining marinade in small saucepan; bring to boiling. Simmer 3 minutes. Serve as dipping sauce for chicken.

Makes 4 servings.

Texas-Style Ribs

(pictured, pages 104 and 105)

4 pounds pork-loin country-style ribs
2 tablespoons water
1 cup ketchup
¼ cup white vinegar
2 tablespoons Worcestershire sauce
1 tablespoon prepared white horseradish
1 small onion, coarsely grated
1½ teaspoons chili powder
½ teaspoon garlic powder
½ teaspoon dried oregano leaves, crushed
½ teaspoon hot-red-pepper sauce
Salad oil

1. Prepare outdoor grill for barbecue. Cut ribs into individual portions; place in a single layer on double thickness of heavy-duty aluminum foil large enough to fold over ribs. Sprinkle ribs with water; fold foil up over ribs, drugstore fashion (see tip below). Using INDIRECT METHOD (see page 108), cook ribs 1 hour, or until tender.

2. Meanwhile, in small bowl, combine remaining ingredients except salad oil. Set aside.

3. Remove foil packet from grill. Carefully open; remove ribs. Drain off fat. Lightly grease grill rack with salad oil. Using DIRECT METHOD (see page 108), cook ribs 15 minutes, turning once and basting frequently with sauce, until lightly browned on both sides. Pass remaining sauce separately.

Makes 6 servings.

■ To wrap food drugstore fashion, place in center of aluminum-foil sheet large enough so that you can bring foil edges together and fold them over several times before reaching surface of food. To finish, join side edges, folding over several times to create an airtight package.

Grilled Sweet-and-Sour Celery

(pictured, page 104)

1 large head celery (about 2 pounds), trimmed and separated into stalks
2 tablespoons white-wine Worcestershire sauce
2 tablespoons salad oil
1 teaspoon salt
¼ teaspoon pepper
1 tablespoon celery seeds
1 bottle (8 ounces) honey-and-orange-flavored dressing

1. Prepare outdoor grill for barbecue. Wash celery stalks; pat dry. Place celery in shallow baking dish. Set aside.

2. In small bowl, with wire whisk, mix Worcestershire with oil, salt and pepper until blended. Brush celery with mixture. Using DIRECT METHOD (see page 108), cook on rack over medium coals, 5 minutes, or until browned. With tongs, turn celery; cook 5 minutes longer. Remove to cutting board.

3. Cut celery diagonally into 3-inch pieces. Place in bowl with celery seeds and dressing; toss well. Serve warm or cold.

Makes 8 servings.

Seafood-Stuffed Grilled Snapper

2½- to 3-pounds red snapper, striped bass or whitefish, dressed and scaled (head and tail intact)
½ pound prepared surimi (fish and lobster or crab blend) salad
¼ cup chopped fennel stalk
1 tablespoon lemon juice
½ teaspoon salt
¼ teaspoon pepper
4 slices bacon
Salad oil

1. Prepare outdoor grill for barbecue. Rinse fish under cold water; pat dry. Set aside.

2. In small bowl, combine surimi salad and fennel. Sprinkle fish cavity with lemon juice, salt and pepper. Spoon surimi mixture into cavity; with small metal skewers or wooden picks, close opening.

3. Wrap bacon slices crosswise around fish; wrap kitchen string around fish over bacon to secure slices. Lightly grease wire fish grill basket with salad oil; place fish in basket.

4. Using INDIRECT METHOD (see page 108), cook fish, with grill covered, 40 minutes, or until fish appears done when tested with fork and stuffing is hot.

5. To serve, remove fish to heated serving platter. Remove and discard string. If desired, place half of a pimiento-stuffed olive over eye, and garnish fish with fennel fern.

Makes 6 servings.

Potato-and-Onion Fans

4 small baking potatoes (about 8 ounces each)
4 small red onions, thinly sliced
⅔ cup butter or margarine, melted
2 tablespoons chopped parsley
1 teaspoon minced fresh thyme or ¼ teaspoon dried thyme leaves, crushed
1 teaspoon coarsely ground pepper
1 teaspoon salt

1. Prepare outdoor grill for barbecue. Slice potatoes crosswise, about two-thirds through and at ½-inch intervals. Place an onion slice into each slit. Place each potato on a piece of aluminum foil large enough to wrap potato completely. Set potatoes aside.

2. In small bowl, combine remaining ingredients. Drizzle mixture over potatoes, dividing evenly. Wrap potatoes loosely with foil.

3. Using INDIRECT METHOD (see page 108), cook potatoes over medium coals, 1 hour, or until fork-tender. Remove potatoes from grill; place on serving platter. Cut each potato crosswise in half; spoon drippings in foil over potatoes.

Makes 8 servings.

Soft-Shell Crabs With Garlic-Tomato Butter

Garlic-Tomato Butter
1 small onion, minced
2 medium cloves garlic, minced
¼ cup balsamic vinegar
2 tablespoons tomato paste
2 tablespoons water
½ cup butter or margarine, cut in pieces
1 tablespoon chopped fresh basil leaves
¼ teaspoon salt
⅛ teaspoon pepper

¼ cup clarified butter (see *Note*)
2 tablespoons lemon juice
4 (about 2 ounces each) soft-shell crabs, cleaned
Seaside Pasta Salad (recipe follows)

1. Make Garlic-Tomato Butter: In medium saucepan, combine onion, garlic, vinegar, tomato paste and water. Bring to boiling; cook, uncovered, 3 minutes, or until mixture thickens. Whisk in butter, a few pieces at a time, allowing pieces to melt completely before adding more. Stir in basil, salt and pepper. Set aside.

2. Prepare outdoor grill for barbecue. In small bowl, combine clarified butter and lemon juice. Brush some of butter-lemon mixture over

crabs; reserve remainder. Using DIRECT METHOD (see page 108), cook crabs, shell side down, 6 inches from heat, 5 minutes. Turn crabs; cook 3 minutes longer, brushing often with remaining butter-lemon mixture, until crabs turn red and legs are slightly crisp. Pass Garlic-Tomato Butter as dipping sauce for crabs; serve crabs with Seaside Pasta Salad.

Makes 4 serving.

Note: To clarify butter, melt butter in saucepan, over low heat. Let stand 5 minutes; carefully pour or spoon clear butter into bowl. Discard remaining milky residue.

Seaside Pasta Salad

Dressing
¼ cup fresh parsley leaves
2 tablespoons fresh basil leaves
1 teaspoon salt
½ teaspoon dried oregano leaves, crushed
½ teaspoon coarsely ground pepper
⅓ cup bottled red-wine vinaigrette dressing
1 tablespoon balsamic vinegar

2 cups medium pasta shells, cooked as package label directs
4 plum tomatoes, quartered and seeds removed
1 small yellow pepper, diced
1 medium cucumber, pared, quartered lengthwise, seeded and thinly sliced crosswise
¼ cup fresh basil leaves, thinly sliced lengthwise

1. Make dressing: In food processor or blender, puree dressing ingredients. Set aside.

2. In large bowl, combine remaining ingredients. Pour dressing over salad mixture; toss well to combine. Refrigerate 30 minutes to allow flavors to mellow. Serve cold or at room temperature.

Makes 4 servings.

Grilled Oriental Cornish Hens

Marinade
2 green onions, thinly sliced
3 tablespoons toasted sesame seeds
2 medium cloves garlic, crushed
¼ teaspoon ground red pepper
½ cup rice vinegar
½ cup soy sauce
¼ cup dry sherry
2 tablespoons dark sesame oil
1 tablespoon minced ginger root

3 (1½ pounds each) Cornish hens, split in half lengthwise

1. In large shallow glass baking dish, combine marinade ingredients. Add hen halves; coat on both sides. Cover with plastic wrap; marinate in refrigerator at least 3 hours, or overnight, turning hens occasionally.

2. Prepare outdoor grill for barbecue. Drain marinade from hens; reserve. Using DIRECT METHOD (see page 108), cook hens, 6 inches from heat, 35 minutes, or until tender, turning often and basting frequently with reserved marinade.

Makes 6 servings.

Spit-Roasted Beef Tenderloin

Marinade
¼ cup cilantro (fresh coriander) leaves, chopped
2 large cloves garlic, crushed
2 tablespoons dry mustard
1 teaspoon ground cumin
1 teaspoon grated orange peel
1 teaspoon paprika
1 teaspoon coarsely ground pepper
1 tablespoon bottled sweetened lime juice
1 tablespoon salad oil

2½-pound beef tenderloin (trimmed weight)

1. In bowl, mix marinade ingredients; rub tenderloin with mixture. Cover with plastic wrap; let stand at room temperature 1 hour.

2. Prepare outdoor grill with rotisserie for barbecue. Place tenderloin on spit, inserting prongs at each end; balance meat on spit. Place drip pan (or fold up edges of a double thickness of heavy-duty aluminum foil 5 inches longer than meat) under meat. Place spit as close to heat as possible without touching coals. Cook 40 to 45 minutes, or until meat thermometer inserted in center registers 140°F for medium rare. Carefully remove meat; cut crosswise into ¼-inch-thick slices.

Makes 8 to 10 servings.

Three-Bean Bake

3 slices bacon
1 apple, cored and cut in ½-inch chunks
1 large onion, chopped
1 can (16 ounces) black beans, drained and rinsed
1 can (16 ounces) pink beans, drained and rinsed
1 can (16 ounces) small white beans, drained and rinsed
½ cup firmly packed dark-brown sugar
½ cup ketchup
¼ cup molasses
2 tablespoons prepared spicy brown mustard

1. Prepare outdoor grill for barbecue. Place bacon in heavy 4-quart saucepan with heat-safe handle; over medium coals, sauté until crisp. Remove bacon; set aside. To drippings, add apple and onion; cook, stirring, until lightly browned. Add remaining ingredients; stir gently.

2. Cover grill; using INDIRECT METHOD (see page 108), cook beans 1 hour, stirring occasionally, until hot and bubbly. Crumble reserved bacon; sprinkle over beans.

Makes 8 to 10 servings.

Quick & Easy: Breads on the Barbecue

Bread on a Skewer

2 plum tomatoes, chopped
¼ cup bottled Italian dressing
2 tablespoons butter or margarine, melted
2 tablespoons olive oil
¼ cup packed fresh basil leaves, finely chopped
3 (7-inch) Italian hoagie rolls
¾ pound whole-milk mozzarella cheese

1. In small bowl, toss tomatoes with dressing; cover with plastic wrap and let stand at room temperature to blend flavors.

2. Prepare outdoor grill for barbecue. In small bowl, mix butter with olive oil and basil; set aside. Cut each roll crosswise into ¾-inch-thick slices; brush cut sides with basil butter. Place on grill; using DIRECT METHOD (see page 108), cook bread 6 inches from heat until toasted on both sides.

3. Cut cheese into 15 slices. On each of three 8-inch skewers, alternate bread with cheese. Wrap skewered breads loosely in square of heavy-duty aluminum foil. Using INDIRECT METHOD (see page 108), cook 6 inches from heat, 3 to 5 minutes, or until cheese melts.

4. Remove breads from foil; place on serving platter. Spoon tomato mixture over breads. Serve breads immediately.

Makes 6 to 8 servings.

Clockwise from top left: Parmesan Fingers, Confetti Cornbread, Bread on a Skewer, Tortilla Roll-Ups.

Parmesan Fingers

2 teaspoons prepared garlic in oil
¼ cup olive oil
¼ cup butter, softened
1-pound long loaf Italian whole-wheat bread
½ cup sliced pitted black olives
4 ounces shredded Parmesan cheese

1. Prepare outdoor grill for barbecue. In food processor or blender, process garlic with oil and butter until smooth; set aside.

2. Slice bread in half lengthwise; spread garlic-butter mixture over cut side of both halves. Sprinkle with olive slices and then cheese. Place on square of heavy-duty aluminum foil; wrap loosely. Using INDIRECT METHOD (see page 108), heat bread in foil packet 4 inches from heat, 10 minutes, turning frequently, until warmed through.

3. Slice each half crosswise into 2-inch pieces. Serve immediately.

Makes 6 servings.

Confetti Cornbread

1 can (8¾ ounces) whole-kernel corn
⅓ cup sour cream
¼ cup chopped green pepper
¼ cup chopped red pepper
2 ounces Cheddar cheese, finely diced
1 large egg, lightly beaten
⅓ cup milk
1 package (12 ounces) cornbread muffin mix
Salad oil

1. In medium bowl, combine corn, sour cream, peppers, cheese, egg and milk; mix well. Add muffin mix; stir until just combined.

2. Prepare outdoor grill for barbecue. With oil, generously grease two cast-iron cornstick pans; place on grill 6 inches from heat. Heat 5 minutes, or until oil sizzles.

3. Spoon 3 tablespoons cornbread batter into each cornstick mold. Using INDIRECT METHOD (see page 108), cook bread, with grill covered, 6 inches from heat, 10 minutes, or until golden-brown. Remove breads immediately from pans. Cook any remaining batter in greased, hot pan. Serve immediately.

Makes about 14 cornsticks.

Tortilla Roll-Ups

2 tablespoons salad oil
1 large green pepper, julienned
1 large red pepper, julienned
1 large yellow pepper, julienned
1½ teaspoons salt-free herb blend
1 package (12.5 ounces) flour tortillas
2 cups (8 ounces) shredded Monterey Jack cheese

1. Prepare outdoor grill for barbecue. In 12-inch skillet, heat oil over medium heat. Add peppers; sauté 5 minutes, or until tender-crisp. Stir in herb seasoning. Remove from heat; set aside.

2. Lay 1 tortilla on smooth surface. Place some mixture in center; sprinkle with some cheese. Beginning from one side, roll into cigar shape; tie with string. Repeat with remaining tortillas.

3. Using INDIRECT METHOD (see page 108), cook tortillas 6 inches from heat, 5 minutes, turning frequently, until peppers are warmed through and cheese is melted. Serve immediately.

Makes 10 servings.

Micro-Way: Easy-on-Dad Barbecue

Plum-Glazed Hens

Glaze
1 tablespooon salad oil
1 medium onion, finely chopped
1/3 cup firmly packed light-brown sugar
1/4 teaspoon ground cinnamon
Dash ground cloves
4 jars (4 1/2-ounce size) pureed plums (baby food)
3 tablespoons soy sauce

2 Cornish hens (1 pound each), halved
Salt
Pepper
6 medium plums, pitted and cut in wedges

1. Make glaze: In medium glass bowl, combine oil with onion. Cook on HIGH 3 minutes, stirring once. Add remaining glaze ingredients; cook on HIGH 5 minutes, stirring once. Cover; set aside.

2. In 13-by-9-by-2-inch microwave-safe baking dish, place hens, skin side down and meaty portions toward sides of dish; sprinkle with salt and pepper. Cover with plastic wrap; turn back one corner to vent. Cook on HIGH 7 minutes. Turn hens over. Cover; vent. Cook on HIGH 4 minutes.

3. Prepare outdoor grill for barbecue. Place hens, skin side up, on grill, 4 inches from heat. Reserve 1 1/2 cups glaze; generously brush hens with remainder. Using INDIRECT METHOD (see page 108), cook hens over low coals with grill covered, 5 minutes. Turn hens;

brush with any remaining glaze. Brush plum wedges with salad oil; place on grill. Cover grill; cook 5 minutes, turning plums once. Serve hens with reserved glaze and plums.

Makes 4 servings.

Barbecued Beef

Barbecue Sauce
2 tablespoons butter or margarine
1 medium onion, finely chopped
2 medium cloves garlic, crushed
½ cup firmly packed light-brown sugar
½ teaspoon dried thyme leaves, crushed
1½ cups ketchup
1 can (5½ ounces) pear nectar
¼ cup red-wine vinegar
2 tablespoons Worcestershire sauce
1 tablespoon Dijon-style mustard
3 drops hot-red-pepper sauce

3¾- to 4-pound beef rump roast
Salt
Pepper
1 cup beef broth
6 to 8 hard rolls, split and toasted

1. Make sauce: In 1-quart microwave-safe casserole, combine butter, onion and garlic. Cook on HIGH 3 minutes, stirring once. Stir in remaining sauce ingredients. Cook on HIGH 5 minutes; stir once.

2. In 12-by-8-by-2-inch microwave-safe baking dish, place beef, fat side down; sprinkle with salt and pepper. Add broth; cover with plastic wrap. Cook on MEDIUM 15 minutes; turn meat over. Cover; cook 15 minutes longer.

3. Prepare outdoor grill for barbecue. In pan with heat-safe handle, mix 1 cup sauce with ¼ cup beef drippings; place on grill. Place beef with fat side up on grill, 4 inches from low coals. Using DIRECT METHOD (see page 108), cook meat, covered, 15 minutes, turning and basting with remaining sauce mixture every 5 minutes.

4. Thinly slice beef across the grain; place beef slices on rolls. Pass sauce separately.

Makes 6 to 8 servings.

July

Starting here, fabulous ways with summer fruit. The list below gives an inkling of the wide range of fruit dishes in this chapter. The photographs that follow show all of these recipes in full glory.

Fruit Gazpacho

Fried Pasta With Plum Sauce

Glazed Peach Tart

Summer-Fruit Cheesecake   Blueberry-Cassis Pie

Oriental Pasta Salad   Tipsy French Toast

Lime-Marinated Spareribs   Raspberry-Grilled Hens

Raspberry Tarts   Banana-Coconut-Cream Pie

Shrimp-and-Fruit Mélange

Kiwi-Banana Bread

Nectarine-Oat-Bran Muffins

Berry Butter

Many-Berry Preserves

cantaloupe

DETECTO

SCALES
1/2
1

DETECTO

Fruit Cookbook

From a tangy fruit gazpacho to a luscious blueberry pie, these recipes capture the best of summer.

Fruit Gazpacho

(pictured, page 117)

3 cups freshly squeezed orange juice
1½ cups tomato puree
¼ cup sugar
1 tablespoon grated orange peel
1 tablespoon grated lime peel
2 tablespoons lemon juice
¼ teaspoon salt
4 cups assorted melon cubes
1 red apple, cored and diced
1 cup blueberries
1 cup halved green and red seedless grapes
1 cup crème fraiche or sour cream

1. In large mixing bowl, combine orange juice, tomato puree, sugar, grated orange and lime peels, lemon juice and salt; stir until sugar dissolves. Stir in fruit. Cover; refrigerate several hours.

2. To serve, ladle into chilled soup bowls. Add a dollop of crème fraîche to each bowl.

Makes 10 servings.

Page 117: (Clockwise from top) Fruit Gazpacho, Fried Pasta With Plum Sauce, Glazed Peach Tart.

Pages 118 and 119: (Clockwise from center) Lime-Marinated Spareribs, Summer-Fruit Cheesecake, Blueberry-Cassis Pie, Oriental Pasta Salad, Tipsy French Toast.

Pages 120 and 121: (Clockwise from right) Raspberry-Grilled Hens, Raspberry Tart, Banana-Coconut-Cream Pie, Shrimp-and-Fruit Mélange, Berry Butter, Kiwi-Banana Bread, Nectarine-Oat-Bran Muffins, Many-Berry Preserves.

Fried Pasta With Plum Sauce

(pictured, page 117)

Sauce
3 large ripe purple plums, quartered and pitted (½ pound)
2 tablespoons grape jam
2 tablespoons ketchup
1 tablespoon brandy
¼ teaspoon grated lemon peel
1 thin slice fresh ginger root

1 package (1 pound) bow-tie pasta or 2 packages (9 ounces each) refrigerated agnolotti, tortellini or cheese ravioli
2 large eggs
4 cups fine fresh bread crumbs
Salad oil

1. Make sauce (not pictured): In food processor or electric blender, puree sauce ingredients. Set aside.

2. If using bow-tie pasta, cook as package label directs. Drain; rinse with cold water. In large bowl, beat eggs until frothy. Add cooked bow-tie pasta or uncooked refrigerated agnolotti, tortellini or ravioli; toss until thoroughly coated with egg. Drain off excess egg. Place bread crumbs in another large bowl; add prepared pasta. Toss until thoroughly coated with bread crumbs.

3. Preheat oven to 250°F. In 5-quart Dutch oven, heat 2 to 3 inches salad oil to 375°F on deep-fat thermometer. Add one-fourth of prepared pasta; fry 6 minutes, or until deep golden-brown. With slotted spoon, remove pasta to paper-towel-lined jelly-roll pan. Place fried pasta in oven to keep warm while frying remaining prepared pasta, one-fourth at a time. Serve immediately with plum sauce as an appetizer, or to accompany Fruit Gazpacho.

Makes 2 cups sauce, 5 cups pasta.

■ To make citrus-peel or tomato roses, remove a continuous strip of peel or skin from fruit with vegetable parer or knife. If necessary, place strip in bowl of hot water until it is flexible. With color side facing in, roll one end tightly to strip's midpoint to form a bud; loosely wrap remaining peel or skin around bud to create outer petal. Secure with wooden pick; place in bowl of cold water. Before serving, drain roses; pat dry with paper towel. Remove wooden pick. Garnish platter with single flowers or make a small bouquet. To complete flowers, insert mint sprigs or parsley leaves at base of flowers.

Glazed Peach Tart

(pictured, page 117)

Pastry

1 cup unsifted all-purpose flour
2 tablespoons granulated sugar
⅛ teaspoon salt
½ cup cold unsalted butter, cut in pieces
1 teaspoon grated lemon peel
1 large egg yolk
1½ tablespoons ice water

¾ cup granulated sugar
1½ teaspoons grated lemon peel
1½ cups water
3¼ teaspoons vanilla extract
9 large ripe peach halves, pitted
3 ounces cream cheese, softened
1 cup heavy cream
¼ cup confectioners' sugar
1 teaspoon lemon juice
¼ teaspoon almond extract
¼ cup raspberries

Glaze

¼ cup peach or apricot preserves
1 tablespoon peach-flavored schnapps or almond-flavored liqueur

Mint sprigs

1. Make pastry: Preheat oven to 400°F. In food processor fitted with steel blade, combine flour, 2 tablespoons granulated sugar and the salt. Add butter and 1 teaspoon grated lemon peel; using pulsing motion, process just until mixture resembles coarse crumbs. In custard cup, mix egg yolk with 1½ tablespoons ice water until blended. With processor running, add egg-yolk mixture to flour mixture through feed tube. Process just until dough begins to form a ball.

2. Remove pastry from processor; place in 9-inch square tart pan. With fingertips, press pastry evenly against bottom and sides of pan. Prick with fork; line with square of aluminum foil. Fill halfway with pie weights or dried beans. Bake 15 minutes. Remove foil and weights; bake until cooked, about 3 minutes longer. Cool in pan on wire rack.

3. In large saucepan, combine ¾ cup granulated sugar, 1 teaspoon grated lemon peel, 1½ cups water and 3 teaspoons vanilla. Bring to boiling, stirring until sugar dissolves. Add peach halves. Cover; simmer until tender, about 8 to 10 minutes. With slotted spoon, transfer peaches to large shallow bowl; when cool, slip off and discard skins. Place peach halves on paper-towel-lined baking sheet to drain; pat dry with additional paper towels.

4. In large bowl of electric mixer, at high speed, beat cream cheese until fluffy. At low speed, gradually beat in heavy cream. Add confectioners' sugar, lemon juice, almond extract and remaining lemon peel and vanilla. Beat mixture until blended and stiff; spread over bottom of prepared crust.

5. With small, sharp knife, thinly slice peach halves lengthwise, keeping peach intact at top; arrange, rounded side up, over filling. Sprinkle raspberries over peaches and filling. Cover with plastic wrap; refrigerate 1 hour, or until firm.

6. Make glaze: In small saucepan, melt preserves; pour through stainless-steel sieve placed over another small saucepan. Press preserves through sieve with back of metal spoon. Discard solids. Stir in schnapps until blended. Bring to boiling; with pastry brush, spread hot glaze over fruit. Cover with plastic wrap; refrigerate until serving. At serving time, garnish tart with fresh mint sprigs.

Makes 9 servings.

Lime-Marinated Spareribs

(pictured, pages 118 and 119)

4 to 5 pounds pork spareribs
6 whole cloves
1 large onion
1 tablespoon salt
Water

Marinade and Dipping Sauce

½ cup firmly packed light-brown sugar
3 large cloves garlic, crushed
1 tablespoon ground ginger
1 teaspoon ground coriander
1 teaspoon ground cumin
1 teaspoon crushed red-pepper flakes
1 cup lime juice
¼ cup honey
¼ cup salad oil
3 tablespoons soy sauce

1. Place ribs in 5-quart Dutch oven. Insert cloves in onion. Place in pan with ribs, salt and enough water to cover. Bring to boiling; simmer, uncovered, 45 minutes.

2. Meanwhile, prepare marinade: In small bowl, whisk all marinade ingredients until blended. Measure and reserve ¾ cup for dipping sauce; refrigerate. Transfer ribs to shallow nonaluminum baking dish; pour remaining marinade over ribs. Cover; refrigerate 12 to 24 hours, turning occasionally.

3. Preheat oven to 350°F. Drain off and reserve marinade. Cook ribs, uncovered, in roasting pan, 45 minutes, basting occasionally with reserved marinade. Cut ribs into serving portions; place on heated platter. If desired, garnish with cilantro leaves and sliced starfruit. In small saucepan, heat reserved ¾ cup dipping sauce until hot; serve sauce with ribs.

Makes 4 servings.

Summer-Fruit Cheesecake

(pictured, pages 118 and 119)

Cake crust
¾ cup butter, softened
1 cup sugar
1 teaspoon grated lemon peel
3 large eggs
1¼ cups unsifted cake flour
1½ teaspoons baking powder
⅛ teaspoon salt

⅔ cup peach preserves
2 tablespoons peach-flavored schnapps
½ cup natural sliced almonds

Cheesecake
1 envelope unflavored gelatine
½ cup water
1 cup heavy cream
3 packages (8 ounces each) cream cheese, softened
1¼ cups sugar
¼ cup peach-flavored schnapps
1 teaspoon vanilla extract

10 small strawberries, hulled and thinly sliced
1 kiwifruit, pared and thinly sliced
1 small peach, halved, pitted and thinly sliced
1 cup raspberries

1. Preheat oven to 375°F. Grease 15½-by-10½-by-1-inch jelly-roll pan. Line with waxed paper; grease paper. Set aside.

2. In large bowl of electric mixer, at medium speed, beat butter, 1 cup sugar and the lemon peel until light and fluffy, about 5 minutes. Beat in eggs, one at a time, until blended. On waxed paper, combine flour, baking powder and salt. Add to butter mixture; beat until smooth. Pour into prepared pan; bake until golden-brown, about 18 minutes. Place on wire rack; cool 5 minutes.

3. With small knife, loosen edges of cake from pan. Invert cake onto cutting board; remove paper. Line side of pan: With a pizza cutter or sharp knife, cut cake lengthwise, 2½ inches from edge; place cake strip around inside of 9-inch springform pan. Cut another 2½-inch-wide strip from edge of cake. Cut 10½-inch length from strip; place on inside of springform pan to finish lining side of pan. Line bottom of pan: From waxed paper, cut an 8¼-inch round. Cut round in half; place halves on remaining cake. Using knife and paper patterns, cut two half-rounds from remaining cake. Line bottom of pan with cake pieces; reserve remaining scraps for other use.

4. In small saucepan, melt peach preserves; pour through stainless-steel sieve placed over another small saucepan. Press through with back of metal spoon; discard solids. Stir in 2 tablespoons schnapps until blended; bring to boiling. With pastry brush, spread half of hot glaze over cake on bottom and side of pan; reserve remaining glaze. Sprinkle sliced almonds over cake bottom; set aside.

5. Make cheesecake: In small saucepan, sprinkle gelatine over ½ cup water; let stand 1 minute, until gelatine softens. Heat gelatine over low heat, stirring until dissolved, about 3 minutes. Set aside. In small bowl of electric mixer, at high speed, beat ½ cup heavy cream until stiff; set aside. In large bowl of electric mixer, with same beaters, beat cream cheese with sugar until fluffy, about 3 minutes. Add remaining heavy cream, beating until blended. Beat in dissolved gelatine, the schnapps and vanilla until blended. With rubber spatula, fold in whipped cream. Pour into cake-lined pan. Cover with plastic wrap; refrigerate 8 hours or overnight. Release and remove side of springform pan. Arrange fruit in rows of arcs on top of cake. Heat remaining glaze; with pastry brush, spread hot glaze over fruit. Refrigerate until serving.

Makes 12 servings.

Blueberry-Cassis Pie

(pictured, page 119)

Filling
6 cups blueberries
½ cup sugar
3 tablespoons quick-cooking tapioca
1 tablespoon grated lemon peel
⅓ cup crême de cassis (black-currant-flavored liqueur)
2 tablespoons lemon juice

Pastry
2½ cups unsifted all-purpose flour
⅓ cup sugar
1 cup cold butter or margarine, cut in small pieces
1 package (2 ounces) walnut pieces (⅔ cup), finely chopped
⅓ cup ice water

1 tablespoon sugar

1. Make filling: In large bowl, combine filling ingredients. With back of spoon, crush berries slightly. Let stand while making pastry.

2. Make pastry: In medium bowl, combine flour and ⅓ cup sugar. With pastry blender or two knives, cut in butter until mixture resembles coarse crumbs. Add walnuts; toss to combine. Sprinkle ice water, 1 tablespoon at a time, over pastry mixture, tossing lightly with fork after each addition; push dampened portion to side of bowl, and sprinkle only dry portion with remaining ice water. (Pastry should be just moist enough to hold together, not sticky.) Shape pastry into a ball; wrap in plastic wrap. Refrigerate pastry at least 1 hour.

3. On lightly floured surface, roll out half of pastry to an 11-inch round. Fold pastry in half; carefully transfer to 9-inch pie plate. Unfold pastry; gently fit into plate. With sharp knife, trim pastry even with edge of plate. Set aside.

4. Make lattice: Roll out remaining pastry to an 11-inch round. With pastry cutter, cut into ½-inch-wide

strips. Using photograph as a guide, weave strips together on aluminum-foil-lined baking sheet. Wrap with plastic wrap; refrigerate 30 minutes.

5. Preheat oven to 375°F. Spoon prepared filling into pastry shell. Moisten edge of pastry shell with cold water; invert pastry lattice over filling. Remove foil. Trim pastry to ½ inch over edge of plate. Pinch pastry to form a rim; crimp edges. Lightly brush pastry with water; sprinkle with 1 tablespoon sugar. Cover edge of pastry top with strip of aluminum foil to prevent overbrowning. Bake 1 hour, or until crust is golden-brown and filling is bubbly, removing foil strip the last 10 minutes if necessary to brown pastry. Serve warm or cold. If desired, garnish with whipped-cream rosettes, mint sprig and additional blueberries.

Makes 8 servings.

Oriental Pasta Salad

(pictured, page 119)

Dressing
2 tablespoons sugar
4 teaspoons grated ginger root
¼ cup dry sherry
¼ cup soy sauce
2 tablespoons dark sesame oil
1 tablespoon mirin (sweet rice wine)

2 cups uncooked penne pasta
1 tablespoon salad oil
3 ripe medium-large nectarines, pitted and cut in ¼-inch slices
1 cup seedless green grapes, halved
1 medium red pepper, cut in 1½-inch-long strips
1 large cucumber, halved, seeded and thinly sliced
¼ cup sliced green onions
⅔ cup coarsely chopped salted cashews
2 tablespoons chopped cilantro (fresh coriander) leaves

1. Prepare dressing: In jar with tight-fitting lid, combine dressing ingredients. Shake well until blended. Set aside.

2. Cook pasta as package label directs for al dente. Drain; in medium bowl, toss with salad oil until coated. Set aside until cool.

3. Add all remaining ingredients except cashews and cilantro to pasta; toss to combine. Shake dressing; pour over pasta mixture. Toss well until coated. If desired, refrigerate salad, covered, ½ hour. Just before serving, add cashews; toss to combine. Sprinkle with cilantro.

Makes 8 to 10 servings.

Tipsy French Toast

(pictured, page 118)

Cinnamon Ice Cream
2½ cups heavy cream
1½ cups half-and-half
1 cup sugar
1 (2½-inch) stick cinnamon
½ teaspoon ground cinnamon
6 large egg yolks

2 pints strawberries, hulled and thickly sliced
¼ cup hazelnut-flavored liqueur
1 loaf (12 ounces) challah (egg bread)
3 large eggs
½ cup light cream or half-and-half
2 tablespoons Cointreau or other orange-flavored liqueur
1 tablespoon water
¼ cup butter or margarine

1. Make ice cream: In large saucepan, combine heavy cream, half-and-half, sugar, cinnamon stick and ground cinnamon. Heat until almost boiling; let steep on low heat 15 minutes. (Do not boil.) In small bowl, whisk egg yolks with ½ cup hot cream mixture; whisk into cream mixture in saucepan. Over low heat, cook, stirring constantly, until mixture coats back of spoon. (Do not boil.) Strain into large heat-safe pitcher; return cinnamon stick to mixture. Cover; refrigerate until cold. Remove cinnamon sticks. Freeze in ice cream freezer according to manufacturer's instructions. Store in covered container in freezer.

2. About 1 hour before serving, in small bowl, combine strawberries and hazelnut liqueur; set aside.

3. Trim and discard ends from challah. Cut challah crosswise in 6 slices, about 1½ inches thick. Set aside. In large shallow baking dish, whisk together eggs, light cream, Cointreau and water; dip challah in egg mixture. Turn slices; let soak in egg mixture 10 minutes.

4. In 12-inch skillet, melt 2 tablespoons butter over medium heat. Add 3 challah slices; cook 5 minutes, or until golden. Turn challah; cook 5 minutes longer. Place on heated platter; keep warm. Repeat with remaining butter and challah slices.

5. To serve: Place 1 slice French toast on serving dish. Top with large scoop Cinnamon Ice Cream and about ½ cup prepared strawberries.

Makes 6 servings, 1 quart ice cream.

■ When softening ice cream, remember to let it warm only to a spoonable stage. The reason: When refrozen, melted ice cream will develop ice crystals.

■ Keep a container of ice cream fresh by wrapping it in foil or freezer wrap. Once a portion has been served, press a piece of plastic wrap over the surface of the ice cream; besides preventing it from sticking to the container, this method keeps ice crystals from forming.

■ For clean, easy cutting, dip your knife in hot water and then wipe it dry.

Raspberry-Grilled Hens

(pictured, pages 120 and 121)

Marinade
¼ cup raspberries
3 small cloves garlic
1 teaspoon salt
½ teaspoon pepper
¼ cup salad oil
¼ cup orange juice
¼ cup raspberry vinegar

4 (1 pound each) Cornish game hens, split lengthwise in half
1 cup raspberries

1. In food processor or electric blender, combine marinade ingredients. Process 1 minute, until ingredients are blended.

2. Place hens in shallow glass baking dish. Pour marinade over hens; refrigerate, covered, 8 hours or overnight, turning occasionally.

3. Prepare outdoor grill for barbecue. Reserve marinade; place hens, skin side down, on grill, directly over medium coals. Cook 10 minutes, or until lightly browned, rearranging hens on grill as they brown, if necessary. Remove hens to platter.

4. Push coals to one side of grill or, if using gas grill, turn off heat on one side. Place hens, skin side up, on grill, away from coals. Brush with marinade; cook hens, covered, 35 minutes, brushing occasionally with marinade and moving pieces on grill as they brown, until joints move easily and juices run clear. Place on warm serving platter; sprinkle with 1 cup raspberries. If desired, garnish with mâche (lamb's lettuce).

Makes 8 servings.

■ Sugar-frosted grapes provide elegant garnishes for roast pork, ham or chicken. To prepare, start with small clusters of red or green seedless grapes. Brush with egg white, sprinkle with sugar and dry on a wire rack.

Raspberry Tarts

(pictured, page 121)

Tart Crust
2 packages (5.29 ounces each) pecan shortbread cookies, crushed (about 3½ cups)
½ cup butter or margarine, melted

Filling
8 ounces strawberry-flavored Neufchâtel cheese, softened
3 tablespoons sugar
3 tablespoons crème de cassis (black-currant-flavored liqueur)
½ cup heavy cream
¼ cup seedless raspberry jam
About 2½ cups raspberries
About 2½ cups blackberries

1. Preheat oven to 425°F. Make tart crust: Grease eight 4½-inch fluted tart pans with removable bottoms. In medium bowl, combine cookie crumbs and butter until crumbs are moistened. With fingers, press mixture onto bottom and side of each tart pan, dividing evenly. Place pans on baking sheet. Bake until lightly browned, about 8 to 10 minutes. Cool on wire rack.

2. Make filling: In large bowl of electric mixer, at high speed, beat cheese, 2 tablespoons sugar and the cassis until blended; set aside. In small bowl of electric mixer, at high speed, beat heavy cream and remaining 1 tablespoon sugar until stiff; with rubber spatula, fold cream into cheese mixture. Spoon into prepared tart shells, dividing evenly. Cover with plastic wrap; refrigerate until well chilled, about 2 hours.

3. In small saucepan, heat jam until melted. Cool 5 minutes; with pastry brush, carefully spread jam over cheese in each crust, dividing evenly. Using photograph as a guide, arrange raspberries on one side of each tart over jam, dividing evenly; fill tarts with blackberries, dividing evenly.

Makes 8 servings.

Banana-Coconut-Cream Pie

(pictured, pages 120 and 121)

Crust
1¼ cups graham-cracker crumbs (about 18 whole graham crackers)
⅓ cup butter or margarine, melted
¼ cup sugar

Custard
½ cup sugar
3 tablespoons cornstarch
¼ teaspoon salt
1¾ cups milk
4 large egg yolks, slightly beaten
1½ teaspoons vanilla extract
½ teaspoon coconut extract

2½ cups heavy cream
4 to 5 large ripe bananas
¼ cup apricot preserves, heated and sieved
½ cup toasted coconut

1. Preheat oven to 375°F. In medium bowl, combine crumbs, butter and ¼ cup sugar until crumbs are moistened. With fingers, press mixture onto bottom and side of 9-inch pie plate. Bake 8 minutes, or until golden-brown. Cool on wire rack.

2. Make custard: In medium saucepan, combine ½ cup sugar, the cornstarch and salt. Gradually whisk in milk until mixture is smooth. Over medium heat, bring mixture to boiling, stirring constantly. On medium-low heat, boil 1 minute, stirring constantly. Place egg yolks in small bowl; whisk in about ½ cup hot-milk mixture. Whisk egg-yolk mixture into remaining milk mixture in pan; simmer 1 minute longer, stirring.

3. Cool custard to room temperature, stirring occasionally. Add 1 teaspoon vanilla and the coconut extract. In small bowl of electric mixer, at high speed, beat ½ cup heavy cream until stiff; with rubber spatula, fold into custard.

4. Cut 2 bananas crosswise into ¼-inch-thick slices; arrange over bottom of prepared crust. Pour custard over bananas; cover with plastic wrap placed directly on custard. Refrigerate at least 4 hours.

5. In large bowl of electric mixer, at high speed, beat remaining 2 cups heavy cream with remaining ½ teaspoon vanilla until stiff. Place 1 cup whipped cream in pastry bag fitted with large star tip; spread remainder over custard in pie. Cut remaining bananas crosswise and diagonally into ¼-inch-thick slices; using photograph as a guide, arrange in rings.

6. In small saucepan, heat strained preserves until boiling; with pastry brush, spread over bananas, covering completely. Sprinkle coconut between rows of bananas. Pipe reserved whipped cream around edge of pie crust. Cover with plastic wrap, using wooden picks to lift plastic away from cream; refrigerate at least 1 hour.

Makes 8 servings.

Nectarine-Oat-Bran Muffins

(pictured, page 120)

2 cups unsifted all-purpose flour
2 teaspoons baking powder
1 teaspoon ground cinnamon
½ teaspoon baking soda
¼ teaspoon salt
2 large eggs
½ cup firmly packed light-brown sugar
1½ cups buttermilk
¼ cup salad oil
3 cups oat-bran-flakes cereal
2 cups finely chopped unpared nectarines (2 medium)

1. Preheat oven to 400°F. Line muffin-pan cups with paper liners. On sheet of waxed paper, combine flour, baking powder, cinnamon, baking soda and salt.

2. In large bowl, whisk eggs with sugar, buttermilk and oil until blended. Add flour mixture, cereal and nectarines; stir just until moistened. Evenly fill prepared muffin cups two-thirds full. Bake 20 minutes, or until golden. Remove muffins from pan; cool on wire rack.

Makes 24 muffins.

Shrimp-and-Fruit Mélange

(pictured, page 120)

Dressing
2 tablespoons sugar
½ teaspoon dry mustard
¼ teaspoon salt
¼ cup raspberry vinegar or lemon juice
½ cup salad oil
1 tablespoon poppy seeds

1½ pounds medium shrimp
3 cups cubed assorted melon
4 green onions, sliced
2 celery stalks, sliced
1 medium peach, pitted and cut in ½-inch slices
1 medium ripe Bartlett pear, cored and coarsely chopped
½ pint blueberries
1 prickly pear, pared and thinly sliced crosswise

Lettuce leaves, washed and crisped

1. Make dressing: In electric blender, combine sugar, mustard, salt and vinegar until blended. With motor running, add oil; blend until thickened. Pour into small bowl; stir in poppy seeds. Refrigerate until chilled.

2. Meanwhile, in 2-quart saucepan, bring 1 quart water to boiling. Add shrimp; return water to boiling. Cook just until shrimp turn pink, about 1½ minutes. Drain; immediately rinse with cold water. Remove and discard shells.

3. In large bowl, combine shrimp and all remaining ingredients except lettuce; toss with dressing until evenly coated. Line serving bowl with lettuce leaves; spoon salad mixture into bowl.

Makes 4 to 6 servings.

Berry Butter

(pictured, page 120)

2 cups mixed berries (hulled strawberries, raspberries, blackberries)
¼ cup confectioners' sugar
¾ cup butter, softened

1. In food processor or electric blender, puree berries; if desired, strain to remove seeds. In small bowl, mix puree with sugar until blended.

2. In small bowl of electric mixer, at high speed, beat butter until light and fluffy. Gradually beat in fruit mixture until blended. Spoon into serving dish; refrigerate. Let soften slightly before serving.

Makes 1½ cups.

Many-Berry Preserves

(pictured, pages 120 and 121)

7 cups mixed berries (hulled strawberries, raspberries, blackberries, blueberries)
1 cup sugar
2 tablespoons lemon juice

1. In food processor or electric blender, puree 3½ cups berries with sugar. In 2-quart saucepan, bring puree, remaining whole berries and the lemon juice to boiling.

2. Over medium-low heat, cook berry mixture, stirring occasionally, 1½ hours, or until thickened and mixture registers 220°F on candy thermometer. Spoon into sterilized jars. Process according to jar manufacturer's instructions.

Makes about 2 quarts.

Kiwi-Banana Bread

(pictured, page 120)

3 kiwifruit, pared and sliced crosswise
1 banana, peeled and cut in chunks
2½ cups unsifted all-purpose flour
1½ teaspoons baking powder
1 teaspoon baking soda
¼ teaspoon salt
½ cup butter or margarine, softened
½ cup sugar
2 large eggs
½ cup buttermilk
2 teaspoons vanilla extract
½ cup toasted pecans, chopped

Glaze
¼ cup sugar
4 teaspoons lemon juice

1. Preheat oven to 350°F. Grease and flour 9-by-5-by-3-inch loaf pan.

2. Reserve 3 kiwifruit slices for garnish. In food processor or electric blender, puree remaining kiwifruit with the banana; set aside. On sheet of waxed paper, combine next 4 ingredients; set aside.

3. In large bowl of electric mixer, beat butter with ½ cup sugar until light, about 3 minutes. Add eggs, one at a time, beating well after each addition. Beat in kiwifruit puree, buttermilk and vanilla until blended. Add flour mixture; beat just until moistened. Stir in pecans.

4. Pour batter into prepared pan. Bake 1 hour and 15 minutes, or until wooden pick inserted in center comes out clean.

5. Meanwhile, make glaze: In small saucepan, over medium heat, combine ¼ cup sugar and the lemon juice, stirring until sugar melts and mixture boils. Remove from heat; cool slightly.

6. Cool bread in pan on wire rack 10 minutes. Invert onto rack; turn top up. Brush top and sides with glaze. Garnish with kiwifruit.

Makes 1 loaf.

Sour-Cream Apple Pie

Pastry for 2-crust pie
3 pounds (about 7) Granny Smith or other tart cooking apples
2 tablespoons lemon juice
1 cup sour cream
1 cup granulated sugar
2 tablespoons flour
1 teaspoon ground cinnamon
⅛ teaspoon ground nutmeg
¼ teaspoon salt

Topping
3 tablespoons dark-brown sugar
3 tablespoons granulated sugar
1 teaspoon ground cinnamon
1 cup chopped walnuts

2 tablespoons butter or margarine
Milk
Granulated sugar

1. Shape pastry into a ball; divide in half. On lightly floured surface, roll out half of pastry into a 12-inch round. Use to line 9-inch pie plate. Refrigerate, along with remaining pastry, until ready to use.

2. Peel, core and thinly slice apples into large bowl. Sprinkle with lemon juice. Toss with sour cream. In small bowl, combine 1 cup granulated sugar, the flour, 1 teaspoon cinnamon, the nutmeg and salt; mix well. Add to apples; toss lightly to combine.

3. Make topping: Combine brown sugar, 3 tablespoons granulated sugar, 1 teaspoon cinnamon and the walnuts; mix well.

4. Roll out remaining half of pastry into a 10-inch round. With knife or pastry wheel, cut into 9 (1-inch-wide) strips.

5. Preheat oven to 400°F. Turn apple mixture into pastry-lined pie plate. Dot top with butter. Sprinkle topping evenly over apple mixture. Moisten rim of pastry slightly with cold water. Arrange 5 pastry strips, ½ inch apart, over filling; press ends to pastry rim. Place remaining strips across first ones at right angle, to make a lattice, and press to rim. Fold overhang of bottom crust over ends of strips, and crimp decoratively. Brush lattice top, but not rim, lightly with milk, and sprinkle with granulated sugar. Bake 50 minutes, or until crust is golden and juice bubbles through lattice. (After 30 minutes, place a foil tent loosely over top to prevent overbrowning.) Cool on wire rack. Serve warm, with ice cream, if desired.

Makes 8 servings.

■ Aluminum foil is the key to baking prettier pies. Keep the fruit filling from overflowing by inserting funnels made of aluminum foil into cuts in the top layer of pastry—the funnels serve as heat vents so filling won't spill out and stain the crust.

■ No pie is complete without that creamy dollop of fresh whipped cream. For best whipping results, pour cream into your mixer bowl and chill with the beaters. Add ½ teaspoon fresh lemon juice just before whipping—guaranteed success!

■ Serving up pies with luscious, flaky crusts is a source of pride for many at-home bakers. The most important step to perfect piecrust is to cut the fat into the flour as well as possible—really work it into small beads. You can't overdo! Another hint: If you think you've added a bit too much water, freeze the unbaked crust overnight before baking; this will help dry it out.

Lite Eating: Savory Grilled Vegetables

Dill Tomatoes

4 large tomatoes
2 tablespoons dry vermouth
1 teaspoon dried dillweed
¼ teaspoon pepper
¼ cup reduced-calorie mayonnaise
2 slices (⅔ ounce each) reduced-calorie Swiss cheese

1. Prepare outdoor grill for barbecue. Remove and discard core from each tomato. Cut tomatoes crosswise in half; with fork, pierce halves several times. Arrange halves, cut side up, in disposable foil pan; sprinkle with vermouth.

2. In small bowl, combine dill, pepper and mayonnaise; spread mixture over tomatoes. Cut cheese slices in half; cut halves crosswise in half. Place 1 square of cheese over topping on each tomato.

3. Place pan with tomatoes on grill, 6 inches from heat; close lid. Using INDIRECT METHOD (see page 108), cook tomatoes 5 minutes, or until cheese melts. Or preheat oven to 425°F. Loosely cover tomatoes with foil; bake 10 minutes.

Makes 8 servings, 59 calories each.

Sesame Asparagus

1 pound asparagus, trimmed
2 tablespoons reduced-calorie margarine, melted
1 tablespoon sesame seeds, toasted
1 tablespoon lemon juice

1. Prepare outdoor grill for barbecue. Place asparagus on square of heavy-duty aluminum foil; set aside. In custard cup, combine remaining ingredients; pour over asparagus.

2. Wrap foil around asparagus, drugstore fashion (see tip, page 109); place on grill, 6 inches from heat. Using INDIRECT METHOD (see page 108), cook 25 minutes, or until asparagus is tender-crisp. Or preheat oven to 425°F; bake asparagus in foil 25 minutes.

Makes 4 servings, 58 calories each.

Green-Bean Bundles

1 pound green beans, trimmed
2 tablespoons reduced-calorie margarine, melted
2 green onions, chopped
2 tablespoons pine nuts, toasted
¼ teaspoon ground savory

1. Prepare outdoor grill for barbecue. Place beans on square of heavy-duty aluminum foil; set aside. In custard cup, combine remaining ingredients; pour over beans.

2. Wrap foil around beans, drugstore fashion (see tip, page 109); place packet on grill, 6 inches from heat. Using INDIRECT METHOD (see page 108), cook 20 minutes, or until beans are tender-crisp. Or preheat oven to 425°F; bake beans in foil 20 minutes.

Makes 6 servings, 55 calories each.

Clockwise from top left: Skillet Coleslaw, Dill Tomatoes, Green-Bean Bundles, Sesame Asparagus.

Skillet Coleslaw

Nonstick cooking spray
4 cups shredded cabbage
1 large carrot, grated
1 medium onion, thinly sliced
1 medium green pepper, julienned
2 tablespoons soy sauce

1. Prepare outdoor grill for barbecue. With nonstick cooking spray, grease cast-iron 10-inch skillet. Add cabbage and remaining ingredients to skillet; toss to combine.

2. Place skillet on grill, 6 inches from heat. Using DIRECT METHOD (see page 108), cook slaw, stirring frequently, 10 minutes, or until hot.

Makes 6 servings, 33 calories each.

Micro-Way: Summer Snacks for Kids

Chewy Caramel Snacks

3 cups cornflakes
1 cup flaked coconut
1 cup raisins
½ cup chopped dried apricots
1 bag (14 ounces) caramels, wrappers removed (about 58)
2 tablespoons water

In large bowl, combine cornflakes, coconut, raisins and apricots; mix well. Place caramels and water in 4-cup glass measure; cook on HIGH 2½ to 3½ minutes, stirring occasionally, until smooth. Pour caramel mixture over cereal mixture; toss until evenly coated. Drop by tablespoonfuls onto waxed-paper-lined baking sheet.

Makes 2 dozen.

Raspberry-Oatmeal Bars

1½ cups unsifted all-purpose flour
1½ cups uncooked old-fashioned rolled oats
½ teaspoon salt
½ teaspoon baking soda
¾ cup butter or margarine, softened
1 cup firmly packed light-brown sugar
1 jar (10 ounces) seedless raspberry jam

1. Line 11-by-7-by-2-inch glass baking dish with two pieces of waxed paper, extending two short sides by 1 inch. On separate sheet of waxed paper, combine flour, oats, salt and baking soda; mix well.

2. In large bowl of electric mixer, at high speed, beat butter and sugar until light and fluffy. With wooden spoon, stir in oat mixture until blended. Press half of oat mixture into bottom of prepared dish. Spread with jam. Crumble remaining oat mixture on top; press lightly.

3. Cover corners of dish with aluminum foil. Cook on MEDIUM 10 minutes, rotating dish every 2 minutes. Remove foil; cook on HIGH 4 minutes, rotating as above. Let cool in baking dish. Grasping both sides of waxed paper, remove cookie from dish. Cut into 1½-by-1-inch bars; peel off waxed paper. If desired, drizzle with icing glaze: In small bowl, mix ¾ cup confectioners' sugar, 1 tablespoon softened butter or margarine and ¾ teaspoon vanilla extract. Stir in 1 tablespoon warm water, a teaspoonful at a time, until icing mixture is of pourable consistency.

Makes about 4 dozen.

Quick Chicken Tacos

1 jar (15 ounces) spaghetti sauce
1 can (4 ounces) chopped mild green chiles
1 tablespoon chili powder
2 cans (5 ounces each) chunk chicken, drained
6 taco shells

1. In medium glass bowl, combine sauce, chiles and chili powder; cover with waxed paper. Cook on HIGH 3 minutes; stir in chicken.

2. Place shells, open side up, in paper-towel-lined 13-by-9-by-2-inch glass baking dish. Spoon mixture into shells. Cook on HIGH 2 to 3 minutes, or until heated through. If desired, top with chopped tomato, shredded lettuce and cheese.

Makes 6 servings.

More-and-Mores

8 whole graham crackers
Creamy peanut butter
Marshmallow creme or grape jelly
1 package (12 ounces) semisweet-chocolate pieces
2 tablespoons shortening

1. Split each cracker crosswise in half to make 2 squares. Spread 1 square with 1 teaspoon peanut butter, and other square with 1 teaspoon marshmallow creme or grape jelly. Press coated sides together. Repeat with remaining crackers.

2. In medium glass bowl, melt chocolate and shortening on MEDIUM 2 to 4 minutes, stirring occasionally, until smooth. Holding one corner and using photograph as a guide, dip filled crackers, one at a time, into melted chocolate mixture, coating half completely. Remove cracker; gently tap off excess. Place crackers on waxed-paper-lined tray; refrigerate until firm.

Makes 8 servings.

Clockwise from top left: Chewy Caramel Snacks, Raspberry-Oatmeal Bars, More-and-Mores, Quick Chicken Tacos.

August

Main-dish salads are perfect meals for hot summer days. Our collection offers lots of tempting combinations. Those listed below are pictured, beginning with the colorful potato salad and stuffed tomato shown here.

Russian Potato Salad

Tonnato-Stuffed Tomatoes

Fresh Pea Salad With Beef Satays

Tortellini Primavera

Calypso Papaya Cups

Taco Salad in Tortilla Baskets

Savory Sweet-Potato Salad

Basque Salad

Lentil Salad With Roasted Lamb Medallions

Szechwan Noodle Toss

Summer Salads Cookbook

Brimming with crisp fresh vegetables, a delicious salad can turn a light summer meal into something special.

Russian Potato Salad

(pictured, page 133)

2½ pounds small new red potatoes
8 cups water
1 teaspoon salt

Vinaigrette
1 teaspoon salt
¼ teaspoon pepper
½ cup salad oil
¼ cup white-wine vinegar

Yogurt Dressing
½ cup low-fat plain yogurt
½ cup mayonnaise
¼ cup chopped chives
1 tablespoon white-wine vinegar
1 tablespoon Dijon-style mustard
1 medium cucumber
¼ cup chopped dill pickle
½ cup sliced pickled beets
Crisp lettuce leaves
3 large hard-cooked eggs, shelled and quartered
½ cup sliced green onion
¼ pound thinly sliced smoked salmon, cut in 1-inch-long strips

1. Quarter or halve potatoes. Place in 5-quart Dutch oven with water and 1 teaspoon salt. Cover and bring to boiling. Simmer until tender, about 10 minutes.
2. Meanwhile, make vinaigrette: In bowl, whisk 1 teaspoon salt, the pepper, oil and ¼ cup white-wine vinegar until blended. Set aside.
3. Make yogurt dressing: In another small bowl, whisk yogurt with mayonnaise, chives, 1 tablespoon white-wine vinegar and the mustard until blended. Set aside.
4. In colander, drain potatoes. Place in large bowl. Add vinaigrette; toss lightly until coated. Cover with plastic wrap; set aside at room temperature. (Salad can be prepared ahead up to this point.)
5. With fork, score cucumber lengthwise. Cut in half lengthwise; with spoon, remove and discard seeds. Cut cucumber halves crosswise into thin slices. Add to potatoes. Stir in pickles. Rinse beets; pat dry. Add to potato mixture.
6. Line serving platter with lettuce leaves; top with potato mixture. Garnish with eggs, green onion and salmon. Pass yogurt dressing separately.

Makes 6 to 8 servings.

Page 133: Russian Potato Salad, Tonnato-Stuffed Tomatoes.

Pages 134 and 135: (Clockwise from top) Tortellini Primavera, Calypso Papaya Cups, Taco Salad in Tortilla Baskets, Fresh Pea Salad With Beef Satays.

Pages 136 and 137: (Clockwise from top) Savory Sweet-Potato Salad, Basque Salad, Lentil Salad With Roasted Lamb Medallions, Szechwan Noodle Toss.

Tonnato-Stuffed Tomatoes

(pictured, page 133)

Stuffing
½ cup bulgur (medium cracked wheat)
2 teaspoons tomato paste
1½ cups water
2 celery stalks, thinly sliced
1 red onion, chopped
½ cup mayonnaise
1 can (3½ ounces) water-packed tuna, drained
¼ cup chopped sun-dried tomatoes in oil, drained
2 tablespoons lemon juice
2 tablespoons chopped mint
2 tablespoons chopped parsley
1 tablespoon capers
1 tablespoon olive oil
3 anchovy fillets, minced
¼ teaspoon hot-red-pepper sauce

6 medium tomatoes

1. In medium bowl, combine bulgur, tomato paste and water. Cover

bowl; let mixture stand 2 hours. Drain well.

2. Add all remaining stuffing ingredients to bulgur; toss to combine. Set aside.

3. With serrated knife, cut each tomato into 8 wedges, not cutting all the way through. Spoon stuffing into tomatoes, dividing evenly.

Makes 6 servings.

Taco Salad in Tortilla Baskets

(pictured, pages 134 and 135)

10 flour tortillas
Corn oil
3 cups shredded lettuce
½ cup julienned radishes
1 can (15 ounces) red kidney beans, drained and rinsed
1 large tomato, seeded and diced
1 small green pepper, diced
1 cup medium-hot prepared salsa
2 tablespoons red-wine vinegar
1 pound lean ground beef
1 small onion, chopped
1 tablespoon chili powder
1 can (7 ounces) whole-kernel corn with sweet peppers
1 cup (4 ounces) shredded Cheddar cheese
½ cup sour cream
1 avocado, pared and cut in 1-inch chunks

1. Make tortilla baskets: Preheat oven to 375°F. Brush tortillas on both sides with corn oil. Using photograph as a guide, arrange each tortilla in cone shape in large (4½-inch) glass custard cup, folding under base of cone to set tortilla in cup; insert a smaller custard cup on inside of tortilla cone to hold cone open. Place tortillas in custard cups on baking sheet; bake 8 minutes. Remove smaller custard cup; bake tortillas 4 minutes longer, or until golden-brown. Keep warm or set aside and reheat before serving.

2. Make filling: In large bowl, combine lettuce and radishes; refrigerate until serving. In medium bowl, toss kidney beans with tomato, green pepper, salsa and red-wine vinegar until well mixed. Set aside. In large skillet, over medium heat, cook beef and onion until meat is browned. With spoon, remove all but 2 tablespoons drippings. Stir in chili powder and corn; cook 2 to 3 minutes longer. Set aside.

3. Assemble tacos: Place some lettuce mixture in each tortilla basket; spoon some meat mixture and green-pepper mixture on top, and sprinkle with cheese, dividing evenly. Serve each taco with sour cream and avocado chunks.

Makes 10 servings.

Fresh Pea Salad With Beef Satays

(pictured, page 134)

Dressing
¾ cup salad oil
¼ cup balsamic vinegar
¼ cup prepared honey-flavored mustard or coarse Dijon-style mustard
3 tablespoons honey
1 teaspoon celery seeds
1 teaspoon salt
¼ teaspoon pepper

Satays
1¼-pound flank steak, partially frozen

Pea Salad
2 pounds peas, shelled (2 cups)
1 medium yellow pepper, thinly sliced
1 cup (4 ounces) toasted slivered almonds
1 cup sliced celery
1 cup sliced green onion
½ cup sliced radishes

Crisped lettuce leaves

1. Make dressing: In jar with tight-fitting lid, combine dressing ingredients; shake vigorously until mixture is blended. Set aside.

2. Soak twelve 6-inch wooden skewers in water. Thinly slice steak diagonally across the grain. Drain skewers; thread steak strips onto each skewer, dividing evenly. Arrange skewers in shallow baking dish; brush with some prepared dressing. Pour ¼ cup additional dressing over meat on skewers. Cover with plastic wrap; refrigerate at least 1 hour.

3. In large bowl, toss uncooked peas with yellow pepper, almonds, celery, green onion, radishes and remaining dressing until well mixed. Cover with plastic wrap; refrigerate while cooking satays.

4. Prepare outdoor grill for barbecue. Place skewers on grill about 6 inches from medium-hot coals. Cook, turning once, until browned, about 10 minutes.

5. Line large bowl with lettuce leaves. Spoon salad on top. Serve with satays.

Makes 5 to 6 servings.

■ Don't throw away those celery leaves—they have a wonderful flavor! Chop them with parsley and use on broiled fish or in casseroles, or add them to soup.

Calypso Papaya Cups

(pictured, page 135)

1 small jicama, pared and coarsely shredded
1 large carrot, pared and finely shredded
1 cup alfalfa sprouts
1 cup watercress leaves
1 grapefruit, peeled and cut in ½-inch cubes
⅓ cup raisins
3 large papayas

Dressing
2 teaspoons grated lime peel
1 teaspoon sugar
½ teaspoon salt
¼ teaspoon celery seeds
⅛ teaspoon pepper
⅓ cup olive or salad oil
3 tablespoons lime juice

3 tablespoons coarsely chopped peanuts

1. In large bowl, combine jicama, carrot, alfalfa sprouts, watercress, grapefruit and raisins; set aside. Pare papayas; slice in half lengthwise. Scoop out and discard seeds. Set aside papayas.

2. Make dressing: In jar with tight-fitting lid, combine dressing ingredients. Shake vigorously to blend. Add to jicama mixture; toss to coat. Spoon mixture into hollow papaya halves, dividing evenly. Sprinkle each with peanuts.

Makes 6 servings.

Tortellini Primavera

(pictured, pages 134 and 135)

Dressing
1 bottle (8 ounces) creamy Italian dressing
½ cup buttermilk
1 tablespoon chopped fresh dill
1 teaspoon celery seeds

Salad
1 medium bunch broccoli, stems pared
1 package (10 ounces) refrigerated tortellini
1 medium yellow squash
1 medium zucchini
1 cup halved cherry tomatoes

1. In small bowl, whisk dressing ingredients until blended. Refrigerate until ready to use.

2. Trim broccoli flowerets to 1½-inch lengths; if large, separate into smaller flowerets. Cut stems on diagonal into 1½-inch lengths. Set aside.

3. In 5-quart Dutch oven, cook tortellini as package label directs, adding broccoli flowerets and stems the last 2 minutes of cooking time. Drain; place in bowl of ice and water until cold. Drain thoroughly.

4. Julienne yellow squash; cut zucchini crosswise in thin slices. In large bowl, combine tortellini and broccoli with remaining ingredients and dressing. Place in serving bowl. If desired, fold thinly sliced salami in quarters to make a loose flower. Place on top of salad.

Makes 8 servings.

■ Everyone loves the look and taste of broccoli flowerets, but what to do with the stems? The answer: serve them, too! First peel with a sharp knife: Cut about ⅛ inch into the stem, and discard the outside. Then cut the stem into three bite-size strips, and serve along with other vegetables and dip. Guests will love their crunchiness.

■ If you're serving fresh asparagus, you'll probably need to blanch it. To keep asparagus from wilting before it's cooked, try this: Snap off the bottom of each spear at the point where it breaks easily—usually just above the beige portion of the stem. Then stand the spears upright in a jar or small pitcher of cold water and place in the refrigerator.

Savory Sweet-Potato Salad

(pictured, pages 136 and 137)

3 pounds sweet potatoes, pared and cut in 1-inch cubes
Water
2 teaspoons salt
1 cup bottled olive-oil-and-vinegar dressing
2 large red peppers, quartered
¾ pound pencil-thin asparagus, cut in 1-inch lengths and blanched
½ pound smoked ham, cut in ½-inch cubes
1 small red onion, diced

Aioli Dressing
2 tablespoons salad oil
1 large leek (white part only), thinly sliced and rinsed
2 small cloves garlic, crushed
⅛ teaspoon pepper
¾ cup mayonnaise
2 teaspoons lemon juice

2 heads radicchio
½ cup chopped pitted Greek black olives

1. In large saucepan, cover potatoes with water. Sprinkle with salt. Bring to boiling; simmer just until tender, about 15 minutes. Drain; place in large bowl. Immediately toss with ¾ cup oil-and-vinegar dressing. Cover with plastic wrap; refrigerate.

2. Place pepper quarters, skin side down, directly on range-top burners. On medium heat, roast peppers until skin is black, about 5 minutes. When peppers are cool enough to handle, peel off and discard charred skin. Cut peppers crosswise into ½-inch pieces. In medium bowl, toss peppers with remaining oil-and-vinegar dressing. Add asparagus, ham and red onion; toss to combine. Toss asparagus mixture with sweet potatoes; refrigerate until cold.

3. Make dressing: Place salad oil in medium skillet over medium

heat. Add leek; sauté until tender, about 5 minutes. Add garlic; sauté 1 minute. Transfer leek mixture to food processor; puree. Add pepper, mayonnaise and lemon juice; process until blended. Refrigerate dressing until cold.

4. Remove inner leaves from 1 head radicchio; fill radicchio "bowl" with Aioli Dressing. Line salad bowl with loose radicchio leaves and leaves from second head of radicchio. Spoon potato salad on top. Sprinkle with olives. Nestle radicchio "bowl" with aioli in salad, as pictured in photograph.

Makes 8 servings.

Basque Salad

(pictured, page 137)

2 packages (6 ounces each) saffron-flavored rice mix
¼ cup orange juice
2 tablespoons olive oil
¼ teaspoon freshly ground pepper
¾ pound medium shrimp, cooked, shelled and cooled
¼ pound sliced cooked ham, cut in ½-inch-wide strips
¼ pound hard salami, cut in ½-inch-wide strips
¼ pound surimi (fish and crab blend)
1 can (4 ounces) whole pimientos, drained and cut in thin strips
½ cup chopped onion
½ small green pepper, julienned
¼ cup chopped parsley
Crisped lettuce leaves

1. Cook rice as package label directs; drain. Spread rice out on jelly-roll pan; freeze until cold, about 15 minutes.

2. In large bowl, whisk together orange juice, olive oil and freshly ground pepper. Add rice, shrimp and all remaining ingredients except lettuce; toss well to coat. Cover lightly with plastic wrap; refrigerate until cold, about 1 hour. Line large serving bowl with lettuce; top with rice mixture.

Makes 10 servings.

Lentil Salad With Roasted Lamb Medallions

(pictured, pages 136 and 137)

Lemon Vinaigrette
1 package (.7 ounce) herb-flavored salad-dressing mix
¼ cup lemon juice

1-pound lamb tenderloin

Lentil Salad
1½ cups dried lentils
2 medium cloves garlic, crushed
½ teaspoon salt
3½ cups water
8 ounces feta cheese, crumbled
1¼ cups pared Jerusalem artichokes (sun-chokes), julienned
1 large tomato, seeded and chopped
¼ cup diced carrots
¼ cup chopped Spanish olives
¼ cup chopped green onion
¼ cup chopped parsley
2 tablespoons chopped cilantro (fresh coriander) leaves
1 tablespoon chopped fresh mint

Lettuce leaves, washed and crisped

1. Prepare Lemon Vinaigrette: In jar with tight-fitting lid, make salad-dressing mix as package label directs except substitute lemon juice for vinegar. Set aside.

2. With kitchen string, tie lamb crosswise at 1-inch intervals; place in shallow bowl. Pour ¼ cup vinaigrette over lamb. Cover lamb with plastic wrap; marinate in refrigerator 1 hour.

3. Meanwhile, place lentils in strainer; rinse under running cold water. Place in 2½-quart saucepan with garlic, salt and water; bring to boiling. Cover; simmer 25 minutes, or until lentils are tender but not mushy. Drain well. Cool to room temperature.

4. Prepare outdoor grill for barbecue. Drain lamb; place on grill 6 inches from medium coals. Cover grill; cook lamb 15 minutes, turning after 7 minutes, until meat thermometer inserted in center of tenderloin registers 135°F for medium rare. Remove string; let stand at room temperature 30 minutes.

5. In medium bowl, combine lentils with remaining salad ingredients and vinaigrette. Arrange lettuce leaves on 6 salad plates; top with lentil mixture, dividing evenly. Slice lamb crosswise in medallions; serve with salad.

Makes 6 servings.

■ Looking for a foolproof way to prepare hollandaise sauce? Just follow these easy steps: In a saucepan, over medium-low heat, beat 2 egg yolks, one at a time, into 3 ounces cream cheese. Stir in 2 tablespoons lemon juice and ¼ teaspoon salt. Cook, stirring, until mixture has thickened, about 4 minutes. Super easy—and the sauce won't curdle!

■ Here are some sure solutions for sauces and gravies that miss the boat! *Too lumpy*: Process in a blender or food processor. *Too thin*: Add some vegetable puree or instant whipped potato flakes or powder. *If a sauce containing eggs begins to curdle*, add about 1 tablespoon ice water or boiling water and beat vigorously with a wire whisk. The results? Perfect sauces or gravies every time.

Szechwan Noodle Toss

(pictured, page 136)

1 package (8 ounces) thin spaghetti
5 tablespoons salad oil
2 large red peppers, julienned
4 green onions, cut diagonally in 1-inch pieces
1 medium clove garlic, crushed
1 pound spinach leaves, washed, drained and cut in 1-inch pieces
1 can (8 ounces) sliced water chestnuts, drained
¾ pound firm tofu, drained and cut in ¾-inch cubes
1½ teaspoons crushed red-pepper flakes
¼ cup low-sodium soy sauce
2 tablespoons dark sesame oil
2 tablespoons rice vinegar
1 teaspoon minced ginger root

1. Cook pasta as package label directs. Drain; rinse with cold water. Drain again. Place in large bowl.

2. In large skillet, heat 2 tablespoons salad oil. Add red peppers, green onions and garlic; sauté until tender-crisp, about 2 minutes. Stir in spinach. Cover; cook until spinach wilts, about 1 minute. Add pepper mixture to pasta; stir in water chestnuts and tofu. Set aside.

3. In small bowl, combine remaining ingredients with remaining salad oil. Add to pasta mixture; toss to coat. Serve immediately, or refrigerate and serve chilled.

Makes 6 servings.

Fresh Corn Salad

4 quarts water
4 to 6 large ears fresh corn
½ cup salad oil
¼ cup cider vinegar
2 teaspoons fresh lemon juice
3 tablespoons chopped parsley
2 teaspoons salt
1 teaspoon sugar
1½ teaspoons minced fresh basil or ½ teaspoon dried basil leaves, crushed
¼ teaspoon ground red pepper
1 medium red pepper, coarsely chopped
1 medium green pepper, coarsely chopped
½ cup chopped green onions
Lettuce leaves

1. In 6- or 8-quart kettle, bring water to boiling. Meanwhile, remove husks from corn. To boiling water, add corn; cover, and return to boiling, about 2 minutes. Immediately remove kettle from heat; let stand, covered, 5 minutes. Drain; plunge corn immediately into a large bowl of ice water.

2. In large bowl, combine oil and next 7 ingredients; whisk.

3. With sharp knife, cut corn off cobs to get 3 cups kernels. Add to bowl along with peppers and onions; mix well. Cover, and chill several hours or overnight.

4. Line 1½-quart salad bowl or 8 salad plates with lettuce. Spoon mixture into bowl or plates.

Makes 8 servings.

■ For an attractive garnish, use turnips, carrots, and capers. First, wash a medium turnip; pare. Cut crosswise into ⅛-inch-thick slices. With tip of paring knife, divide each slice into eights by cutting out thin slivers from center section to edge. Be careful not to cut through center of turnip. Trim each eighth to a point; place in a bowl of ice water to which a little lemon juice has been added. Refrigerate, covered. Next, repeat procedure, using a large carrot. When ready to use, drain all flowers well on paper towels. Secure carrot flower to center of turnip flower with part of a wooden pick. Last, place a caper in center. Use to garnish a cheese board.

Cobb Salad

2 heads Bibb lettuce
½ head Romaine lettuce
1 small bunch watercress
½ small head chicory
1 pound boneless chicken breasts, cooked and diced (2 cups)
2 medium tomatoes, diced
1 medium avocado, pared, halved, seeded and sliced crosswise
2 large hard-cooked eggs, shelled and quartered lengthwise
¼ pound bacon, cooked and crumbled
2 ounces blue cheese, crumbled
2 tablespoons chopped chives

Special Vinaigrette (recipe follows)

Rinse and pat dry lettuces, watercress and chicory. Tear into bite-size pieces. Place on both sides of large platter; arrange chicken, tomatoes, avocado, eggs, bacon and cheese on platter. Sprinkle chicken with chives. Just before serving, toss salad with enough vinaigrette to coat; pass remainder.

Makes 6 to 8 servings.

Special Vinaigrette

1 teaspoon sugar
1 teaspoon dry mustard
1 medium clove garlic
½ teaspoon salt
⅛ teaspoon pepper
⅓ cup red-wine vinegar
2 tablespoons balsamic vinegar
½ teaspoon Worcestershire sauce
1 cup olive oil

In blender, combine all ingredients except oil until smooth. With blender motor running, add oil in a thin, steady stream; blend until dressing is slightly thickened.

Makes 1⅓ cups.

Easy, Extra-Special Birthday Cakes

These party cakes are almost as much fun to look at as they are to eat. The Watermelon Cake, the Birthday Balloon Cake or the Kong Cake will delight children of all ages.

Birthday Balloon Cake

1 pint each frozen chocolate-, strawberry- and vanilla-flavored yogurt, softened
2 (9-inch) yellow cake layers
¼ cup malted-milk powder
¼ cup sugar
Red food coloring
2 cups heavy cream, chilled
Candy sprinkles
Mint-flavored candy wafers
1 tube (4.25 ounces) green decorating icing
Birthday candles
Large animal-shape marshmallow candies or candle holders
Ribbon

1. Line three 9-inch round cake pans with waxed paper; spoon 1 flavor yogurt into each pan. Freeze until firm.

2. Slice cake layers horizontally in half. Place 1 half-layer, cut side up, on serving plate. Arrange 1 of each frozen-yogurt rounds between remaining cake layers. Freeze until all are firm.

3. In large bowl of electric mixer, at high speed, beat malted-milk powder with sugar, a few drops red food coloring and the cream until soft peaks form. With metal spatula, frost cake with cream mixture. Using photograph as a guide, decorate cake with candy sprinkles, candy wafers and decorating icing. Place birthday candles in marshmallow candies; arrange on cake top. Refrigerate cake until serving. Just before serving, tie ribbon around base of cake.

Makes 12 servings.

Say "Happy Birthday" with one of these party cakes: (clockwise from top) Birthday Balloon Cake, Watermelon Cake.

Watermelon Cake

1 package (about 19 ounces) chocolate-chip cake mix with pudding
1 cup water
½ cup salad oil
3 large eggs
Red food coloring

Frosting
1 cup butter or margarine, softened
2 cups confectioners' sugar
2 tablespoons milk
1½ teaspoons vanilla extract

Green food coloring
½ teaspoon water
1⅔ cups flaked coconut
1 tablespoon semisweet-chocolate pieces

1. Preheat oven to 350°F. Grease and flour two 9-inch round cake pans. Prepare and bake cake mix as package label directs, using the water, salad oil, eggs and 10 drops red food coloring. Pour batter into prepared pans, dividing evenly.

2. Make frosting: In large bowl of electric mixer, at medium speed, beat butter until smooth. Add confectioners' sugar; beat until fluffy. Beat in milk and vanilla. In small bowl, blend 1 cup frosting with 5 drops red food coloring.

3. Place 1 cake layer on serving dish; spread with ½ cup pink frosting. Top with second cake layer; spread top only with remaining pink frosting. Cover side with white frosting. With sharp knife, score frosting on top of cake into 8 wedges. In small bowl, mix a few drops green food coloring with ½ teaspoon water. Reserve 1 tablespoon coconut; toss remainder in colored water until evenly colored. Press green coconut onto side and around 1 inch of top of cake. Sprinkle reserved coconut around inside of green-coconut circle. Press chocolate pieces into top to resemble seeds.

Makes 16 servings.

Kong Cake

1 package (about 19 ounces) chocolate-cake mix
½ cup butter or margarine, melted
2 squares (1 ounce each) semisweet chocolate, melted and cooled
3 cups heavy cream
1½ cups milk-chocolate baking pieces, coarsely chopped
1 container (12 ounces) frozen nondairy whipped topping, thawed
2 creme-filled chocolate-sandwich cookies
1 prune
2 green candy-coated chocolate candies
1 tube (4.25 ounces) each: blue, red, yellow decorating icing
1 tablespoon semisweet-chocolate pieces
Chocolate sprinkles
Multicolored sprinkles
Birthday candles

1. Preheat oven to 350°F. Grease and flour one 13-by-9-by-2-inch baking pan.

2. Prepare chocolate cake as package label directs, except use melted butter and melted semisweet chocolate in place of salad oil in the mix recipe.

3. In small saucepan, heat 1½ cups heavy cream to boiling, but do not boil. Place the chopped milk-chocolate pieces in large bowl of electric mixer; at low speed, add hot cream. Beat until chocolate melts and mixture is blended. Add remaining cream. Remove beaters; chill beaters, cream mixture and bowl until very cold.

4. (See *Note*, below recipe.) Meanwhile, with marker and tracing paper, trace Kong Cake pattern pieces; enlarge patterns to scale. Label all pieces; cut out with scissors. Place pattern pieces on cake; with sharp knife, cut out cake pieces. Using photograph as a guide, arrange cake pieces to make gorilla on tray or large foil-covered cardboard rectangle. (If desired, use leftover cake pieces to make longer arms on gorilla.)

5. When chocolate-cream mixture is chilled, with electric mixer at high speed, beat mixture until soft peaks form. With metal spatula, cover gorilla with whipped chocolate cream. With spatula, using photograph as a guide, spread nondairy topping over birthday cake and gorilla's chest. Refrigerate cake until frosting is firm.

6. Using photograph as a guide, decorate gorilla cake with chocolate-sandwich-cookie ears, prune nose, candy-coated chocolate-candy eyes, red-icing smile and chocolate pieces for claws. Sprinkle chocolate sprinkles over whipped topping on chest for hair. Sprinkle birthday cake with multicolored sprinkles; decorate with blue and yellow icing. Insert birthday candles. Refrigerate cake until serving.

Makes 12 servings.

Note: To make pattern for cutting out and assembling cake, use the pattern on page 252.

Kid-Pleasing Treats

No party would be complete without some goodies to munch on. Our selection is great-tasting and nutritious too.

Happy Cereal Cones

¼ cup butter or margarine
1 bag (10 ounces) marshmallows
1 box (14 ounces) ready-sweetened high-fiber cereal with oat and wheat bran, coarsely crushed
1 cup raisins
½ cup flaked coconut
1½ pints favorite ice cream
6 paper muffin-cup liners
Assorted candies

1. In large saucepan, over low heat, melt butter. Add marshmallows; cook, stirring occasionally, until melted. Remove from heat; stir in cereal, raisins and coconut. Cool slightly. With greased hands, shape 1 cup mixture into a cone shape. Repeat with remaining mixture. Let stand until firm, about 1 hour.

2. Meanwhile, scoop ice cream into 6 balls, using ½-cup ice cream scoop; place on baking sheet. Freeze until ready to serve. To serve, slightly flatten paper muffin-cup liners. Place 1 liner on each of 6 dessert plates. Place 1 ice cream ball on each paper liner; gently press wide end of each cereal cone onto each ball. Decorate ice cream with assorted candies to resemble faces. Serve immediately.

Makes 6 servings.

Cookiewiches

6 squares (1 ounce each) semisweet chocolate
2 packages (6½ ounces each) oatmeal-raisin, chocolate-chunk or milk-chocolate-chip cookies (or sixteen 3-inch-diameter favorite cookies)
⅓ cup chopped peanuts
1 pint favorite ice cream, slightly softened

1. Line large baking sheet with waxed paper; set aside. In small saucepan, over low heat, melt chocolate, stirring until smooth. Using tongs, dip cookies into chocolate; shake off excess. Place flat side down on prepared baking sheet; sprinkle top of cookies with peanuts. Chill until chocolate hardens.

2. With metal spatula, spread ice cream on flat side of each of 8 cookies, dividing evenly. Top with one of remaining cookies, placing flat side on ice cream. Press lightly. Wrap each sandwich with plastic wrap. Freeze until firm.

Makes 8 servings.

Clockwise from top: Berry Float Punch, Cocoa Gorp, Cookiewiches, Happy Cereal Cones, Frozen Banana Pops.

Cocoa Gorp

¼ cup butter or margarine
¼ cup unsweetened cocoa powder
¼ cup sugar
3 cups toasted oat cereal
1½ cups ready-sweetened, high-fiber oat- and wheat-bran cereal
1½ cups bite-size corn cereal
2 cups salted mixed nuts
2 cups thin pretzel sticks
1 cup raisins
½ cup dried apricots, quartered

1. Preheat oven to 250°F. In small saucepan, over medium-low heat, combine butter, cocoa powder and sugar. Heat, stirring, until butter melts and sugar dissolves. Set aside.

2. In large roasting pan, combine remaining ingredients. Stir in butter mixture; with hands, toss mixture until evenly coated. Bake 1 hour, stirring occasionally. Cool completely; store in airtight containers.

Makes 12 servings.

Frozen Banana Pops

4 large bananas
8 flat wooden sticks
1 container (4 ounces) frozen nondairy whipped topping, thawed
Coating suggestions: chopped candy, chocolate sprinkles, toasted coconut
Styrofoam block

1. Peel bananas; cut crosswise in half. Insert wooden stick into cut side of each banana.

2. With metal spatula, spread enough whipped topping over each banana to cover completely; sprinkle with one or more of suggested coatings. Insert sticks into Styrofoam to stand bananas upright. Freeze until firm.

Makes 8 servings.

Berry Float Punch

1 package (10 ounces) frozen strawberries in syrup, thawed
6 cups orange-strawberry-banana juice blend
1 pint vanilla ice cream
1 pint strawberry sorbet

In food processor, puree strawberries with 1 cup juice blend and 1 cup each ice cream and sorbet. Pour mixture through fine sieve into 3-quart punch bowl; discard seeds. Stir in remaining juice blend. Refrigerate punch mixture until ready to serve. Just before serving, add scoops of remaining ice cream and sorbet to punch.

Makes 8 to 16 servings.

Caramel Popcorn Balls

Nonstick cooking spray
8 cups popped popcorn (see *Note*)
½ cup dark seedless raisins
1 cup unsalted dry-roasted peanuts
1 can (6 ounces) frozen apple-juice concentrate, thawed and undiluted
¾ cup sugar
¼ cup light corn syrup
½ teaspoon cider vinegar
¼ teaspoon salt

1. Line a 15½-by-10½-by-2¼-inch roasting pan with aluminum foil for easy cleanup. Spray foil with nonstick cooking spray, or lightly oil. Place popped popcorn in prepared pan; add raisins and peanuts to popcorn. Toss to mix. Set popcorn mixture aside.

2. In small saucepan, combine apple-juice concentrate, sugar, corn syrup, cider vinegar and salt. Over medium-high heat, bring mixture to boiling, stirring until well mixed. Reduce heat; simmer until syrup reaches soft-crack stage on candy thermometer (about 280°F). Remove mixture from heat; immediately pour syrup evenly over popcorn mixture in pan. With wooden spoon, toss until mixture is well coated.

3. When popcorn mixture has cooled enough to handle but is still quite warm, with lightly oiled hands quickly shape into 3-inch balls; set aside to cool. (If mixture becomes too stiff to form into balls, place pan in a 350°F oven for 2 to 3 minutes, or until popcorn mixture is warm and pliable.)

Makes 10 popcorn balls.

Note: About ¼ cup popcorn kernels will make 8 cups of popped popcorn.

Chocolate-Covered Pretzels

1 package (12 ounces) semisweet-chocolate pieces
2 tablespoons butter or margarine
2 tablespoons shortening
5 cups 1½-inch pretzel twists

1. In heavy medium saucepan, over low heat, melt semisweet-chocolate pieces, butter and shortening, stirring constantly. Or in microwave oven, cook semisweet-chocolate pieces, butter and shortening in glass bowl on HIGH 2 to 3 minutes, stirring each minute.

2. In large bowl, pour chocolate mixture over pretzels, tossing gently until all surfaces of pretzels are well covered.

3. Using small tongs, place pretzels individually on wire rack over waxed paper. Allow pretzels to dry at room temperature for several hours. Store in airtight container in refrigerator.

Makes 5 cups.

Lite Eating: Summery Desserts

Clockwise from top: Nectarine-Chocolate Angel Cake, Tropical-Fruit Sorbet, Fruit-Filled Meringues.

Nectarine-Chocolate Angel Cake

1 package (16 ounces) angel-food cake mix
⅓ cup unsweetened cocoa powder
½ teaspoon ground ginger

Sauce
3 cans (5½ ounces each) peach nectar
4 teaspoons cornstarch
3 tablespoons water
1 tablespoon minced crystallized ginger root
1½ teaspoons grated lemon peel
1 teaspoon lemon juice
½ teaspoon imitation butter flavor
3 large nectarines, pitted and sliced

1. Make cake as package label directs, adding cocoa and ground ginger to dry mix. Set aside to cool. Remove cake from pan; place on large serving dish.

2. Make sauce: In medium saucepan, heat nectar until hot. In custard cup, blend cornstarch with water until smooth; stir into nectar. Bring to boiling, stirring constantly; simmer until thickened. Remove from heat; stir in crystallized ginger and next 3 ingredients. Cool 5 minutes; stir in nectarine slices.

3. Cut cake into 12 slices; place each slice on a dessert plate. Top with sauce, dividing evenly.

Makes 12 servings, 209 calories each.

Fruit-Filled Meringues

2 large egg whites, at room temperature
½ teaspoon vanilla extract
⅛ teaspoon cream of tartar
½ cup sugar
3 cups strawberries, hulled and sliced
3 kiwifruit, pared and sliced
2 tablespoons Grand Marnier

1. Preheat oven to 250°F. Line baking sheet with parchment paper, or grease with nonstick cooking spray; set aside.

2. In large bowl of electric mixer, at medium speed, beat egg whites with vanilla and cream of tartar until frothy. At high speed, beat in sugar, two tablespoons at a time, until stiff peaks form. Spoon six mounds of mixture onto parchment paper; with metal spatula, spread each into small rectangle shape. Place remaining meringue in pastry bag fitted with star tip; using photograph as a guide, pipe around edge of each rectangle, making a high decorative border. Bake 1 hour. Turn off heat; let stand in oven 1 hour, or until dry. Carefully peel meringues off paper; place on serving dish. Set aside in dry place.

3. In bowl, combine 1 cup strawberries with the kiwifruit. Place remaining strawberries in blender or food processor; add Grand Marnier. Puree. To serve, spoon some sauce into meringues; fill with fruit mixture. Pass remaining sauce.

Makes 6 servings, 93 calories each.

Tropical-Fruit Sorbet

1 medium papaya, pared, seeded and sliced
1 large mango, pared, pitted and sliced
½ medium pineapple, pared, cored and sliced
1 can (12 ounces) guava nectar, chilled
Mint sprigs

1. Reserve several slices of papaya, mango and pineapple; refrigerate. Cube remaining fruit; place in a single layer on baking sheet. Freeze until solid but can be pierced with tip of paring knife.

2. Place frozen fruit in food processor; process until fruit is in small flakes. With motor running, add nectar; process just until mixture is a firm sorbet. Garnish with reserved fruit and mint; serve immediately.

Makes 6 servings, 86 calories each.

Micro-Way: Super-Easy Barbecue

Minted Leg of Lamb

Marinade
½ cup firmly packed light-brown sugar
1 teaspoon grated lemon peel
½ teaspoon salt
¼ teaspoon pepper
½ cup lemon juice
½ cup salad oil
¼ cup red-wine vinegar
¼ cup chopped fresh mint leaves
1 teaspoon dried rosemary leaves, crushed

6½-pound leg of lamb
2 large cloves garlic, slivered

1. In glass bowl, mix marinade ingredients. Cook on HIGH 3 minutes, or until boiling; set aside.
2. With knife tip, make slits in lamb; insert garlic in slits. Place in 13-by-9-by-2-inch glass baking dish; pour marinade over lamb. Cover; refrigerate 4 hours or overnight.
3. Pour off marinade; reserve. Place lamb, meaty side down, in dish. With aluminum foil, wrap 2 inches of shank end. Cover with plastic wrap; turn back one corner to vent. Cook on HIGH 10 minutes; rotate dish a half turn. Cook on MEDIUM 20 minutes. Turn leg over; remove aluminum foil. Cook 35 minutes longer, until meat thermometer registers 135°F for rare.
4. Prepare outdoor grill for barbecue. Place lamb on grill, 4 inches from heat; brush with marinade. Using INDIRECT METHOD (see page 108), cook, covered, 5 minutes. Turn; brush with marinade. Cook 5 minutes longer. If desired, garnish with mâche (lamb's lettuce) and lemon halves.

Makes 8 to 10 servings.

■ To use a microwave without a turntable, rotate dish and stir, or rearrange food at least once.

Pineapple-Honey-Glazed Ribs

4 to 5 pounds pork spare ribs (2 racks)
1 medium pineapple
½ teaspoon ground ginger
1½ cups pineapple juice
⅓ cup honey
⅓ cup cider vinegar
1 tablespoon soy sauce
3 tablespoons cornstarch

1. Cut racks into 2- or 3-rib portions. In 13-by-9-by-2-inch microwave-safe baking dish, place ribs with meaty side down and thickest sections toward sides of dish. Cover with sheet of waxed paper; cook on MEDIUM 30 minutes.

2. Turn ribs over and rearrange, placing less cooked sections toward edge of dish. Cover with sheet of waxed paper; cook on MEDIUM 35 minutes.

3. Meanwhile, remove leaves from pineapple; pare. Cut pineapple crosswise into ½-inch-thick slices; set aside.

4. In glass bowl, combine ginger with 1 cup pineapple juice, the honey, cider vinegar and soy sauce. Cook on HIGH 3 minutes.

5. In small cup, blend remaining pineapple juice with cornstarch; stir into honey mixture. Cook on HIGH 1 minute, or until mixture boils and thickens, stirring once.

6. Prepare outdoor grill for barbecue. Place ribs, meaty side up, 4 inches from low coals. Place pineapple slices around ribs; baste with sauce. Using INDIRECT METHOD (see page 108), cook ribs, covered, 5 minutes. Turn ribs and pineapple slices; baste with sauce. Cover; cook 5 minutes longer. Remove to serving platter. If desired, garnish ribs with rosemary sprigs.

Makes 6 servings.

September

Back for an encore appearance, the recipes most often requested by readers. Most of the 15 favorites—those listed below—are pictured. To start things off, the numbers one and two favorites: Perfect Chocolate Cake, first published in the 1940s, and The Ultimate Cheesecake, from 1963.

Perfect Chocolate Cake

The Ultimate Cheesecake

Refrigerator Potato Rolls

Veal Parmigiana

Ratatouille Quiche

Cucumber-Sauced Salmon

Boston Cream Pie

Minestrone

Mile-High Meringue Pie

Creamy Macaroni and Cheese

Mouth-Watering Meat Loaf

Chicken Paprika With Galuska

1933
APRIL 1931
McCALL'S

FALL
Fashion
Number
October
1917
10 cts.
NUMBER 10
THE QUEEN OF FASHION

November

Best of McCall's *Cookbook*

For your eating enjoyment, a taste of our best recipes, listed in order of popularity.

In this chapter we present a collection of our most popular recipes, each one a hit with readers since it first appeared in the magazine. Because we get so many requests for copies of these recipes week after week, we decided to reprint the top 15. And to prove that even a good thing can be made better, we've added a few new twists to some of these old favorites. For instance, The Ultimate Cheesecake recipe, first published in the magazine in 1963, has a new fruit glaze and a choice of two sauces, while our lemon meringue pie pleaser has an updated "mile high" crown of meringue topping.

Now, without further ado, for your eating enjoyment, a taste of *McCall's* best recipes, listed in order of popularity.

Page 151: (From top) Perfect Chocolate Cake, The Ultimate Cheesecake.

Pages 152 and 153: (Clockwise from top right) Refrigerator Potato Rolls, Veal Parmigiana, Ratatouille Quiche, Cucumber-Sauced Salmon, Boston Cream Pie.

Pages 154 and 155: (Clockwise from top right) Minestrone, Mile-High Meringue Pie, Creamy Macaroni and Cheese, Mouth-Watering Meat Loaf, Chicken Paprika With Galuska.

1. Perfect Chocolate Cake

(pictured, page 151)

Cake
1 cup unsweetened cocoa powder
2 cups boiling water
2¾ cups unsifted all-purpose flour
2 teaspoons baking soda
½ teaspoon baking powder
½ teaspoon salt
1 cup butter, softened
2½ cups granulated sugar
4 large eggs
1½ teaspoons vanilla extract

Filling
4 bars (2 ounces each) white baking chocolate, chopped
2 cups heavy cream

Frosting
1 package (12 ounces) semisweet-chocolate pieces
½ cup half-and-half
1 cup butter
1 box (1 pound) confectioners' sugar

Chocolate-Marble Tiles
½ cup chocolate-flavored candy melting wafers
½ cup vanilla-flavored candy melting wafers

Silver dragées

1. Preheat oven to 350°F. Grease and flour three 9-inch round cake pans; set aside. Place cocoa in medium bowl; gradually stir in water, stirring until blended. Set aside to cool completely.

2. On sheet of waxed paper, combine flour, baking soda, baking powder and salt; set aside. In large bowl of electric mixer, at high speed, beat 1 cup butter with granulated sugar until light and fluffy. Add eggs, one at a time, beating well after each addition. Beat in vanilla. Alternately add one-fourth flour mixture with one-third cocoa mixture until well blended, repeat with remaining flour and cocoa mixture. Place in prepared pans, dividing evenly. Bake 25 minutes. Cool layers in pans 10 minutes; remove layers and cool on wire racks.

3. Make filling: In top of double boiler placed over hot, not boiling, water, combine white chocolate and ¼ cup heavy cream. Heat, stirring, until white chocolate melts and mixture is smooth. Remove from heat; pour into large bowl of electric mixer. Stir in remaining 1¾ cups heavy cream; refrigerate until very cold. With mixer at high speed, beat

filling ingredients together until stiff. Reserve 1¼ cups mixture; spread remainder between cooled cake layers, dividing evenly.

4. Make frosting: In medium saucepan, over medium heat, combine chocolate pieces, half-and-half and 1 cup butter. Cook, stirring, until mixture is smooth. Transfer mixture to large mixing bowl; with portable electric mixer, at high speed, beat in confectioners' sugar. Place bowl in larger bowl of ice and water; at high speed, beat until frosting is firm enough to spread. With metal spatula, cover top and sides of cake with frosting. Refrigerate cake while making tiles.

5. Make Chocolate-Marble Tiles: Grease bottom and sides of 8-inch round cake pan; line bottom with two 8-inch waxed-paper rounds. Set aside. Place chocolate-flavored and vanilla-flavored candy wafers in separate custard cups. In microwave, heat each cup on MEDIUM 2 minutes, or until candy melts. Or separately melt chocolate-flavored and vanilla-flavored candy wafers in top of double boiler placed over hot, not boiling, water. Drop dollops of melted candies in prepared pan, alternating flavors. With spoon handle, swirl candies decoratively, being careful not to blend flavors completely. Let stand at room temperature until candy is hardened. Carefully invert hardened candy round onto cutting board; remove waxed paper. Using X-acto knife or sharp paring knife, cut round into 8 even wedges.

6. Decorate cake: Place reserved filling in pastry bag fitted with star tip. Pipe mixture into 6 large rosettes, spacing evenly around top edge of cake. Sprinkle each with dragées. Using photograph as a guide, arrange 1 tile, smooth side down and large end toward edge of cake, over each rosette. (There will be 2 extra tiles in case of breakage.) Refrigerate cake until ready to serve.

Makes 12 servings.

2. The Ultimate Cheesecake

(pictured, page 151)

Crust

2½ cups graham cracker crumbs
½ cup butter, melted
½ cup sugar

Filling

5 packages (8 ounces each) cream cheese, softened
1¾ cups sugar
3 tablespoons all-purpose flour
2 teaspoons grated lemon peel
1½ teaspoons grated orange peel
¼ teaspoon vanilla extract
5 large eggs
2 large egg yolks
¼ cup heavy cream

¾ cup sour cream
1 ripe mango
¼ cup sugar
1 package (10 ounces) frozen raspberries in light syrup, thawed
2 tablespoons cornstarch
1 kiwifruit, pared and thinly sliced
¼ cup fresh raspberries

1. Preheat oven to 375°F. Make crust: In bowl, with fork, toss crumbs with butter and ½ cup sugar until moistened. Pour into 9-inch springform pan. With fork, evenly press onto bottom and sides of pan. Bake until golden-brown, about 5 minutes. Cool on wire rack.

2. Heat oven to 450°F. Make filling: In large bowl of electric mixer, at high speed, beat cream cheese with 1¾ cups sugar, the flour, grated lemon and orange peels and vanilla until blended. At medium speed, beat in eggs and egg yolks, one at a time, until blended, scraping bowl occasionally. Beat in heavy cream until blended. Pour mixture into prepared pan. Bake 10 minutes. Lower oven temperature to 300°F. Bake 1 hour and 10 minutes. (Filling mixture will be loose but will set upon standing.) Cool cake on wire rack 2 hours. With spatula, spread sour cream over top of cake to within ½ inch of edge; refrigerate 3 hours or overnight.

3. Pare mango; slice flesh from pit. Cut enough slices into small triangles to make ¼ cup. Set aside. Place remainder in food processor; add ¼ cup sugar. Process until pureed; pour into small bowl. Set aside. In clean food processor, puree thawed raspberries with their syrup; pour through sieve placed over medium saucepan. Stir in cornstarch until blended. Bring to boiling, stirring constantly; simmer 1 minute, or until sauce is thickened and clear. Pour into small bowl. Cover with plastic wrap; refrigerate until cold.

4. Remove cake from pan; place on serving dish. Using photograph as a guide, spoon enough mango and raspberry sauces over top of cake to cover. Garnish with reserved mango, kiwifruit slices and fresh raspberries. Pass remaining fruit sauces separately.

Makes 16 servings.

■ For your next piecrust, substitute cold apple juice or cider for water. The result? Added flavor and a wonderfully flaky crust.

3. Mouth-Watering Meat Loaf

(pictured, page 154)

2 large eggs
1 teaspoon dry mustard
¾ teaspoon salt
¼ teaspoon pepper
½ cup milk
4 slices firm-textured bread, finely crumbled
2½ pounds ground beef
1 large onion, minced
½ cup minced celery
¼ cup chopped parsley

Glaze
2 tablespoons brown sugar
¼ teaspoon dry mustard
½ cup ketchup

2 slices (¾ ounce each) American cheese

1. Preheat oven to 350°F. Line roasting pan with aluminum foil.

2. In large bowl, whisk eggs with 1 teaspoon mustard, the salt and pepper until blended. Stir in milk and bread crumbs; let stand 5 minutes. Add ground beef, onion, celery and parsley. With hands, mix lightly until well blended.

3. Turn mixture into prepared pan. Moisten hands with water; shape mixture into an 8-by-5-inch loaf. Bake 1 hour and 15 minutes.

4. In small bowl, mix glaze ingredients until blended. Spread mixture over top of meat loaf; bake 15 minutes longer. Cut cheese in half crosswise into triangles; using photograph as a guide, arrange over top of glaze. Transfer meat loaf to platter. If desired, serve with roasted potatoes; garnish with celery leaves.

Makes 8 servings.

■ For extra savory meat loaf, spread a layer of mashed potato on top and sides of cooked loaf; sprinkle with grated Parmesan cheese. Bake until mashed potato is light golden-brown.

4. Veal Parmigiana

(pictured, page 153)

2 large eggs
1 cup fine dry seasoned bread crumbs
1 pound thin veal scallops
¼ cup olive or salad oil

Tomato Sauce (recipe follows)

1 package (8 ounces) mozzarella cheese, sliced
¼ cup grated Parmesan cheese

1. Preheat oven to 350°F. In shallow bowl, beat eggs with fork; set aside. Place bread crumbs on sheet of waxed paper. Dip veal in eggs; drain off excess. Coat veal pieces on both sides with bread crumbs.

2. In large skillet, heat half the oil until hot. Over medium heat, cook veal, a few pieces at a time, until golden-brown on both sides, about 5 minutes in all. Remove from pan; keep warm. Repeat with remaining oil and veal. Place half of veal in shallow baking dish; cover with half of Tomato Sauce. Sprinkle with half each of mozzarella and Parmesan cheese. Repeat layering with remaining veal, sauce and cheeses. Bake, uncovered, 30 minutes, or until bubbly. If desired, serve with cooked pasta; garnish with Italian parsley sprigs.

Makes 4 to 6 servings.

Tomato Sauce

2 tablespoons olive or salad oil
½ cup chopped onion
1 medium clove garlic, crushed
1 can (1 pound, 1 ounce) Italian plum tomatoes, undrained
2 teaspoons sugar
¾ teaspoon salt
½ teaspoon dried oregano leaves, crushed
¼ teaspoon dried basil leaves, crushed
¼ teaspoon freshly ground black pepper

In hot oil in medium skillet, sauté onion and garlic until golden-brown, about 5 minutes. Add remaining ingredients, breaking up tomatoes with fork. Bring to boiling; simmer, covered, 10 minutes.

Makes about 2 cups.

5. Mile-High Meringue Pie

(pictured, page 155)

Pastry
1 cup unsifted all-purpose flour
¼ cup blanched almonds
2 tablespoons sugar
½ teaspoon grated lemon peel
½ teaspoon salt
⅓ cup cold butter, cut in chunks
3 tablespoons ice water

Filling
1¼ cups sugar
¼ cup cornstarch
3 tablespoons all-purpose flour
¼ teaspoon salt
2 cups water
5 large egg yolks
1 tablespoon grated lemon peel
½ cup lemon juice
1 tablespoon butter

Meringue
6 large egg whites
¼ teaspoon cream of tartar
½ cup sugar

1. Make pastry: In food processor, combine 1 cup flour, the almonds, 2 tablespoons sugar, ½ teaspoon lemon peel and ½ teaspoon salt. Process 30 seconds, or until almonds are finely ground. Add butter chunks; using pulsing motion, process until mixture resembles coarse crumbs. With motor running, add 3 tablespoons ice water. Process just until mixture begins to hold together. Remove to lightly floured pastry board. With lightly floured

rolling pin, roll out pastry to an 11-inch round. Carefully transfer to 9-inch pie plate; press lightly to line plate. Trim off excess pastry; crimp edges. Refrigerate 15 minutes.

2. Meanwhile, preheat oven to 375°F. Line inside of pastry shell with sheet of aluminum foil; prick foil with fork. Bake 15 minutes; remove foil. Bake 5 minutes longer, or until pastry is golden-brown. Cool completely on wire rack.

3. Make filling: In medium saucepan, combine 1¼ cups sugar, the cornstarch, 3 tablespoons flour and ¼ teaspoon salt. Gradually add 2 cups water, stirring until smooth. Bring to boiling, stirring; boil mixture 1 minute.

4. In small bowl, whisk egg yolks until smooth; whisk in a little of the hot cornstarch mixture. Whisk egg-yolk mixture into remaining cornstarch mixture in pan; simmer, stirring, 5 minutes. Remove pan from heat; stir in 1 tablespoon lemon peel, the lemon juice and 1 tablespoon butter. Pour into prepared pie shell.

5. Preheat oven to 400°F. Make meringue: In large bowl of electric mixer, at medium speed, beat egg whites with cream of tartar until frothy. At high speed, beat in ½ cup sugar, 2 tablespoons at a time, until stiff peaks form. Spread meringue over lemon filling to edge of crust. Bake 9 minutes, or until meringue is golden-brown. Let cool on wire rack; do not refrigerate or meringue will weep. If desired, garnish meringue with knots of lemon peel.

Makes 8 servings.

■ Caught without cake flour while baking desserts? Try this simple stand-in: For each cup of cake flour your recipe calls for, measure out one cup of all-purpose flour; then simply remove one tablespoon of the flour, and replace with one tablespoon of cornstarch.

6. Lady Baltimore Cake

Cake

3½ cups unsifted cake flour
4 teaspoons baking powder
1 teaspoon salt
1 cup butter or margarine, softened
2 cups sugar
2 teaspoons vanilla extract
1 cup milk
8 large egg whites, at room temperature

Filling

1 cup chopped pecans
¾ cup chopped dates
½ cup chopped candied cherries
½ cup chopped raisins
¼ cup brandy or bourbon

Frosting

2¼ cups sugar
¾ teaspoon cream of tartar
½ cup water
6 large egg whites, at room temperature
¾ teaspoon vanilla extract

Garnish

Maraschino cherries
Pitted dates
Pecan halves
Candied pineapple

1. Make cake: Preheat oven to 350°F. Grease and flour three 9-by-1½-inch round cake pans; set aside. On sheet of waxed paper, combine flour, baking powder and salt; set aside. In large bowl of electric mixer, at high speed, beat butter until fluffy. Add 1½ cups sugar and 2 teaspoons vanilla; at high speed, beat 2 minutes, or until mixture is light and fluffy. With rubber spatula, fold flour mixture into butter mixture alternately with milk, beginning and ending with flour mixture. Transfer mixture to large mixing bowl. In clean, large bowl of electric mixer, with clean beaters, at medium speed, beat 8 egg whites until frothy. At high speed, beat until soft peaks form. Beat in remaining ½ cup sugar until stiff peaks form. With rubber spatula, fold beaten whites into flour mixture just until no white streaks remain. (Do not overfold.) Spread batter in prepared pans; bake 25 minutes, or until cake springs back when gently pressed with fingertip. Cool in pans on wire racks 10 minutes; turn out onto wire racks to cool completely.

2. Make filling: In medium bowl, combine filling ingredients. Let stand at room temperature 1 hour.

3. Meanwhile, make frosting (see *Note*): In medium saucepan, mix 2¼ cups sugar, the cream of tartar and water. Bring to boiling, stirring; boil until mixture registers 240°F on candy thermometer. In large bowl of electric mixer, at high speed, beat 6 egg whites until soft peaks form. With mixer at high speed, slowly pour sugar syrup into egg whites in a thin stream. Add ¾ teaspoon vanilla; beat until stiff.

4. With rubber spatula, fold 2 cups frosting into filling mixture. Place 1 cake layer on serving plate; top with half of the filling mixture. Repeat with another cake layer and remaining filling. Top with remaining cake layer. Frost top and sides of cake with remaining frosting; garnish top with cherries, dates, pecan halves and candied pineapple arranged in a ring near edge.

Makes 16 servings.

Note: It's best not to make frosting on a humid day.

■ Cakes freeze better without icing or filling. For best results, place cooled, baked layers in freezer bags or plastic wrap; then seal and freeze. Keep in mind that cakes with uncooked frosting can be frozen successfully, while cakes with cooked frostings or whipped-cream toppings do not freeze well.

7. Refrigerator Potato Rolls

(pictured, pages 152 and 153)

6 to 7 cups unsifted all-purpose flour
2 packages fast-rising or regular dry yeast
½ cup sugar
1 tablespoon salt
1½ cups water
½ cup butter or margarine
2 large eggs, beaten
½ cup plain mashed potatoes

1 tablespoon melted butter (for crescents only)
1 large egg
1 tablespoon water
Toppings: poppy seeds, sesame seeds, coarse salt, salt-free herb blend

1. In large bowl of electric mixer, combine 3 cups flour, the yeast, sugar and salt; mix well. Over low heat, in small saucepan, heat 1½ cups water and ½ cup butter until butter melts and mixture is 120° to 130°F. With mixer at low speed, pour butter mixture into flour mixture. Beat at low speed 2 minutes, scraping bowl with rubber spatula. Add 2 beaten eggs, mashed potatoes and ½ cup flour. Beat at medium speed 2 minutes, scraping bowl occasionally. With wooden spoon, gradually add enough remaining flour until dough leaves side of bowl. On lightly floured surface, knead dough until smooth and elastic, about 5 minutes. Place in lightly greased bowl; turn dough over to bring greased side up. Cover bowl with plastic wrap and towel; let dough rise in refrigerator 2 hours, or until doubled in bulk.

2. Remove dough from refrigerator. With fist, punch down dough. Cover; refrigerate. Dough can be refrigerated one to three days, but punch it down once a day. About 2 hours before serving, grease three large baking sheets; set aside. Remove dough from refrigerator; break into 3 dozen pieces or follow instructions for crescents. Shape each piece into a braid, ball, crescent, knot or twist; place on prepared baking sheets. (For crescents, place one-third of dough on lightly floured surface; divide in half. With rolling pin covered with floured stockinette, roll each half into a 10-inch round. Brush with 1 tablespoon melted butter. Cut into 6 wedges. Starting at wide end, roll up each wedge toward the point. Place on prepared baking sheet, 2 inches apart, point side down. Curl ends inward slightly.) In small bowl, beat 1 egg with 1 tablespoon water; brush mixture over tops of rolls. Sprinkle each with desired topping. Cover with towel; let rise in warm place, free from drafts, until doubled, about 30 minutes.

3. Preheat oven to 350°F. Bake rolls 30 to 40 minutes, covering loosely with sheet of aluminum foil during last 10 minutes if rolls brown too quickly.

Makes about 3 dozen.

8. Creamy Macaroni and Cheese

(pictured, pages 154 and 155)

½ package (16-ounce size) tomato-and-egg pasta rosettes
¼ cup butter or margarine
¼ cup unsifted all-purpose flour
1 teaspoon dry mustard
1 teaspoon salt
⅛ teaspoon pepper
2 cups milk
2 cups (8 ounces) grated Cheddar cheese
¼ cup salad oil
2 cups ½-inch cubes Italian bread
1 ounce sun-dried tomatoes, thinly sliced

1. Cook pasta as package label directs; drain. Set aside.

2. Preheat oven to 375°F. In medium saucepan, over medium-high heat, melt butter. Remove pan from heat; stir in flour, mustard, salt and pepper. Cook, stirring, until bubbly. Gradually stir in milk. Bring to boiling, stirring; simmer 1 minute. Stir in 1½ cups cheese and the cooked pasta. Pour mixture into shallow 1½-quart casserole; sprinkle with remaining cheese. Bake 15 minutes, or until golden-brown and bubbly.

3. Meanwhile, in large skillet, heat oil over medium heat. Add bread cubes; cook, stirring, until golden-brown. Remove pan from heat; stir in tomatoes. Sprinkle crouton mixture over casserole.

Makes 6 servings.

9. Minestrone

(pictured, pages 154 and 155)

3-pound shin of beef
4 quarts water
4 medium carrots, pared
4 celery stalks, coarsely chopped
4 parsley sprigs
2 beef-flavored bouillon cubes, crushed
1 large onion, quartered
1 bay leaf
1 can (10½ ounces) chickpeas, drained
1 can (10½ ounces) kidney beans, drained
1 can (14 ounces) Italian plum tomatoes
2 cups chopped cabbage
1 package (10 ounces) frozen cut green beans
1 package (10 ounces) frozen peas
2 teaspoons salt
¼ teaspoon pepper
¼ pound uncooked spaghetti

1. In covered 8-quart Dutch oven or stockpot, bring beef and water to

boiling. Skim off and discard any foam. Add carrots, celery, parsley, crushed bouillon, onion and bay leaf; simmer, uncovered, 2½ hours.

2. Remove beef and carrots; set aside. Strain broth. (There should be about 7 cups.) Discard cooking vegetables and bay leaf.

3. In same pan, combine broth, chickpeas, kidney beans, tomatoes and their liquid, cabbage, green beans, peas, salt and pepper; bring mixture to boiling, stirring occasionally. Break spaghetti into 1-inch pieces; add to broth mixture. Simmer, covered, 12 minutes, or until pasta is cooked.

4. Meanwhile, slice cooked carrots and cut meat from bone into small pieces. Add to soup; heat through.

Makes 3½ quarts.

10. Cucumber-Sauced Salmon

(pictured, page 152)

1 cup white wine
1 cup water
1 bay leaf
½ teaspoon salt
¼ teaspoon pepper
4 salmon steaks, ¾-inch thick (about 2¼ pounds)
1 (14-inch) seedless cucumber
6 tablespoons butter
2 teaspoons fresh dill
2 teaspoons parsley sprigs
2 tablespoons all-purpose flour
Fresh dill sprigs

1. In large skillet, combine wine, water, bay leaf, salt and pepper. Bring to boiling. Add salmon; cover pan. In simmering liquid, poach salmon 10 minutes, or until fish is just firm and cooked through.

2. Cut 10 thin slices crosswise from cucumber; set aside. Pare and chop remaining cucumber.

3. With slotted spatula, remove salmon to warm platter. Cover to keep warm. Pour cooking liquid through sieve into large glass measure; set aside.

4. In clean skillet, over medium-high heat, melt 2 tablespoons butter. Add chopped cucumber; sauté until tender-crisp. Spoon sautéed cucumber into food processor or blender; add dill and parsley. Puree; set aside.

5. In same skillet, over medium-high heat, melt remaining butter. Stir in flour; cook 1 minute, until bubbly. Gradually stir in pureed cucumber mixture and 1½ cups reserved cooking liquid from salmon. Cook, stirring, until boiling and thickened. Spoon some sauce around salmon steaks; pass remainder. Garnish with reserved cucumber slices and dill sprigs.

Makes 4 servings.

11. Luscious Brownies

¾ cup unsifted all-purpose flour
¼ teaspoon baking powder
¼ teaspoon salt
¾ cup butter or margarine
4 squares (1 ounce each) unsweetened chocolate
1¼ cups sugar
3 large eggs
1 teaspoon vanilla extract
¾ cup chopped walnuts
¾ cup semisweet-chocolate minipieces
1 ounce vanilla-flavored candy melting wafers (optional)
1 ounce chocolate-flavored candy melting wafers (optional)

1. Preheat oven to 325°F. Lightly grease 8-by-8-by-2-inch cake pan; set aside.

2. On sheet of waxed paper, combine flour, baking powder and salt; set aside. In medium saucepan, over medium heat, melt butter and chocolate, stirring with wooden spoon. (Do not boil.) Remove from heat; stir in sugar. Add eggs and vanilla; stir until blended. Stir in flour mixture, the walnuts and chocolate pieces; mix until dry ingredients are moistened. Pour batter into prepared pan. Bake 45 minutes, or until wooden pick inserted in center comes out clean.

3. Cool completely on wire rack. Melt vanilla-flavored and chocolate-flavored candy melting wafers. Place each in a small icing bag fitted with small plain writing tip. Pipe lines of melted candies on brownie layer. Cut into 2-inch squares.

Makes 16 servings.

■ When you're melting chocolate, a drop or two of water splashed into the pan can cause the chocolate to thicken. To remedy the situation, add one teaspoon shortening (not butter) for every ounce of chocolate.

■ If you're caught short of confectioners' sugar while making cake or cookie frosting, try this simple trick: Combine 1 cup granulated sugar with 1 tablespoon cornstarch in the electric blender, and process at high speed for several minutes, until sugar is powdery.

■ Here's an easy and efficient way to grease baking pans. Simply slip your hand inside a sandwich-size plastic bag, dip into shortening and evenly coat the pan with it. Best of all, you can leave the "mitt" in the shortening can for later use.

■ Do you ever lose count when measuring out ingredients, such as four cups of flour? Here's a fail-safe method for getting it right: Before you begin, line up four peanuts, raisins or bits of cheese in front of you. Pop one into your mouth after emptying each flour cup full.

12. Boston Cream Pie

(pictured, page 152)

Filling
2 packages (3.5 ounces each) vanilla-flavored pudding-and-pie-filling mix
3 cups milk
2 teaspoons vanilla extract
½ cup heavy cream, chilled

Cake
1¼ cups unsifted all-purpose flour
1 cup granulated sugar
1½ teaspoons baking powder
¾ cup milk
⅓ cup shortening
1 large egg
1 teaspoon vanilla extract

Glaze
3 tablespoons butter or margarine
3 tablespoons water
2 squares (1 ounce each) unsweetened chocolate
¾ cup confectioners' sugar
¾ teaspoon vanilla extract

1. In medium saucepan, combine pudding mix with 3 cups milk; cook as package label directs. Remove from heat; stir in 2 teaspoons vanilla. Place in bowl; cover with plastic wrap. Refrigerate until cold.

2. In small bowl of electric mixer, at high speed, beat heavy cream until stiff peaks form. With spatula, fold into cold pudding. Cover; refrigerate until ready to fill cake.

3. Make cake: Preheat oven to 350°F. Grease and flour 9-inch round cake pan; set aside. In large bowl of electric mixer, combine cake ingredients. At low speed, beat 30 seconds, scraping bowl frequently, or until ingredients are blended. At high speed, beat 3 minutes, scraping bowl occasionally. Pour batter into prepared pan; bake 35 minutes, or until cake tester inserted in center comes out clean. Cool in pan on wire rack.

4. Make glaze: In saucepan, heat butter and water until boiling. In food processor, process chocolate with confectioners' sugar until chocolate is finely chopped. With processor running, add hot-butter mixture; process until chocolate melts and mixture is smooth. Blend in ¾ teaspoon vanilla. If too thick, add teaspoonfuls of boiling water until of desired consistency.

5. Assemble cake: With serrated knife, cut cake in half horizontally; place one half, cut side up, on platter. Spoon filling into pastry bag fitted with large plain tip; pipe over top of cake. Place remaining half, cut side down, over filling. With metal spatula, spread glaze over cake, letting excess drip over side. Refrigerate 30 minutes.

Makes 8 servings.

13. Chicken Paprika With Galuska

(pictured, page 154)

4 tablespoons butter or margarine
6 whole chicken breasts (about ¾ pound each), split
16 small white onions (1½ pounds)
1 cup chopped onion
1 tablespoon paprika
1 pound baby carrots, trimmed and pared
2 cans (10¾ ounces each) condensed chicken broth, undiluted
1 teaspoon salt

Galuska
3¼ cups unsifted all-purpose flour
1 teaspoon salt
1 cup water
3 large eggs
2 quarts water
2 teaspoons salt
2 tablespoons butter or margarine
1 tablespoon chopped parsley

Gravy
⅓ cup unsifted all-purpose flour
½ cup dry white wine
2 cups sour cream

1. In large skillet or Dutch oven, over medium-high heat, melt 2 tablespoons butter. Add half the chicken; brown on all sides, about 20 minutes in all. Remove from pan. In drippings in pan, brown remaining chicken-breast halves.

2. Remove chicken from pan; set aside. Melt remaining 2 tablespoons butter. Add whole and chopped onions and the paprika; sauté until onions are lightly browned. Add carrots; sauté 2 minutes. Stir in undiluted broth and 1 teaspoon salt.

3. Arrange chicken on top of vegetables; bring liquid to boiling. Cover; simmer 45 minutes, or until chicken and vegetables are tender.

4. Meanwhile, make galuska dough: In large bowl, with wooden spoon or portable electric mixer, mix 3¼ cups flour, 1 teaspoon salt, 1 cup water and the eggs until dough is smooth; set aside.

5. Preheat oven to 250°F. With tongs and slotted spoon, remove chicken and vegetables to platter. Cover; keep warm in oven. Set aside skillet and cooking liquid.

6. Grease 2-quart casserole; set aside. In large saucepan, heat 2 quarts water with 2 teaspoons salt until boiling. With metal spatula, spread about 2 teaspoons galuska dough on metal pancake turner. Wet spatula; hold pancake turner over boiling water. With spatula, cut off long, thin pieces of dough, letting them drop into water. Continue until one-quarter of dough is used. Boil gently, uncovered, until galuska are firm and rise to top of water. With slotted spoon, remove and place in colander or strainer. Quickly rinse with hot water; drain, and place in prepared casserole. Keep warm in oven while shaping and cooking remaining galuska.

When all galuska are cooked, toss with 2 tablespoons butter and the chopped parsley. Keep warm while making gravy.

7. In skillet, heat cooking liquid from chicken until boiling. In small bowl, mix ⅓ cup flour with wine until blended and smooth. Stir into skillet; bring to boiling, stirring. Simmer 2 minutes, stirring. Slowly stir in sour cream; heat gently 1 minute. Serve gravy with chicken, vegetables and galuska.

Makes 8 servings.

14. Neapolitan Cookies

1 package (7 or 8 ounces) almond paste
1 cup butter or margarine
1 cup sugar
4 large eggs, separated
1 teaspoon almond extract
2 cups unsifted all-purpose flour
Red and green food coloring
¼ cup seedless raspberry jam
¼ cup apricot preserves
1 package (6 ounces) semisweet-chocolate pieces

1. To cook in microwave (to cook in conventional oven, see *Note*): Grease bottom and sides of 13-by-9-by-2-inch microwave-safe baking dish. Line with waxed paper; grease paper. Set aside.

2. In large bowl of electric mixer, at high speed, beat almond paste, butter, sugar, egg yolks and almond extract until fluffy; stir in flour. In small bowl of electric mixer, with clean beaters, beat egg whites until soft peaks form. With rubber spatula, fold into flour mixture just until no white streaks remain. Place 1⅓ cups batter in each of two small bowls. Add red food coloring to one bowl and green food coloring to the other.

3. Spread red batter in prepared dish. Cook on MEDIUM 5 minutes, rotating dish after 2 minutes. Cook on HIGH 2 minutes more. Holding edge of waxed paper, lift layer onto wire rack. Reline dish, and cook, in turn, the green batter and white batter as above. Cool completely.

4. Invert green layer; remove waxed paper. Spread with raspberry jam. Invert white layer over jam; remove waxed paper. Spread with apricot preserves. Invert red layer over preserves; remove waxed paper. Set heavy pan on top of cookie layers; refrigerate overnight.

5. The next day, in a small glass bowl, melt chocolate pieces on HIGH 3 minutes, stirring once. Spread over red layer; trim edges of cookie layers. Let chocolate set slightly. With sharp knife, cut through layers into ½-inch-wide strips. Cut strips into 4 pieces.

Makes about 8 dozen.

Note: To cook in a conventional oven, preheat oven to 350°F. Grease bottom and sides of 13-by-9-by-2-inch baking pan. Line with aluminum foil; grease foil. Set aside. To make batter, follow instructions in Step 2. Spread red batter in prepared pan. Bake 8 minutes, or until cookie layer springs back when gently pressed with fingertip. Holding edge of foil, carefully lift layer to cooling rack. Reline pan with foil and bake, in turn, the green and white batters following instructions as above. Repeat remaining instructions for filling, frosting and cutting cookies. To melt chocolate, place in top of double boiler over hot, not boiling water. Stir occasionally, until melted and smooth.

■ Use your microwave to melt chocolate; it's simpler than working with a double boiler. Set the microwave on MEDIUM, and melt one cup of morsels or four 1-ounce squares of chocolate in 2½ minutes; stir after one minute to ensure smoothness.

15. Ratatouille Quiche

(pictured, page 153)

Filling
½ small eggplant (¼ pound)
1 small zucchini (¼ pound)
3 tablespoons salad oil
½ cup chopped onion
½ cup chopped green pepper
1 medium clove garlic, crushed
½ teaspoon salt
Dash pepper
1 ripe tomato, cut in wedges

½ package (15-ounce size) refrigerated all-ready pie crust (1 crust)
1½ cups (6 ounces) grated Swiss cheese
4 large eggs
¾ cup half-and-half
¼ teaspoon salt
⅛ teaspoon grated nutmeg
Dash pepper

1. Make ratatouille: Cut eggplant and zucchini crosswise into ¼-inch-thick slices. Cut eggplant slices crosswise in half. In large skillet, heat oil until hot. Add eggplant, zucchini, onion, green pepper and garlic; sauté until vegetables are tender-crisp. Sprinkle with ½ teaspoon salt and dash pepper. Place tomato wedges on top of mixture. Cover; over low heat, cook ratatouille 5 minutes. Set aside.

2. Preheat oven to 375°F. Roll out pastry as package label directs. Line 10-inch quiche dish with pastry; place on baking sheet. Sprinkle cheese over bottom of pastry. Drain ratatouille; evenly spread mixture over cheese. Using photograph as a guide, arrange vegetables over top. Set aside.

3. In bowl, whisk eggs with half-and-half, ¼ teaspoon salt, the nutmeg and dash pepper until combined but not frothy. Pour over ratatouille. Bake quiche on lower rack 50 minutes, or until custard is puffy and set in center. Cool on wire rack 10 minutes before serving.

Makes 8 servings.

Quick & Easy: Light Chicken 'n' Rice Dishes

Creole Chicken

Salsa Rice Ring
Nonstick cooking spray
4 cups cooked white rice
¾ cup medium-hot salsa
¼ cup minced parsley

Creole Chicken
1 tablespoon salad oil
1½ pounds boneless chicken breasts, skinned and cut in ¾-inch cubes
¾ pound medium shrimp, peeled and deveined
1 green pepper, chopped
1 teaspoon dried oregano leaves, crushed
½ teaspoon salt
¼ teaspoon pepper
½ cup medium-hot salsa
2 green onions, chopped
¼ pound okra, cut in 1-inch pieces

1. Make Salsa Rice Ring: Preheat oven to 325°F. Grease 4-cup ring mold with nonstick cooking spray. In bowl, mix rice with ¾ cup salsa and the parsley. Spoon into mold; warm through in oven.

2. Meanwhile, make Creole Chicken: In 12-inch skillet, heat oil over medium-high heat. Add chicken, shrimp, green pepper, oregano, salt and pepper. Sauté 3 minutes. Stir in remaining ingredients; simmer 5 minutes.

3. Unmold the rice ring onto a serving platter. Spoon chicken mixture into center of rice ring and serve immediately.

Makes 6 servings, 340 calories each.

Chicken Fried Rice

1 pound boneless chicken breasts, skinned and cut in ¼-inch-wide strips
1 tablespoon cornstarch
1 tablespoon soy sauce
1 tablespoon salad oil
3 green onions, chopped
½ pound mushrooms, sliced
½ red pepper, chopped
1 tablespoon butter or margarine
1 package (4.7 ounces) teriyaki-flavored stir-fry rice mix
1 large egg, beaten
1 can (8 ounces) sliced water chestnuts, drained
1 cup cooked black beans

1. In bowl, toss chicken with cornstarch and soy sauce. In 12-inch skillet, heat oil over medium-high heat. Add chicken; sauté until golden, about 3 minutes; remove to plate. In drippings in pan, sauté green onions, mushrooms and pepper until tender-crisp, about 3 minutes; remove to plate. In same pan, using butter, cook rice as package label directs.

2. Meanwhile, in 6-inch nonstick skillet, over medium-low heat, cook egg until set, tilting pan so egg covers bottom. Turn out onto plate; roll up. Cut crosswise into ¼-inch-wide strips.

3. To rice in pan, add reserved chicken, mushrooms and vegetables, the water chestnuts, beans and egg; heat through.

Makes 4 servings, 382 calories each.

Chicken Roulades

1 package (10 ounces) frozen chopped spinach, thawed and well drained
1 cup (4 ounces) shredded Gruyère cheese
¼ cup pine nuts
1 teaspoon dried basil leaves, crushed
¾ teaspoon salt
½ teaspoon pepper
2 tablespoons apple juice
2 whole boneless chicken breasts, skinned and split (1½ pounds)
8 thin slices prosciutto
1 tablespoon butter or margarine
1 tablespoon salad oil
1 package (6 ounces) white or wild rice mix

1. In food processor, blend spinach with next 6 ingredients.

2. Place each chicken breast between 2 sheets of waxed paper; with meat mallet, pound to ¼-inch thickness. Remove top sheet of paper; place 2 slices prosciutto over each breast. Spread with spinach mixture. Roll up; tie with kitchen string.

3. In large skillet, over medium-high heat, melt butter in oil. Add chicken rolls; cook, turning, until browned, about 5 minutes. Remove from pan; set aside.

4. In same pan, using drippings, prepare rice mix as package label directs. Add chicken during last 12 minutes of cooking time. Remove string; cut each roulade crosswise into quarter-inch slices.

Makes 6 servings, 380 calories each.

Clockwise from left: Creole Chicken, Chicken Fried Rice, Chicken Roulades.

■ Here's an easy, safe way to empty the container of a food processor—without the blade falling out: Simply insert your finger into the hole from the bottom of the bowl, and then press the blade column against the side. It's safe and simple!

Lite Eating: Late-Summer Salads

Chicken-and-Basmati Mold

½ cup uncooked long-grain American brown basmati rice
1 cup water

Dressing
1½ tablespoons cornstarch
1 cup chicken broth
1 can (14 ounces) hearts of palm
3 tablespoons low-sodium soy sauce
1 teaspoon lemon juice

½ large red pepper, cut in ¼-inch-wide strips
½ cup chopped green onion
½ cup chopped celery
2 cups diced cooked chicken
6 lettuce leaves, washed

1. In medium saucepan, combine rice and water. Bring to boiling. Cover; simmer 15 minutes. Let stand 5 minutes. Drain; place in shallow bowl. Cover; chill thoroughly.

2. Meanwhile, make dressing: In small saucepan, mix cornstarch with broth until blended. Drain hearts of palm, reserving ¼ cup liquid. Add ¼ cup liquid, the soy sauce and lemon juice. Bring to boiling; simmer until thickened, about 3 minutes. Transfer to shallow bowl. Cover; chill.

3. Line a 4-cup mold with plastic wrap. Cut 4 hearts of palm in half lengthwise; evenly space pieces with ends up and cut sides in around side of mold. Between each piece place a red-pepper strip, round side out; set aside.

4. In large bowl, mix rice with green onion, celery, chicken and dressing until combined. Spoon mixture into prepared mold. Cover; refrigerate until thoroughly chilled, about 3 hours.

5. Line serving plate with lettuce; invert mold on top. Remove plastic wrap. Serve immediately.

Makes 4 servings, 251 calories each.

Warm Turkey Oriental

1 pound boneless turkey cutlets, cut in ¼-inch-wide strips
2 tablespoons cornstarch
2 tablespoons salad oil
1 small red onion, thinly sliced
1 cup snow pea pods
½ red pepper, cut in ¼-inch-wide strips
4 large mushrooms, thinly sliced
¼ cup water
¼ cup bottled low-calorie Oriental-style dressing
1 teaspoon salt
¼ teaspoon pepper
1 medium tomato, cut in wedges
2 cups spinach leaves, washed
2 small heads Bibb lettuce, leaves separated and washed
1 tablespoon pine nuts

1. In medium bowl, toss turkey with cornstarch until coated. In large skillet, heat oil over high heat. Add half the turkey; sauté until golden-brown, about 5 minutes. Remove to bowl. Repeat with remaining turkey.

2. To drippings in skillet, add onion, pea pods, red pepper and mushrooms; sauté 2 minutes. Return turkey to pan; add water, dressing, salt and pepper. Bring to boiling; cook, stirring, 1 minute. Add tomato; heat through.

3. On serving dish, arrange spinach and lettuce; spoon turkey mixture on top. Sprinkle with pine nuts.

Makes 4 servings, 297 calories each.

Fruited Pork Salad

1 medium cantaloupe, quartered
1½ cups diced cooked pork
1½ cups fresh pineapple chunks
1 cup low-fat lemon-flavored yogurt
1 tablespoon crumbled blue cheese

Place cantaloupe, rind side down, on large serving plate; set aside. In bowl, combine remaining ingredients; spoon into cantaloupe pieces. If desired, garnish with mint sprigs and lemon slices.

Makes 4 servings, 286 calories each.

Clockwise from left: Chicken-and-Basmati Mold, Warm Turkey Oriental, Fruited Pork Salad.

SALT
PER

Micro-Way: Super Savory Soups

Cabbage Soup
(pictured, left)

8 slices bacon, chopped
2 medium cloves garlic, crushed
1 large onion, chopped
1 large new potato, pared and cut in ½-inch cubes
½ teaspoon dried dillweed
4 cups shredded cabbage
2 cans (about 10½ ounces each) condensed beef broth, undiluted
1 can (28 ounces) crushed tomatoes
1½ cups water
⅛ teaspoon pepper

1. Place bacon in 3-quart microwave-safe casserole; loosely cover with waxed paper. Cook on HIGH 4 minutes, or until browned, stirring once. Remove with slotted spoon; set aside. To drippings, add garlic, onion, potato and dillweed. Cover and vent; cook on HIGH 5 minutes, stirring occasionally.
2. Stir in cabbage; cook on HIGH 5 minutes longer. Stir in broth, tomatoes and their juice, water and pepper. Cover and vent; cook on HIGH 5 minutes, or until hot. Before serving, add bacon. If desired, serve with croutons.

Makes 8 servings.

■ When seasoning foods in the microwave oven, go lightly—especially with pepper and dried herbs. But garlic loses flavor, so you may want to add an extra clove to the food.

■ For croutons, cut ½-inch cubes from sliced bread; place them on a paper towel. Microwave on HIGH about 1 minute per slice, tossing cubes occasionally during cooking so bread dries out evenly. If desired, place croutons in a bowl with about a teaspoon of olive oil and ½ teaspoon of salt-free herb blend per slice of bread, and stir until croutons are evenly coated.

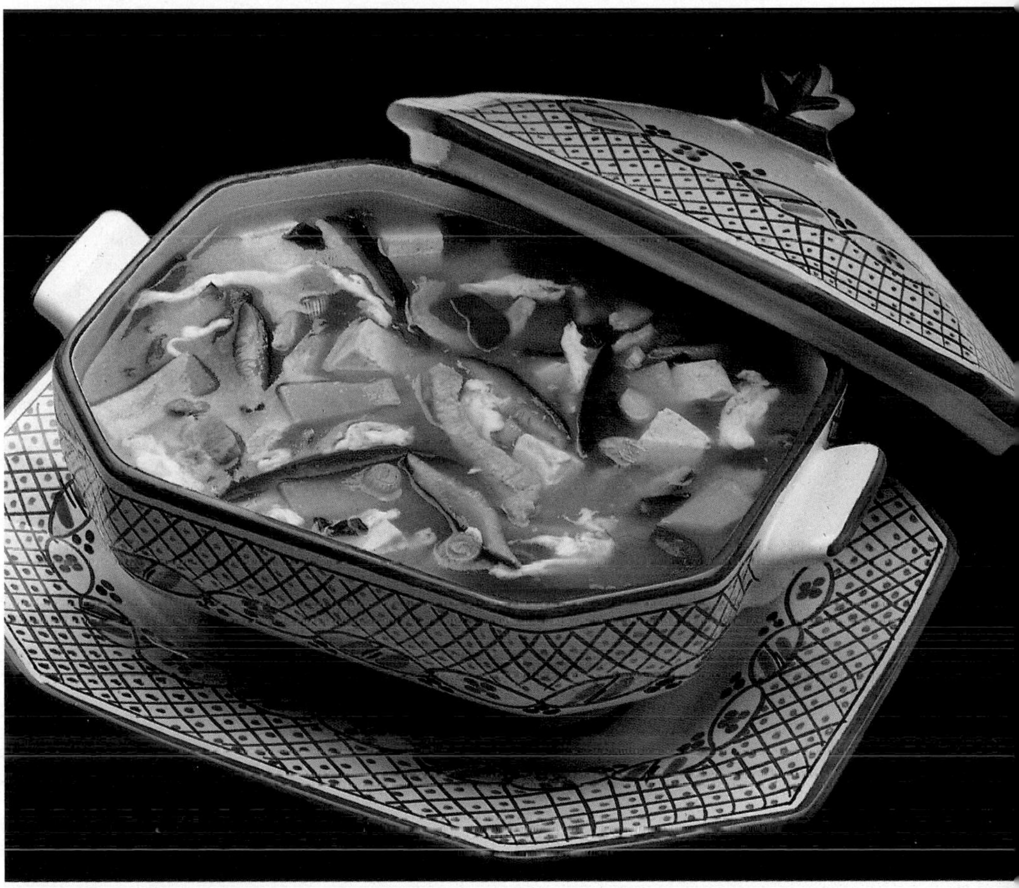

Hot-and-Sour Soup

1 ounce dried shiitake mushrooms
2 cans (about 14 ounces each) chicken broth
3 tablespoons white vinegar
2 tablespoons soy sauce
¼ pound boneless pork, cut in thin strips
¼ pound firm tofu, cut in ½-inch cubes
1 small red pepper, julienned
1 can (8 ounces) bamboo shoots, drained
2 tablespoons cornstarch
1 large egg, beaten
1 teaspoon dark sesame oil
½ teaspoon hot-red-pepper sauce
3 green onions, sliced

1. In medium bowl, cover mushrooms with hot water; soak 20 minutes, or until soft. Drain, reserving liquid. Remove and discard stems; slice caps into ¼-inch-thick strips. Set aside.

2. In 3-quart microwave-safe casserole, combine broth, ½ cup mushroom liquid, the vinegar and soy sauce. Cover with plastic wrap and fold back one corner to vent; cook on HIGH 10 minutes, or until boiling. Stir in pork, tofu, red pepper, bamboo shoots and mushrooms. Cover and vent; cook on HIGH 3 minutes.

3. In small bowl, blend the cornstarch with ¼ cup mushroom liquid until smooth; stir into soup. Cover and vent; cook on HIGH 6 minutes, stirring occasionally. With fork, stir egg into soup until strands form. Stir in oil, pepper sauce and green onions. Cook on HIGH 1 minute.

Makes 6 servings.

Soup Toppings From the Microwave

■ **Cheese-and-Crackers:** Arrange 6 Melba toast rectangles on a paper plate. Sprinkle each with 2 teaspoons French-fried onions. Top each with 2 teaspoons shredded Swiss cheese. Microwave on HIGH 1 minute, or until cheese melts, turning plate once during cooking. Add crackers to soup just before serving.

■ **Lemon-Butter Swirl:** In a medium glass bowl, melt 1 tablespoon butter. Add 1 minced shallot and 1 small clove garlic. Cover with plastic wrap; turn back one corner to vent. Cook on HIGH 1 minute, or until shallot is tender. Add 7 tablespoons of cold butter, cut in 1-inch chunks. Heat on MEDIUM 30 seconds, or until butter is softened. With wooden spoon, beat until mixture is blended; beat in 1 tablespoon minced parsley, 1 teaspoon grated lemon peel and 1 tablespoon lemon juice. Place flavored butter on sheet of freezer-safe plastic wrap; roll up to make a ¾-inch-wide cylinder. Wrap tightly; store in freezer, and slice off ¼-inch-thick pieces for each serving of hot soup. Use this tangy butter to flavor a mild broth or cool down a too-hot mug or bowl of soup.

October

Dress up your dinner menu with one of our delicious accompaniment dishes. To start things off, two molded delights: a creamy pasta-and-cheese combination and an elegant but easy layered vegetable pâté, wonderful with roast chicken!

Ziti-Zucchini Timbale

Three-Vegetable Terrine With Roasted-Pepper Sauce

Couscous-Stuffed Peppers

Tomatoes Fontina

Potatoes Italiano

Creamy Vegetable Bake

Bacon Dumplings

Patchwork-Quilt Rice

Hot Broccoli Slaw

Eggplant-Artichoke Savarin

German-Style Red Cabbage

Brussels Sprouts Stir-Fry

Corn Fritters With Yellow-Pepper Salsa

Great Side Dishes Cookbook

Perfectly seasoned side dishes make any meal special. And some of these offerings add an international flavor as well.

Ziti-Zucchini Timbale

(pictured, page 171)

¼ cup butter or margarine
2 pounds zucchini, julienned
½ cup minced parsley
½ teaspoon salt
½ package (1-pound size) ziti
1 package (1.8 ounces) white-sauce mix
1 cup ricotta cheese
½ cup grated Parmesan cheese

1. In large skillet, over medium-high heat, melt butter. Add zucchini; sauté until tender, about 3 minutes. Sprinkle zucchini with parsley and salt; set aside.

2. Cook ziti as package label directs; drain well. Set aside. Grease 10-cup soufflé dish or deep casserole; line with aluminum foil. Generously grease foil. Set aside.

3. Preheat oven to 400°F. Prepare sauce mix as package label directs. Place in medium bowl. Add ricotta, ¼ cup Parmesan and the ziti; mix until combined. Place half of ziti mixture in prepared soufflé dish. Top with half of the zucchini mixture, pressing down lightly. Top with remaining ziti and zucchini mixture; sprinkle with remaining ¼ cup Parmesan. Bake 20 minutes, or until heated through.

4. Remove dish from oven; let stand on wire rack 15 minutes. Place serving plate over timbale; invert plate and dish. Let timbale stand 10 minutes. Carefully remove foil, using spatula to press timbale back into shape, if necessary. If desired, garnish timbale with additional minced parsley and zucchini asters (see *Note*). To serve, cut into wedges.

Makes 6 to 8 servings.

Note: To make zucchini asters, cut a medium zucchini in half lengthwise. With vegetable parer, remove wide strips from cut side of zucchini. With paring knife, make crosswise cuts along the length of each strip, cutting through peel only on one long side. Roll up each strip, pinwheel fashion.

Page 171: Ziti-Zucchini Timbale, Three-Vegetable Terrine With Roasted-Pepper Sauce.

Pages 172 and 173: (Clockwise from top right) Couscous-Stuffed Peppers, Tomatoes Fontina, Potatoes Italiano, Creamy Vegetable Bake, Bacon Dumplings, Patchwork-Quilt Rice.

Pages 174 and 175: (Clockwise from top left) Hot Broccoli Slaw, Eggplant-Artichoke Savarin, German-Style Red Cabbage, Brussels Sprouts Stir-Fry, Corn Fritters With Yellow-Pepper Salsa.

Three-Vegetable Terrine With Roasted-Pepper Sauce

(pictured, page 171)

1½ pounds carrots
1½ teaspoons salt
1 cup heavy cream, at room temperature
5 large eggs
1 large egg yolk
½ teaspoon pepper
¼ teaspoon ground nutmeg
2 jars (7 ounces each) roasted red peppers, well drained
2 tablespoons butter or margarine
2 medium zucchini, shredded (2 cups)
1 package (10 ounces) frozen spinach, thawed and squeezed dry
¼ cup grated Parmesan cheese
1 package (0.9 ounce) hollandaise-sauce mix

1. Line 8½-by-4½-by-2½-inch loaf pan with aluminum foil. Grease foil; set aside. Pare carrots; cut crosswise into ½-inch pieces. Place in large saucepan with ¼ teaspoon salt and cold water to cover. Cook, covered, until carrots are tender, about 15 minutes. Drain thoroughly.

2. In food processor, puree carrots; place puree in same saucepan. Cook, stirring, until excess moisture evaporates, about 5 minutes. Stir in

⅔ cup heavy cream. Bring to boiling; simmer, stirring, until the heavy cream reduces and mixture thickens, about 8 minutes. Pour into shallow bowl; cool mixture slightly.

3. In bowl, whisk 3 eggs and the egg yolk until blended. Gradually whisk in carrot mixture; stir in 1 teaspoon salt, ½ teaspoon pepper and the nutmeg. Spoon half of mixture over bottom of prepared pan.

4. Julienne two-thirds of peppers; reserve remainder. Arrange half of the pepper strips in lengthwise rows over carrot mixture in loaf pan.

5. In skillet, over medium heat, melt butter. Add zucchini; sauté until tender, about 5 minutes. In food processor, puree zucchini with spinach; pour into same skillet. Cook, stirring, until excess moisture evaporates, about 5 minutes. Stir in remaining cream. Bring to boiling; simmer, stirring, until cream is reduced and mixture thickens, about 5 minutes. Pour into shallow bowl; cool slightly.

6. Preheat oven to 375°F. In medium bowl, whisk remaining eggs until blended. Gradually whisk in zucchini mixture; stir in 2 tablespoons Parmesan and ¼ teaspoon salt. Spoon mixture evenly over carrot mixture and pepper strips in loaf pan. Arrange remaining pepper strips in lengthwise rows over spinach mixture; spoon remaining carrot mixture evenly over all.

7. Grease a sheet of aluminum foil large enough to cover terrine; place over mixture, sealing edges tightly. Place loaf pan in small roasting pan; place in oven. Pour in enough boiling water to come halfway up sides of loaf pan. Bake 2½ hours, or until firm to the touch and wooden pick inserted in center comes out clean, adding more boiling water to roasting pan if necessary. Remove pan from water; cool terrine in pan on wire rack at least 30 minutes before serving.

8. Meanwhile, in small saucepan, prepare hollandaise-sauce mix as package label directs; set aside. In food processor, puree remaining red peppers; add to hollandaise. Stir in remaining Parmesan; keep warm.

9. Remove foil from top of pan. Invert terrine onto platter. If necessary, remove foil. If desired, garnish with parsley sprig, red-pepper triangles and pared, blanched baby carrots. Pass sauce separately.

Makes 12 servings, 2 cups sauce.

Note: Terrine can be prepared ahead and reheated, or served at room temperature.

Couscous-Stuffed Peppers

(pictured, pages 172 and 173)

6 medium green, red or yellow peppers
¼ cup butter or margarine
1 large carrot, pared and shredded
3 green onions, chopped
1 medium clove garlic, crushed
1 can (14 ounces) chicken broth
1 cup uncooked couscous
½ cup raisins
¼ teaspoon ground cinnamon
¼ teaspoon dried thyme leaves, crushed
½ cup water

1. Preheat oven to 350°F. Cut off and reserve a thick, lengthwise slice from side of each pepper. Remove and discard seeds from peppers; set peppers aside. Chop reserved pepper slices; set aside.

2. In large skillet, over medium-high heat, melt butter. Add chopped pepper, the carrot, green onions and garlic; sauté until tender-crisp, about 3 minutes. Add broth; bring to boiling. Stir in couscous and next three ingredients until well mixed. Remove pan from heat. Cover; let stand 5 minutes, until liquid is absorbed. With fork, stir mixture.

3. Spoon ¾ cup mixture into each prepared pepper. Arrange peppers in shallow baking dish; pour water in bottom of dish. Bake, uncovered, 35 minutes, or until peppers are tender and filling is hot.

Makes 6 servings.

Patchwork-Quilt Rice

(pictured, page 172)

3 tablespoons butter or margarine
1 cup sliced celery
1 cup chopped onion
¾ cup chopped carrot
¾ cup chopped green pepper
1 cup chopped unpared tart red apple
1 cup sliced mushrooms
1 package (6.25 ounces) long-grain and wild rice mix
1 can (10½ ounces) condensed chicken broth
¼ cup toasted slivered almonds

1. In skillet, over medium-high heat, melt butter. Add celery, onion, carrot and pepper; sauté until carrot is tender, about 8 minutes. Add apple and mushrooms; sauté 2 minutes longer. Add rice from mix; toss to combine. Stir in seasoning from mix. In glass measure, combine broth with enough water to make 2 cups; stir into rice mixture.

2. Bring to boiling; cover. Simmer until broth is absorbed, about 10 minutes. Add almonds; toss to combine. Serve immediately.

Makes 6 servings.

Tomatoes Fontina

(pictured, page 173)

6 tablespoons butter or margarine
2 shallots, minced
1½ cups uncooked tubetti or other small pasta
1 can (about 14 ounces) chicken broth
1¼ cups water
½ teaspoon salt
8 large firm tomatoes
Salt
Pepper
½ cup chopped fresh basil leaves
3 cups (12 ounces) shredded fontina cheese
½ cup water

1. In medium saucepan, over medium heat, melt butter. Add shallots; sauté until tender, about 2 minutes. Stir in pasta; cook until lightly browned, about 3 minutes. Add broth, 1¼ cups water and ½ teaspoon salt. Bring to boiling; simmer, uncovered, 15 minutes, or until liquid is absorbed, stirring often.

2. Preheat oven to 350°F. Cut off tops of tomatoes. With spoon, remove and discard seeds and center pulp from tomatoes. Sprinkle inside of each with salt, pepper and half of the basil. Stir shredded cheese into pasta mixture; spoon into tomatoes, dividing evenly.

3. Place tomatoes in shallow baking dish; pour ½ cup water in bottom of dish. Cover; bake 20 minutes. Remove cover; bake 10 minutes longer, or until hot and bubbly. Sprinkle top edge of tomatoes with remaining basil, dividing evenly.

Makes 8 servings.

Potatoes Italiano

(pictured, pages 172 and 173)

2 tablespoons olive oil
1 large onion, diced
2 medium cloves garlic, crushed
1 can (28 ounces) crushed tomatoes
2 tablespoons tomato paste
2 tablespoons minced parsley
2 teaspoons dried Italian seasoning, crushed
1 teaspoon dried basil leaves, crushed
1 teaspoon salt
¼ teaspoon cracked pepper
2 pounds medium red potatoes, unpared and thinly sliced
1½ cups (6 ounces) shredded fontina cheese

1. In 5-quart Dutch oven, heat olive oil over medium heat. Add onion and garlic; sauté 3 minutes. Add tomatoes, tomato paste, parsley, Italian seasoning, basil, salt and pepper. Bring to boiling. Simmer, covered, 15 minutes; stir occasionally.

2. Preheat oven to 400°F. Spread one-third of the sauce over bottom of shallow 2-quart baking dish. Arrange half of the potatoes over the sauce; sprinkle with ½ cup fontina cheese. Spoon half of the remaining sauce over the cheese. Cover with the remaining potatoes; sprinkle with ½ cup cheese. Spread remaining sauce over all.

3. Bake until potatoes are tender, about 45 minutes. Sprinkle with remaining ½ cup cheese; bake until cheese melts, about 5 minutes longer.

Makes 8 servings.

■ Store mushrooms correctly. To prevent excess moisture from creating brown spots and causing spoilage, remove plastic wrap from carton before refrigerating. Place in a brown paper bag or in a bowl covered with a damp cloth.

■ To get rid of soil that clings to fresh mushrooms, don't wash them! Place mushrooms in a paper bag, add several tablespoons flour and shake. Refrigerate mushrooms in the paper bag for up to a week.

Creamy Vegetable Bake

(pictured, page 173)

1½ pounds russet potatoes, pared
1½ pounds turnips or rutabagas, pared
5 large carrots, pared
2 teaspoons salt
¾ cup butter or margarine
2 cups sliced leeks, white part only (from about 5 medium)
2 cups sliced mushrooms
¼ cup half-and-half
½ teaspoon ground nutmeg
¼ teaspoon pepper
2 tablespoons chopped parsley
Paprika

1. Cut potatoes and turnips into ½-inch cubes; cut carrots crosswise into ¼-inch-thick slices. In 6-quart Dutch oven, place potatoes, turnips, carrots, 1 teaspoon salt and enough cold water to cover vegetables by 1 inch. Cover; bring to boiling. Simmer 25 minutes, or until tender.

2. In large skillet, over medium-high heat, melt ½ cup butter. Add leeks and mushrooms; sauté until tender. Set aside.

3. In small saucepan, over medium-high heat, bring half-and-half and remaining butter to boiling. Stir in 1 teaspoon salt, the nutmeg and pepper; set aside.

4. Drain potato mixture; puree, in batches, in food processor, adding hot half-and-half mixture to each batch. Transfer puree to large bowl. Fold in leek mixture and parsley. Refrigerate 4 hours or overnight to mellow flavors.

5. Preheat oven to 350°F. Place potato mixture in large pastry bag fitted with 1-inch star tip. Pipe mixture into eight 1-cup ramekins (small soufflé dishes); sprinkle with paprika. Bake 30 minutes, or until mixture is heated through and tops are browned.

Makes 8 servings.

Bacon Dumplings

(pictured, pages 172 and 173)

1 package (12 ounces) sliced bacon, diced
3 cups bread cubes, cut from firm-textured bread
½ cup diced onion
⅔ cup milk
2 tablespoons minced chives
⅔ cup unsifted all-purpose flour
1 large egg, beaten
3 tablespoons minced parsley
1 teaspoon dried thyme leaves, crushed
¼ teaspoon salt
⅛ teaspoon pepper

Onion Gravy
2 cups sliced onions
1 package (1.2 ounces) brown-gravy mix
1½ cups water

1. In medium skillet, over medium heat, cook bacon until crisp; using slotted spoon, transfer to paper towels. Set aside. Pour off and reserve drippings.

2. Over medium heat, in same skillet, heat 5 tablespoons drippings until hot. Add bread cubes; sauté until golden. Pour into large bowl.

3. Over medium heat, in same skillet, heat 2 tablespoons drippings until hot. Add diced onion; sauté until lightly browned. Add to bowl with bread cubes; with fork or hands, gently stir in cooked bacon, milk, chives, flour, egg, parsley, thyme, salt and pepper until ingredients are blended. Let stand until milk is absorbed, about 15 minutes.

4. Preheat oven to 350°F. Grease large baking sheet. With hands, form mixture into 20 balls; arrange on prepared baking sheet. Bake 20 minutes, or until golden-brown.

5. Meanwhile, make gravy: Over medium heat, in same skillet, heat 3 tablespoons reserved bacon drippings until hot. Add sliced onions; sauté until golden-brown, about 8 minutes. Add gravy mix; cook as package label directs, except use 1½ cups water. Serve gravy with dumplings.

Makes 8 servings.

Corn Fritters With Yellow-Pepper Salsa

(pictured, page 174)

Yellow-Pepper Salsa
1 tablespoon salad oil
1 small onion, chopped
1 medium yellow pepper, chopped
2 to 3 pickled jalapeño peppers, minced
1 jar (10 ounces) apple jelly
1 tablespoon cilantro (fresh coriander) or parsley leaves, chopped
4 teaspoons cornstarch
2 tablespoons water

Corn Fritters
½ cup unsifted all-purpose flour
½ cup yellow cornmeal
1½ teaspoons baking powder
2 teaspoons sugar
½ teaspoon salt
3 large eggs
⅔ cup milk
¼ cup butter or margarine, melted
1 can (1 pound) whole-kernel corn, drained
3 green onions, chopped
Salad oil

Green-pepper half (optional)

1. Day before or early in day, make salsa: In medium saucepan, heat 1 tablespoon salad oil over medium-high heat. Add onion, yellow pepper and jalapeños; sauté 1 minute. Add jelly and cilantro; heat, stirring, until jelly melts. In small cup, mix cornstarch with water until blended; stir into pepper mixture. Cook, stirring, until mixture boils and thickens. Pour into bowl. Cover; chill.

2. Make fritters: On sheet of waxed paper, mix flour, cornmeal, baking powder, sugar and salt; set aside. In medium bowl, whisk eggs with milk, melted butter, corn and green onions until mixed. Add flour mixture; mix just until dry ingredients are moistened. In large skillet, heat 2 tablespoons oil over medium heat. Drop tablespoonfuls of batter into hot oil; cook until golden on both sides, turning once. Add more oil to pan if necessary.

3. To serve, pour salsa into green-pepper half, if desired. Arrange on platter with fritters. If desired, garnish fritters with fresh jalapeños. Serve immediately.

Makes 3 dozen fritters, about 1¾ cups sauce.

Hot Broccoli Slaw

(pictured, pages 174 and 175)

1 bunch (2 pounds) broccoli
2 tablespoons salad oil
4 green onions, julienned
1 large red pepper, julienned
2 tablespoons balsamic vinegar
2 tablespoons white-wine vinegar
2 tablespoons soy sauce
1 teaspoon celery seeds
1 cup water

1. Trim and reserve broccoli flowerets; set aside. Trim, pare and julienne stems; set aside.

2. In large skillet or wok, heat salad oil over high heat; add julienned vegetables. Sauté or stir-fry until tender-crisp, about 3 minutes. Remove pan from heat. Add vinegars, soy sauce and celery seeds; toss to coat vegetables. Place slaw in serving dish; keep warm.

3. In same pan, bring water to boiling. Add reserved broccoli flowerets; cook until tender-crisp, about 3 minutes. Drain well; arrange on slaw. If desired, garnish with green-onion flowers.

Makes 5 to 6 servings.

Eggplant-Artichoke Savarin
(pictured, page 175)

2 small eggplants
5 large eggs
¾ cup seasoned fine dry bread crumbs
1 cup grated Parmesan cheese
⅓ cup olive oil
2 packages (9 ounces each) frozen artichoke hearts
¼ cup chopped parsley
¼ cup mayonnaise
3 ounces prosciutto ham, coarsely chopped
¼ teaspoon pepper

Tomato Sauce
2 tablespoons butter or margarine
1 medium onion, chopped
1 large clove garlic, crushed
1 can (14 ounces) Italian plum tomatoes
3 tablespoons tomato paste
2 teaspoons dried basil leaves, crushed
1 teaspoon dried oregano leaves, crushed
1 teaspoon sugar

1. Grease 6- to 7-cup ring mold. Trim eggplants; cut lengthwise into ¼-inch-thick slices. Reserve 10 slices; coarsely chop remainder.

2. In pie plate, with fork, beat 2 eggs until mixed; set aside. On sheet of waxed paper, combine ½ cup bread crumbs with ¼ cup cheese; dip eggplant slices into eggs, draining off excess, and then into crumb mixture. Shake off excess; set aside on sheets of waxed paper.

3. In large skillet, heat 2 tablespoons olive oil over medium heat until hot. Cook eggplant slices, a few at a time, adding more oil as necessary, turning once, until golden-brown on both sides. Arrange fried slices crosswise and overlapping slightly in prepared mold so there are no gaps, allowing ends to extend over edges of pan. Set aside. In skillet, in remaining oil, sauté chopped eggplant until tender, about 5 minutes; set aside.

4. Preheat oven to 350°F. Cook artichoke hearts as package directs. Cut each heart in half; set aside.

5. In large bowl, whisk remaining eggs until mixed. Add parsley, mayonnaise, prosciutto, remaining bread crumbs and cheese, the sautéed eggplant, artichokes and the pepper; stir until mixed. Spoon into eggplant-lined mold; with hand, pat down firmly. Fold ends of eggplant slices over filling. Place mold in small roasting pan; set pan in oven. Pour enough boiling water into pan to come halfway up side of mold. Cover mold loosely with foil; bake 45 minutes, or until filling sets.

6. Meanwhile, make sauce: In same skillet, over medium heat, melt butter. Add onion and garlic; sauté until tender, about 5 minutes. Stir in tomatoes and next 4 ingredients, breaking up tomatoes with a spoon. Bring to boiling; simmer 10 minutes, stirring occasionally.

7. To serve, invert savarin onto platter; if desired, garnish with oregano sprigs. Pass sauce separately.

Makes 10 servings, 2¼ cups sauce.

German-Style Red Cabbage
(pictured, page 175)

¼ pound salt pork, diced
2 medium onions, sliced
2 medium red cooking apples
1½ pounds red cabbage, shredded
¼ cup sugar
2 teaspoons caraway seeds
1 teaspoon salt
¼ teaspoon pepper
1 cup chicken broth
½ cup cider vinegar
¼ cup dry red wine

1. In 5-quart Dutch oven, over medium heat, cook diced salt pork, stirring occasionally, until crisp and all fat is rendered. With slotted spoon, remove salt pork; set aside.

2. Drain off all but 2 tablespoons fat from pan. Add onions; over medium heat, sauté 5 minutes. Core and dice apples; add to onions with cooked salt pork, the cabbage, sugar, caraway seeds, salt, pepper, broth, vinegar and wine. Bring to boiling; simmer, covered, until cabbage is tender, about 40 minutes.

Makes 8 servings.

Brussels Sprouts Stir-Fry
(pictured, pages 174 and 175)

1 medium clove garlic, crushed
1 tablespoon cornstarch
1 tablespoon sugar
1 teaspoon salt
½ teaspoon ground ginger
¼ teaspoon crushed red-pepper flakes
¾ cup chicken broth
2 tablespoons lemon juice
2 tablespoons light soy sauce
1 pint (¾ pound) brussels sprouts
½ small head cauliflower
2 medium celery stalks
1 medium onion
1 medium yellow pepper
1 tablespoon sesame seeds
3 tablespoons salad oil

1. In medium bowl, mix garlic, cornstarch, sugar, salt, ginger, red-pepper flakes, chicken broth, lemon juice and soy sauce until blended; set aside.

2. Trim brussels sprouts; cut in half lengthwise. Set aside. Cut cauliflower into flowerets; set aside. Cut celery diagonally into ¼-inch-thick slices; set aside. Cut onion into ¼-inch-thick wedges; set aside. Julienne pepper; set aside.

3. In large skillet, over medium-high heat, toast sesame seeds, stirring frequently, until golden-brown.

Remove to small cup; set aside. In same skillet, heat salad oil over medium-high heat. Add brussels sprouts, cauliflower and celery; sauté 2 minutes. Add onion and pepper strips; sauté mixture 2 minutes longer.

4. Stir cornstarch mixture to recombine; stir into vegetable mixture. Over medium heat, cook, stirring, until sauce is thickened and vegetables are tender-crisp, about 5 minutes. Sprinkle with toasted sesame seeds.

Makes 4 to 6 servings.

Vegetable Stir-Fry on Squash Lo Mein

1 large (3- to 3½-pound) spaghetti squash
¼ cup olive oil
½ teaspoon salt
⅛ teaspoon pepper
6 ounces asparagus
4 green onions
6 ounces snow peas, trimmed
1 red pepper, julienned
2 large cloves garlic, crushed
⅛ teaspoon crushed red-pepper flakes
1 can (8 ounces) bamboo shoots, drained
1 can (8 ounces) sliced water chestnuts, drained
⅓ cup light soy sauce

1. Preheat oven to 350°F. Line jelly-roll pan with aluminum foil; set aside. Slice squash in half lengthwise. With large spoon, scoop out and discard seeds. Drizzle 1 tablespoon olive oil over halves; sprinkle each with salt and pepper, dividing evenly. Place halves, cut side down, on prepared pan. Bake until squash is tender when pierced with a fork, about 1 hour and 15 minutes.

2. Meanwhile, cut asparagus and green onions diagonally into 2-inch pieces; set aside. In large skillet or wok, heat remaining olive oil over medium-high heat. Add asparagus, green onions, snow peas, red-pepper strips, garlic and red-pepper flakes; stir-fry vegetables until tender-crisp, about 5 minutes. Add bamboo shoots, water chestnuts and soy sauce; stir-fry until heated through. Keep warm.

3. With large fork, scoop spaghetti squash into shallow bowl. Top with vegetable stir-fry. Serve immediately.

Makes 4 to 6 servings.

Do-Ahead Cheese-Stuffed Potatoes

8 hot baked potatoes (4 pounds)
¾ cup hot milk
½ cup butter or margarine
1 package (3 ounces) cream cheese, softened
2 tablespoons chopped chives
1 teaspoon salt
⅛ teaspoon pepper
½ cup (2 ounces) shredded extrasharp Cheddar cheese
Paprika

1. Cut off a ¼-inch-thick lengthwise slice from one long side of each potato. With a spoon, scoop out potatoes, being careful not to break skin; set aside. In large bowl of electric mixer, at medium speed, beat potatoes and milk until smooth. Add butter, cream cheese, chives, salt and pepper; beat until fluffy.

2. Spoon mixture into potato skins, mounding slightly. Top each potato with some shredded cheese, dividing evenly. Sprinkle each with paprika. (Potatoes may be prepared ahead to this point; cover with plastic wrap. Refrigerate.)

3. Preheat oven to 350°F. Unwrap potatoes; place on jelly-roll pan. Bake until golden and heated through, about 30 minutes.

Makes 8 servings.

Mushrooms Scandia

4 cups water
4 cups broccoli flowerets and stems, cut in ½-inch slices (¾ pound)
1 medium potato, pared and diced
5 tablespoons unsalted butter or margarine
1 teaspoon salt
¼ teaspoon ground white pepper
⅛ teaspoon ground nutmeg
2 teaspoons lemon juice
1 tablespoon chopped fresh dill or 1 teaspoon dried dillweed
12 very large mushrooms (about 3 inches in diameter), stems removed

1. In medium saucepan bring water to boiling. Add broccoli and potato; cook until tender-crisp, about 12 minutes. Drain. Place in food processor. Add 3 tablespoons butter, the salt, pepper, nutmeg and lemon juice. Puree; stir in dill. (Filling may be refrigerated at this point, bring to room temperature before using to fill mushroom caps.)

2. Preheat oven to 450°F. Place mushrooms, stem side up, in lightly-buttered shallow baking dish. With filling in pastry bag fitted with large plain tip, pipe mixture into mushroom caps. Bake until golden-brown, about 20 minutes. Melt remaining butter; drizzle over filling.

Makes 12 servings.

■ Here's the way to frost-proof plastic-wrapped frozen foods: Before you seal the plastic bag, insert a drinking straw, holding the bag's opening snugly around the straw, and gently suck as much air as possible out of the bag. Then, remove the straw, and quickly seal the bag—an easy airtight container!

Lite Eating: Terrific Halloween Treats

Jack-O'-Lantern Cookie

Nonstick cooking spray
½ cup light corn-oil spread
⅓ cup firmly packed brown sugar
1 large egg
¾ teaspoon vanilla extract
1½ cups uncooked rolled oats
¾ cup unsifted all-purpose flour
½ teaspoon baking soda
½ teaspoon ground cinnamon
½ teaspoon salt
1 large egg white
⅔ cup granulated sugar
¼ teaspoon cream of tartar
3 tablespoons water
Red and yellow food color

1. Preheat oven to 350°F. Line 12-inch pizza pan with foil. Grease with cooking spray.
2. In bowl, beat corn-oil spread, brown sugar, egg and ½ teaspoon vanilla until fluffy. On waxed paper, combine oats, flour, baking soda, cinnamon and salt; stir into sugar mixture.
3. Spread batter in prepared pan. Bake 15 minutes or until done. Cool.

Clockwise from top left: Jack-O'-Lantern Cookie, Broomstick Pears, Witchy Pumpkin Cakes, Happy Ghost Mold.

4. Make frosting: In top of double boiler, combine egg white, sugar, cream of tartar and water. With portable electric mixer, beat until frothy. Place double-boiler top over bottom containing rapidly boiling water (bottom of container should not touch water). At high speed, beat until stiff peaks form, about 7 minutes. Remove double-boiler top from pan; add ¼ teaspoon vanilla. Beat until stiff. Place one-third of frosting in bowl. With food colors, tint remaining frosting orange.

5. Spread cookie with orange frosting. Spread white frosting over pumpkin to make eyes and mouth. If desired, decorate with black and green gel icing and candy.

Makes 16 servings, 143 calories each.

Broomstick Pears

Nonstick cooking spray
8 flat wooden sticks
8 Seckel pears or lady apples
24 caramel candies
3 tablespoons water
1 large biscuit shredded-wheat cereal, shredded

Line baking sheet with waxed paper; grease paper with cooking spray. Insert stick into stem end of each pear. In small saucepan, over low heat, melt candies with water, stirring. Remove pan from heat. Dip each pear into mixture, turning to coat evenly. Remove excess caramel mixture from bottom of pan by wiping along edge. Drain. Sprinkle with cereal; place on baking sheet. Refrigerate. Let stand at room temperature 15 minutes before serving.

Makes 8 servings, 229 calories each.

Witchy Pumpkin Cakes

1½ cups unsifted all-purpose flour
1 teaspoon baking powder
½ teaspoon baking soda
½ teaspoon ground cinnamon
½ teaspoon salt
½ cup firmly packed brown sugar
1 cup canned pumpkin
¼ cup reduced-calorie syrup
1 large egg
2 tablespoons salad oil
½ package (8-ounce size) Neufchâtel cheese, softened
½ cup confectioners' sugar
½ teaspoon vanilla extract
Green food color

1. Preheat oven to 350°F. Insert paper liners in 12 muffin-pan cups.

2. In bowl, mix first 5 ingredients. In small bowl, mix brown sugar and next 4 ingredients; whisk into flour mixture. Spoon into pans. Bake 15 minutes, until done. Cool in pans 10 minutes; turn out to cool.

3. In bowl, beat cheese, confectioners' sugar and vanilla; tint green. Spread icing on cakes. If desired, decorate to resemble witch faces.

Makes 12 servings, 181 calories each.

■ To make an ice block for punch, the day before using: Fill a bowl with 2 quarts water; let stand at room temperature 1 hour. Stir occasionally. Mound 2 trayfuls of ice cubes in a 2-quart, fancy round mold; fill with the water. Freeze until firm. To unmold: Dip mold in warm water until ice loosens; turn out on waxed paper. Return to freezer if not using at once.

Happy Ghost Mold

5 packages (0.3 ounce each) sugar-free orange-flavored gelatin
1½ cups boiling water
3 cups cold water
4 cups nonfat plain yogurt
2 navel oranges, peeled and chopped
1 container (8 ounces) frozen nondairy whipped topping, thawed
Black string licorice
Chewy chocolate candies

1. In bowl, dissolve gelatin in boiling water. Stir in cold water and yogurt. Chill 30 minutes, until slightly thickened. Fold in oranges. Pour into ghost pan or 10-cup mold. Chill until firm, at least 3 hours.

2. Unmold onto platter. With topping in pastry bag fitted with star tip, using photograph as a guide, decorate mold. Add licorice and candies.

Makes 16 servings, 92 calories each.

Party Cranberry Punch

1 quart bottled low-calorie cranberry juice, chilled
1 can (1 pint, 7 ounces) pineapple juice, chilled
1 cup orange juice
½ cup lemon juice
2 bottles (28-ounce size) sugar-free ginger ale, chilled
8 cups crushed ice

In punch bowl, combine juices. Just before serving, add ginger ale and ice. If desired, make some punch ahead and freeze in an ice tray; make an ice block (see tip).

Makes 20 to 25 punch-cup servings, about 40 calories each.

Micro-Way: Quick Chicken Suppers

Chicken Strata Olé

4 slices whole-wheat bread, toasted
1 tablespoon salad oil
1 pound boneless chicken breasts, skinned and cut in ½-inch-wide strips
1 small onion, chopped
1 can (4 ounces) chopped green chiles, drained
1 medium clove garlic, crushed
1 can (17 ounces) Mexican-style corn, drained
1 cup (4 ounces) shredded Monterey Jack cheese
1 cup (4 ounces) shredded Cheddar cheese
3 large eggs
½ teaspoon salt
⅛ teaspoon pepper
¾ cup half-and-half
½ cup sour cream

1. Cut each slice toast diagonally in half; set aside. In large glass bowl, combine salad oil, chicken, onion, chiles and garlic. Cover with plastic wrap; turn back one corner to vent. Cook on HIGH 5 minutes, stirring occasionally, until chicken is just tender.

2. With slotted spoon, remove chicken mixture to 1½-quart microwave-safe baking dish. Add corn and cheeses. In medium bowl, whisk eggs with salt, pepper, half-and-half and sour cream; add to chicken mixture. Arrange toast triangles, spoke fashion, on top. Cook on HIGH 6 minutes, rotating dish after 3 minutes. Cook on MEDIUM 12 minutes, rotating dish every 4 minutes. Let stand 10 minutes. If desired, garnish with parsley and serve in wedges, with salsa.

Makes 8 servings.

■ One of the nicest things about a microwave is the variety of products you can use in it. You can heat a roll on a napkin or rewarm a meal on a dinner plate (instead of warming up food in pans that have to be washed). You can use plastic, paper, glass, ceramic and china dishes that can go from the freezer to the microwave to the table—and even into the dishwasher.

■ Microwave-safe dinnerware is now pretty enough to grace your table, even when you are entertaining guests. Keep in mind that there should be no metallic trim on a plate to be used in the microwave oven—including any signature on the underside. Some paints and glazes can contain metallic substances.

Chicken Sloppy Joes

1 tablespoon salad oil
1 small green pepper, chopped
1 small onion, chopped
1 tablespoon brown sugar
½ teaspoon dry mustard
1 can (8 ounces) tomato sauce
¾ cup ketchup
1 tablespoon Worcestershire sauce
1 tablespoon red-wine vinegar
3 cans (5 ounces each) chunk-style white-meat chicken, drained
6 sandwich buns, split
1 cup (4 ounces) shredded Cheddar cheese

1. In large glass bowl, combine salad oil, chopped green pepper and onion. Cook on HIGH 3 minutes, stirring once. Stir in brown sugar, mustard, tomato sauce, ketchup, Worcestershire and vinegar until blended. Cook mixture on HIGH 2 minutes. Add chicken; stir to combine. Cook on HIGH 2 minutes longer, until mixture is bubbly.

2. Spoon rounded ½ cup chicken mixture onto bottom half of each bun; sprinkle each with cheese, dividing evenly. Cover each with top of bun. Wrap each sandwich with plastic wrap. Place sandwiches in a ring in microwave; heat on HIGH 2 minutes. (To heat 1 sandwich, heat 30 seconds; 2 sandwiches, 45 seconds; 3 sandwiches, 1 minute; 4 sandwiches, 1½ minutes; 5 sandwiches, 1 minute 45 seconds; 6 sandwiches, 2 minutes.) If desired, serve sandwiches with potato chips.

Makes 6 servings.

■ Keep some cheese snacks on hand: Cube 10 ounces Cheddar cheese, 3 ounces cream cheese and ¼ cup butter; place in glass bowl. Soften in microwave on HIGH 5 minutes; mix well. Add 1 teaspoon dried onion flakes; roll into balls. Coat with sesame seeds; store in refrigerator.

November

Start a holiday tradition with country-style turkey and all the trimmings. Here, three-bread stuffing with oysters, pear-and-cranberry relish and pecan-topped sweet potatoes make the meal special.

Roast Turkey With Three-Bread Stuffing

Pear-Cranberry Conserve

Praline-Topped Sweet Potatoes

Deep-Dish Apple-Cider Pie

Broccoli and Celery Pesto

Savory Artichoke Cheesecake

Parmesan Potato Skins   Silver-Onion Soup

Roasted Capon With Chestnut Stuffing

Frozen Banana-Toffee Soufflé

Brussels Sprouts Bisque   Mini Potato Scones

Molded Salmon Mousse   Amaretto Apricot Sauce

Hostess Peas   Citrus Jellied Wine

CORIANDER

Thanksgiving Cookbook

Begin with a twist on onion soup—pearl onions in a sherried chicken broth, paired with crisply baked, Parmesan-flavored potato skins. Finish with our spiced apple-raisin pie, sprinkled with brown-sugar crumble and drizzled with a sweet glaze.

Pear-Cranberry Conserve

(pictured, page 187)

1 package (12 ounces) cranberries
½ cup sugar
3 medium pears, cored and coarsely chopped
1 cup bite-size dried figs, quartered
½ cup port wine
1 tablespoon minced preserved ginger
1 tablespoon grated lemon peel

In food processor or blender, process cranberries and sugar until berries are minced; spoon mixture into medium bowl. Add pears, figs, wine, ginger and lemon peel; toss gently to mix. Cover; refrigerate at least 4 hours to blend flavors.

Makes 8 servings (5 cups).

Praline-Topped Sweet Potatoes

(pictured, page 187)

3 cans (1 pound each) yams in light syrup, drained
½ cup butter or margarine, melted
½ cup heavy cream
2 large eggs
1 cup firmly packed light-brown sugar
¾ cup chopped pecans
¼ teaspoon ground cinnamon
¼ teaspoon ground nutmeg
¼ teaspoon salt
1 teaspoon vanilla extract

1. In food processor, puree yams with 6 tablespoons melted butter and 2 tablespoons cream. Add eggs and ½ cup brown sugar; process until blended. Spread half the potato mixture in shallow 2-quart baking dish; with remaining potato mixture in pastry bag fitted with large star tip, using photograph as a guide, pipe large rosettes over mixture.

2. Preheat oven to 375°F. In small saucepan, combine remaining melted butter, cream and brown sugar, the pecans, cinnamon, nutmeg and salt. Bring to boiling; simmer 5 minutes. Remove from heat; stir in vanilla. Spoon over center of potato mixture. Bake 20 minutes, or until bubbly. If desired, garnish with toasted pecan halves.

Makes 6 to 8 servings.

Roast Turkey With Three-Bread Stuffing

(pictured, pages 187 and 188)

Stuffing
48 shucked oysters (2 pints), liquor reserved
3 large onions
1 cup butter or margarine
3 cups chopped celery
1½ cups shredded carrots
8 cups ½-inch cubes white bread, toasted
6 cups ½-inch cubes pumpernickel bread, toasted
6 cups ½-inch cubes rye bread, toasted
2 large eggs, slightly beaten
½ cup heavy cream
¾ cup minced parsley
3 tablespoons chopped fresh sage leaves
1½ teaspoons salt
¼ teaspoon ground red pepper

Page 187: (Clockwise from top) Roast Turkey With Three-Bread Stuffing, Pear-Cranberry Conserve, Praline-Topped Sweet Potatoes.

Pages 188 and 189: (Clockwise from top left) Roast Turkey With Three-Bread Stuffing, Deep-Dish Apple-Cider Pie, Broccoli and Celery Pesto, Savory Artichoke Cheesecake, Parmesan Potato Skins, Silver-Onion Soup.

Pages 190 and 191: (Clockwise from top left) Frozen Banana-Toffee Soufflé, Brussels Sprouts Bisque, Mini Potato Scones, Molded Salmon Mousse, Amaretto Apricot Sauce, Hostess Peas, Citrus Jellied Wine, Roasted Capon With Chestnut Stuffing.

16- to 18-pound turkey, thawed if frozen
¼ teaspoon salt
⅛ teaspoon pepper
3 cups chicken broth
¼ cup unsifted all-purpose flour

1. Make stuffing: Coarsely chop oysters; set aside. Coarsely chop 1 onion. In 8-quart Dutch oven, over medium heat, melt half the butter. Add chopped onion, celery and carrots; sauté until tender, about 5 minutes. Remove pan from heat; add oysters and their liquor, bread cubes, eggs, cream, parsley, sage, 1½ teaspoons salt and red pepper. Toss gently.

2. Remove turkey giblets and neck; set aside. Remove and discard excess fat. Wash turkey; pat dry.

3. Preheat oven to 325°F. Lightly spoon stuffing into neck cavity. Bring neck skin over stuffing; secure with poultry pins. Spoon some of remaining stuffing into body cavity; do not pack. (Place extra stuffing in greased baking dish; cover and bake last hour turkey is in oven.) Close body cavity with poultry pins; lace with string. Tie legs together. Pin wings to breast.

4. Place turkey, breast side up, on rack in large, open roasting pan. Cut remaining 2 onions into wedges; place around turkey with giblets and neck. In small saucepan, melt remaining ½ cup butter. Brush turkey with some melted butter; sprinkle with ¼ teaspoon salt and ⅛ teaspoon pepper. Insert meat thermometer into thickest portion of thigh, away from bone. Roast, uncovered, 5½ hours, basting every 30 minutes, until meat thermometer registers 170°F. After 1 hour, add 1 cup chicken broth to pan. When skin turns golden, cover turkey loosely with aluminum-foil tent.

5. Place turkey on warm serving platter. Remove poultry pins and string. Let stand 15 minutes for easier carving. If desired, garnish platter with mâche (lamb's lettuce), crab apples and small squashes.

6. Skim off and discard all fat from pan juices. Blend flour with remaining 2 cups broth; add to pan juices. Bring gravy to boiling, stirring to loosen any browned bits. Simmer, stirring until thickened, about 5 minutes; strain into gravy boat. Serve with turkey and stuffing.

Makes 16 to 18 servings.

Silver-Onion Soup

(pictured, page 188)

2 pounds pearl onions
¼ cup butter or margarine
1½ cups sliced celery
2 tablespoons all-purpose flour
6 cups chicken broth
1 tablespoon sugar
½ teaspoon dried thyme leaves, crushed
¼ teaspoon ground nutmeg
½ cup sherry

Parmesan Potato Skins (page 194)

1. Peel onions; cut larger ones in half. In large saucepan, over medium-low heat, melt butter. Add onions and celery; sauté 15 minutes. Stir in flour until blended; cook, stirring, until bubbly.

2. Gradually add broth, stirring until blended. Stir in sugar, thyme and nutmeg. Bring to boiling, stirring; cook 1 minute. Simmer, covered, until onions are tender, about 15 minutes. Add sherry; heat through. Serve with Parmesan Potato Skins.

Makes 8 servings.

Broccoli and Celery Pesto

(pictured, page 189)

1 large clove garlic
1 jar (3 ounces) pine nuts
½ cup packed fresh basil leaves
¼ cup grated Parmesan cheese
¼ teaspoon salt
¼ cup olive oil
1 small onion
6 celery stalks (¾ pound)
1 large head broccoli
2 tablespoons salad oil

1. Make sauce: In food processor or blender, mince garlic. Reserve 2 tablespoons pine nuts; to garlic, add remaining pine nuts, the basil, Parmesan and salt. Process until smooth. With motor running, pour in olive oil in a steady stream; process until blended. Set aside.

2. Cut onion crosswise into thin slices; set aside. Cut celery crosswise and diagonally into thin slices; set aside. Cut broccoli into flowerets. Pare stems; cut diagonally into thin slices. Set aside. In skillet, over medium-low heat, sauté reserved pine nuts until golden-brown; set aside. Add oil to pan; heat over medium-high heat until hot. Add onion; sauté 2 minutes. Add celery and broccoli; sauté until tender-crisp, about 5 minutes.

3. Remove pan from heat; add pesto sauce, stirring until mixture is coated. Spoon into dish; sprinkle with reserved sautéed pine nuts.

Makes 6 servings.

■ To defrost a frozen turkey, thaw it in its wrapper in the refrigerator or in cool water, changing the water frequently. For a 16-pound turkey, thaw in refrigerator three to four days.

Savory Artichoke Cheesecake

(pictured, page 189)

1 tablespoon butter or margarine, softened
¼ cup fine dry bread crumbs
2 packages (8 ounces each) cream cheese, softened
¾ cup (4 ounces) crumbled feta cheese
1 cup sour cream
3 large eggs
1 package (9 ounces) frozen artichoke hearts, thawed
1 medium red pepper, chopped
½ cup sliced green onions
1 large clove garlic, crushed
1 teaspoon dried tarragon leaves, crushed
½ teaspoon dried basil leaves, crushed
Rye and pumpernickel toast points

1. Preheat oven to 375°F. With butter, grease inside of 9-inch springform pan. Sprinkle with bread crumbs to coat thickly; reserve remaining crumbs. Set pan aside.

2. In large bowl of electric mixer, at medium-high speed, beat cream cheese until fluffy. Add feta, sour cream and eggs; beat until blended and smooth. Pat dry and finely chop artichoke hearts; add to bowl with cheese mixture. Beat in chopped pepper, onions, garlic, tarragon and basil until blended. Spoon into prepared pan; spread evenly.

3. Bake 35 minutes, or until puffed and golden. Cool on wire rack to room temperature; refrigerate 3 hours or overnight.

4. Remove springform side. Pat remaining bread crumbs onto side of cheesecake. If desired, garnish top of cheesecake with fresh basil leaves, red-pepper strips and cooked artichoke hearts. To serve, slice cheesecake in wedges; serve with toast points.

Makes 24 servings.

Parmesan Potato Skins

(pictured, page 188)

1½ pounds (4 large) baking potatoes, scrubbed
¼ cup butter or margarine, melted
⅓ cup freshly grated Parmesan cheese
Freshly ground black pepper
Paprika

1. Preheat oven to 425°F. With knife, remove skins from potatoes in ¼-inch-thick strips. (Save inside of potatoes for another use.)

2. In large bowl, toss skins with butter; arrange skin-side up in a single layer on large jelly-roll pan. Bake 10 minutes; turn over. Sprinkle with cheese and pepper, dividing evenly. Bake 15 minutes longer. Sprinkle with paprika before serving.

Makes 8 servings.

Deep-Dish Apple-Cider Pie

(pictured, page 189)

1 cup apple cider
½ cup granulated sugar
3 pounds (6 medium) Granny Smith apples, pared, cored and thinly sliced
1½ cups golden raisins
1 teaspoon grated lemon peel
2 tablespoons lemon juice
½ teaspoon ground cinnamon
2 tablespoons cornstarch
1 cup chopped pecans
9½-inch baked deep-dish pie shell (recipe follows)
½ cup firmly packed light-brown sugar
½ cup unsifted all-purpose flour
¼ cup butter or margarine
½ cup confectioners' sugar
2 to 3 teaspoons milk

1. Preheat oven to 400°F. In large saucepan, bring ¾ cup cider and the granulated sugar to boiling. Add apples, raisins, lemon peel, lemon juice and cinnamon; mix well. Reduce heat; simmer, uncovered, until apples are tender, about 4 minutes. In small glass measure, blend cornstarch with remaining cider; stir into apple mixture. Bring to boiling; cook, stirring until thickened, about 2 minutes. Stir in ½ cup pecans; spoon into prepared pie shell.

2. In small bowl, combine brown sugar and flour; with pastry blender or two knives, cut in butter until mixture resembles coarse crumbs. Stir in remaining ½ cup pecans. Sprinkle nut mixture evenly over apples. Bake 30 minutes, or until topping is golden. Remove from oven; cool on wire rack. In small bowl, blend confectioners' sugar and just enough milk to make mixture of spoonable consistency; drizzle over pie. Using photograph as a guide, arrange pastry "leaves" (see pie shell recipe, below) over apples. Refrigerate until ready to serve.

Makes 8 servings.

Pie Shell

1½ cups unsifted all-purpose flour
½ teaspoon salt
½ cup cold butter, cut in small pieces
5 tablespoons ice water
1 large egg yolk

1. In food processor, combine flour and salt. Add butter; turn machine on and off until mixture resembles coarse crumbs. In small glass measure, blend ice water with egg yolk; with machine running, pour liquid into flour mixture. Process just until mixture begins to form a ball.

2. Remove ¼ cup dough; set aside. On lightly floured surface, with lightly floured rolling pin, roll out dough to an 11-inch round. Carefully transfer to deep 9½-inch pie plate; crimp edges. Roll reserved

pastry to 1/8-inch thickness. With small paring knife, cut out leaf shapes, using blunt side of knife to make "veins." Place on baking sheet; set aside.

3. Lightly press sheet of aluminum foil over pastry in pie plate; with fork, prick pastry through foil. Refrigerate pastry 20 minutes, or until thoroughly chilled.

4. Preheat oven to 400°F. Bake pie shell and pastry leaves 12 minutes. Remove foil from pie plate; bake pastry 4 minutes longer. Cool completely on wire rack. If necessary, bake pastry leaves a few minutes longer, until golden-brown. Cool on wire rack.

Makes 1 pie shell.

Citrus Jellied Wine

(pictured, page 190)

1/2 cup fresh orange juice
1/4 cup fresh lemon juice
1/2 cup sugar
2 envelopes unflavored gelatine
1 bottle (750 milliliters) Asti spumante or other sweet sparkling white wine
1/4 cup syrup from 10-ounce jar preserved stem ginger
Sweetened whipped heavy cream
Gingered Orange Sauce (recipe follows)

1. In nonaluminum 2-quart saucepan, combine orange juice, lemon juice and sugar; stir until sugar dissolves. Sprinkle gelatine over juice mixture; let stand until softened, about 5 minutes.

2. Heat, stirring, over low heat, until gelatine dissolves. Stir in wine and ginger syrup. When foam subsides, pour mixture into each of 6 compote dishes, dividing evenly. Cover; refrigerate 6 hours, or until set. (May be prepared up to 3 days in advance.)

3. To serve, place whipped cream in pastry bag fitted with star tip; pipe a rosette of cream onto top of each jelly. Spoon some sauce over whipped cream. Serve immediately.

Makes 6 servings.

Gingered Orange Sauce

1/4 cup sugar
1 1/2 teaspoons cornstarch
1/2 cup fresh orange juice
2 teaspoons fresh lemon juice
2 teaspoons light corn syrup
2 tablespoons diced preserved stem ginger
1 tablespoon julienne lemon peel
1 tablespoon julienne lime peel

In small nonaluminum saucepan, combine sugar and cornstarch. Stir in orange juice, lemon juice and corn syrup. Bring to boiling, stirring; boil 1 minute. Remove from heat; stir in ginger, lemon peel and lime peel. Cover; refrigerate until cold, about 2 hours.

Makes about 2/3 cup.

Mini Potato Scones

(pictured, page 191)

3 cups unsifted all-purpose flour
2 tablespoons baking powder
2 tablespoons sugar
1 teaspoon salt
3/4 cup butter or margarine, cut in pieces
2 cups cold plain mashed potatoes
2 large eggs, beaten
1/4 cup milk
1 large egg yolk
1 tablespoon water
1 tablespoon poppy seeds

1. Preheat oven to 425°F. Lightly grease 2 large baking sheets; set aside. In large bowl, combine flour, baking powder, sugar and salt. Using pastry blender or two knives, cut in butter until mixture resembles coarse crumbs.

2. With wooden spoon, stir in potatoes, beaten eggs and milk all at once, stirring until dough leaves side of bowl. Turn dough out onto lightly floured surface; gently knead 5 times. With lightly floured rolling pin, roll dough to 1/2-inch thickness. Cut out scones with a 2-by-3-inch diamond-shape cutter.

3. Place scones about 1 inch apart on prepared baking sheets. In cup, with fork, beat egg yolk with water until blended; brush some of mixture over top of each scone. Sprinkle each with poppy seeds. Bake 20 to 25 minutes, or until golden-brown.

Makes 2 1/2 dozen.

Hostess Peas

(pictured, pages 190 and 191)

2 medium leeks
4 slices bacon, chopped
1 medium red pepper, julienned
2 packages (10 ounces each) frozen peas, thawed
1/4 cup chopped parsley
1 teaspoon salt
1/8 teaspoon pepper

1. Wash leeks; cut crosswise into thin slices. Set aside. In 3-quart saucepan, over medium heat, sauté bacon until crisp, about 3 minutes. With slotted spoon, remove bacon; set aside.

2. To drippings in pan, add leeks and red pepper; sauté until tender, about 5 minutes. Stir in peas, half the parsley, the salt and pepper. Cook until mixture is heated through. Spoon into serving dish; sprinkle with reserved bacon and remaining chopped parsley.

Makes 8 servings.

Molded Salmon Mousse

(pictured, page 191)

Salad oil
6 ounces sliced smoked salmon
1 can (16 ounces) salmon, drained and skin removed
1 cup heavy cream
1 envelope unflavored gelatine
¼ cup white wine
½ cup boiling water
½ cup mayonnaise
3 small limes
1 tablespoon grated onion and its juice
Dash hot-red-pepper sauce
1 teaspoon ground coriander
½ teaspoon paprika
½ cup chopped pistachios
1 tablespoon minced chives
1 tablespoon minced fresh dill

Cocktail Triangles
1 loaf (about 20 slices) cocktail rye or pumpernickel bread
¼ cup butter or margarine, softened
½ cup minced fresh dill

1. With oil, lightly grease two 2-cup fish-shape molds. Set aside.

2. Cut half of smoked salmon in ½-inch-thick strips. Wrap in plastic wrap; refrigerate. Chop remaining salmon in ¼-inch pieces; set aside. Place canned salmon in food processor or blender. Add ½ cup heavy cream; process until mixture is smooth. Set aside.

3. In medium bowl, sprinkle gelatine over wine; let stand 5 minutes, or until softened. Add boiling water, stirring until gelatine dissolves; set aside until cool. Stir in mayonnaise, the juice of half a lime, the grated onion and onion juice, hot-red-pepper sauce, coriander and paprika until blended.

4. Set bowl in larger bowl of ice and water. Let stand, stirring occasionally, until consistency of unbeaten egg white, about 5 minutes.

5. In small bowl, beat remaining cream until stiff peaks form; with rubber spatula, fold whipped cream, reserved chopped salmon, pureed salmon mixture, chopped pistachios, chives and 1 tablespoon dill into thickened gelatine mixture until no white streaks remain. Pour into prepared molds, dividing evenly. Refrigerate until mousse is firm, about 3 hours or overnight.

6. Make Cocktail Triangles: Trim crust from cocktail loaf; cover all sides of loaf with softened butter. Press ½ cup minced fresh dill into butter. Arrange bread slices in several stacks; cut each stack diagonally in half. Cover with damp paper towels and plastic wrap; refrigerate until serving time.

7. To serve: Unmold each mousse onto serving platter. Thinly slice remaining limes. Using photograph as a guide, arrange lime slices and reserved smoked-salmon strips, overlapping, on top of each mousse. If desired, garnish with lemon-peel bow, sprinkle additional minced fresh dill on top of mousse, and arrange sliced stuffed olives for eyes. Serve with Cocktail Triangles.

Makes about 40 servings.

Roasted Capon With Chestnut Stuffing

(pictured, pages 190 and 191)

8-pound capon
Chestnut Stuffing (recipe follows)
¼ cup butter or margarine, melted
¼ teaspoon salt
⅛ teaspoon pepper
Amaretto Apricot Sauce (recipe follows)

1. Preheat oven to 325°F. Remove giblets and neck from capon; set aside for another use. Remove and discard excess fat. Wash capon; pat dry.

2. Lightly spoon stuffing into neck cavity. Bring neck skin over stuffing; secure with poultry pins. Spoon some of remaining stuffing into body cavity; do not pack. (Place extra stuffing in greased baking dish; cover and bake last 30 minutes capon is in oven.) Close body cavity with poultry pins; lace with string. Tie legs together. Pin wings to breast.

3. Place capon, breast side up, on rack in roasting pan. Brush with melted butter. Sprinkle with salt and pepper. Insert meat thermometer into thickest portion of thigh, away from bone. Roast, uncovered, basting every 30 minutes with drippings, until meat thermometer registers 170°F, about 2½ hours.

4. Place capon on warm serving platter. Remove poultry pins and string. Let stand 15 minutes for easier carving. If desired, garnish with radish sprouts and steamed baby vegetables. To serve, spoon stuffing in turkey into serving bowl; pass sauce separately.

Makes 6 to 8 servings.

Chestnut Stuffing

½ package (1-pound size) bulk pork sausage
1 medium onion, chopped
2 celery stalks, chopped
1½ cups apple juice or cider
1 can (1 pound) whole chestnuts, drained
1 cup raisins
2 tablespoons chopped parsley
½ package (14-ounce size) cubed country-style stuffing mix (4 cups)

In large skillet, over medium-high heat, cook sausage, stirring, until evenly browned. Add onion and celery; sauté 3 minutes longer. Add apple juice, chestnuts, raisins and parsley. Place in large bowl; add stuffing mix. Set aside to cool.

Makes 8 cups.

Amaretto Apricot Sauce

(pictured, page 191)

1 can (1 pound) apricot halves in heavy syrup
2 tablespoons butter or margarine
1 small onion, minced
¼ cup apricot preserves
2 tablespoons lemon juice
¼ cup Amaretto or other almond-flavored liqueur
4 teaspoons cornstarch

Drain apricots, reserving syrup. Slice apricots; set aside. In small saucepan, over medium-high heat, melt butter. Add onion; sauté 2 minutes. Add preserves; stir until melted. Add reserved apricot syrup and the lemon juice. In small cup, blend liqueur with cornstarch. Add to saucepan; cook, stirring, until sauce boils and thickens, about 2 minutes. Add reserved sliced apricots; heat through.

Makes 2½ cups.

Brussels Sprouts Bisque

(pictured, page 191)

½ cup butter or margarine
½ pound mushrooms, sliced
3 medium carrots, pared and julienned
2 pints (1¼ pounds) brussels sprouts, trimmed and halved
1 large onion, chopped
3 cans (about 14 ounces each) chicken broth
½ cup dry white wine
1 tablespoon white-wine Worcestershire sauce
3 tablespoons all-purpose flour
2 cups half-and-half
1¼ teaspoons salt
¼ teaspoon pepper
⅛ teaspoon ground nutmeg
3 tablespoons chopped parsley

1. In 5-quart Dutch oven, over medium-high heat, melt 3 tablespoons butter. Add mushrooms and carrots; sauté until tender, about 5 minutes. With slotted spoon, transfer mushrooms and carrots to bowl; set aside.

2. In same pan, melt remaining butter. Add brussels sprouts and onion; sauté 3 minutes. Stir in broth, wine and Worcestershire. Bring to boiling; simmer, covered, until vegetables are tender, about 10 minutes. Remove pan from heat.

3. Pour soup through colander placed over large bowl or pan. Set aside about ¾ cup brussels-sprouts mixture. Place remaining brussels-sprouts mixture in food processor or blender; puree. Return puree and broth mixture to Dutch oven.

4. Place flour in small bowl; gradually add half-and-half, stirring until smooth. Pour into broth mixture, stirring until blended. Add mushroom mixture, reserved brussels-sprouts mixture, the salt, pepper and nutmeg. Bring to boiling, stirring; simmer 10 minutes, or until thickened, stirring occasionally. Stir in parsley; pour soup into tureen.

Makes 8 servings.

Frozen Banana-Toffee Soufflé

(pictured, page 190)

6 bars (1.4 ounces each) milk-chocolate-covered toffee candy
2 envelopes unflavored gelatine
½ cup orange juice
4 to 5 small ripe bananas
4½ teaspoons lemon juice
8 large egg yolks
1 cup sugar
4 cups heavy cream

1. Using sharp paring knife, cut 1 candy bar crosswise in half. Cut each piece diagonally in half to make 4 triangles; set aside. Finely chop remaining 5 bars; set aside.

2. Prepare soufflé dish: Fold a 26-inch-long piece of aluminum foil lengthwise into thirds. Generously grease one side. Wrap foil strip around outside of 1-quart soufflé dish, placing greased side against dish, so collar stands 3 inches above rim. Secure with string or tape. Set prepared dish aside.

3. In small bowl, sprinkle gelatine over orange juice; let stand 5 minutes, or until softened. Meanwhile, in food processor or blender, puree enough bananas with lemon juice to make 1½ cups. Set aside.

4. In top of double boiler, set over hot, not boiling, water, whisk egg yolks with sugar until thickened, about 10 minutes. Add softened gelatine; stir until dissolved, about 1 minute. Transfer custard to medium bowl; set over larger bowl of ice and water. Cool 2 minutes, stirring constantly. Chill, stirring frequently, until custard is consistency of unbeaten egg white, about 20 minutes. Whisk in banana puree until blended.

5. In large bowl of electric mixer, at high speed, beat 3½ cups heavy cream until soft peaks form. With rubber spatula, fold cream into banana mixture until no white streaks remain. Pour half of soufflé mixture into prepared dish; sprinkle with all but ¼ cup reserved chopped candy. Top with remaining soufflé mixture. Freeze until firm, about 6 hours or overnight.

6. To serve: Remove foil collar from soufflé; pat reserved chopped candy onto soufflé side. Beat remaining heavy cream until stiff; place in pastry bag fitted with star tip. Using photograph as a guide, decorate top of soufflé with cream; garnish with reserved candy triangles.

Makes 10 servings.

■ Spruce up your holiday stuffing with fruit juice. Try substituting apple juice, orange juice or apricot nectar for the water required by your favorite recipe.

Easy Party Appetizers

Easy Chinese Flatbreads

1 package (10 ounces) refrigerated white-bread dough
2 tablespoons salad oil
1 tablespoon dark sesame oil
All-purpose flour
2 green onions, thinly sliced
¼ teaspoon garlic powder
¼ teaspoon salt
2 teaspoons sesame seeds

1. Preheat oven to 400°F. Equally divide dough into four pieces. In small cup, mix salad oil with sesame oil; set aside.
2. On lightly floured board, roll one piece dough to 8-by-4-inch rectangle. Brush with some of oil mixture; sprinkle with some of the green onions and a dash each garlic powder and salt.
3. Starting with long side, roll up dough jelly-roll fashion. With seam side down, shape dough into coil. Flatten with hand; roll to 5-inch round. Repeat procedure with remaining dough.
4. Arrange flatbreads on ungreased baking sheet. Brush each with oil mixture; sprinkle with sesame seeds. Bake 15 minutes, or until golden. Serve warm.

Makes 4 servings.

Cheese-Filled Gouda

2-pound ball Gouda cheese, at room temperature
8 ounces blue cheese, at room temperature
1½ packages (8-ounce size) cream cheese, softened
¾ cup dry sherry
2 cups chopped toasted pecans
Assorted crackers
Fresh pear slices

1. With sharp knife, cut a large slice—about one-third of the cheese—from top of Gouda. If desired, make a zigzag design around the rim of the large portion of the cheese. Scoop out cheese from both cut portions, leaving a ¼-inch-thick shell of large part.
2. Make filling: In large bowl of electric mixer, at low speed, blend cheeses and sherry until well mixed. Fold in pecans. Fill reserved shell with cheese mixture; cover and chill several hours to develop flavors. Bring cheese ball to room temperature before serving; serve with crackers and pear slices.

Makes 24 servings.

Teriyaki Wings

2 tablespoons brown sugar
1 medium clove garlic, minced
¼ teaspoon pepper
⅓ cup lemon juice
¼ cup ketchup
¼ cup salad oil
¼ cup teriyaki sauce
3 pounds chicken wings, cut at joint and wing tips removed

1. Make marinade: In medium bowl, combine brown sugar, minced garlic, pepper, lemon juice, ketchup, salad oil and teriyaki sauce. Blend mixture well.
2. Place chicken pieces in 9-by-14-inch baking dish; pour marinade over pieces. Cover and refrigerate at least 6 hours, turning chicken pieces occasionally.
3. Preheat oven to 375°F. Arrange chicken on wire rack in shallow roasting pan. Bake 40 minutes, basting occasionally with marinade, until tender, turning once.

Makes 3 dozen pieces.

Clockwise from top: Easy Chinese Flatbreads, Cheese-Filled Gouda, Teriyaki Wings.

Spirited Drinks Without Spirits

Creamsicle Punch

3 large eggs
2 tablespoons honey
2 cups orange juice, chilled
⅓ cup lemon juice
1 quart vanilla ice cream
1 bottle (32 ounces) lemon-lime-flavored soft drink, chilled
Ground nutmeg

In large bowl of electric mixer, beat eggs with honey until thick and lemon colored. Stir in juices. Cover; refrigerate. Just before serving, spoon ice cream into large punch bowl. Add juice mixture, then soft drink. Sprinkle with nutmeg.

Makes 14 (6-ounce) servings.

Clockwise from bottom: Creamsicle Punch, Mandarin Berry Tea, Pineapple-Lemon Punch, Orange Prune Nog.

Mandarin-Berry Tea

8 orange-spice tea bags
3 cups boiling water
2 cups raspberry-cranberry drink
Juice and pulp of 1 orange
2 tablespoons honey
Orange slices

Place tea bags in heat-safe pitcher. Add water; let steep 5 minutes. Remove tea bags; stir in drink, orange juice and pulp and honey. Add orange slices. Serve hot or cold.

Makes 5 to 6 servings.

Pineapple-Lemon Punch

1 gallon cranberry-apple drink
1 can (46 ounces) pineapple juice
1 can (6 ounces) frozen lemonade concentrate
Ice cubes
3 slices pineapple
Mint sprigs

In large punch bowl, combine cranberry-apple drink, pineapple juice and lemonade. Add ice cubes; garnish with pineapple and mint.

Makes 32 (6-ounce) servings.

■ Holiday entertaining doesn't mean you have to prepare a formal, sit-down dinner. Invite friends over for our assortment of easy-to-make appetizers and refreshing punch or tea before an evening at the theater, for example, or a program at the children's school. You'll find this an easy way to entertain.

Orange-Prune Nog

1 cup plain yogurt
⅔ cup pineapple-orange juice
½ cup apple juice
½ cup prune juice
1 large egg
8 ice cubes
Whipped topping

In blender, combine yogurt with juices and egg. Blend until smooth. Add ice cubes. Blend until smooth. Pour into 4 glasses, dividing evenly; garnish with whipped topping.

Makes 4 servings.

Deluxe Holiday Desserts

Dark-Chocolate-Covered Fruitcake

1 package (16.6 ounces) date-bread mix
1 large egg
1 tablespoon salad oil
½ cup water
½ cup chopped dried apricots
½ cup chopped pecans
½ cup dark rum
8 ounces semisweet chocolate
1 ounce unsweetened baking chocolate
⅓ cup light corn syrup
¼ cup red-currant jelly
1 tube (4 ounces) red decorating icing
Dragées

1. Prepare fruitcake 1 week ahead. Preheat oven to 350°F. Lightly grease 8-by-4-inch loaf pan; line with foil. Lightly grease and flour foil; set aside. In bowl, combine bread mix, egg, oil and water; mix as package label directs. Stir in apricots and pecans; pour into loaf pan. Bake 1 hour, or until done. Cool. Brush with rum. Wrap in plastic wrap; cover with foil. Let rest in refrigerator 1 week.

2. Line large baking sheet with aluminum foil; set aside. In top of double boiler, over hot, not boiling, water, melt semisweet and unsweetened chocolates; stir in syrup. Pour onto prepared baking sheet; cover with waxed paper. With rolling pin, roll to a 14-by-12-inch rectangle. Cool 10 minutes in refrigerator.

3. Remove cake and chocolate from refrigerator. Unwrap cake; place on dish. In saucepan, melt jelly; while jelly is hot, brush over outside of cake. Set aside.

4. With kitchen scissors, cut out panels of chocolate covering the size of cake top and each side. From remaining chocolate, cut 1¼-inch-wide strips. Remove waxed paper. Place panels, foil side out, on cake; carefully remove foil. With hands, press lightly to mold chocolate around cake; pinch seams together and trim bottom edge of chocolate. Remove foil from chocolate strips; using photograph as a guide, and working with one strip at a time, loop strip along length of cake top, using hands to warm chocolate enough to make it pliable without breaking and to join strips.

5. Pipe icing over top edge of chocolate ruffles; attach dragées to icing. Store, covered, in refrigerator. Allow to come to room temperature before slicing.

Makes 12 servings.

Clockwise from top: Dark-Chocolate-Covered Fruitcake, Eggnog-Mousse Pie, Festive Bombe.

Eggnog-Mousse Pie

24 gingersnaps
5 tablespoons melted butter
⅓ cup pecan halves
3 envelopes unflavored gelatine
½ cup water
3½ cups prepared eggnog
2 tablespoons brandy
¼ teaspoon ground nutmeg
1 cup heavy cream, whipped
4 canned pear halves, chopped
¼ cup toasted chopped pecans

1. Preheat oven to 350°F. In food processor, grind gingersnaps. Add butter and ⅓ cup pecan halves; process until nuts are finely chopped. Press mixture over bottom and side of 9-inch pie plate; bake 10 minutes. Cool on wire rack.

2. In large bowl, sprinkle gelatine over water. Let stand 5 minutes. In saucepan, heat 1 cup eggnog until very hot; stir into gelatine mixture until gelatine dissolves. Add remaining eggnog, the brandy and nutmeg. Place bowl in larger bowl of ice and water; chill, stirring occasionally, until thickened, about 15 minutes. Fold in whipped cream, pears and toasted pecans until no white streaks remain. Chill over ice and water until mixture begins to set; spoon into pie shell. Refrigerate until set, about 4 hours. If desired, garnish with sweetened whipped cream and pecan halves.

Makes 8 servings.

Festive Bombe

½ cup chopped red and green candied cherries
½ cup golden raisins
1 package (8 ounces) chopped dates
½ cup chopped hazelnuts
½ cup brandy
3 quarts vanilla ice cream, softened
1 cup crushed bittersweet almond-flavored Italian cookies
1 cup heavy cream, whipped

1. In bowl, combine first 5 ingredients; let stand at room temperature 1 hour.

2. Fold ice cream into fruit mixture; fold in ½ cup crushed cookies. Spoon into 3-quart plum-pudding mold. Cover; freeze overnight.

3. Dip mold into large bowl of very warm water; pat dry. Invert onto platter; remove mold. Place in freezer 1 hour. Pat remaining crumbs over bombe. With whipped cream in pastry bag fitted with star tip, pipe onto bombe. If desired, garnish with mint and raspberries.

Makes 16 servings.

Special Breakfast Section: Weekend Brunch

TOMATO JUICE
CRISP ONION BREAD
HAM-AND-EGG RING
CITRUS COMPOTE
COFFEE OR TEA

Crisp Onion Bread

¼ cup butter or margarine
4 large yellow onions, sliced
1 package (16 ounces) hot-roll mix
2 tablespoons cornmeal
¾ teaspoon caraway seeds

1. In large skillet, melt butter. Add onions; over medium heat, sauté 20 minutes, stirring, until golden-brown. Set aside.

2. Meanwhile, in large bowl, make hot-roll mix as package label directs. Turn out dough onto floured surface. Knead 5 minutes. With lightly floured rolling pin, on floured surface, roll out dough to 14-by-11-inch rectangle. Grease 15½-by-10½-by-1-inch jelly-roll pan; sprinkle with cornmeal. Transfer dough to pan; pat to fit pan. With fork, prick dough. Cover with plastic wrap; let rise 15 minutes.

3. Preheat oven to 400°F. Distribute onions evenly over dough; sprinkle with caraway seeds. Bake 20 minutes or until bread is golden. Cool slightly; cut into pieces.

Makes 8 servings.

Ham-and-Egg Ring

1½ cups finely chopped cooked ham (10 ounces)
2 tablespoons chopped parsley
⅛ teaspoon pepper
Nonstick cooking spray
14 large eggs
2 packages (12 ounces each) mushrooms, cleaned and quartered
2 tablespoons butter or margarine
1 package (0.9 ounce) hollandaise-sauce mix

1. Preheat oven to 350°F. Toss ham with parsley and pepper; set aside. Grease 6-cup ring mold with spray; break 6 eggs into mold. Spoon ham mixture over eggs; break remaining eggs over ham. With spray, grease piece of aluminum foil; arrange, greased side down, over mold. Place mold in roasting pan. Pour hot water in pan to come halfway up side of mold. Bake egg ring 45 minutes, until set.

2. Meanwhile, sauté mushrooms in butter until golden-brown, about 10 minutes.

3. Prepare hollandaise sauce as package label directs; keep warm. Remove foil and invert mold with egg ring onto platter; drain off liquid. Remove mold; spoon mushrooms in center of ring. Pass sauce.

Makes 8 servings.

■ Serve a quick Sunday-style breakfast. Gently simmer prunes or dried pears in cranapple juice with a cinnamon stick for about 5 minutes. Add two oranges, peeled and sectioned; cover and cool. Use as a topping on waffles or pancakes.

Clockwise from top: Crisp Onion Bread, Tomato Juice, Citrus Compote, Coffee, Ham-and-Egg Ring.

Citrus Compote

½ cup sugar
½ cup water
1 small lemon
1 small lime
4 navel oranges
2 grapefruit

In medium saucepan, combine sugar with water; bring to boiling, stirring. Remove peel from lemon and lime in thin strips; add peel to hot syrup. (Save fruit for another use.) Simmer 5 minutes. Peel and slice oranges crosswise; peel, seed and slice grapefruit crosswise. Place fruit in serving bowl; cover with syrup. Serve immediately or chilled.

Makes 8 servings.

How To Get Kids To Love Breakfast

Corn-Muffin Scrambler

4 slices Canadian bacon
4 large eggs
2 tablespoons cream cheese, in small pieces
⅛ teaspoon salt
2 tablespoons butter or margarine
4 corn-muffin toaster cakes, toasted
8 tomato slices

In medium skillet, over medium heat, lightly brown Canadian bacon on both sides. Roll each bacon slice into cornucopia shape; set aside. In small bowl, combine eggs, cream cheese and salt. In clean skillet, over medium heat, melt butter. Add egg mixture; cook 3 minutes, stirring occasionally, until set. On each corn cake, place 2 tomato slices; cover with scrambled eggs, dividing evenly. Top each with bacon slice.

Makes 4 servings.

Little-Man Muffins

1 package (11 ounces) frozen muffins swirled with cinnamon-sugar
1 container (8 ounces) whipped cream cheese with pineapple pieces
12 raisins
2 red apples, cored and thinly sliced

Heat muffins as package label directs; slice crosswise in half. Spread 1 tablespoon cream cheese over cut side of bottom half of each muffin; cover with top half of muffin, cut side down. Place remaining cream cheese in small pastry bag fitted with star tip. Using photograph as a guide, make eyes and hair on each muffin top. Attach raisins to cream-cheese eyes; press apples into muffin for hair, nose and mouth.

Makes 6 servings.

Fruited French Muffins

2 large eggs
⅓ cup orange juice
1 tablespoon cinnamon-sugar
¼ teaspoon vanilla extract
4 English muffins, split and toasted
2 tablespoons butter or margarine
2 cups assorted fruit: sliced kiwifruit, sliced strawberries, pineapple chunks
¾ cup pourable apricot preserves

In pie plate, whisk eggs, orange juice, cinnamon-sugar and vanilla. Add four muffin halves; turn to coat both sides. In 12-inch skillet, over medium heat, melt 1 tablespoon butter. Place prepared muffin halves, cut side down, in skillet; cook until lightly browned on both sides, about 5 minutes in all. Repeat with remaining muffins, egg mixture and butter. Meanwhile, in medium bowl, toss fruit with preserves. Serve mixture over prepared muffins.

Makes 4 servings.

Mouse Muffins

2 slices (¾ ounce each) pasteurized processed American cheese
1 honey-wheat English muffin, split and toasted
2 sausage patties, cooked
1 small carrot
2 slices celery

Place one slice cheese over cut side of each muffin half; broil until cheese melts. Place each muffin half on plate. Cut each sausage patty crosswise in half; set aside. Cut carrot crosswise into 6 thin slices; julienne enough of remainder to make 12 pieces. Using photograph as a guide, arrange sausage ears, carrot eyes, mouth, whiskers, and celery nose on each muffin half.

Makes 2 servings.

Clockwise from right: Corn-Muffin Scrambler, Little-Man Muffins, Mouse Muffin, Fruited French Muffins.

Lite Eating: A Savory Holiday Feast

Roasted Game Hens With Harvest Vegetables

2 tablespoons lemon juice
2 tablespoons salad oil
4 medium cloves garlic, crushed
1 tablespoon Worcestershire sauce
4 teaspoons prepared cayenne-pepper sauce
2 teaspoons dried thyme leaves, crushed
1 teaspoon dried sage leaves, crushed
2 teaspoons lemon pepper
1 teaspoon paprika
½ teaspoon ground allspice
3 Cornish hens (¾ pound each)
1 quart water
1 teaspoon salt
4 medium turnips, pared and sliced
1 package (12 ounces) baby carrots, pared
12 green onions, cut in 2-inch lengths
½ pound cherry tomatoes

1. In small bowl, mix lemon juice, oil, garlic, Worcestershire, pepper sauce, thyme, sage, lemon pepper, paprika and allspice. Set mixture aside.

2. With poultry shears, split hens lengthwise; remove and discard backbone and neck. In large roasting pan, arrange hens skin side up. Brush with half the lemon-juice mixture, dividing evenly.

3. Preheat oven to 425°F. In large saucepan, bring water and salt to boiling. Add turnips; simmer, covered, until tender-crisp, about 4 minutes. Drain; place in large bowl. Add carrots, onions and tomatoes; toss with remaining lemon-juice mixture. Place vegetables around hens in roasting pan. Bake 50 minutes, or until hens are cooked. To serve, arrange hens and vegetables on a serving platter; if desired, garnish platter with sage leaves.

Makes 6 servings, 469 calories each.

Apple Tart Deluxe

Nonstick cooking spray
3 pounds assorted apples (Golden Delicious, Granny Smith, McIntosh)
2 teaspoons julienne lemon peel
¼ cup low-calorie apricot conserve
2 tablespoons lemon juice
¼ teaspoon ground nutmeg
⅛ teaspoon ground allspice
1 ounce dried apricots, thinly sliced
Mint sprig

1. Preheat oven to 375°F. With aluminum foil, cover outside of 8-inch springform pan; grease inside with cooking spray. Set aside. Core and thinly slice apples; place in large bowl. Add remaining ingredients except mint sprig; toss to combine.

2. Using photograph as a guide, arrange apples, overlapping and with skin side facing side of pan, in layers. Cover tightly with foil; place on jelly-roll pan. Bake 50 minutes; remove foil. Bake until apples are tender, about 15 minutes longer. Cool in pan. Serve at room temperature, garnished with mint sprig. For ease in slicing, use electric knife.

Makes 9 servings, 98 calories each.

Mixed Green Salad

5 cups bite-size pieces of mixed salad greens, washed and crisped
1 small cucumber, scored and thinly sliced
1 jar (4 ounces) roasted red peppers, drained and quartered
¼ cup lemon juice
½ teaspoon freshly cracked black pepper

In large salad bowl, arrange salad greens, cucumber slices and pepper quarters. Add lemon juice and cracked black pepper; toss until salad greens are coated. Serve in large salad bowl or spoon into individual salad plates or bowls.

Makes 6 servings, 17 calories each.

Clockwise from top left: Mixed Green Salad, Apple Tart Deluxe, Roasted Game Hens With Harvest Vegetables.

Micro-Way: Festive First Courses

Clams Casino

6 slices bacon
24 littleneck clams, shucked and on the half shell
¼ cup butter or margarine
1 medium clove garlic, crushed
¼ cup finely chopped green onions
¼ cup finely chopped tomato
2 tablespoons lime juice
Lemon and lime wedges (optional)

1. Place bacon on microwave-safe rack in glass baking dish; cover with paper towel. Cook on HIGH 3 minutes, or until partially cooked. Cut each piece crosswise into quarters; set aside. Place clams, hinge side toward rim, around side of 12-inch round microwave-safe serving dish or tray.

2. In small bowl, cook butter and garlic on LOW 30 seconds, or until softened, stirring once. Place ½ teaspoon garlic-butter mixture on each clam. Spoon green onions and tomato onto each clam, dividing evenly. Sprinkle lime juice on top of filled clams, dividing evenly. Top each filled clam with a piece of partially cooked bacon.

3. Cover clams with sheet of waxed paper; cook on MEDIUM 8 minutes, or until clams and bacon are cooked. Let stand, covered, 2 minutes. If desired, pass lemon and lime wedges separately.

Makes 6 servings.

Clams Casino (left), Madeira Pâté, served with assorted toasts.

Madeira Pâté

2 tablespoons butter or margarine
1 large onion, chopped
¼ pound mushrooms, chopped
1 pound chicken livers
3 tablespoons Madeira or port wine
¼ teaspoon dried tarragon leaves, crushed
½ teaspoon salt
⅛ teaspoon freshly cracked pepper
Chopped parsley
Sieved hard-cooked egg yolk
Melba and other toasts

1. In 2-quart microwave-safe baking dish, cook butter, onion and mushrooms on HIGH 4 minutes, stirring once. Add livers, Madeira, tarragon, salt and pepper; mix well. Cook, covered, on MEDIUM 10 minutes, or until livers are no longer pink, stirring occasionally. (Do not overcook livers.) Let stand, covered, 5 minutes.

2. In food processor, puree liver mixture; place in 3-cup crock. Cover; let mellow in refrigerator at least 6 hours or overnight. Using photograph as a guide, garnish with chopped parsley and sieved hard-cooked egg yolk. Serve with assorted toasts.

Makes 8 to 10 servings.

Sherried Zucchini Bisque

2 tablespoons butter or margarine
1 medium onion, chopped
1 medium clove garlic, crushed
2 medium potatoes, pared and grated (2 cups)
1 pound zucchini, shredded
1 can (about 14 ounces) chicken broth
1 medium carrot, pared and shredded
2 tablespoons sherry
1 tablespoon chopped fresh dill
⅛ teaspoon ground nutmeg
1 cup heavy cream
½ teaspoon salt
⅛ teaspoon pepper

1. In 3-quart microwave-safe casserole, cook butter, onion and garlic on HIGH 2 minutes. Add potatoes; cover. Cook on HIGH 8 minutes, stirring after 4 minutes. Set aside ½ cup shredded zucchini; add remainder to potato mixture. Cook, covered, on HIGH 5 minutes, stirring once, until mixture boils and vegetables are tender. Place mixture in food processor or electric blender; puree. Return to casserole.

2. Add water to chicken broth to make 2 cups; stir into puree in casserole. Add carrot, sherry, dill and nutmeg; cook, covered, on HIGH 6 minutes, or until boiling. Add reserved zucchini; cook on HIGH 5 minutes longer, or until vegetables are tender. Stir in cream, salt and pepper. To serve, pour soup into tureen. If desired, garnish soup with a dill sprig.

Makes 8 servings.

Right: Sherried Zucchini Bisque.

■ Embellish party punches with jumbo "fruit cubes"—juices frozen with cherries or lemon or lime slices in muffin-pan cups—for prettier, tastier ice cubes.

December

'Tis the season for serving your very best recipes. Two to try this holiday: bouillabaisse, chock-full of seafood in a wine-laced tomato broth, and a honey-and-mustard-glazed turkey breast stuffed with spinach, ham and peppers. Or choose from other dressed-up dishes listed below and pictured in the next two lavish spreads.

Bouillabaisse With French-Bread Twists

Turkey Breast Florentine With Citrus-Glazed Carrots

Prime Rib a l'Orange

Orange Béarnaise

Wild-Rice Yorkshire Pudding   Zuppa Inglese

Shrimp and Leek Tarts   Acorn Squash Rings

Consommé Bellevue   Chicken Livers Montrachet

Baked Broccoli-Stuffed Tomatoes

Holiday Stuffed Goose

Christmas Cloud Cake

Old-fashioned Christmas Cookbook

Enjoy a classic English meal—rib roast with Yorkshire pudding or a dressed-up holiday goose.

Bouillabaisse With French-Bread Twists

(pictured, page 209)

¼ cup olive oil
1 cup chopped onion
2 large cloves garlic, crushed
1 can (28 ounces) peeled, crushed tomatoes in puree
2 cups water
1 cup dry white wine
1 teaspoon grated orange peel
1 teaspoon salt
½ teaspoon dried thyme leaves, crushed
¼ teaspoon fennel seeds
2 bay leaves
Dash hot-red-pepper sauce
1-pound "chicken" lobster
¾ pound mussels, scrubbed
½ pound steamer or littleneck clams, scrubbed
1 pound halibut or cod fillet
½ pound large shrimp, shelled and deveined
French-Bread Twists (recipe follows)

1. In 6-quart Dutch oven, heat olive oil over medium-high heat. Add onion and garlic; sauté until soft, about 3 minutes. Add tomatoes, water, wine, orange peel, salt, thyme, fennel, bay leaves and hot-red-pepper sauce. Bring to boiling; simmer, covered, 30 minutes. (If desired, cool and refrigerate.)

2. Add lobster. Return mixture to boiling; simmer, covered, 10 minutes. Turn lobster over. Add mussels and clams. Cover; simmer 10 minutes, or until lobster turns red and shellfish open. Cut fish into 2-inch chunks; add with shrimp to mixture. Cover; simmer 5 minutes, or until fish and shrimp are just cooked.

3. Remove pan from heat. With tongs, place lobster on cutting board. Using paper towels or potholders, twist off tail; with large chef's knife, cut tail crosswise through shell into 3 or 4 pieces. Twist off large claws; with hammer, lightly crack. With large chef's knife, cut claws in half. Discard feelers and body. Return tail and claw pieces to soup; heat through. Remove bay leaves. Ladle into tureen; if desired, garnish with fresh thyme. Serve with French-Bread Twists.

Makes 8 servings.

Page 209: Bouillabaisse With French-Bread Twists, Turkey Breast Florentine With Citrus-Glazed Carrots.

Pages 210 and 211: (Clockwise from top left) Orange Béarnaise, Prime Rib a l'Orange, Wild-Rice Yorkshire Pudding, Zuppa Inglese, Shrimp and Leek Tarts, Acorn Squash Rings.

Pages 212 and 213: (Clockwise from top) Consommé Bellevue, Chicken Livers Montrachet, Holiday Stuffed Goose, Baked Broccoli-Stuffed Tomatoes, Christmas Cloud Cake.

French-Bread Twists

1 package (2 pounds) frozen bread dough, thawed, at room temperature (2 loaves)
¼ cup butter or margarine, melted
2 large cloves garlic, crushed
1 tablespoon grated Parmesan cheese
1½ teaspoons dried dillweed
1½ teaspoons dried oregano leaves, crushed
½ teaspoon paprika

1. Lightly grease 2 large baking sheets; set aside.

2. Cut each loaf of dough lengthwise into quarters for a total of 8 pieces. On lightly floured surface, with hands, roll each dough strip into a thin rope about 24 inches long. Tightly twist 2 ropes together; place diagonally on a prepared baking sheet. Repeat with remaining dough, arranging 2 twists on each baking sheet; set aside. (See *Note.*)

3. In small bowl, mix butter with garlic; brush over twists, dividing

evenly. Sprinkle one with Parmesan, one with dillweed, one with oregano and one with paprika.

4. Let bread rise in a warm place (about 80°F), free from drafts, until doubled in bulk, about 30 minutes.

5. Preheat oven to 375°F. Bake twists 18 minutes, or until deep golden-brown.

Makes 4 twists.

Note: If baking sheets are not large enough to accommodate 2 bread twists each, twist, raise and bake half of bread dough at a time.

Turkey Breast Florentine With Citrus-Glazed Carrots

(pictured, page 209)

Stuffing
2 tablespoons olive oil
1 medium onion, chopped
1 medium clove garlic, crushed
2 cups sliced mushrooms
1 package (10 ounces) whole-leaf spinach, thawed
1 red pepper, diced
½ cup (2½ ounces) diced ham
1 carrot, pared and shredded
1 cup (4 ounces) shredded mozzarella cheese
½ cup fine dry bread crumbs
2 large eggs, beaten
½ teaspoon salt
¼ teaspoon freshly ground black pepper
¼ teaspoon dried thyme leaves, crushed

6¼-pound boneless turkey breast (skin on)
2 tablespoons honey
2 tablespoons Dijon-style mustard
Citrus-Glazed Carrots (recipe follows)

1. Make stuffing: Heat olive oil in large skillet over medium heat. Add onion and garlic; sauté until softened, about 4 minutes. Add mushrooms; sauté 4 minutes. Squeeze spinach dry; add to mushroom mixture. Sauté 2 minutes. Add red pepper, ham and carrot; sauté until all moisture evaporates, about 3 minutes. Set mixture aside to cool. Stir in mozzarella, bread crumbs, eggs, salt, black pepper and thyme. Set stuffing aside.

2. Preheat oven to 425°F. Remove any excess fat from turkey breast. Place skin side down on work surface. Fold breast fillets to the outside. With sharp knife, butterfly thicker portions of breast to make it uniformly thick, turning the pieces to the outside to make a rectangle. Cover breast with waxed paper; with meat mallet, pound to flatten slightly.

3. Spoon stuffing down center over length of breast, pressing lightly to compact mixture in a 2- to 3-inch-wide strip. Bring sides of turkey breast together; secure with poultry pins. Grease large sheet of heavy-duty aluminum foil; place on another sheet of heavy-duty aluminum foil, greased side up. Place turkey breast on greased foil; wrap in double thickness of foil, sealing tightly.

4. Place wrapped turkey roll in roasting pan. Bake 40 minutes. Reduce heat to 350°F; carefully open foil packet to expose turkey. In custard cup, blend honey with mustard; brush mixture over turkey. Bake 30 minutes longer, basting turkey every 10 minutes with honey-mustard mixture. Let turkey roll rest 10 minutes before removing pins and slicing. Arrange turkey roll on a serving platter along with Citrus-Glazed Carrots.

Makes 8 to 10 servings.

Citrus-Glazed Carrots

3 pounds baby carrots, untrimmed
2 oranges
2 limes
¼ cup butter or margarine
2 tablespoons sugar
⅔ cup water

1. Trim carrots, leaving ½-inch green top. Pare; set aside. Using a citrus stripper, remove peel from oranges and limes; place peel in bowl of cold water. Set aside.

2. Squeeze juice from fruits into large skillet. Add butter, sugar and water; stir until sugar dissolves. Add carrots. Cover; bring to boiling. Simmer 5 minutes, or until carrots are tender-crisp.

3. With slotted spoon, remove carrots to bowl; keep warm. Bring cooking liquid to boiling; boil 1 minute, or until syrupy. Add carrots to syrup; stir to coat. Spoon carrots into serving dish; garnish with reserved citrus-peel strips.

Makes 8 servings.

■ Timing the serving of homemade dinner rolls is easy. Bake a favorite recipe of rolls to within five minutes of being done; they'll be golden-brown and firm on top, crusty on the bottom. Remove pan from oven; brush rolls with melted butter, and slide them onto an aluminum-foil-lined wire rack, not breaking rolls apart. Wrap tightly in foil and freeze. Thaw at room temperature for two hours; place, wrapped, on baking sheet, and peel back foil. Brush with melted butter, if desired. Heat ten minutes at 350°F.

Prime Rib à l'Orange
(pictured, pages 210 and 211)

Tarragon-Glazed Orange Peel
1 medium navel orange
1 tablespoon salt
½ cup sugar
1 large sprig fresh tarragon or 2 teaspoons dried tarragon leaves
⅓ cup tarragon-flavored wine vinegar
⅔ cup water

11- to 12-pound beef rib roast (4 ribs)
2 tablespoons coarse salt
1 teaspoon freshly ground black pepper
1 carrot, coarsely chopped
1 celery stalk, coarsely chopped
1 medium onion, coarsely chopped

Au Jus
1 carrot, coarsely chopped
1 celery stalk, coarsely chopped
1 large onion, coarsely chopped
3 parsley sprigs
4 cups water
4 beef-flavored bouillon cubes

Fresh tarragon sprigs
Orange Béarnaise
Wild-Rice Yorkshire Pudding

1. Day before: Quarter orange lengthwise. Remove pulp; reserve for another use. Remove and discard pith from peel; cut peel into ¼-inch-wide strips. Mix peel with 1 tablespoon salt and enough water to cover. Weight down peel to immerse; cover and soak overnight. Drain; rinse under cold water.

2. In non-aluminum-lined saucepan, combine sugar, tarragon, vinegar and water. Bring to boiling; add peel. Simmer, uncovered, until peel is glazed, about 25 minutes. Cool slightly; drain. Set aside. Glazed peel can be refrigerated up to 3 days.

3. Allow roast to come to room temperature, leaving meat unrefrigerated no longer than 2 hours. Adjust oven rack to the lowest position. Preheat oven to 500°F.

4. In custard cup, mix coarse salt and the black pepper. Rub mixture over fat on top of the roast. Place vegetables in large roasting pan; place roast on top. Insert meat thermometer in meat in center of the roast, away from bones. Roast 20 minutes. Reduce oven temperature to 325°F. Roast until the meat thermometer registers 130°F for medium-rare, about 2 hours.

5. Remove roast from oven; transfer to serving platter. Reserve drippings in pan for Wild-Rice Yorkshire Pudding. Cover roast loosely with aluminum foil; set aside in a warm place 30 minutes to allow juices to set. (Meat will continue to cook as it stands.)

6. Meanwhile, make au jus: In saucepan, combine carrot, celery, onion, parsley and water. Bring to boiling; stir in bouillon cubes until dissolved. Simmer until vegetables are tender, about 25 minutes. Strain broth and reserve; discard vegetables. Pour off and reserve drippings from roast; pour broth into pan. Bring to boiling, stirring to loosen brown bits; simmer 5 minutes.

7. Garnish roast with tarragon-glazed orange peel and tarragon sprigs. Serve roast with au jus, Orange Béarnaise and Wild-Rice Yorkshire Pudding.

Makes 12 servings.

Orange Béarnaise
(pictured, page 210)

¼ cup tarragon-flavored wine vinegar
3 tablespoons orange juice
2 tablespoons minced shallots
2 tablespoons minced fresh tarragon or 2 teaspoons dried tarragon leaves
3 large egg yolks
½ teaspoon grated orange peel
½ teaspoon salt
¼ teaspoon ground white pepper
1 cup unsalted butter, melted and warm

1. In small, non-aluminum-lined saucepan, combine vinegar, orange juice, shallots and tarragon; bring to boiling. Boil until liquid is reduced to 1 tablespoon, about 10 minutes. (Watch mixture carefully after first 5 minutes.) Cool.

2. Strain vinegar mixture into electric blender; reserve solids. To liquid in blender, add egg yolks, orange peel, salt and white pepper. Turn blender on and off once or twice to combine ingredients. With motor running on BLEND, add butter in a fine, steady stream, until mixture is blended and thick. Transfer to bowl; stir in reserved shallot mixture. Sauce can be made up to 1 hour before serving. To keep sauce until serving, cover surface directly with plastic wrap; set in larger bowl of warm, not hot, water.

Makes 1 cup.

■ You don't have to worry about meat mishaps. *If your roast is too rare,* arrange end slices on platter and return roast to oven, or slice and broil rare slices to desired doneness. *If meat is overcooked,* dip slices into gravy and arrange on platter. It's also a good idea to keep parsley on hand to add color; then just chop and sprinkle over meat.

■ Here's a quick, simple hint for prettier potatoes—especially attractive when served with your holiday roast. All you need to do is to use a melon baller to scoop out small spheres from unpared potatoes; then boil in salted water for about 10 minutes, or until potatoes are tender. Toss potatoes with butter and parsley—delicious and fancy.

Wild-Rice Yorkshire Pudding

(pictured, page 211)

¼ cup beef drippings (see *Note*)
5 large eggs
2 cups milk
1 teaspoon Worcestershire sauce
1½ teaspoons salt
1½ cups unsifted all-purpose flour
2½ cups cooked seasoned wild rice, at room temperature

1. Preheat oven to 450°F. Place 1 teaspoon beef drippings in each of twelve 3-by-1½-inch muffin-pan cups. Heat in oven 3 minutes, or until very hot.

2. Meanwhile, in electric blender, combine eggs, milk, Worcestershire and salt; blend until mixed. Add flour; blend until smooth. Pour into large bowl; stir in rice.

3. Pour into hot drippings in muffin cups, dividing evenly. Bake 30 minutes, until puffed and brown.

Makes 12 servings.

Note: Reserve drippings from prime rib.

Zuppa Inglese

(pictured, page 211)

6 large egg yolks
½ cup sugar
⅓ cup almond-flavored liqueur
½ package (11-ounce size) frozen pound cake, thawed
¼ cup seedless raspberry jam
1½ cups heavy cream
½ cup crushed bittersweet almond-flavored Italian cookies
Whole small bittersweet almond-flavored Italian cookies
Raspberries

1. In top of double boiler, with portable electric mixer, beat egg yolks and sugar until thick and lemon-colored. Gradually beat in liqueur. Place over simmering, not boiling, water. Beat until mixture mounds and is almost double in volume, about 5 minutes. Remove from heat; transfer mixture to medium bowl. Cover; refrigerate until cool.

2. Cut cake into 16 thin slices. Spread each slice with about ½ teaspoon raspberry jam. Arrange slices, jam side up, around side and bottom of 1½- to 2-quart glass bowl.

3. In large bowl of electric mixer, at high speed, beat cream until stiff, moist peaks form. With rubber spatula, fold two-thirds of the whipped cream into egg-yolk mixture. Spoon half of mixture over cake slices; sprinkle with half of cookie crumbs. Repeat layers, sprinkling crumbs in center only of top layer.

4. Spoon remaining whipped cream into pastry bag fitted with star tip; pipe around cookie crumbs on top of Zuppa Inglese. Garnish with whole cookies and raspberries.

Makes 8 servings.

Acorn Squash Rings

(pictured, page 210)

2 large (about 1½ pounds each) acorn squash
2 tablespoons butter or margarine
2 tablespoons maple syrup

Filling
1 medium onion
1 large Golden Delicious apple
1 large Red Delicious apple
1 navel orange
1 banana
2 tablespoons butter or margarine
¼ teaspoon curry powder
½ teaspoon salt
¼ teaspoon freshly ground black pepper
2 tablespoons toasted almonds, chopped

1. Preheat oven to 350°F. Cover large baking sheet with aluminum foil; grease. Set aside.

2. Cut off and discard ends from squash. Slice each crosswise into 4 rings. Discard seeds. Place on prepared baking sheet; set aside.

3. In small saucepan, bring 2 tablespoons butter and the maple syrup to boiling; boil until syrupy, about 30 seconds. Brush some of syrup mixture over squash rings; reserve remainder. Cover with aluminum foil; bake 30 minutes. Uncover; bake, basting occasionally with syrup mixture, until tender, about 25 minutes.

4. Meanwhile, make filling: Quarter and slice onion; set aside. Cut apples into ½-inch cubes; set aside. Peel, section and cut orange into 1-inch pieces; place in small bowl and set aside. Slice banana; add to orange. In skillet, over medium-high heat, melt 2 tablespoons butter. Add onion; sauté until softened, about 3 minutes. Add apples; sauté until tender but not mushy, about 3 minutes. Stir in curry powder; add orange mixture, salt and pepper. Cook, stirring, until heated.

5. Place squash rings on serving dish; spoon filling into centers, dividing evenly; sprinkle with almonds. Use wide spatula to serve.

Makes 8 servings.

■ For a flavor extravaganza, make your own curry: In a heavy skillet, combine 3 tablespoons coriander seeds, 3 tablespoons dried red-pepper flakes, 5 tablespoons mustard seed and 1 tablespoon black peppercorns. Cook over very low heat 15 minutes, stirring occasionally. In blender or spice grinder, combine roasted spices with 3 tablespoons ground turmeric, 1 tablespoon each of ground cinnamon, cloves and cardamom seeds. Process until fine powder. Store in airtight jar.

Shrimp and Leek Tarts

(pictured, page 210)

Pastry
2 cups unsifted all-purpose flour
½ cup cold butter or margarine
½ teaspoon salt
2 large eggs
2 tablespoons ice water

Filling
8 large leeks
6 tablespoons butter or margarine
1 large egg white
1 tablespoon water
1¼ cups heavy cream
5 large egg yolks
1¼ teaspoons salt
¼ teaspoon freshly ground black pepper
⅛ teaspoon ground nutmeg
24 medium shrimp, shelled and deveined
½ teaspoon dried oregano leaves, crushed

1. Make pastry: In food processor, combine flour, cold butter and ½ teaspoon salt. Process until mixture resembles coarse crumbs. In custard cup, with fork, beat eggs with ice water until mixed; add to flour mixture. Mix, turning machine on and off 4 times, or until dough begins to hold together. Turn out onto surface; press together to form a disk. Wrap in plastic wrap; chill until firm, at least 1 hour or overnight.

2. Make filling: Trim, split and rinse leeks; thinly slice. In skillet, over medium heat, melt 4 tablespoons butter; add leeks. Cook, covered, 6 minutes. Uncover; over medium-high heat, sauté 4 minutes, or until liquid evaporates. Set aside.

3. Preheat oven to 400°F. Divide pastry into 8 equal pieces. On lightly floured surface, with lightly floured rolling pin, roll each piece into a 5-inch round. Fit each into a 4-inch tart pan with removable bottom. With fork, prick pastry on bottom. Place tart shells on baking sheet; bake 10 minutes. In custard cup, with fork, beat egg white with water. Brush mixture over inside of tart shells. Bake 2 minutes longer. Cool on wire rack. Reduce oven temperature to 375°F.

4. In medium bowl, whisk heavy cream with egg yolks, 1 teaspoon salt, the black pepper and nutmeg. Sprinkle prepared leeks over bottom of tart shells, dividing evenly. Pour cream mixture into tart shells, dividing evenly. Bake 15 minutes, or until custard is set. Meanwhile, in large skillet over medium-high heat, melt remaining butter. Add shrimp, oregano and remaining ¼ teaspoon salt; sauté 4 minutes, or until shrimp are cooked. Using photograph as a guide, arrange 3 shrimp over custard in each tart. If desired, garnish each with a sprig of fresh oregano. Remove tarts from pans; serve hot.

Makes 8 servings.

Consommé Bellevue

(pictured, pages 212 and 213)

6 cups chicken broth
4 bottles (8 ounces each) clam juice
1 small clove garlic, crushed
⅛ teaspoon ground white pepper
¼ cup julienne carrot (1½ inches long)
½ cup heavy cream
Dash salt
12 thin slices lemon
2 tablespoons minced parsley

1. In 4-quart saucepan, bring broth, clam juice, garlic and white pepper to boiling. Simmer 10 minutes. Strain broth into another large saucepan; add carrot. Bring to boiling; simmer until carrot is tender, about 10 minutes.

2. Meanwhile, in small bowl of electric mixer, beat cream with salt until soft peaks form. Serve soup in bowls, garnished with whipped cream, lemon slice and parsley.

Makes 12 servings.

Chicken Livers Montrachet

(pictured, page 213)

1 pound chicken livers
4 slices bacon
½ cup sliced green onion
1½ cups sliced mushrooms
4½ teaspoons all-purpose flour
⅓ cup chicken broth
2 large tomatoes, seeded and coarsely chopped
1¼ teaspoons salt
¼ teaspoon freshly ground pepper
2 cups water
¾ cup butter or margarine
2 cups unsifted all-purpose flour
8 large eggs
2 large egg yolks, beaten

1. Separate and trim livers; set aside. Cut bacon into ½-inch pieces. In large skillet, over medium-high heat, sauté bacon until crisp, about 6 minutes. With slotted spoon, remove to bowl. To hot drippings in skillet, add livers; sauté until brown on the outside but pink inside, about 3 minutes. With slotted spoon, remove livers and add to bacon. To hot drippings in skillet, add green onion; sauté 2 minutes. Add mushrooms; sauté 2 minutes. Stir in 4½ teaspoons flour until blended; cook until bubbly. Stir in broth, tomatoes, ¾ teaspoon salt and the pepper until blended; bring to boiling, stirring. Simmer 5 minutes; set aside.

2. In large saucepan, bring water, butter and ½ teaspoon salt to boiling. Remove pan from heat; immediately add 2 cups flour all at once. With wooden spoon, beat until dough leaves side of pan. Over medium heat, cook dough, beating

constantly, 1 minute. Away from heat, beat in 8 eggs, one at a time, blending egg completely into dough before each addition. Beat until dough is smooth.

3. Preheat oven to 400°F. Spoon dough into 8 large custard cups, dividing evenly. Using back of metal spoon, spread dough to line each cup. With pastry brush, brush some beaten egg yolk over dough in each cup; spoon chicken-liver mixture into each cup. Place filled cups on baking sheet. Bake 40 minutes, or until pastry is puffed and brown.

Makes 8 servings.

Baked Broccoli-Stuffed Tomatoes

(pictured, pages 212 and 213)

2 packages (10 ounces each) frozen chopped broccoli, thawed and drained
3 tablespoons butter or margarine
1 cup (4 ounces) shredded fontina cheese
¼ cup heavy cream
1 teaspoon salt
⅛ teaspoon pepper
⅛ teaspoon ground nutmeg
4 medium tomatoes

1. In food processor, puree broccoli; set aside. In large saucepan, over medium heat, melt butter. Add broccoli; sauté until tender, about 3 minutes. Add cheese, heavy cream, salt, pepper and nutmeg. Heat until cheese melts; set aside.

2. Preheat oven to 350°F. Lightly grease 13-by-9-by-2-inch baking dish. Cut tomatoes horizontally in half; with spoon, remove seeds. Place tomatoes in prepared dish.

3. Spoon broccoli mixture into pastry bag fitted with ½-inch star tip. Pipe into each tomato half, dividing evenly. Bake until tomatoes are tender, about 10 minutes.

Makes 8 servings.

Holiday Stuffed Goose

(pictured, pages 212 and 213)

16-pound young goose
Salt
2 cups water
½ teaspoon salt

Stuffing
1 pound bacon, coarsely chopped
1 pound seasoned bulk pork sausage, coarsely chopped
2 large celery stalks, coarsely chopped
2 large onions, coarsely chopped
½ pound mushrooms, sliced
1 package (14 ounces) herb-seasoned stuffing mix
1 package (12 ounces) fresh cranberries
1 can (about 14 ounces) chicken broth
1 tablespoon dried sage leaves, crushed
1 tablespoon dried thyme leaves, crushed

Lingonberry Sauce
1 tablespoon grated orange peel
1 jar (14 ounces) lingonberry sauce or 1 can (16 ounces) whole-berry cranberry sauce
⅓ cup red-currant jelly
⅓ cup freshly squeezed orange juice
⅓ cup butter or margarine

1. Line large roasting pan with heavy duty aluminum foil; set aside. Prepare goose: About 5 hours before serving, remove neck and giblets from body cavity; set aside. Remove and discard excess fat and neck skin. Rinse bird well; drain. With paper towels, pat dry on inside and outside. Lightly sprinkle inside cavities with salt. Place goose, breast side up, on rack in prepared roasting pan; cover loosely with plastic wrap. Refrigerate goose while cooking giblets and preparing stuffing.

2. In large saucepan, bring water and ½ teaspoon salt to boiling. Add neck and all giblets except liver; simmer, covered, 1½ hours, or until tender, adding liver last 5 minutes of cooking time. Drain giblets; cool. Chop coarsely; set aside. Reserve broth for another use.

3. Make stuffing: Preheat oven to 400°F. In large skillet, over medium-high heat, sauté bacon until almost cooked. Add sausage to skillet; sauté until sausage is lightly browned and bacon is crisp. Add celery, onions and mushrooms; sauté 5 minutes longer. With slotted spoon, transfer mixture to large bowl. Add stuffing mix, fresh cranberries, chicken broth, sage, thyme and reserved giblets; stir mixture lightly until well blended.

4. Spoon stuffing into breast and neck cavities of goose—do not pack (place extra stuffing in greased baking dish; cover and bake last hour goose is in oven). Close cavities with poultry pins. Lace with string; tie legs together. Pin wings to breast. Insert meat thermometer deep into inside thigh muscle, away from bone. Pour 2 cups water in pan to prevent grease from spattering. Roast goose, uncovered, on rack in prepared pan, 1 hour, spooning or siphoning off accumulated fat every half hour. Reduce oven temperature to 325°F. Roast goose until thermometer registers 175°F, about 2 hours longer. Cool goose, loosely covered, 15 minutes before carving. Remove legs or slice meat from legs; place on sheet of aluminum foil. Fold edges over to seal. Return to oven to cook until of desired doneness, about 20 minutes. Meanwhile, remove breast from goose; carve crosswise into slices.

5. Make sauce: In small saucepan, bring all sauce ingredients to boiling. Simmer 15 minutes. Serve hot with goose.

Makes 8 to 10 servings.

Christmas Cloud Cake

(pictured, page 212)

Cake

3½ cups unsifted cake flour
4 teaspoons baking powder
1 teaspoon salt
1 cup butter or margarine, softened
2 cups sugar
2 teaspoons vanilla extract
1 cup milk
8 large egg whites, at room temperature

Filling

1 cup chopped pecans
¾ cup chopped dates
½ cup chopped candied cherries
½ cup chopped raisins
¼ cup brandy or bourbon

Frosting

2¼ cups sugar
¾ teaspoon cream of tartar
½ cup water
6 large egg whites, at room temperature
¾ teaspoon vanilla extract

Garnish

Pitted dates, small dried figs, maraschino cherries with stems, candied-pineapple rings, pecan halves

1. Make cake: Preheat oven to 350°F. Grease and flour three 9-by-1½-inch round cake pans; set aside. On sheet of waxed paper, combine flour with baking powder and salt; set aside. In large bowl of electric mixer, at high speed, beat butter until fluffy. Add 1½ cups sugar and 2 teaspoons vanilla; at high speed, beat 2 minutes, or until mixture is light and fluffy. With rubber spatula, fold flour mixture into butter mixture alternately with milk, beginning and ending with flour mixture. Transfer to large mixing bowl.

2. In clean large bowl of electric mixer, at medium speed, beat 8 egg whites until frothy. At high speed, beat until soft peaks form. Beat in remaining ½ cup sugar until stiff peaks form. With rubber spatula, fold egg-white mixture into flour mixture just until no white streaks remain. (Do not overfold.) Spread batter into prepared pans; bake 25 minutes, or until cake layers spring back when gently pressed with fingertip. Cool cakes in pans on wire racks 10 minutes; turn out onto wire racks to cool layers completely.

3. Make filling: In medium bowl, combine filling ingredients. Let stand at room temperature 1 hour.

4. Meanwhile, make frosting (see *Note*): In medium saucepan, mix 2¼ cups sugar, the cream of tartar and water. Bring to boiling, stirring; boil until mixture registers 240°F on candy thermometer. In large bowl of electric mixer, at high speed, beat 6 egg whites until soft peaks form. With mixer at high speed, slowly pour sugar syrup into egg whites in a thin stream. Add ¾ teaspoon vanilla; beat until stiff.

5. With rubber spatula, fold 2 cups frosting into filling mixture. Place 1 cake layer on serving plate; top with half the filling mixture. Repeat with another cake layer and remaining filling. Top with remaining cake layer. Frost top and side of cake with remaining frosting; using photograph as a guide, garnish top with dates, figs, cherries, pineapple and pecans.

Makes 16 servings.

Note: It is best not to make frosting on a humid day.

■ Dried fruits can be chopped easily in the food processor by using a quick, on-off pulsing motion. For use in baked goods, add 1 tablespoon of the flour required for the recipe; this keeps the fruit from sticking. For other uses, add 1 tablespoon of salad oil per pound of dried fruit. Note: To chop dried fruits by hand, always oil the knife blade or scissors.

Cinnamon-Pumpkin Cake

Cake

2 cups granulated sugar
1¼ cups salad oil
1 can (16 ounces) pumpkin
4 large eggs
3 cups unsifted all-purpose flour
2 teaspoons baking powder
2 teaspoons baking soda
2 teaspoons ground cinnamon
1 teaspoon salt
1 cup chopped walnuts or pecans
½ cup raisins
½ cup golden raisins

Cream-Cheese Frosting

1 package (1 pound) confectioners' sugar
½ cup butter, softened
1 package (8 ounces) cream cheese, softened
2 teaspoons vanilla extract

1. Preheat oven to 350°F. Grease 10-inch tube pan; set aside.

2. Make cake: In large bowl of electric mixer, combine granulated sugar, salad oil and pumpkin; at medium speed, beat until blended. Add eggs, one at a time, beating well after each addition.

3. On sheet of waxed paper, combine flour, baking powder, baking soda, cinnamon and salt. Fold into batter, mixing just until blended. Stir in nuts and raisins.

4. Pour mixture into prepared tube pan; bake until cake tester inserted in center comes out clean, about 1 hour and 15 minutes. Cool cake in pan 10 minutes. Turn out onto wire rack to allow cake to cool completely.

5. Make frosting: In large bowl of electric mixer, at high speed, beat all ingredients together until frosting mixture is smooth and fluffy. With metal spatula, spread cake with frosting.

Makes 12 servings.

Fabulous Fruitcake Finale

Silver and Gold Fruitcake

1 package (16 ounces) pound-cake mix
⅔ cup lemonade
2 large eggs
½ cup mixed green and red candied cherries
½ cup chopped mixed nuts
½ cup golden raisins
½ cup orange-flavored liqueur or orange juice
2 packages (10 ounces each) vanilla-flavored candy melting wafers or 20 ounces white chocolate
⅓ cup light corn syrup
Shelled and unshelled nuts covered with vark or with silver and gold foil (see *Note*)

1. Preheat oven to 325°F. With aluminum foil, line 9-inch springform pan. Grease and flour foil.

2. In large bowl, combine cake mix, lemonade and eggs. Mix as package label directs; stir in cherries, chopped nuts and raisins. Pour into prepared pan. Bake 1 hour, or until cake tester inserted in center comes out clean. Cool cake in pan on wire rack 15 minutes. Remove pan side; cool completely. Remove foil. Brush cake with liqueur or orange juice. Wrap in cheesecloth and then foil. Refrigerate at least 2 days or several weeks before decorating.

3. Unwrap cake. Place on plate; let come to room temperature.

4. Meanwhile, in top of double boiler placed over simmering, not boiling, water, melt candy wafers, stirring. Remove from heat; stir in corn syrup just until blended.

5. Line 2 large baking sheets with foil. On foil on 1 baking sheet, spread three-fourths of melted-candy mixture. Cover with sheet of waxed paper; roll into a 14-by-12-inch rectangle. On second baking sheet, spread remaining mixture; cover with waxed paper. Roll into a 9-inch round. Refrigerate until firm. Remove waxed-paper sheets; with sharp knife, cut two 14-by-2-inch strips from candy rectangle, cutting through foil. Place 1 strip, foil side out, around sides of cake; remove foil. Repeat with remaining candy strip, trimming strip to fit. With hands, press strips around cake. With tip of warm knife, smooth seams. Place candy round, foil side out, on cake top. Remove foil; with tip of warm knife, smooth seams. With small knife, cut out leaves from remaining candy strip. If necessary, remelt scraps to make additional leaves. Roll small pieces of candy mixture into berries. Using photograph as a guide, arrange leaves, berries and nuts on cake. If desired, add gold and silver decorations.

Makes about 16 servings.

Note: Vark is edible gold and silver leaf, available at East Indian grocery stores. To use vark to cover shelled and unshelled nuts: Place vark on work surface; remove covering tissue. Brush nuts with lightly beaten egg white. Without touching vark with hands, using knife tip, roll nuts in vark until coated. Use tweezers or chopsticks to move nuts.

A World of Christmas Cookies

Our annual Christmas collection features an array of 24 delicious easy-to-make cookies. This year we're presenting sweet treats with an international flavor.

Kourambiedes

1 cup unsalted butter or margarine, softened
¾ cup confectioners' sugar
1 large egg yolk
2 tablespoons orange juice
2 teaspoons grated orange peel
1½ teaspoons vanilla extract
2¼ cups unsifted all-purpose flour
½ cup blanched whole almonds, ground
¾ teaspoon baking powder
¼ teaspoon salt

1. In large bowl of electric mixer, at medium speed, beat butter until light and fluffy. Beat in ½ cup confectioners' sugar until blended. Beat in egg yolk, orange juice, orange peel and vanilla. On sheet of waxed paper, combine flour, almonds, baking powder and salt; gradually add to butter mixture, beating just until dry ingredients are moistened. Cover dough with plastic wrap; refrigerate until firm, about 1 hour.

2. Preheat oven to 350°F. For each cookie, shape 1 tablespoon dough into a 3-inch-long rope. Place on ungreased baking sheet; curve ends to form crescent shape. Repeat with remaining dough, spacing cookies 1 inch apart.

3. Bake 15 minutes, or until very lightly browned on bottom. Place a sheet of waxed paper under wire racks; place cookies on wire racks. Cool 5 minutes. Sprinkle warm cookies generously with remaining confectioners' sugar. Let cookies cool completely.

Makes about 2 dozen.

Butterscotch-Cream Bells

Cookies
2 cups unsifted all-purpose flour
½ teaspoon baking powder
¼ teaspoon salt
½ cup butter or margarine, softened
⅓ cup granulated sugar
1 large egg
1½ teaspoons vanilla extract

Filling
½ package (3-ounce size) cream cheese, softened
¾ cup confectioners' sugar
2 tablespoons light-brown sugar
1 teaspoon molasses
½ teaspoon vanilla extract

1 square (1 ounce) semisweet chocolate, melted

1. Preheat oven to 350°F. Grease 2 large baking sheets; set aside.

2. Make cookies: On sheet of waxed paper, combine flour, baking powder and salt; set aside. In large bowl of electric mixer, at medium speed, beat butter and sugar until light and fluffy. Beat in egg and vanilla until blended. Stir in flour mixture until blended.

3. On lightly floured surface, with lightly floured rolling pin, roll dough to ⅛-inch thickness. Using a 2-inch bell-shape cutter, cut out cookies. Place 1 inch apart on prepared baking sheets. Bake 12 minutes, or until lightly browned. Cool on wire racks.

4. Make filling: In small bowl of electric mixer, at medium speed, beat cream cheese until smooth. Beat in confectioners' sugar, brown sugar, molasses and vanilla until blended. With metal spatula, spread bottom of each of half the cookies with filling, dividing evenly; top each with flat side of a remaining cookie.

5. With spoon, drizzle melted chocolate over 1 side of each cookie-sandwich, dividing evenly. Set aside until chocolate hardens.

Makes about 30.

■ Give a gift everyone appreciates—freshly baked cookies. To ensure that edible delicacies are served in their prime, include any storage or serving instructions.

Candy Canes

¾ cup butter or margarine, softened
1 cup confectioners' sugar
1 large egg
1 teaspoon vanilla extract
2⅓ cups unsifted all-purpose flour
2 tablespoons red cinnamon candies
Red food color
2 tablespoons crushed peppermint candies
2 tablespoons granulated sugar

1. In large bowl of electric mixer, at medium speed, beat butter and confectioners' sugar until light and fluffy. Beat in egg and vanilla extract until blended. At low speed, gradually beat in enough flour to make a soft dough; stir or knead in remaining flour to make a smooth, not sticky, ball.

2. Cut dough in half. Wrap one half in plastic wrap; refrigerate. In blender or food processor, chop red cinnamon candies. Knead or work chopped candies and red food color into dough in mixing bowl. Wrap dough in plastic wrap; refrigerate until firm, about 30 minutes.

3. Preheat oven to 350°F. On lightly floured surface, with hands, roll a rounded teaspoonful red dough into a 7-inch rope. Repeat with a rounded teaspoonful plain dough. Place the two ropes side by side; twist together, being careful not to blend doughs. Place twist on ungreased baking sheet; curve one end to form cane. Repeat procedure with remaining dough.

4. Bake cookies 10 minutes, or until lightly browned. Meanwhile, in custard cup, combine crushed peppermint candies and granulated sugar; sprinkle mixture over hot cookies, dividing evenly. Cool cookies completely on wire rack.

Makes about 2 dozen.

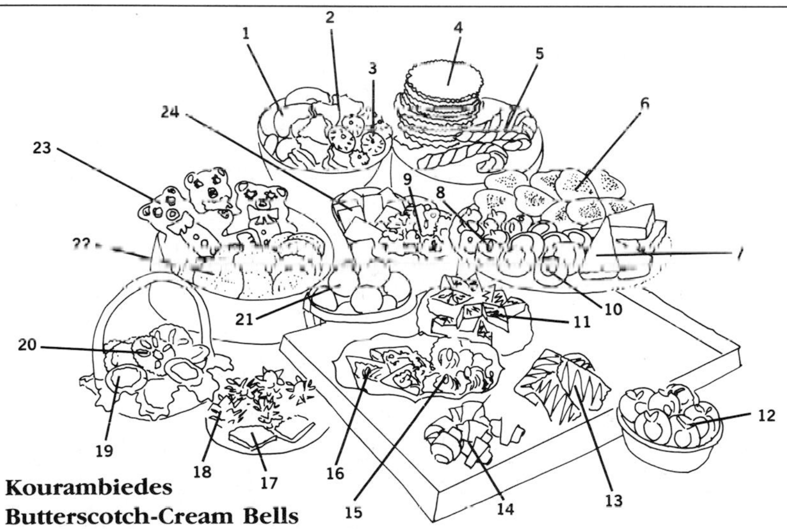

1 Kourambiedes
2 Butterscotch-Cream Bells
3 Nut Spirals
4 Anise Pizzelles
5 Candy Canes
6 Snowflakes
7 Marble-Topped Hazelnut Shortbread
8 Caramel Acorns
9 Marbled Spritz Cookies
10 Poppy-Seed Thumbprints
11 Fruitcake Diamonds
12 Pistachio Wreaths
13 Cranberry-Raisin Tarts
14 Mincemeat Rugelach
15 Mini Lace Cups
16 Lemon-Fig Bites
17 Cranberry-Apple Streusel Bars
18 Marzipan Pinecones
19 Coconut-Eggnog Tarts
20 Cherry-Almond Wreaths
21 Pfeffernuesse
22 Coffee-Butter Snaps
23 Chocolate Sugar Bears
24 Springerle
Photograph, pages 222 and 223.

Nut Spirals

1 cup butter or margarine, softened
⅔ cup granulated sugar
1 large egg
1 teaspoon almond extract
2 cups unsifted all-purpose flour
1 cup ground blanched almonds
¼ teaspoon salt
Confectioners' sugar
Chopped green and red candied cherries

1. Preheat oven to 350°F. Line 36 mini-muffin-pan cups with paper liners; set aside.

2. In large bowl of electric mixer, at medium speed, beat butter and granulated sugar until light and fluffy. Beat in egg and almond extract. Stir in flour, almonds and salt until blended.

3. Spoon mixture into large pastry bag fitted with large star tip. Pipe mixture into prepared muffin cups, dividing evenly. Bake 20 minutes, or until lightly browned. Let cookies cool on wire racks. Place some confectioners' sugar in fine wire sieve; sprinkle confectioners' sugar over cookies. Decorate each cookie with a piece of chopped candied cherry.

Makes 36.

Anise Pizzelles

3½ cups unsifted all-purpose flour
1½ cups sugar
1 cup butter or margarine, melted
4 teaspoons baking powder
6 large eggs
1 bottle (1 ounce) anise extract
½ teaspoon lemon extract

1. Preheat 5-inch pizzelle iron according to the manufacturer's directions.

2. In large bowl of electric mixer, at low speed, beat all ingredients until well blended. Spoon a heaping tablespoonful of mixture onto center of pizzelle iron (or use amount recommended by manufacturer); cover and bake until golden-brown, about 30 seconds. Lift cover; with fork, carefully loosen pizzelle. Place on wire rack to cool. Repeat with remaining batter.

Makes about 4½ dozen.

Marble-Topped Hazelnut Shortbread

2¼ cups unsifted cake flour
½ cup ground toasted hazelnuts
½ cup confectioners' sugar
¼ teaspoon salt
1 cup butter or margarine, softened
4 squares (1 ounce each) semisweet chocolate, melted
¼ cup vanilla-flavored candy melting wafers, melted

1. Preheat oven to 325°F. Line 9-inch round cake pan with aluminum foil, allowing foil to extend 2 inches up side of pan; set aside.

2. In large bowl, combine flour, hazelnuts, sugar and salt. Cut butter into small pieces; knead into flour mixture until dough holds together. Pat dough into prepared pan. Bake 40 minutes, or until shortbread is lightly browned.

3. When shortbread is done, remove from oven; immediately spread melted semisweet chocolate over top of shortbread. With spoon, drizzle melted candy wafers in lines, about ¾ inch apart, over semisweet chocolate. Using a wooden pick, swirl melted wafers into semisweet chocolate to make a marbled design, being careful not to overmix and blend mixtures.

4. Cool shortbread in pan on wire rack 40 minutes; cut into 12 wedges. Let shortbread cool completely in pan before removing, using foil to carefully lift shortbread from pan.

Makes 1 dozen.

Snowflakes

Cookies
½ cup butter or margarine, softened
1 cup granulated sugar
1 large egg
2 teaspoons grated lemon peel
2 tablespoons milk
2 teaspoons vanilla extract
½ teaspoon lemon extract
2 cups unsifted all-purpose flour
2 teaspoons baking powder
¼ teaspoon salt

¾ cup flaked coconut
Red and green food color

Glaze
1 cup confectioners' sugar
1 tablespoon lemon juice
2 teaspoons milk

1. Make cookies: In large bowl of electric mixer, at medium speed, beat butter and granulated sugar until light and fluffy. Beat in egg, lemon peel, milk, vanilla and lemon extract until blended. On sheet of waxed paper, combine flour, baking powder and salt; beat into butter mixture until blended. Divide dough in half. Wrap each half in plastic wrap; refrigerate until firm, about 1 hour.

2. Preheat oven to 350°F. On lightly floured surface, with floured rolling pin, roll one half to ¼-inch thickness. With floured, 2-inch heart-shape cutter, cut out dough.

3. On ungreased baking sheets, using photograph as a guide, arrange 4 hearts together, with sides of hearts touching and points toward center of each group. Repeat with remaining dough half, re-rolling dough scraps and cutting out additional hearts. Bake cookies 10 minutes, or until edges are lightly browned. Cool on wire racks.

4. Tint coconut: In each of 2 small jars with tight-fitting lids, place ¼ cup coconut. To one jar add a few drops of green food color; to the other jar add a few drops of red food color. Fasten lids; shake coconut to color evenly. Set aside.

5. Make glaze: In small bowl, combine confectioners' sugar, lemon juice and milk until blended. With small metal spatula, spread glaze on top of each of the 4 hearts in each cookie, dividing evenly. While glaze is soft, sprinkle with some coconut.

Makes 1 dozen.

Caramel Acorns

2¾ cups unsifted all-purpose flour
½ teaspoon baking powder
1 cup butter or margarine, softened
¾ cup firmly packed light-brown sugar
3 large egg yolks
1½ cups finely chopped walnuts or pecans
1 teaspoon vanilla extract
½ pound caramels
¼ cup water

1. Preheat oven to 350°F. On sheet of waxed paper, mix flour with baking powder; set aside. In large bowl of electric mixer, at medium speed, beat butter, sugar and egg yolks until smooth and fluffy. Stir in ½ cup chopped nuts, the vanilla and flour mixture until blended.

2. Roll 1 slightly heaping teaspoonful dough into a ball for each cookie. With fingers, pinch dough to form a rounded point, and shape dough to resemble an acorn. Place acorns, point side up, 1 inch apart on ungreased baking sheets. Bake 12 minutes, or until golden-brown. Cool completely on wire racks.

3. Place remaining chopped nuts on sheet of waxed paper; set aside. In top of double boiler placed over hot water, or in small saucepan over low heat, melt caramels in water, stirring until blended. Remove from heat; dip large end of each cookie into caramel and then into chopped nuts. Place on sheet of waxed paper until caramel hardens. Store cookies covered, in refrigerator.

Makes about 6 dozen.

Marbled Spritz Cookies

1 cup butter or margarine, softened
¾ cup sugar
1 large egg
1 teaspoon vanilla extract
2⅓ cups unsifted all-purpose flour
1 square (1 ounce) unsweetened chocolate, melted and cooled

1. In large bowl of electric mixer, at medium speed, beat butter and sugar until light and fluffy. Beat in egg and vanilla. Stir in flour just until blended. Divide dough in half; mix chocolate into one half until blended. Cover halves with plastic wrap; refrigerate 20 minutes.

2. Preheat oven to 350°F. Form each dough half into 6 ropes. Alternately arrange chocolate and plain doughs in cookie press fitted with desired disk. Force dough through press onto ungreased baking sheets, placing cookies about 1 inch apart. Bake 8 minutes, or until cookies are firm. Cool on wire racks.

Makes about 5 dozen.

Poppy-Seed Thumbprints

1 cup butter or margarine, softened
½ cup firmly packed light-brown sugar
2 large egg yolks
1 teaspoon vanilla extract
2½ cups unsifted all-purpose flour
2 tablespoons poppy seeds
About ⅔ cup favorite jelly or jam

1. In large bowl of electric mixer, at medium speed, beat butter, sugar, egg yolks and vanilla until blended. Stir in flour and poppy seeds, mixing just until dough holds together. Cover with plastic wrap; refrigerate until firm, about 30 minutes.

2. Preheat oven to 350°F. Roll 1 tablespoonful dough into a ball for each cookie; place 1 inch apart on ungreased baking sheets. With floured thumb, press top center of each ball to make a deep thumbprint. Bake 15 minutes, or until golden. Let cookies cool on wire racks; fill each thumbprint with 1 teaspoonful jelly.

Makes 32 cookies.

■ Aluminum foil is the key to easy cleanup after baking. Simply line pans or sheets with foil—no need to grease or flour—and, when you remove from oven, just throw away the foil!

Fruitcake Diamonds

1 cup raisins
¾ cup candied green cherries, coarsely chopped
¾ cup candied red cherries, coarsely chopped
¾ cup pitted dates, coarsely chopped
½ cup dark rum
1½ cups unsifted all-purpose flour
½ cup butter or margarine, softened
½ cup granulated sugar
3 large eggs
⅓ cup unsweetened pineapple juice
¾ teaspoon baking powder
¾ teaspoon ground cinnamon
½ teaspoon salt
¼ teaspoon ground cloves
¼ teaspoon ground nutmeg
¾ cup chopped walnuts

Glaze
1 cup confectioners' sugar
1 tablespoon dark rum
1 teaspoon milk

1. Preheat oven to 350°F. Grease 13-by-9-by-2-inch baking pan; set aside. In medium bowl, combine raisins, candied cherries, dates and ⅓ cup rum; let stand 1 hour.

2. In large bowl of electric mixer, combine flour, butter, granulated sugar, eggs, pineapple juice, baking powder, cinnamon, salt, cloves and nutmeg; at medium speed, beat until well blended. Stir in walnuts and undrained fruit mixture. Spread mixture in prepared pan; bake 35 minutes, or until lightly browned and cake tester inserted in center comes out clean. Cool in pan on wire rack.

3. Make glaze: In small bowl, mix confectioners' sugar with 1 tablespoon rum and the milk until smooth. With spoon, drizzle glaze over top of cooled fruitcake; cut into diamonds.

Makes 2 dozen.

Pistachio Wreaths

3 large egg whites, at room temperature
1/4 teaspoon cream of tartar
1/8 teaspoon salt
2/3 cup sugar
1 teaspoon vanilla extract
1/4 teaspoon almond extract
1/4 cup finely chopped pistachios
About 10 candied red cherries, slivered

1. Preheat oven to 200°F. Line 2 large baking sheets with parchment paper; set aside.

2. In large bowl of electric mixer, at high speed, beat first 3 ingredients until soft peaks form. At medium speed, beat in sugar, 2 tablespoons at a time, beating well after each addition. At high speed, beat until stiff peaks form. Beat in vanilla and almond extracts until blended.

3. Spoon mixture into pastry bag fitted with medium star tip; pipe into 2-inch-wide rings 1 inch apart on prepared baking sheets. Sprinkle rings with pistachios, dividing evenly. Using photograph as a guide, garnish with candied cherries. Bake 1 hour, or until set. Turn off oven; leave in oven until dry, about 1 hour. Cool on wire rack.

Makes about 40.

Mini Lace Cups

1/3 cup ground almonds
1/4 cup sugar
1/4 cup butter (no substitute)
1 tablespoon milk
1 1/2 teaspoons all-purpose flour

Filling
1/2 cup heavy cream
2 tablespoons sugar
1 tablespoon unsweetened cocoa powder
1 teaspoon instant-coffee powder
Chocolate-covered coffee beans

1. Preheat oven to 350°F. Grease and flour 2 large baking sheets. Set prepared sheets aside.

2. In large skillet, place almonds, 1/4 cup sugar, the butter, milk and flour. Cook over low heat, stirring constantly, until butter melts and mixture thickens slightly; keep mixture warm.

3. Drop rounded teaspoonfuls batter, 2 inches apart, onto prepared baking sheets, allowing only 6 cookies per baking sheet. Bake cookies, 6 at a time, 5 minutes, or until golden. Remove baking sheet from oven; cool cookies 1 minute. With metal spatula, quickly and gently loosen each cookie; fit each into a 1 3/4-inch muffin pan, forming a mini cup. (If cookie hardens while fitting into pan, heat in warm oven to soften slightly.) When cookies harden, remove from pans; store in an airtight container.

4. Just before serving, make filling: In small bowl of electric mixer, at high speed, beat heavy cream, 2 tablespoons sugar and the cocoa and instant-coffee powders until stiff peaks form. Place whipped-cream mixture in pastry bag fitted with star tip; pipe mixture into each cookie-cup, dividing evenly. Garnish each cookie with a chocolate-covered coffee bean.

Makes about 1 dozen.

Marzipan Pinecones

1 package (7 ounces) almond paste
1 2/3 cups confectioners' sugar
1 to 2 tablespoons water
Toasted sliced, unblanched almonds

1. In medium bowl, break almond paste into small pieces; knead until pliable. Gradually knead in sugar and water, until mixture is blended but not sticky.

2. With palms of hands, shape 1 scant tablespoon almond-paste mixture into a 1 1/2-inch-high cone. Dip pointed end of each sliced almond into water; using photograph as a guide, insert almonds, pointed end in, into marzipan at slight angle and overlapping slightly, to make horizontal rows along length of cone. Store in refrigerator.

Makes 28.

Lemon-Fig Bites

1 package (8 ounces) dried figs, coarsely chopped
3/4 cup sugar
4 teaspoons grated lemon peel
2/3 cup water
3 tablespoons lemon juice
3/4 cup butter or margarine, softened
2 large egg yolks
2 cups unsifted all-purpose flour

1. In food processor, finely chop figs with 1/4 cup sugar and 2 teaspoons grated lemon peel. Transfer mixture to medium saucepan; stir in water and 2 tablespoons lemon juice. Bring to boiling; simmer until thickened, about 8 minutes. Set mixture aside.

2. In large bowl of electric mixer, at medium speed, beat butter with remaining sugar until light and fluffy. Beat in egg yolks and remaining lemon juice and lemon peel. At low speed, gradually beat in flour until blended. Divide dough into 4 pieces. Roll each piece into a 12-inch-long, 1-inch diameter rope. Place ropes at least 2 inches apart on ungreased baking sheet.

3. With finger, make a 1/2-inch-wide, 1/4-inch-deep depression down center of each rope; fill with fig mixture, dividing evenly. Refrigerate 20 minutes.

4. Preheat oven to 350°F. Cut each rope crosswise into 2-inch

diagonal slices, but do not separate into bars. Bake 25 minutes, or until lightly browned. Cut through slices while still warm; cool completely on wire racks.

Makes 2 dozen.

Cranberry-Raisin Tarts

¼ cup cranberries
¼ cup plus 2 tablespoons granulated sugar
1 tablespoon raisins, diced
¼ teaspoon cornstarch
1 tablespoon water
1 package (11 ounces) pie-crust mix
½ teaspoon ground cinnamon
1 large egg
1 teaspoon water
½ cup confectioners' sugar
2½ teaspoons orange juice
Dragées

1. In small saucepan, combine cranberries, 2 tablespoons granulated sugar, the raisins, cornstarch and 1 tablespoon water. Heat, stirring, until boiling. Cook, stirring, 1 minute, or until mixture is thickened, breaking up cranberries with back of spoon. Set aside to cool.

2. Preheat oven to 350°F. In medium bowl, make pie crust as package label directs, adding cinnamon and ¼ cup granulated sugar to dry mix. Cut dough in half. On lightly floured surface, with floured rolling pin, roll each dough half into a 9-inch square. Cut each square horizontally into 3-inch-wide strips; cut strips crosswise at 1½-inch intervals to make 18 rectangles per square.

3. Spoon ½ teaspoon cranberry mixture over length of 18 pastry rectangles about ¼ inch from edges. Top each with a remaining pastry rectangle to make 18 tarts. With fork tines, press edges together. Place on ungreased baking sheets. Beat egg with 1 teaspoon water; brush top of each cookie with some egg mixture. Bake 12 minutes, or until lightly browned. Cool on wire rack.

4. In bowl, mix confectioners' sugar with orange juice. With spoon or with icing in pastry bag fitted with small plain tip, drizzle tarts with icing. Sprinkle with dragées; let stand until glaze sets.

Makes 18.

Mincemeat Rugelach

1 package (8 ounces) cream cheese, softened
¾ cup butter or margarine, softened
½ cup plus 1 tablespoon sugar
1 teaspoon vanilla extract
¼ teaspoon salt
3 cups unsifted all-purpose flour
1½ cups prepared mincemeat
1 tablespoon brandy or orange juice
1 cup plus 2 tablespoons ground walnuts
1 large egg white
1 teaspoon water

1. In food processor, process cream cheese, butter, ½ cup sugar, the vanilla and salt until blended. Add flour; process until blended and mixture holds together. Shape pastry into a ball; refrigerate until firm, about 2 hours.

2. Preheat oven to 350°F. Grease 2 large baking sheets; set aside. In food processor, process mincemeat and brandy until blended. Transfer mixture to bowl; stir in 1 cup ground walnuts. Set aside.

3. Divide pastry into 4 pieces. On lightly floured surface, with lightly floured rolling pin, roll 1 piece of dough into a 10-inch round; trim edge. Spread pastry to within ¼ inch of edge with heaping ⅓ cup mincemeat mixture; with sharp knife, cut into 16 wedges. Roll up each wedge, beginning at end on outside of pastry round. Place cookies with pastry point down on prepared baking sheets. Repeat with remaining pastry and mincemeat.

4. In small bowl, with fork, lightly beat egg white with 1 teaspoon water; set aside. In custard cup, combine remaining ground walnuts and sugar; brush each cookie with some of the egg-white mixture and sprinkle with some of the walnut mixture. Bake 25 minutes, or until lightly browned. Cool on wire racks.

Makes 64.

Cranberry-Apple Streusel Bars

2 cups plus 3 tablespoons unsifted all-purpose flour
½ cup firmly packed light-brown sugar
½ teaspoon ground cinnamon
¼ teaspoon salt
⅔ cup butter or margarine, softened
1 can (12 ounces) apple filling
1 cup whole-berry cranberry sauce
1 teaspoon grated orange peel

1. Preheat oven to 400°F. Grease 13 by 9 by 2-inch baking pan.

2. In large bowl, combine 2 cups flour, the brown sugar, ¼ teaspoon cinnamon and the salt. With pastry blender or two knives, cut in butter until mixture resembles coarse crumbs. Remove ½ cup mixture; set aside. Press remaining mixture into bottom of prepared pan. Bake 10 minutes, or until lightly browned. Cool 10 minutes.

3. Meanwhile, in medium bowl, combine apple filling, cranberry sauce, grated orange peel and the remaining flour and cinnamon. Spread evenly over crust in pan. Sprinkle with reserved flour mixture. Bake 25 minutes, or until lightly browned. Cool in pan on wire rack. Cut into bars.

Makes 28.

Coconut-Eggnog Tarts

1 cup unsifted all-purpose flour
5 tablespoons sugar
¼ teaspoon ground nutmeg
½ cup butter or margarine, softened
⅓ cup flaked coconut
¼ cup light corn syrup
¼ teaspoon rum extract
1 large egg, beaten

1. Preheat oven to 350°F. Generously grease 18 mini-muffin-pan cups; set aside.

2. In medium bowl, mix flour, 4 tablespoons sugar and ⅛ teaspoon nutmeg. With hands, knead in 7 tablespoons butter until blended and mixture can be formed into a ball. Divide evenly into 18 pieces; press each into a prepared muffin-pan cup to line sides and bottom. Sprinkle coconut into each, dividing evenly.

3. In small saucepan, melt remaining butter. Remove pan from heat; stir in syrup, rum extract and remaining sugar and nutmeg. Stir in egg just until blended. Pour over coconut in each tart shell, dividing evenly. Bake 25 minutes, or until cake tester inserted in center comes out clean. Cool in pans on wire racks 10 minutes. With small, sharp knife, loosen tarts from pans; carefully remove to wire racks to cool completely.

Makes 18.

Cherry-Almond Wreaths

1 cup butter or margarine, softened
1 cup plus 2 tablespoons sugar
2 cups ground toasted almonds
2 cups unsifted all-purpose flour
¼ teaspoon salt
1 large egg yolk
1 teaspoon vanilla extract
Slivered green and red candied cherries

1. Preheat oven to 350°F. In large bowl of electric mixer, at medium speed, beat butter with 1 cup sugar until light and fluffy. Add almonds, flour, salt, egg yolk and vanilla; beat until blended.

2. Divide dough in half. Wrap one half in plastic wrap; set aside. Place remaining half between 2 sheets of waxed paper. With rolling pin, roll dough to ⅛-inch thickness. Remove top sheet of paper; with 2½-inch fluted round cutter, cut out cookies. With 1-inch fluted round cutter, cut out center of each cookie, reserving centers. Place cookies, 1 inch apart, on ungreased baking sheets. Using photograph as a guide, decorate with candied cherries. Add scraps and cut-out centers to remaining dough; roll, cut out and decorate as for first half of dough.

3. Sprinkle cookies with remaining sugar, dividing evenly. Bake 10 minutes, or until lightly browned. Cool on wire racks.

Makes about 4 dozen.

Pfeffernuesse

6 cups unsifted all-purpose flour
1 tablespoon ground cinnamon
2 teaspoons baking powder
1 teaspoon ground allspice
1 teaspoon ground cloves
¾ teaspoon ground nutmeg
½ teaspoon pepper
½ teaspoon salt
⅛ teaspoon ground cardamom
5 large eggs
2 cups firmly packed light-brown sugar
3 tablespoons black coffee
1 cup ground blanched almonds
1 teaspoon grated lemon peel
½ cup confectioners' sugar

1. In large bowl, combine flour, cinnamon, baking powder, allspice, cloves, nutmeg, pepper, salt and cardamom; set aside. In large bowl of electric mixer, at high speed, beat eggs until fluffy. Gradually beat in light-brown sugar until blended. At low speed, alternately beat in flour mixture and coffee. With rubber spatula, fold in almonds and lemon peel. Wrap in plastic wrap; refrigerate until firm, about 2 hours.

2. Preheat oven to 300°F. Grease 2 large baking sheets; set aside. Roll 1 tablespoon dough into a ball; place on prepared baking sheet. Repeat with remaining dough, placing cookies 1 inch apart on baking sheets. Bake 18 minutes, or until cookies are lightly browned. Cool on wire racks. Place confectioners' sugar on sheet of waxed paper; roll cookies in sugar until coated.

Makes about 8 dozen.

Coffee-Butter Snaps

1 tablespoon instant-coffee powder
1 teaspoon hot water
1 large egg
1 teaspoon vanilla extract
2 cups unsifted all-purpose flour
¾ cup butter or margarine, softened
¾ cup sugar
1½ teaspoons baking powder
¼ teaspoon salt

1. In small cup, dissolve coffee in hot water; add egg and vanilla. With fork, beat until blended; set aside. In large bowl of electric mixer, at medium speed, beat flour, butter, sugar, baking powder, salt and egg mixture until blended. Shape dough into a ball; cover with plastic wrap. Refrigerate until firm, about 1 hour.

2. Preheat oven to 350°F. Divide dough in half. On lightly floured surface, with lightly floured rolling pin, roll half of dough to ⅛-inch thickness. With 3-inch fluted round cutter, cut out cookies. Place 1 inch apart on ungreased baking sheets.

Using end of metal or wooden skewer, press holes into cookies in decorative pattern without scoring completely. Add dough scraps to remaining dough; roll, cut out and score as for first half of dough. Bake 10 minutes, or until firm. Cool on wire racks.

Makes about 30.

Chocolate Sugar Bears

2¾ cups unsifted all-purpose flour
⅔ cup unsweetened cocoa powder
½ teaspoon baking soda
½ teaspoon salt
1½ cups granulated sugar
1 cup butter or margarine, softened
1 teaspoon vanilla extract
2 large eggs

Frosting
3 cups confectioners' sugar
2 large egg whites
¼ teaspoon cream of tartar
Assorted food colors

Assorted candies for garnish

1. On sheet of waxed paper, combine flour, cocoa, baking soda and salt. In large bowl of electric mixer, at medium speed, beat granulated sugar, butter, vanilla and eggs until light and fluffy. Gradually beat in flour mixture until blended. Cover with plastic wrap; refrigerate until thoroughly chilled, about 1 hour.

2. Preheat oven to 350°F. Grease 2 large baking sheets; set aside.

3. Divide dough in half. On lightly floured surface, with lightly floured rolling pin, roll one-half of dough to ¼-inch thickness. Using 6-inch teddy-bear cookie cutter, cut out cookies; place about 1½ inches apart on prepared baking sheets. Reroll scraps; cut out cookies. Repeat with remaining dough and scraps. Bake 10 minutes; cool on wire racks.

4. Make frosting: In small bowl of electric mixer, at medium speed, beat confectioners' sugar, egg whites and cream of tartar until stiff peaks form. With food colors, tint as desired. Using photograph as a guide, decorate cookies with frosting and candies.

Makes 9.

Springerle

4 cups unsifted all-purpose flour
1 teaspoon baking powder
½ teaspoon salt
4 large eggs
2 cups sugar
2 teaspoons grated lemon peel
2 tablespoons anise seeds
Confectioners' sugar

1. Two days before baking cookies: In large bowl, combine flour with baking powder and salt; set aside. In large bowl of electric mixer, at high speed, beat eggs until thick and lemon-colored, about 5 minutes. At medium speed, beat in sugar, 2 tablespoons at a time; continue to beat until mixture is thick and smooth, about 10 minutes.

2. Add flour mixture and lemon peel; with wooden spoon, stir until blended. Cover with plastic wrap; refrigerate dough and springerle rolling pin overnight.

3. Lightly grease 2 large baking sheets; sprinkle each with half the anise seeds. Divide dough into 3 parts. Cover each with plastic wrap; refrigerate until ready to roll out.

4. On work surface lightly sprinkled with confectioners' sugar, place 1 part dough. Sprinkle regular rolling pin with confectioners' sugar; roll out dough to a rectangle 8 inches long by length of springerle rolling pin. Sprinkle chilled springerle rolling pin with confectioners' sugar; starting from long side of dough, roll pin once, firmly and evenly, pressing hard enough on pin to make designs in surface of dough. (Use spatula to peel off dough if it sticks to pin while rolling.)

5. With sharp, floured knife, carefully cut along lines in dough to make individual cookies; with wide spatula, transfer cookies to prepared baking sheets. Repeat with remaining dough. Let cookies stand, uncovered, at room temperature, overnight.

6. Next day, preheat oven to 325°F. Bake cookies 12 minutes, or until lightly golden. Remove to wire rack; cool completely. Store in tightly covered container 2 to 3 weeks before using.

Makes about 4¼ dozen.

■ To add colorful sparkle to your holiday dessert tray, roll refrigerator cookie dough into a log and mix in a combination of candied fruit and chopped almonds or walnuts. Refrigerate until firm, then slice and bake according to package directions.

■ Toasted walnuts add an unusual flavor to any holiday dish. Bake the shelled nuts at 350°F. in a shallow baking pan for 12 minutes or until golden. In a real rush? Microwave! Spread 1 cup walnut pieces in a glass pie plate. Cook on HIGH 5 minutes, stirring every 2 minutes.

■ When melting squares of chocolate in the microwave, be sure to keep these points in mind: Stir often to ensure even melting, but never with a wet utensil—it can ruin chocolate. If for any reason the chocolate does harden, add one to two tablespoons shortening—not butter or margarine—for every six ounces of chocolate, and stir until smooth.

Santa's Dream House

Fantasyland begins here with Santa's Dream House. It's a Christmas dream come true—a house created from candies and cookies with a fence made of gingerbread men.

Santa's Dream House
(pictured, right)

HOUSE PATTERN PIECES
(pages 260 and 261)
Section A: #1-9, front room; B, C, D, E1, E2, F, G, main house; elf; Santa

PROPS AND SUPPORT
X-acto knife; ruler; 2 (48-by-32-inch) sheets, 1/4-inch-thick foam-core board; glue; tape; marker; tracing paper; scissors; small metal spatula; small paintbrush; disposable pastry bags; pastry tips: Nos. 3, 16 (two), 352; tall juice cans; 1 (10-inch) Styrofoam cone; 1 (12-inch) Styrofoam cone

8 recipes Royal Icing, page 234 (make in separate batches before using)

Food paste colors: red, brown, yellow, leaf green

Candies
2 ounces semisweet chocolate, melted; about 325 strawberry-flavored soft, chewy candies; about 80 milk-chocolate-covered candy bars with chopped almonds in nougat, topped with caramel; about 50 milk-chocolate-covered, caramel- and crunchy-cookie candy bars; 10 each lemon-, orange- and strawberry-flavored soft chewy candies; 6 (3½-inch) candy canes; 1 bag (1 pound) candy-covered chocolate candies; 1 (6-inch) candy cane; about 10 small gingerbread men cookies; sugar

1. With X-acto knife and ruler, cut out two 17-by-28-inch pieces foam-core board for base. Stack and tape or glue pieces together; set aside. With marker and tracing paper, trace pattern pieces; enlarge to scale. Label all pieces; cut out with scissors. Place patterns on remaining foam core. Cut out with X-acto knife.

2. Assemble house front (Section A): Glue and tape A4 to sides A3 and to A8. Glue and tape sides A2 to A1. Glue and tape A1 to A3. Glue and tape A7 to sides A9. Glue and tape assembled house front to one foam-core piece B. Lay front section on flat surface. With metal spatula and Royal Icing, evenly cover all Section-A foam-core pieces except A4 and A7, swirling icing to resemble rough stucco. Let dry 4 hours.

3. Make windows and door: Thin 1/4 cup icing to painting consistency. With paintbrush and thinned icing, cover foam-core piece (house front) A4 and each of two foam-core (window) pieces F and A6; color gloves on foam-core elf. Set aside. With red food color, tint 1/4 teaspoon thinned white icing pink; with paintbrush, using photograph as a guide, color foam-core Santa's face and elf's face and ears. With red food color, tint remaining thinned white icing red; with paintbrush, using photograph as a guide, paint elf's jacket and socks, and Santa's hat and suit on Santa piece, flowers and hearts on (window) A6, (door) A5 and (front) A4 pieces. Set aside.

With 2 tablespoons white icing and green food color, tint icing green. With paintbrush and thinned green icing, cover foam-core (window) G piece and paint elf's hat, shoes and shirt.

With 2 tablespoons white icing and brown food color, tint icing brown. With paintbrush and thinned brown icing, cover (door) piece A5. Set aside. Darken remaining brown icing; paint eyes and mitten on Santa piece and, using photograph as a guide, door hinges and "wood" markings on (door) piece A5 and (window) pieces A6.

With 1 teaspoon white icing and yellow food color, tint icing yellow. With paintbrush and yellow icing, paint flower centers on (front) piece A4 and (window) pieces A6 and elf's trousers and bow.

Right: Santa gives a cheery welcome to his candy-cookie house, appropriately named Santa's Dream House.

Designed and executed by Pat Darling.

Let windows, door, elf and Santa dry 4 hours.

4. With melted chocolate in pastry bag fitted with number-3 tip, pipe diagonal lines in a diamond pattern over icing on (window) F pieces. Let dry 2 hours.

5. On (front) foam-core B piece, with metal spatula and white icing, using photograph as a guide, attach (window) F and G pieces. Attach Santa to G piece. On section A, with white icing, attach (window) A6 pieces and (door) A5 piece. Let dry 4 hours.

6. Meanwhile, using photograph as a guide, with small metal spatula and white icing, attach strawberry-flavored chewy candies to (front) B, (sides) C and D pieces. Let dry overnight.

7. Assemble house: Carefully stand decorated (front) section B on double-thickness 17-by-28-inch foam core; support with cans. Glue and tape (side) D piece to right side; glue and tape (side) C piece to left side. Glue and tape (back) B piece to side pieces. Glue and tape (roof) E1 and E2 pieces to house.

8. Decorate roofs: Using photograph as a guide, with small metal spatula and white icing, attach milk-chocolate-covered, chopped-almond candy bars to roof, using X-acto knife to cut candy to fit as necessary. With X-acto knife, cut milk-chocolate-covered caramel- and crunchy-cookie bars crosswise into 1- to 2-inch pieces. Using photograph as a guide, with small metal spatula and white icing, attach candy, cut side facing front, to (roof) A7 piece, beginning at bottom of roof and stacking candy. Let dry overnight.

9. Next day: With pastry bag fitted with number-16 tip and white icing, pipe a thick line of icing over top edge of house frame. Using photograph as a guide, attach lemon-, orange- and strawberry-flavored soft chewy candies to icing. Pipe a thick line of icing over front edge of house roof and at all seams of section A. With icing, using photograph as a guide, attach candy canes to section A.

With green food color, tint about 3 cups icing green. With pastry bag fitted with number-16 tip and ¼ cup green icing, decorate edges of (window) F pieces. While icing is wet, using photograph as a guide, attach candy canes to sides. With remaining green icing in pastry bag fitted with number-352 tip, using photograph as a guide, decorate house and 6-inch candy cane with leaves; cover Styrofoam cones with green-icing leaves, starting at bottom of cone. While icing is wet, insert candy-covered chocolate candies into "trees." With red food color, tint 2 tablespoons icing red; with pastry bag fitted with number-3 tip and red icing, pipe dots of icing onto leaves on roof edge and on 6-inch candy cane.

10. Make fence: With white icing in pastry bag fitted with number-3 tip, using photograph as a guide, decorate remaining milk-chocolate-covered, caramel- and crunchy-cookie candy bars and the gingerbread cookies.

11. With white icing in pastry bag fitted with number-3 tip, pipe hair and beard on Santa and elf. Let dry.

12. Arrange scene: Heap sugar "snow" around house and onto roofs. Stand elf with candy-cane staff, fence pieces and trees in "snow." (Or attach elf and candy cane to small foam-core square; let icing harden.) Arrange fruit-flavored chewy candies and candy-covered chocolate candies in a winding path.

■ Milk to be used in hot chocolate should be cooked in a double boiler or on very low heat to prevent the formation of a skin. The Aztecs were very clever; they used a wooden mixer called a *molinillo*. Today, we use a rotary beater to blend the cocoa and milk. This helps to reduce the settling of the cocoa once it is served and it enhances the chocolate flavor.

■ What to do if you want to decorate a cake directly on its serving plate? Slip strips of waxed paper under the edge of the cake, allowing the strips to hang over the rim of the plate. Frost the cake; then, with a quick motion, pull out the paper.

Royal Icing

3 large egg whites, at room temperature
1 package (1 pound) confectioners' sugar (sift if lumpy)
½ teaspoon cream of tartar

1. In small bowl of electric mixer, combine all ingredients. Beat at high speed until icing is stiff enough to hold its shape. (Add more sugar if necessary.)

2. Cover with a damp cloth or moist paper towel, or place plastic wrap directly on icing surface. If you have filled pastry bags with icing, cover tips with plastic wrap. Store excess icing in sealed container in refrigerator.

Makes about 2 cups.

Notes: When icing is used as mortar, the stiffer it is, the faster it will dry. To match icing color with gingerbread, add cocoa by tablespoonfuls while beating.

To prepare icing for decoration, use wooden picks to add dots of paste colors to icing until color is achieved. If painting with icing, place a small amount of icing in a custard cup. Color; thin with drops of water until spreadable with a paintbrush. If too thin, add more icing.

Over the River and Through the Woods

Designed and executed by Pat Darling.

Our version of the holiday song comes to life in a trio of whimsical creations made from purchased cookies and candies and a little imagination. This page begins the instructions for creating the tasteful town house.

Town House

(pictured, page 235)

PATTERN PIECES
(pages 252, 253, 254, 255, 256)
A, A1-5, B, C, D, E, F, F1-2, G, G1-3, H, I, J, J1-3, K, K1-3, caroler

PROPS AND SUPPORTS
Marker; tracing paper; scissors; X-acto knife; ruler; 2 (40-by-32-inch) sheets, ¼-inch- thick foam-core board; glue; tape; tall juice cans; 7 disposable pastry bags; pastry tips: Nos. 3 (four), 9, 18, 352; rolling pin; about 20 (10-inch) wooden skewers; baking sheet; pastry brush; small metal spatula; wire rack; small paintbrush; plastic wrap; waxed paper; 1 (12-inch) Styrofoam cone

8 recipes Royal Icing, page 234 (make in separate batches before using)

Food paste colors: true brown, leaf green, super red, yellow

DECORATION, CANDIES AND COOKIES
Flour; ½ package (17¼-ounce size) frozen puff pastry, thawed (1 sheet); 1 large egg white, beaten; 2 packages (7¼ ounces each) rectangular butter cookies embossed with chess-piece designs; 3 packages (10 ounces each) rectangular crackers topped with sesame seeds; 12 packages (5½ ounces each) biscuit wafers topped with chocolate and pecans; 1 box (7½ ounces) pumpernickel cracker sticks; 1 package (26 ounces) tiny fish-shape pretzels; 5 chocolate-covered candy bars; red cinnamon candies; sugar

1. With marker and tracing paper, trace pattern pieces; enlarge to scale. Label all pieces; cut out with scissors. With X-acto knife and ruler, cut out 20-by-25-inch piece foam-core board for base; set aside. Place pattern pieces except G, G3, J3 and K3 on remaining foam core. Cut out with X-acto knife. Reserve one 4-by-1-inch piece foam core for caroler support.

2. On foam-core base, using photograph as a guide, assemble center front: Glue and tape one side of A to one side of each A1 piece, using tall juice cans to support structure. Glue and tape A1 to A2. Glue and tape A1 to A3. Glue and tape one B to A2 and other B to A3. Glue and tape one short side of C to each B. With icing in pastry bag fitted with number-3 tip, attach house frame to base. Make roofs: With glue and tape, attach A5 pieces to A and A1, and D and E pieces to house frame. Make chimney: Glue and tape each F piece to F1 pieces; attach F2 (chimney bottom). Set aside. Let stand until glue and icing dry, about 2 hours.

3. Meanwhile, preheat oven to 375°F. On floured surface, with floured rolling pin, roll out puff pastry to 12-inch square. With X-acto knife and ruler, cut pastry crosswise to make nine ½-inch-wide strips. Reserve remaining pastry for another use; twist each strip around a wooden skewer to cover the length of skewer. Place prepared pastry twists on baking sheet; brush with egg white. Bake 20 minutes, until golden-brown. Cool on baking sheet on wire rack. With metal spatula, transfer twists to wire rack; cool completely.

4. With X-acto knife, cut remaining wooden skewers into two 6-inch lengths, two 6¼-inch lengths, one 7¼-inch length, one 7¾-inch length and four 8-inch lengths. Set aside.

5. In custard cup, thin ½ cup icing to painting consistency. With paintbrush and thinned icing, cover foam-core pieces A4, J, J1, K, K1, H and I. Let stand until dry, about 6 hours. Cover remaining thinned icing with plastic wrap; set aside.

6. Tape G, G3, J3 and K3 pattern pieces to work surface. Tape a sheet of waxed paper over each; with pastry bag fitted with number-3 tip and icing, outline all pieces on the waxed paper. While icing is wet, press respectively sized length of wooden skewer in top and bottom of each icing railing and into edges of door opening and on all outside edges of G piece for support. Pipe enough icing over all edges to make ¼-inch-thick border, making sure to cover skewers. Pipe ¼-inch-thick rails spaced ¼ inch apart between railings. With paintbrush and remaining thinned icing, fill in top of G. Let stand until dry, about 6 hours.

7. Meanwhile, with pastry bag fitted with number-3 tip and icing, pipe icing over one long edge of G1 and G2 foam-core pieces. Using photograph as a guide, place on A, centering G1 2½ inches from bottom edge of A and placing G2 6 inches above G1 to allow for insertion of G. Pipe icing over seams. Repeat with J2 and K2 foam-core pieces, attaching J2 to A2 10 inches from base of A2; attach K2 to E 4 inches from

base of E. Place 6 ¼-inch lengths of wooden skewers on G1 to support G2, and tape all pieces crosswise to house frame. Let stand until icing dries, about 2 hours.

8. With metal spatula and icing, using photograph as a guide, attach plain side of butter cookies with chess-piece designs to A2, A3, B and C pieces with short side of cookies on base of house and design right side up.

9. With X-acto knife, score back side of each sesame cracker crosswise into thirds. Cut or break cracker at score lines. With metal spatula and white icing, using photograph as a guide, attach plain side of each cracker piece to flat sides of foam-core house frame, beginning at lower end of house frame above butter cookies and working toward top, using enough icing to resemble mortar around cracker "stones." Let stand until icing dries, about 4 hours.

10. With ¼ cup icing and brown food color, tint icing brown. With brown icing in pastry bag fitted with number-3 tip, using photograph as a guide, decorate door, outline windows, panes of glass on windows and caroler's lamp. Thin icing to painting consistency. With paint brush, using photograph as a guide, fill in borders around windows. Reserve thinned icing, covered with plastic wrap. Let pieces stand until icing dries, about 4 hours.

11. With white icing in pastry bag fitted with number-3 tip, using photograph as a guide, attach chimney to roof; decorate inside edge of A4 with dots of icing; attach windows to house; attach plain side of one biscuit wafer topped with chocolate and pecans to door; attach J and K to respective J2 and K2 platforms on house; attach J1 roof pieces to J; attach K1 roof pieces to K. Let stand until dry, about 1 hour. When dry, with icing, attach door and A4 to house. Carefully peel G, G3, J3 and K3 from waxed paper; with icing in pastry bag, attach G to G1; G3 to G2; J3 to J2; and K3 to K2, using tall juice cans to hold in place until icing dries, about 2 hours.

12. With X-acto knife, cut pumpernickel cracker sticks in half crosswise. With white icing in pastry bag fitted with number-3 tip and using photograph as a guide, attach cracker-stick "bricks" to chimney frame. Let stand until dry, about 2 hours.

13. With icing in pastry bag fitted with number-9 tip, pipe a thick line of icing over roof seams and edges. With X-acto knife, trim puff-pastry twists to fit seams and edges and, using photograph as a guide, attach twists to icing. Let stand until icing dries, about 2 hours. With icing in pastry bag fitted with number-18 tip, using photograph as a guide, pipe thick dots of icing over pastry twists on roof top. Attach mouth side of a fish-shape pretzel to each dot. With icing, attach plain side of biscuit wafers topped with chocolate and pecans to roof, beginning at bottom of roof and stacking cookies to resemble shingles; cut cookies to fit with X-acto knife.

14. With white icing in pastry bag fitted with number-18 tip, using photograph as a guide, pipe zigzag strips over peaks and edges of J1 and K1 roofs and platform edges of G.

15. With white icing in pastry bag fitted with number-9 tip, using photograph as a guide, pipe snow mounds in corners of roof; attach candy bars to each other to form front steps. Let dry.

16. With 1 cup icing and green food color, tint icing green. With metal spatula and some green icing, cover Styrofoam cone. With green icing in pastry bag fitted with number-352 tip, pipe leaves over cone, beginning at bottom edge. Pipe leaves in wreath shape on all windows and, using photograph as a guide, make bunting on balconies. While icing is wet, attach red cinnamon candies for berries on tree. In custard cup, with red food color, tint 2 tablespoons icing red. With red icing in pastry bag fitted with number-3 tip, pipe icing berries onto wreaths and bunting. Let stand until icing dries, about 2 hours.

17. Decorate caroler: In custard cup, with red icing, tint spoon icing flesh color. Thin to painting consistency; with paintbrush, paint caroler's face and hands. In custard cup, thin 1 tablespoon red icing to painting consistency. With paintbrush, cover foam-core caroler except for face, hands and lamp with red icing. Paint mouth on face. With reserved thinned brown icing and paintbrush, paint eyes on face and fill in lamp. Let dry 1 hour. With (unthinned) red icing in pastry bag fitted with number-3 tip, make candle and pipe ruffle collar on dress and fabric fold lines at skirt waist. Using photograph as a guide, with remaining green icing in pastry bag fitted with number-3 tip, outline bow on caroler's hat. In custard cup, thin ½ teaspoon green icing to painting consistency. With paintbrush, fill in lines of hat with green icing. In custard cup, with yellow food color, tint 1 tablespoon icing yellow. With yellow icing in pastry bag fitted with number-3 tip, using swirling motion, pipe hair on caroler and flame on candle. With white icing in pastry bag fitted with number-3 tip, pipe fabric folds in dress and swirls at edge of dress and cape; pipe outline of caroler's book, and fill in.

18. Tape reserved 4-by-1-inch piece foam core to back of caroler for standing support. Arrange tree and prop caroler near house. Arrange sugar to make snow drifts around house.

■ To keep fine white-flour "dust" from clinging to the sides of home-baked chocolate cakes, "flour" your pans with cocoa instead—it even adds flavor.

Here's the sweet route to holiday fun: a cookie-candy-covered bridge, complete with pistachio-nut supports. The horse-drawn sleigh is made of pastillage (sugar paste).

Sleigh Scene

(pictured, pages 238 and 239)

3 recipes Pastillage, page 242 (make in separate batches before using)
Nonstick cooking spray
1 package (3 ounces) powdered gum arabic (see *Note*)

PATTERN PIECES
(pages 256 and 257)
A, B, C, D, E, F, F1, F2, G, H, I, J, J1, K, K1, L, L1, M, N, N1

PROPS AND SUPPORTS
Marker; tracing paper; scissors; X-acto knife; 8-by-12-inch sheet thin cardboard; eight 4½-inch bamboo skewers; 8-by-12-inch file folder; waxed paper; small paintbrush; cans; aluminum foil; 2 pieces medium or fine sandpaper; wire cutters; 1 thin wire coat hanger; floral wire; 16-by-24-inch sheet, ¼-inch-thick foam-core board

DECORATIONS AND CANDIES
Nontoxic colored felt markers; nontoxic black felt drawing pen; 1 piece red string licorice; assorted small colored candies

1. About 2 weeks ahead of making house, with marker and tracing paper, trace pattern pieces; enlarge pieces to scale. Label all pieces and cut out with scissors. On cardboard, trace 2 sleigh side pieces; cut out with X-acto knife. With tip of knife and wooden skewer, make holes in cardboard as marked on sleigh sides. On file folder, trace 2 seat backs and 1 sleigh front; cut pieces out with scissors.

2. Grease several sheets of waxed paper and a rolling pin with nonstick cooking spray. On prepared waxed paper, roll out pastillage, 1 recipe at a time, to ⅛-inch thickness. Set aside pattern pieces B, C and I. Lay as many remaining patterns as possible on the pastillage. With X-acto knife, cut out around patterns, cutting through waxed paper. Combine and reroll trimmings. Carefully remove paper patterns and all excess pastillage. With fingers, using photograph as a guide, form some of trimmings into package shapes and cushions for inside sleigh. Save remaining trimmings; wrap in plastic wrap to use for patching, if necessary.

3. Carefully invert pastillage pieces onto clean sheets of waxed paper, using baking sheets to support pieces while turning. Carefully remove greased waxed paper. With skewers, make holes as marked on sleigh sides and horse pieces. Set aside all pieces in a dry place 1 to 3 days, until dry.

4. Meanwhile, make glue: In small jar with tight-fitting lid, combine gum arabic with enough water to make creamy consistency. Let stand, covered, 12 hours to cure.

5. Assemble sleigh: With small paintbrush, brush glue over one side of each cardboard sleigh side piece;

Pages 238 and 239: Our Christmas family travels on their holiday journey. Right: The destination is Grandma's Gingerbread House.

Covered Bridge designed by Victoria Scocozza Hayes.
Sleigh designed and executed by the Sugar Association.

Designed and executed by Holly Sheppard.

press lightly to attach to pastillage sleigh side piece. Carefully insert one skewer into each hole on one sleigh side piece and extend it to corresponding hole on remaining sleigh side piece. Brush glue over each hole on inside and outside of sleigh. Prop with cans placed around outside of sleigh frame; prop from the inside of sleigh with a crushed piece of aluminum foil. Let stand 12 hours, until glue hardens. When dry, with sandpaper, sand lightly to remove excess glue. If necessary, sand sleigh seats and floor to fit inside of sleigh. Brush glue over edges of seats and floor pieces; press lightly to arrange in place over skewers inside sleigh. Let stand 24 hours, or until glue dries. Roll out pastillage and cut out sleigh front and seat backs as directed above. With nonstick cooking spray, grease file-folder sleigh front and seat-back patterns. Place paper supports in place inside sleigh, curving to fit; trim if necessary. Carefully stand sleigh on back end. Place pastillage seat backs and sleigh front in place, using paper to support curve of each piece. Let stand 12 hours, or until pastillage dries. Brush glue over side edges of pastillage seat backs and sleigh front pieces; attach to sleigh. Let stand 24 hours, or until glue dries. When sleigh is completely dry, stand it on its runners. Carefully remove paper supports from seats and front. With colored felt markers, using photograph as a guide, decorate sleigh.

6. Make people: Glue each pastillage arm piece to front of respective person. Let stand 24 hours, or until glue dries. With sandpaper, smooth edges of top pastillage piece. With colored felt markers, using photograph as a guide, decorate people. Use drawing pen to mark details on people.

7. Make horse and dog: Glue horse pieces together. Using photograph as a guide, glue harness pieces to horse. Let stand 24 hours, or until glue dries. With colored felt markers, using photograph as a guide, decorate horse. Using markers, color dog.

8. Make connecting bars: Roll out remaining pastillage as directed above. Cut out I pattern pieces. Cut coat hangers to make two lengths slightly longer than I piece. Place wires over I piece; bend slightly where I piece bends. Set aside. In center of each 6-inch length of floral wire, make a 1/3-inch-wide loop. Place one piece of coat hanger wire over one I pastillage piece, matching at bend; place one piece of floral wire over coat hanger wire, placing loop outside lower edge of pastillage. Brush glue over wires. Press second I pastillage piece over all, hiding wires within pastillage. Repeat procedure with remaining pastillage and wires to make second rod. Let stand 24 hours, or until glue dries. If necessary, smooth edges with sandpaper. With black felt marker, color connecting bars.

9. Place sleigh in position on foam-core board. Place end of one connecting bar in hole in front of sleigh. Loop one end of 5-inch length of floral wire through loop of bar; thread wire through holes in horse and into loop of second bar. Twist slightly to hold in place while positioning second bar into remaining hole in sleigh front. Twist wires; cut off excess. Glue the horse and sleigh in place. Glue one end of each licorice string to each side of the horse's mouth. Glue the other ends to hands of driver, trimming off excess licorice.

10. With glue, using photograph as a guide, attach candies to decorate sleigh, connecting rods and harness. Let stand 12 hours, or until glue dries. Meanwhile, with markers and candies, using photograph as a guide, decorate packages and cushions. With glue, attach cushions, people, dog and packages in place in sleigh. Let stand 24 hours, or until glue dries.

Pastillage

1 package (1 pound) confectioners' sugar
1 tablespoon gum tragacanth
1/4 cup water
Cornstarch

1. In small bowl of electric mixer, at medium speed, combine sugar and gum tragacanth. Mix in water until blended. With wooden spoon, stir until pastillage forms a ball.

2. Turn out onto a countertop lightly dusted with cornstarch. Knead until smooth and pliable, adding more water, a teaspoon at a time, if necessary. Dust with cornstarch; place in plastic bag or airtight container. Let rest 1 hour.

Makes 1 cup.

Note: Gum tragacanth is available at candy-making supply stores.

Covered Bridge

(pictured, pages 238 and 239)

BRIDGE FRAME PIECES

Cut according to dimensions:
2 (19 by 6 inches) for roof; 1 (18 by 8 1/2 inches) for floor; 2 (18 by 8 inches) for sides; 2 (8 1/2 by 1 inch) for beams; 4 (12 by 4 inches) for base sides; 2 (12 by 4 inches) for base top and bottom; 4 (4 by 2 inches) for base ends

BRIDGE PATTERN PIECES *(page 257)*
Roof end; side (for size and placement of windows)

TREE PIECES

Cut one square each size:
2 3/4 inches; 2 1/2 inches; 2 1/4 inches; 2 inches; 1 3/4 inches; 1 1/2 inches; 1 1/4 inches; 1 inch; 3/4 inch; 1/2 inch

PROPS AND SUPPORT

Marker; ruler; tracing paper; scissors; X-acto knife; 2 (40-by-30-inch) sheets, 3/16-inch thick, foam-core board; glue; white masking tape; disposable pastry bags; pastry tips: Nos. 0, 2B, 4, 4B, 6, 6B, 18; metal spatula; gold star; iridescent paper or cellophane (or see *Note*)

COOKIES, CRACKERS AND CANDIES

16 honey graham crackers; 3½ packages (8½-ounce size) vanilla sugar wafers; 1½ packages (9½-ounce size) shredded whole-wheat wafers; 2 rolls (.9 ounce each) wild-cherry-flavored roll candy; 4 (6-inch) candy canes; 1 package (.5 ounce) green oval spearmint candies; red cinnamon candies; 2 round peppermint-flavored candies; silver dragées; 40 green candy-coated chocolate candies; 6 sticks cherry-flavored striped stick bubble gum; 6 round green soft jelly candies; 6 round red soft jelly candies; 4 bags (5.5 ounces each) red pistachios; 1 small green gumdrop; granulated sugar or coarse (kosher) salt

7 recipes Royal Icing (page 234; make in separate batches before using)

Food paste colors: leaf green, Christmas red

1. With marker, ruler and tracing paper, trace pattern pieces; enlarge to scale. (There are no patterns for bridge frame and tree pieces; use marker and ruler to cut out these pieces according to dimensions given.) Label; cut out with scissors. Place bridge frame pieces on foam-core board; cut out with X-acto knife. With marker, outline windows on foam-core bridge side pieces; cut out with X-acto knife. Outline tree pattern pieces on 4 graham crackers, fitting several squares on one cracker. With X-acto knife, score crackers several times around pattern edges; cut out, trimming off excess crackers. Set aside.

2. Assemble bridge frame: With glue and masking tape, attach bridge floor to bridge side pieces. Attach flat side of one short end of each bridge beam to top edge of opposite side, placing each beam about 4 inches from short side edge. Let glue dry. Meanwhile, assemble roof: With glue and masking tape, join one long edge of each roof piece, and to each end glue and tape one roof end piece. Let stand until glue dries. Attach roof to bridge. Let stand until glue dries.

3. Assemble bridge base: Using glue and tape, join each long edge of base top at right angles to one long edge of a base side. Attach one base end to each end. Repeat with remaining foam-core base pieces to make second base. Let stand until glue dries.

4. With Royal Icing in pastry bag fitted with number-0 tip, pipe icing on one flat long side of sugar wafer. Lightly press wafer onto lower edge of end of bridge, placing short side of wafer at bottom edge. Pipe a thin line of icing over edges of wafer. Repeat with enough remaining icing and wafers to cover both sides of bridge, using X-acto knife to cut wafers as necessary to fit. Attach wafers at each end of bridge for a finished look. With additional icing, in same pastry bag, attach whole graham crackers to floor inside bridge, making 4 crosswise rows of 3 whole graham crackers each. If necessary, with X-acto knife, score crackers several times and cut to fit. With icing in same pastry bag, attach sugar wafers to inside walls of bridge as for outside. Let stand 4 hours, until icing dries.

5. Decorate roof: With icing in pastry bag fitted with number-4 tip, pipe a thick, horizontal line of icing onto roof about ½ inch from lower edge of roof. While icing is soft, attach flat side of enough shredded whole-wheat wafers to cover length of roof, using X-acto knife to trim wafers to fit. Repeat, overlapping shredded whole-wheat wafers to make 4 more rows. Repeat on remaining side of roof. (If desired, wafers can also be attached by piping icing directly onto one flat side of each wafer.) With X-acto knife, cut remaining shredded whole-wheat wafers in half. Pipe a thick line of icing on seam of roof. While icing is wet, press half-wafers into icing to make a row along each side of peak. Let icing dry, about 4 hours.

With icing in pastry bag fitted with number-6B star tip, pipe a thick line over roof peak. While icing is wet, using photograph as a guide, press wild-cherry-flavored roll candies into icing. Attach gold star at one end. With dots of icing, attach candy canes to roof.

With icing in pastry bag fitted with number-4B star tip, using photograph as a guide, pipe a line of icing along edge of each roof end and three stars at peak of roof end. While icing is wet, attach green oval spearmint candies in each line and a red cinnamon candy in each star.

With icing in pastry bag fitted with number-2B star tip, pipe stars of icing to cover each roof end. While icing is wet, attach a round peppermint-flavored candy in center. Pipe stars of icing along lower edge of each roof side; press a red cinnamon candy into each star. Pipe stars of icing along lower edge of roof end at front of bridge. Press a silver dragée into each star.

6. Decorate sides of bridge: With icing in pastry bag fitted with number-4B star tip, using photograph as a guide, pipe a line of icing over edges of sugar wafers at ends of bridge. While icing is wet, attach a

cinnamon candy at top of line on inside edge; attach green candy-covered chocolate candies to each outside line.

With icing in pastry bag fitted with number-18 star tip, pipe enough icing stars around each window edge to form a continuous line. While icing is wet, attach a silver dragée to each star.

With icing in pastry bag fitted with number-18 star tip, pipe lines of icing over foam-core piece in center of each window. While icing is wet, attach a stick of gum.

With a dot of icing, attach a green jelly candy over each window and a red jelly candy under each window.

With icing in pastry bag fitted with number-18 star tip, pipe a window-size *X* on bridge at side of each window. While icing is wet, attach cinnamon candies at ends and center of *X*'s; press silver dragées into remaining portion of *X*'s.

7. With metal spatula, spread icing thickly over sides and ends of bridge bases. While icing is wet, attach enough pistachios to cover icing. Let icing dry.

8. Make tree: With icing in pastry bag fitted with number-6 tip, pipe a large circle of icing over largest graham-cracker square. Press cracker square just smaller than first onto icing, so corners of second square are not directly over corners of first square. Repeat, stacking squares in order of size, ending with smallest. Let stand until icing hardens.

In small bowl, with green food color, tint ½ cup icing green. Place in pastry bag fitted with number-18 tip. Pipe "leaves" onto each graham-cracker corner of tree. With dot of green icing, attach gumdrop to top of tree.

In another small bowl, with red food color, tint ½ cup icing red. Place in pastry bag fitted with number-4 tip. Pipe "berries" onto leaves.

9. Place bridge bases on flat surface with long sides facing and about 16 inches apart. Crinkle iridescent paper; flatten slightly. Arrange paper "stream" between bases. Place bridge on top, resting each end of bridge on a base piece. Spread exposed top edges of bases with icing; while icing is wet, attach pistachios. Place tree near bridge. Sprinkle tree and bridge with sugar "snow." Pile sugar around tree, bridge and stream.

Note: To make a candy stream, preheat oven to 350°F. Line baking sheet with aluminum foil; set aside. Unwrap 1 package (7½ ounces) hard blue-mint candies; place in thick plastic bag. With hammer, crush candies coarsely. Place on baking sheet to form a 10-by-4-inch strip (strip can be slightly wavy). Bake until candies begin to melt to form "water," about 5 minutes. (Leave some pieces unmelted to give rippling effect.) Cool on baking sheet on wire rack. Carefully peel off foil when ready to set up scene.

■ Trimmings from gingerbread dough make stunning (and fragrant!) tree ornaments, gift tags and place cards. Reroll trimmings and chill dough as for gingerbread houses, except roll dough to ⅛-inch thickness. To make ornaments: With ¼-inch round cutter or metal tip from a pastry bag or plastic drinking straw, cut a hole near the top of each cookie. Make holes about ½-inch inside edges so when cookies soften by the heat of tree lights they will not tear through. To make tags and cards: Cut holes all around edges of cookies to lace tags and cards with ribbons. Decorate cookies with decorating icing, and "paint" them with thinned icing. (Liquid food colors may be used to tint icing, but paste colors will be more intense.) Do not use too much icing, as this will soak the cookies, softening them and adding to their weight. Store cookies in an airtight container.

An icing wreath in the window welcomes guests to Grandma's gingerbread house. Cotton-candy smoke wafts from the chocolaty peanut chimney, and frosted pretzels line the roof.

Grandma's Gingerbread House

PATTERN PIECES
(pages 258 and 259)
A, A1-2, B, B1-3, C, C1, D, E, E1, F, F1-4, G, G1-3, H, I, J, K, L, M, N

PROPS AND SUPPORT
Marker; ruler; tracing paper; scissors; 2 (40-by-32-inch) sheets, ¼-inch-thick foam-core board; X-acto knife; tape; parchment paper; rolling pin; large baking sheets; wire rack; glue; tall juice cans; nonstick cooking spray; about 12 disposable pastry bags; pastry tips: Nos. 1 (four), 3 (four), 5, 9, 16, 67; small metal spatula; small paintbrush; waxed paper; 28 small red twisted birthday candles; 1 (10-inch) Styrofoam cone; light

2 recipes Gingerbread dough, page 247

About 6 recipes Royal Icing, page 247 (make in separate batches before using)

3 recipes Sugar-Syrup Glass, page 247 (make in separate batches before using)

Food paste colors: leaf green, Christmas red, yellow

DECORATIONS, CANDIES AND COOKIES

Flour; about 150 pieces seashell-shape candies; silver dragées; 2 packages (4 ounces each) pink bubble-gum tape; about 24 sticks peppermint candy; 2 boxed (16 ounces each) small cinnamon graham crackers; about 400 red cinnamon candies; about 500 brown candy-coated peanuts; 8 pieces hot-dog-shape bubble gum; 1 oval cookie; about 12 assorted licorice candies; 10 miniature white-chocolate-covered or yogurt-covered pretzels; assorted miniature gumdrops; shelled sunflower seeds; cotton candy; sugar

1. With marker, ruler and tracing paper, trace pattern pieces; enlarge to scale. Label all pieces; cut out with scissors. With X-acto knife and ruler, cut out two 18-by-24-inch pieces foam-core board for base. Tape pieces together to make double thickness. Set aside.

2. Make foam-core backing: On remaining foam-core board, outline all pattern pieces except B2, C1, D, E, F and F1-4 (these are to be made of unsupported gingerbread). On foam-core pattern pieces A, A1, A2, and B, extend window opening ¼ inch on all sides, on patterns A and A1, mark foam core to measure ¼ inch less at rooftop than outline of pattern. (Differences in foam-core board and gingerbread pieces are to allow for trimming any uneven edges on baked gingerbread.) Cut out foam-core pieces with X-acto knife; set aside.

3. Make gingerbread pieces: On floured 22-by-12-inch sheet parchment paper or aluminum foil, with floured rolling pin, roll 1 piece of dough to ¼-inch thickness. Place rolled dough and paper on baking sheet; chill 15 minutes. Roll out and chill remaining dough as above. Flour reverse side of patterns except C, H, L, M and N. Lay as many patterns as possible (except C, H, L, M and N) on the chilled rolled dough, ½ inch apart. With X-acto knife, cut out around patterns. Carefully remove paper patterns and all excess dough. (Save dough trimmings in plastic bag; chill to reroll later.)

4. Preheat oven to 350°F. Bake gingerbread pieces 15 to 25 minutes, or until very firm and dark brown. (Soft gingerbread is not advised for use in houses.) Remove small pieces as they brown to wire rack, since they bake faster; cool completely. Store in airtight container until ready to assemble house.

5. On foam-core base, using photograph as a guide, assemble house frame from foam-core pieces: Glue and tape each side of A to one long side of one B piece, using tall juice cans to support structure. Glue and tape each remaining side of B piece to one long side of each remaining B piece, supporting structure with juice cans. Glue and tape one side of each A1 piece to each remaining side of B pieces. Glue and tape each remaining side of each A1 piece to one long side of each A2 piece. Glue and tape remaining side of each A2 piece together.

6. Make chimneys: Glue and tape straight long side of each G foam-core piece to each long side of G1 piece. Glue and tape G3 to join wide portion of G pieces. Glue and tape G2 pieces together to form a box.

7. With X-acto knife, score any uneven edges of gingerbread pieces; trim edges evenly. Set aside all pieces without windows.

8. Make "glass" windows and door: Place gingerbread pieces with windows and the door piece on enough baking sheets to arrange pieces in a single layer. With nonstick cooking spray, grease area on baking sheet under door and window openings except large window on A piece (to be covered with bay window) and the bottom window space on one B piece (to be used as a door opening onto front porch). Working quickly with one recipe hot sugar syrup at a time, pour enough syrup into each window opening to fill but not overflow opening. Let stand until completely cool. Carefully remove gingerbread pieces from baking sheet; set aside.

9. Make clapboard markings: Arrange gingerbread wall pieces on flat surface with long sides touching. With ruler and tip of X-acto knife, mark horizontal lines ⅝ inch apart over walls, making sure lines match from wall to wall. Tint 3 recipes icing with enough unsweetened cocoa powder to match gingerbread. With brown icing in pastry bag fitted with number-3 tip, cover markings in gingerbread. Let stand 2 hours, until icing is dry.

10. Beginning with A2 pieces, with one recipe white icing in pastry bag fitted with number-9 tip, pipe over back of each gingerbread wall; press onto corresponding section of foam-core house frame, holding gingerbread on foam-core frame until secure, about 1 minute.

11. With brown icing in pastry bag fitted with number-3 tip, using photograph as a guide, attach one side of one bay-window panel to gingerbread A piece; with icing, attach sides of remaining panels to each other, using tall juice cans to support structure. Attach remaining side of window to gingerbread A piece. With brown icing, using photograph as a guide, attach B1 to right side of A. Let stand until icing dries, using tall juice cans to support porch side. Meanwhile, with brown icing in pastry bag fitted with number-3 tip, cover each seam with a

thick line of icing. Let stand 4 hours, until icing dries.

12. With small metal spatula and brown icing, using photograph as a guide, attach seashell-shape candies to base of house except on B pieces, using enough icing to resemble mortar in a 1½-inch-thick strip around base of house. Thickly cover H foam-core piece with brown icing; press shells into icing. Let stand until dried, about 4 hours.

13. Attach roofs and trim supports: Using photograph as a guide, glue and tape foam-core I piece to house. Glue and tape 4 foam-core J pieces to house. Glue and tape foam-core K piece to house. Glue and tape L trim-support pieces onto angled roof edges; glue and tape M trim-support to edge of K roof piece.

14. Attach chimneys: Glue and tape assembled wide end (with G3 piece) of long chimney to cutout section of I roof piece and over seam of A2 pieces of house side. Glue and tape assembled G2 pieces to K roof piece.

15. With green food color, tint one recipe icing green. With 1 cup green icing in pastry bag fitted with number-3 tip, outline top edges of all shutters. Let stand 1 hour, or until icing dries. Thin ½ cup green icing to painting consistency; with paintbrush and thinned green icing, cover shutter inside of green-icing edge. Let stand 2 hours, or until dried. With green icing in pastry bag fitted with number-1 tip, using photograph as a guide, pipe 3 horizontal lines 1/16 inch apart at top and bottom of painted side of each shutter. Let stand 2 hours, or until dried.

16. With red food color, tint ¼ cup white icing red. With icing in pastry bag fitted with number-1 tip, pipe a tiny heart under green-icing lines at top of each shutter. With spatula, spread red icing on door around "glass"; with red icing in pastry bag fitted with number-1 tip, outline edges and pipe tiny dots of icing at top and bottom of door. While icing is wet, attach a silver dragée near glass at each inside corner of door and a brown candy-covered peanut on door for doorknob. On sheet of waxed paper, pipe one 1-inch-high and one 2-inch-high red bow. Set aside 1 hour, or until icing dries. Carefully remove from paper; set aside.

17. With yellow food color, tint ½ cup icing yellow. With yellow icing in pastry bag fitted with number-3 tip, pipe an arch around top of each window. Place all but 4 candles on sheet of waxed paper; with yellow icing in pastry bag fitted with number-3 tip, pipe a flame onto each candle wick. Set aside 2 hours, or until icing dries. Carefully remove from paper; set aside.

18. Tape C pattern piece to work surface. Tape a sheet of waxed paper over pattern. With white icing in pastry bag fitted with number-3 tip, pipe diagonal lines of icing ¼ inch apart extending from top of porch support to bottom of support; repeat, reversing directions, to make diamond-shape lattice. Let stand 4 hours, or until icing dries. Carefully remove from paper. Set aside.

19. With brown icing in pastry bag fitted with number-3 tip, spread icing over side of one foam-core board porch support (C) that fits against house under window. Pipe a line of brown icing over edge of second C piece to fit against house. With brown icing, attach steps to join support pieces; attach front-porch floor and door. With X-acto knife, cut sticks of gum the length of steps. With brown icing, attach sticks of gum to cover each step and porch floor; with icing, attach a silver dragée at end of each stick of gum to resemble a nail head. Let stand 1 hour, or until icing hardens.

20. Meanwhile, with X-acto knife, cut candy sticks so that there is one piece for each window width and a 5½-inch length for porch post. With brown icing in pastry bag fitted with number-3 tip, attach candy-stick windowsill to each window; using photograph as a guide, attach a shutter to each side of a respective-size window. With icing, attach candy-stick post to porch; attach front- and back-porch roofs to house and post and side supports, sloping roofs slightly and using juice cans for support. Attach bay-window roof. Let stand 2 hours, or until icing dries.

21. Decorate roofs of house: With metal spatula and white icing, working in small sections at a time, spread roofs with icing. While icing is wet, using photograph as a guide, attach rows of small graham crackers placed ⅛ inch apart, using X-acto knife to cut crackers in half diagonally to fit at roof edges; with icing, attach cracker halves onto roof-trim supports. With brown icing in pastry bag fitted with number-3 tip, attach a red cinnamon candy to each cracker on house roofs only. Pipe a line of brown icing over each sloping seam and short edge of J roof pieces.

22. Decorate chimneys of house: With brown icing in pastry bag fitted with number-3 tip, thickly coat chimney with icing. While icing is wet, using photograph as a guide, attach brown candy-coated peanuts to chimney sides and a hot-dog-shape piece of bubble gum to each edge on chimneys.

23. With green icing in pastry bag fitted with number-67 tip, pipe leaves in center of each candy-stick windowsill. While icing is wet, attach a candle with yellow-icing flame, cutting candle with X-acto knife to fit inside each window. Using photograph as a guide, pipe leaves on window above front porch to form a wreath.

24. With red icing in pastry bag fitted with number-1 tip, attach candles to front-porch floor for rails; with icing, attach N foam-core railing to candles, wall and candy-stick post. With icing, attach a red-icing bow to wreath and candy-stick post. Pipe berries onto wreath. With

icing, cover center of cookie to make doormat; attach to porch under door. With icing, attach several pieces of licorice together and decorate to make packages.

25. With white icing in pastry bag fitted with number-5 tip, using photograph as a guide, pipe a thick line of icing over roof seams and edges. While icing is wet, attach pretzels to top of roof and a brown-candy-covered peanut to each roof edge. With dots of icing, decorate crackers on roof trim. Attach icing lattice under porch floor.

26. With green icing and metal spatula, cover Styrofoam cone. With green icing in pastry bag fitted with number-67 tip, pipe leaves over icing on cone. While icing is wet, attach red cinnamon candies, silver dragées, gumdrops and sunflower seeds. With white icing in pastry bag fitted with number-1 tip, pipe snowflakes onto tree. With yellow icing in pastry bag fitted with number-1 tip, decorate tree with garlands of icing; outline star on yellow piece of licorice; attach star to top of tree.

27. Place light in house. Place seashell-coated walkway in front of steps. Place cotton candy in each chimney. Sprinkle sugar as snow around house. Arrange tree and packages near porch.

Royal Icing

3 large egg whites, at room temperature
1 to 1½ packages (1-pound size) confectioners' sugar (sift if lumpy)
½ teaspoon cream of tartar
Unsweetened cocoa powder

In small bowl of electric mixer, combine egg whites, 1 package sugar and the cream of tartar. Beat at high speed until icing is stiff enough to hold its shape. If not stiff, add more sugar. Place plastic wrap directly on icing surface to keep from drying out; if icing is in pastry bags, wrap tips with plastic wrap.

Makes about 2 cups.

Notes: When icing is used as mortar, the stiffer it is, the faster it will dry. To match icing color with gingerbread, add cocoa powder by tablespoonfuls to icing while beating.

To prepare icing for decoration, use wooden picks to add dots of paste colors to icing until the desired depth of color is achieved.

Gingerbread Dough

8½ to 9 cups unsifted all-purpose flour
1 tablespoon ground ginger
2 teaspoons ground cinnamon
½ teaspoon salt
1 cup butter-flavored shortening
1 bottle (16 ounces) dark corn syrup
1½ cups lightly packed brown sugar

1. In large bowl of heavy-duty electric mixer, mix together 4 cups flour, the ginger, cinnamon and salt. Set mixture aside.

2. In medium saucepan, over low heat, melt shortening. Add corn syrup and sugar; stir until sugar dissolves. Remove from heat.

3. With mixer at low speed, gradually beat syrup mixture into flour mixture. At medium speed, beat in 2 cups flour. With wooden spoon or hands, mix in remaining 2½ to 3 cups flour until stiff dough forms. (Dough should be firm, not sticky.) Divide dough into four parts; if not using immediately, wrap in plastic wrap and refrigerate up to a week. If dough is refrigerated, let it come to room temperature before rolling (about 3 hours).

Sugar-Syrup Glass

1 cup sugar
¼ cup water

In small saucepan, dissolve sugar in water. Bring to boiling, stirring. Boil without stirring, until syrup is amber-colored, swirling pan to color sugar evenly. Remove pan from heat; immediately use as directed for making "glass" windows for house.

Packing Tips for Homemade Foods

■ Bake and send brownies or other bar cookies in a disposable foil pan. Wrap in a strong plastic bag; overwrap in enough foil or packing material to stabilize it in a gift box.

■ To pack cookies for mailing, wrap them first in plastic wrap, then place in a gift box. Put the box in a sturdy shipping box lined with a thick wall of packing material. Solid, bar-type cookies are better for shipping than are iced or crisp cookies. Avoid shapes with pointed edges, which can break off.

■ In lieu of tins, wrap empty coffee or shortening cans in holiday paper or aluminum foil. Fill the tins with cookies, separating the layers with waxed paper.

■ For a festive, tasty gift, wrap baked cookies individually in plastic wrap, and pack them in a basket along with the recipe and some of the ingredients used to bake them.

■ Include the pan or casserole your food gifts were baked in as part of the gift. Or nestle your cooked goodies in a piece of brand-new cooking equipment.

Holiday Centerpieces to Savor

Dazzle family and friends with our sweet sensations. Create a tree spun with purchased pirouette cookies—and that's just the start of our good-enough-to-eat holiday decorations.

Pirouette Cookie Tree compliments of Pepperidge Farm, Inc.

Pirouette Cookie Tree
(pictured, left)

3 packages (12 ounces each) chocolate-flavored (imitation) pieces (see *Note*)
Styrofoam cone, 4″ base, 9″ high
6 to 8 packages (5½ ounces each) pirouette cookies
6 ounces pecan halves
Red and green candied cherries, halved

1. In top of double boiler, melt chocolate-flavored morsels over warm, not boiling, water. Spread a little chocolate on bottom of cone, and anchor in center of 14-inch platter or cake board. Lightly coat cone with melted chocolate.
2. Arrange pirouette cookies in star-burst fashion around base of cone, using chocolate as "glue." Build rows of cookies on top of each other. Reduce number of cookies as you move up cone in a circle. It may also be necessary to trim and shorten some cookies.
3. As you reach top of cone, stack cookies in teepee fashion. Drizzle all over with melted chocolate.
4. Sandwich pecan halves together with chocolate to make pinecones; attach to tree with a little chocolate. Trim tree with red and green cherries. If desired, place a bow and small ornament at top.

Note: Real chocolate morsels will discolor or "bloom" upon melting and rehardening unless they undergo a tempering process. Using chocolate-flavored morsels makes this process unnecessary.

Truffle Wreath

(pictured, below right)

Truffles

1½ cups unsalted butter or margarine
6 cups sugar
1½ cups milk
1½ cups unsweetened cocoa powder
6 cups quick-cooking oats, uncooked
1½ cups finely chopped toasted almonds
1½ cups finely chopped dried apricots
¼ cup almond extract
Cocoa coating (see *Note*)

Chocolate Stand

2 packages (12 ounces each) semisweet-chocolate pieces
4 ounces paraffin
14-by-3-by-2-inch Styrofoam ring
Straight pins
2½ yards (2-inch) ribbon

Wreath

1 package (12 ounces) semisweet-chocolate pieces
3 tablespoons shortening
12 unshelled almonds
12 to 16 dried apricot halves

1. Make truffles: In very large saucepan, combine butter, sugar and milk. Bring to boiling; simmer 4 to 5 minutes. Remove pan from heat; stir in cocoa. Blend in oats, almonds, apricots and almond extract. Lightly grease 15½-by-10½-by-1-inch jelly-roll pan. Spread mixture in pan. Cover with plastic wrap; chill until just firm. With hands or a melon-ball or small ice-cream scoop, form in about one hundred 1-inch balls. Roll balls in cocoa coating; allow to dry overnight.

2. Make chocolate stand: In top of double boiler, over hot, not boiling, water, melt 2 packages chocolate with paraffin, stirring until smooth. Place Styrofoam ring on a wire rack set on a sheet of aluminum foil. With metal spatula, completely cover ring with melted chocolate. Remelt drippings, if necessary, for a second coating. Set aside to harden.

3. Pin ribbon to outside of ring. Make a bow from remaining ribbon; pin over ribbon seam.

4. Make wreath: In top of double boiler, over hot, not boiling, water, melt chocolate with shortening, stirring until smooth. With spoonfuls of melted-chocolate mixture, attach a layer of truffles to Chocolate Stand. Let harden.

5. With additional melted-chocolate mixture, attach remaining truffles to first layer. Let harden. Use remaining melted-chocolate mixture to attach almonds and apricots.

Note: To make cocoa coating, in medium bowl, combine 1½ cups unsweetened cocoa powder with 1½ cups confectioners' sugar.

Truffle Wreath compliments of Hershey Foods.

Micro-Way: Holiday Party Drinks

Apricot Nog

5 large egg yolks
½ cup sugar
¼ teaspoon ground cinnamon
2 cups milk
1 cup apricot-flavored brandy
1 can (12 ounces) apricot nectar
1 cup heavy cream
Additional ground cinnamon
Cinnamon sticks

1. Place egg yolks in large glass bowl; with wire whisk, beat in sugar and ¼ teaspoon ground cinnamon until mixture is thick and the sugar dissolves. Set aside.

2. In 4-cup glass measure, heat milk and brandy on HIGH 4 minutes. Gradually add hot milk mixture to egg-yolk mixture, whisking constantly until blended. Cook on HIGH 1½ minutes, stirring after 45 seconds. Whisk in apricot nectar. Cover; refrigerate apricot mixture until cold.

3. Just before serving, with electric mixer, whip cream until soft peaks form; fold into milk mixture. Pour into punch bowl. Sprinkle with additional ground cinnamon; garnish with cinnamon sticks.

Makes 12 servings (8 cups).

■ Don't throw away that half-empty bottle of ginger ale or lemon-lime-flavored soda. Instead, pour the beverage into an ice-cube tray and freeze. Keep on hand and later use the ice cubes to chill and to add flavor to a party punch.

Holiday Currant Punch

1 cup currant jelly
2 cups pineapple juice
1 can (6 ounces) frozen limeade concentrate
3 cups water
1 bottle (1 liter) club soda
Ice mold

In large glass bowl, melt jelly on MEDIUM, about 6 minutes, stirring every 2 minutes. Stir in juice, limeade and water; chill. Before serving, place punch in punch bowl; stir in soda until blended. Garnish with ice mold (see tip, next column).

Makes 16 servings (12 cups).

Hazelnut Mocha Café

½ cup instant-coffee powder
2 squares (1 ounce each) unsweetened chocolate, finely chopped or grated
1½ cups water
½ cup sugar
4 cups half-and-half or light cream
½ cup hazelnut-flavored liqueur
1 cup heavy cream, whipped

1. In large glass bowl, combine coffee powder, chocolate and water. Cook on HIGH 2 minutes, stirring after 1 minute. Stir in sugar; cook on HIGH 6 minutes, stirring after each minute. Set aside.

2. In 4-cup glass measure, heat half-and-half on HIGH 5 minutes; stir into chocolate mixture. Stir in liqueur. With wire whisk or portable electric mixer, beat mixture until frothy. Pour into eight 6-ounce mugs, dividing evenly; top each with a dollop of whipped cream. If desired, garnish cream with chocolate curls or grated chocolate.

Makes 8 servings.

■ To make ice mold, fill star-shape or other mold ¾ full with water. Freeze. Pour about ¼ inch water on top of ice; arrange sliced starfruit, lime wedges and maraschino cherries with stems. Freeze. Just before serving punch, unmold ice mold. Place in punch. Arrange fresh-mint sprigs on top.

Serve a holiday beverage: Apricot Nog (top), Holiday Currant Punch.

Cake and Cookie Patterns

Kong Cake Cutting Diagram
(Recipe, page 144.)

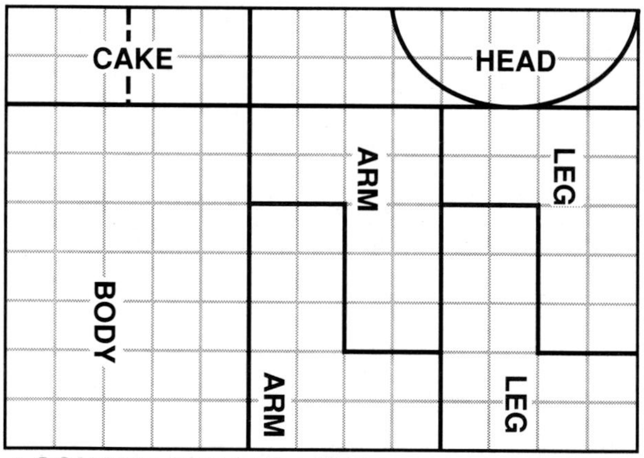

1 SQUARE EQUALS 1 INCH

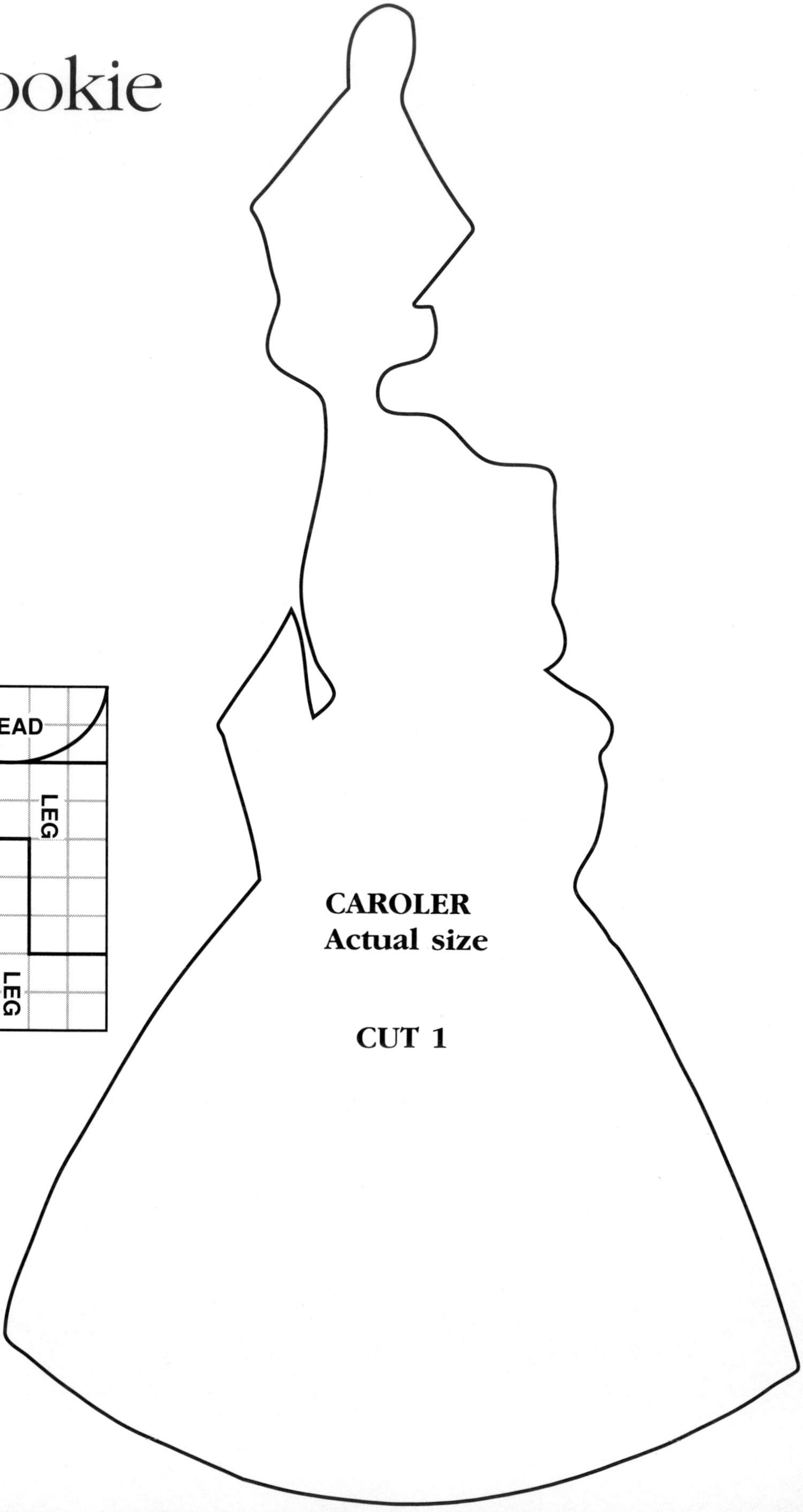

Town House
Patterns are one-fourth actual size.

(Instructions begin on page 236.)

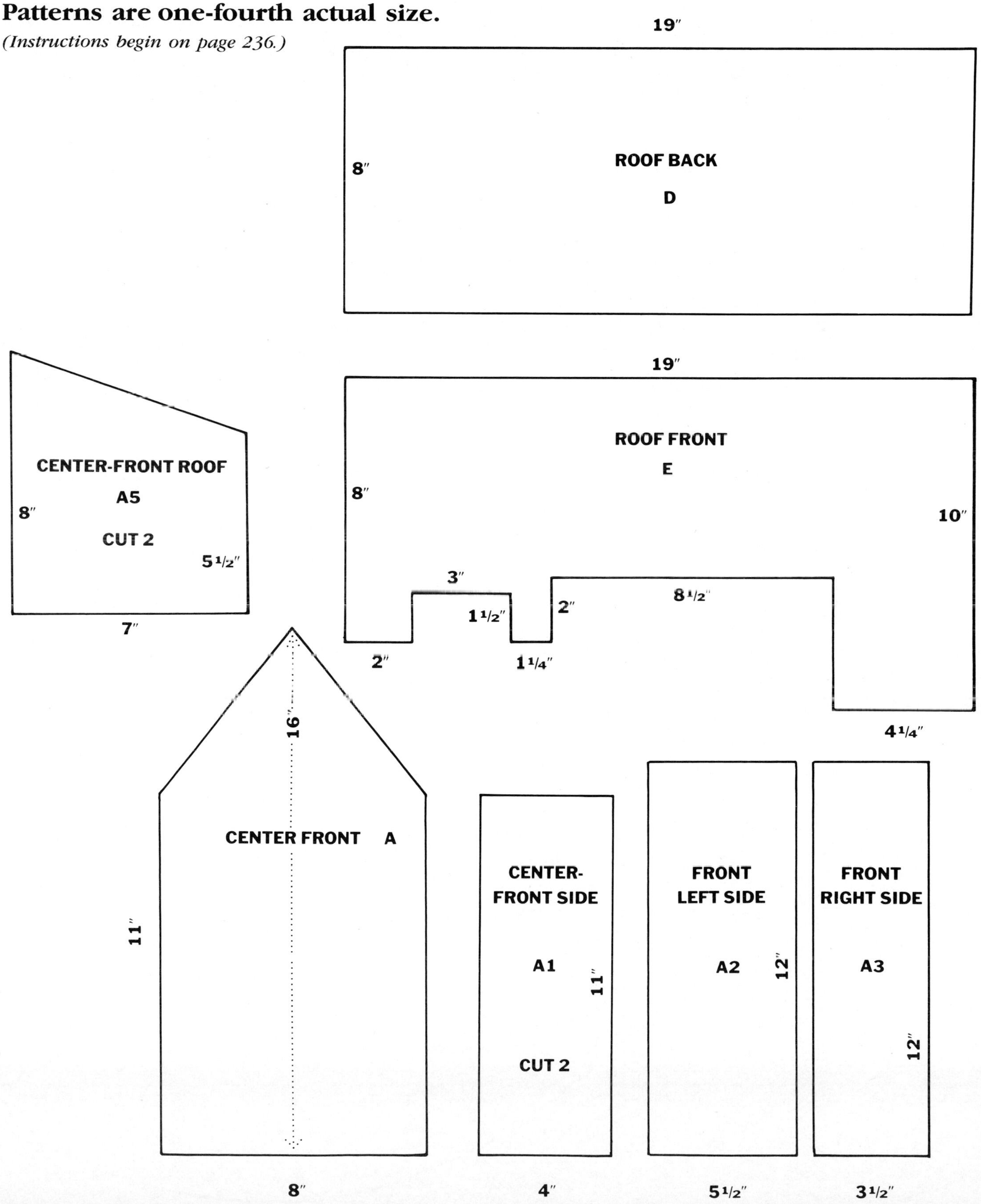

Town House
Patterns are one-fourth actual size.

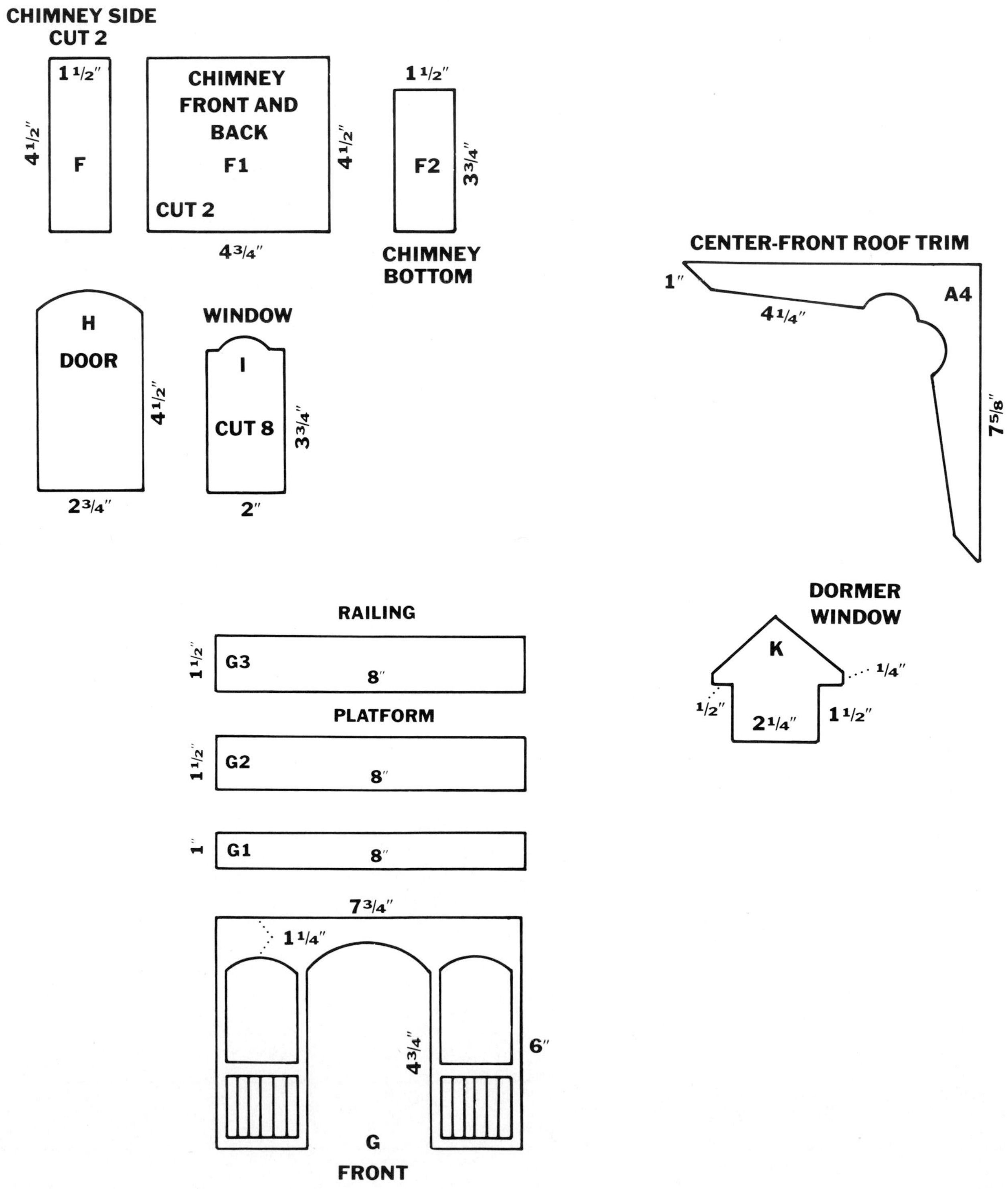

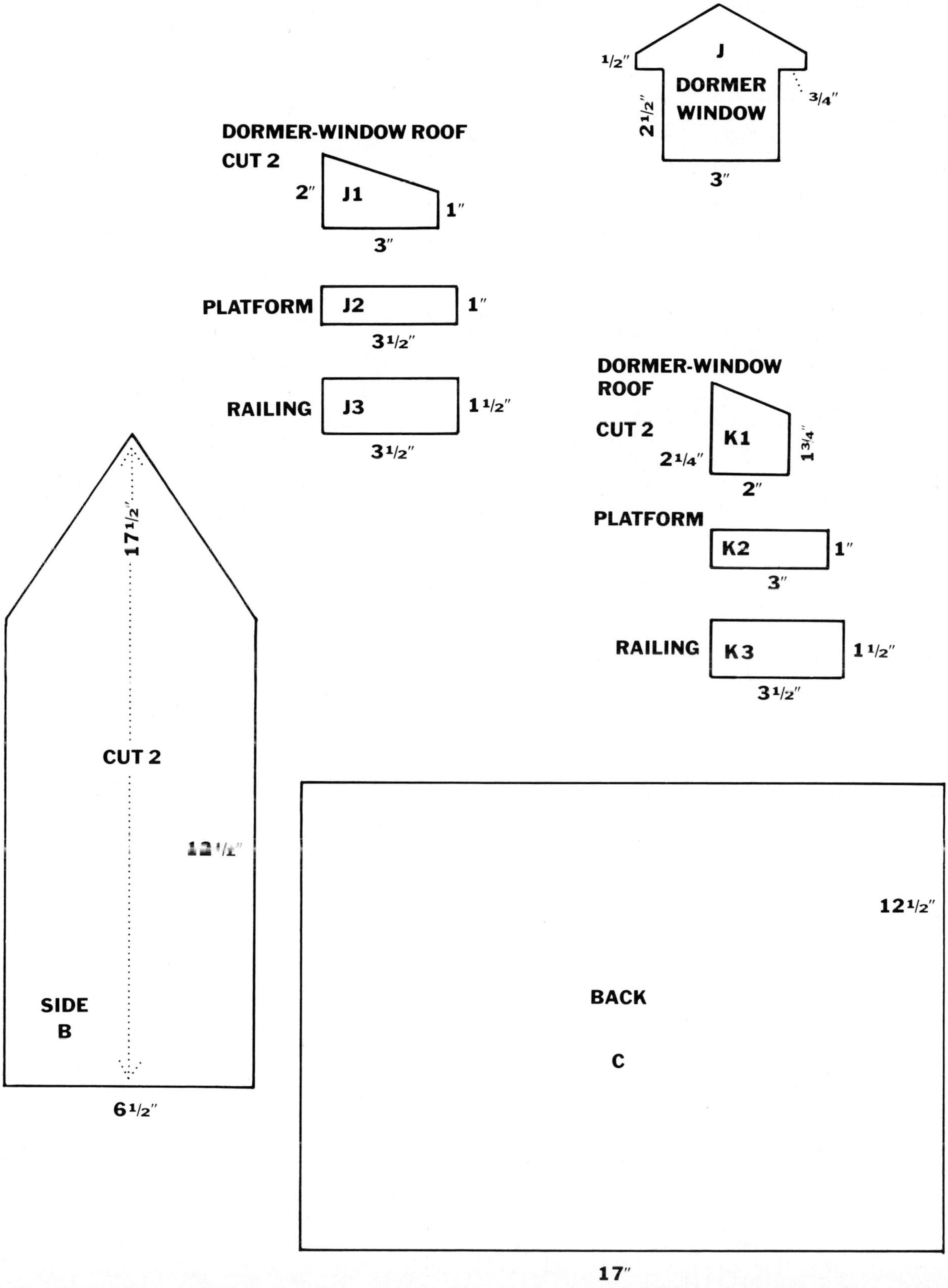
J
DORMER WINDOW
1/2"
2 1/2"
3/4"
3"
DORMER-WINDOW ROOF
CUT 2
J1
2"
1"
3"
PLATFORM
J2
1"
3 1/2"
RAILING
J3
1 1/2"
3 1/2"
DORMER-WINDOW ROOF
CUT 2
K1
2 1/4"
1 3/4"
2"
PLATFORM
K2
1"
3"
RAILING
K3
1 1/2"
3 1/2"
17 1/2"
CUT 2
12 1/2"
SIDE
B
6 1/2"
BACK
C
12 1/2"
17"

Sleigh Scene with Covered Bridge
Patterns are one-fourth actual size.

(Instructions begin on page 240.)

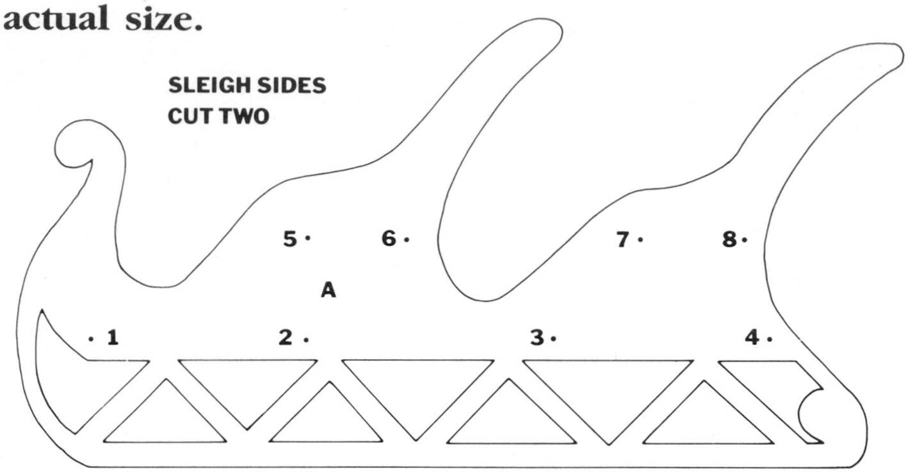

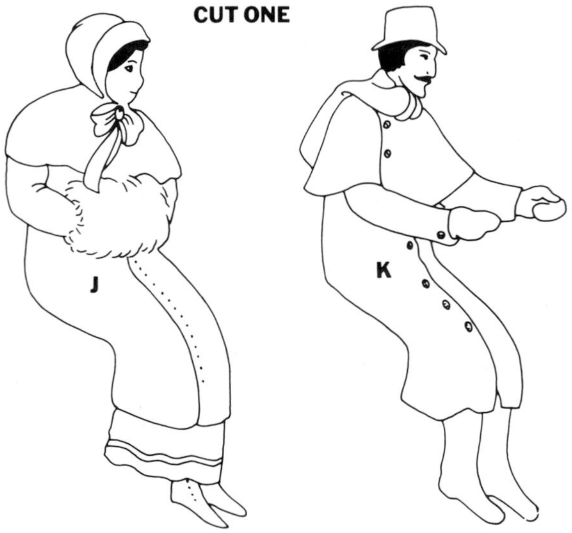

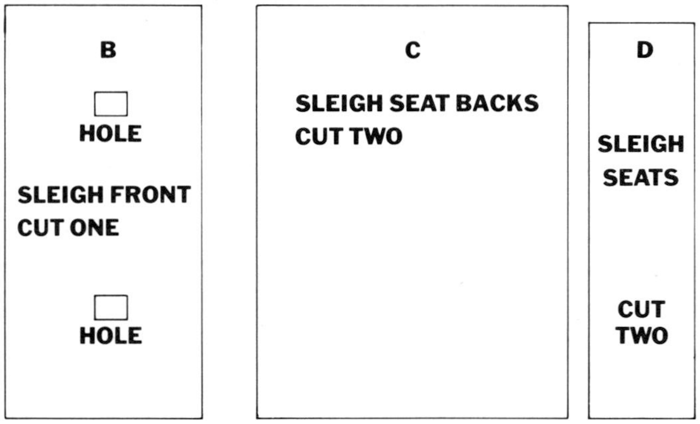

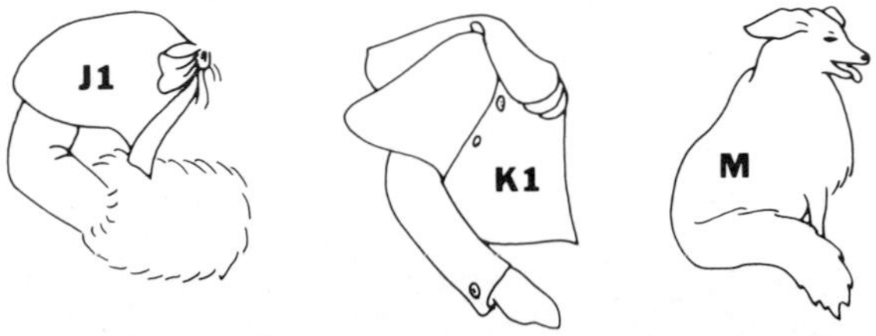

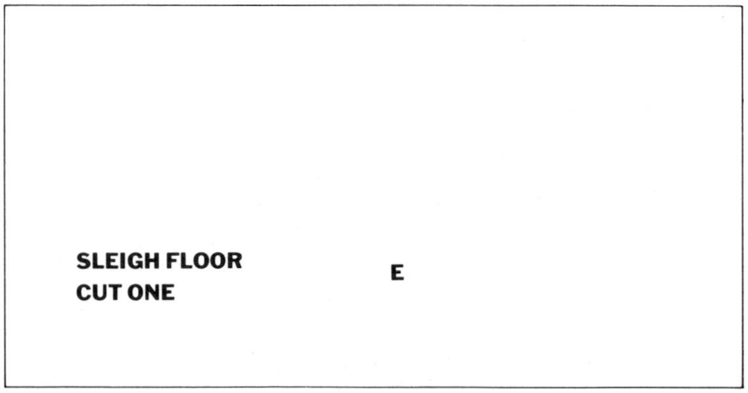

COVERED BRIDGE

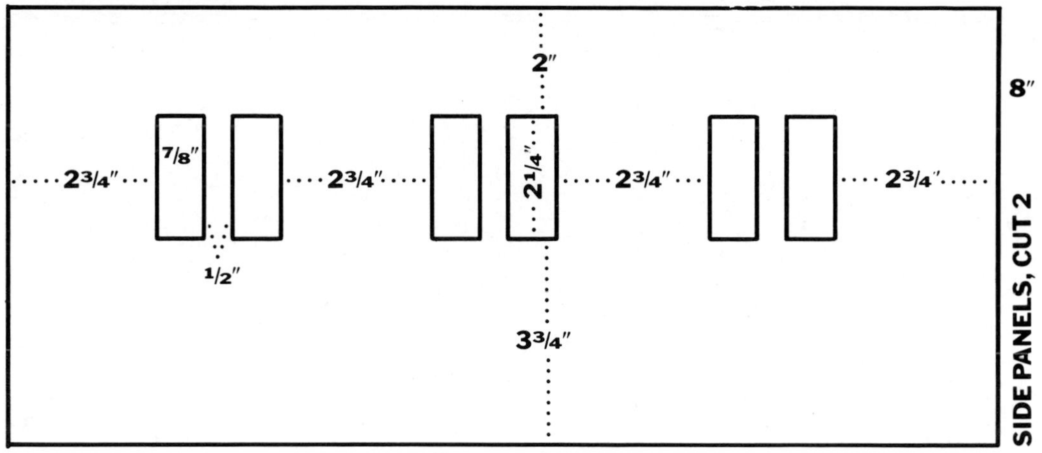

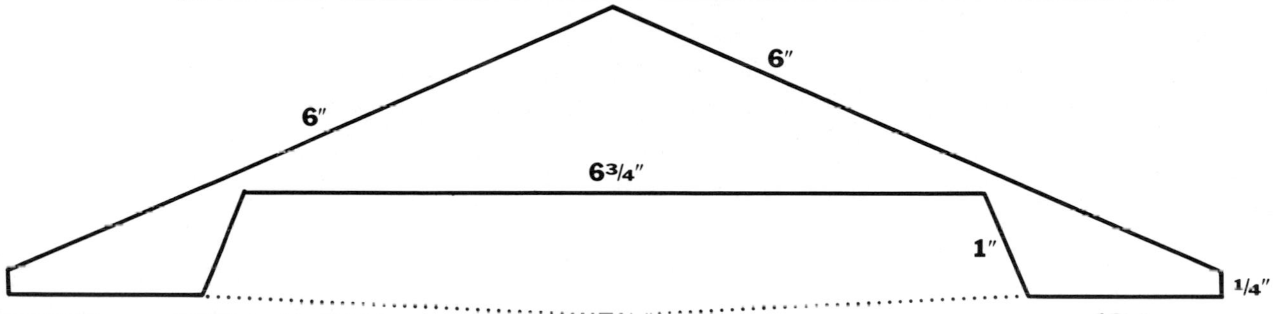

COVERED BRIDGE **ROOF END, CUT 2**

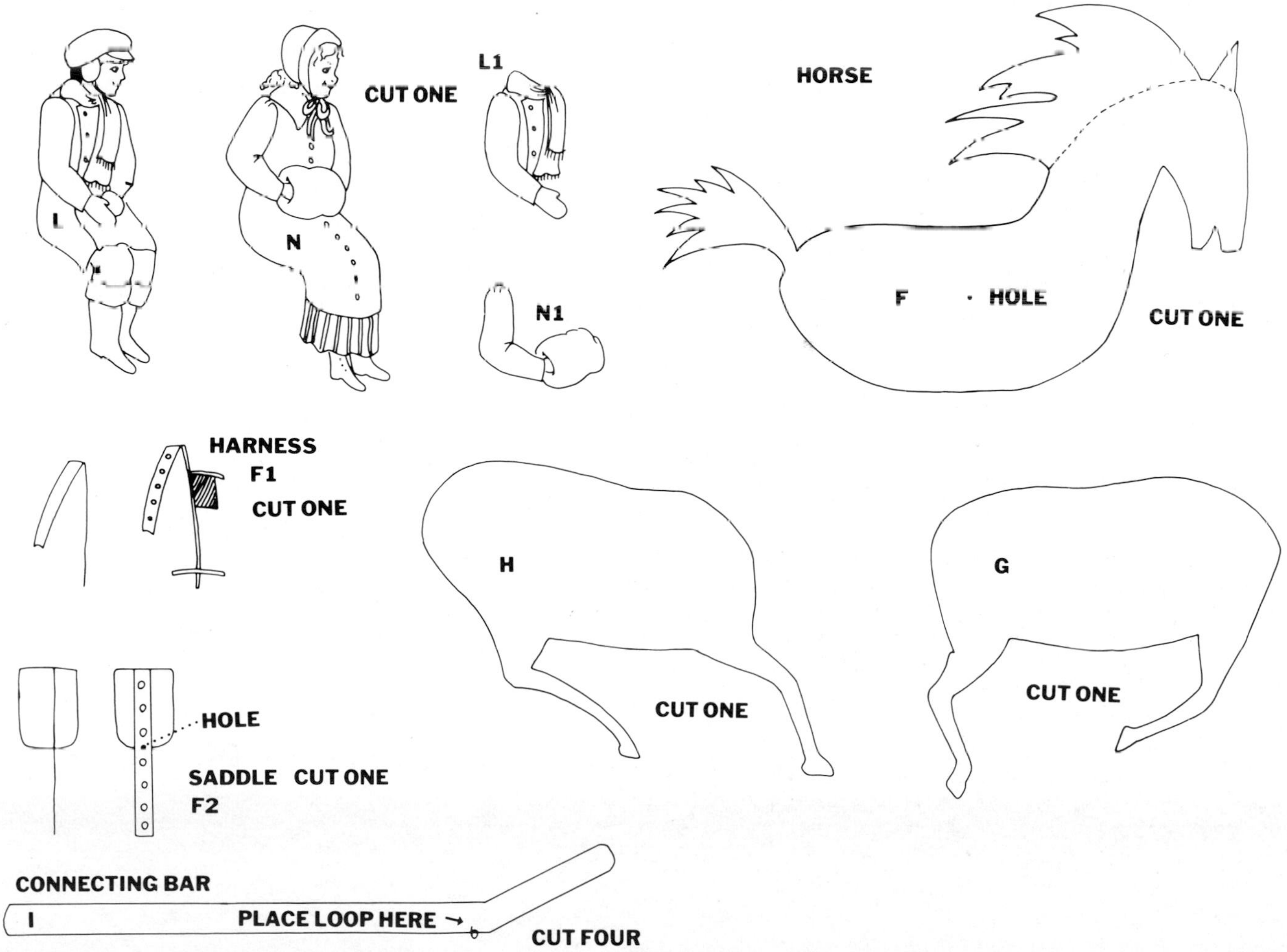

Grandma's Gingerbread House
Patterns are one-fourth actual size.

(Instructions begin on page 244.)

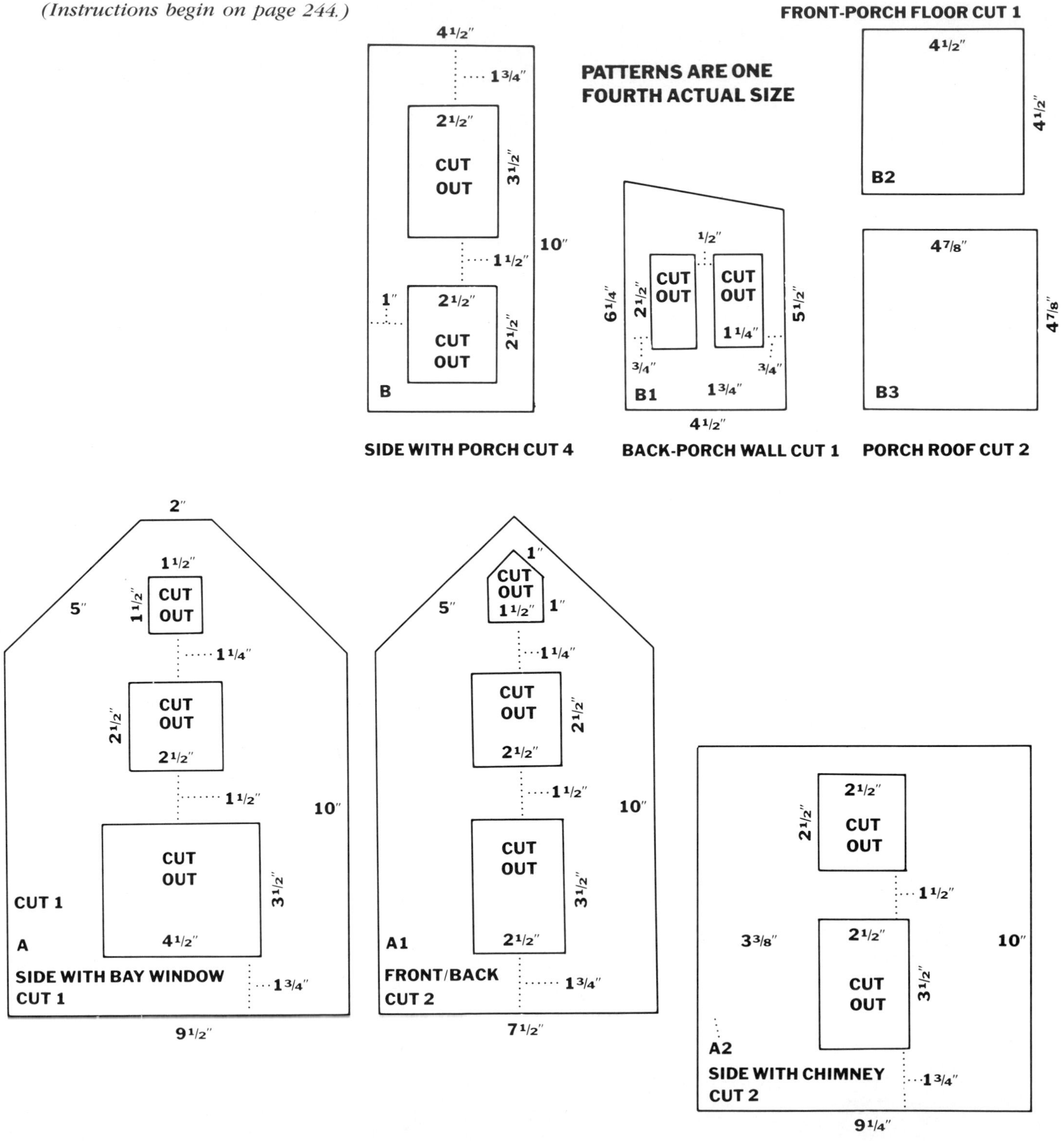

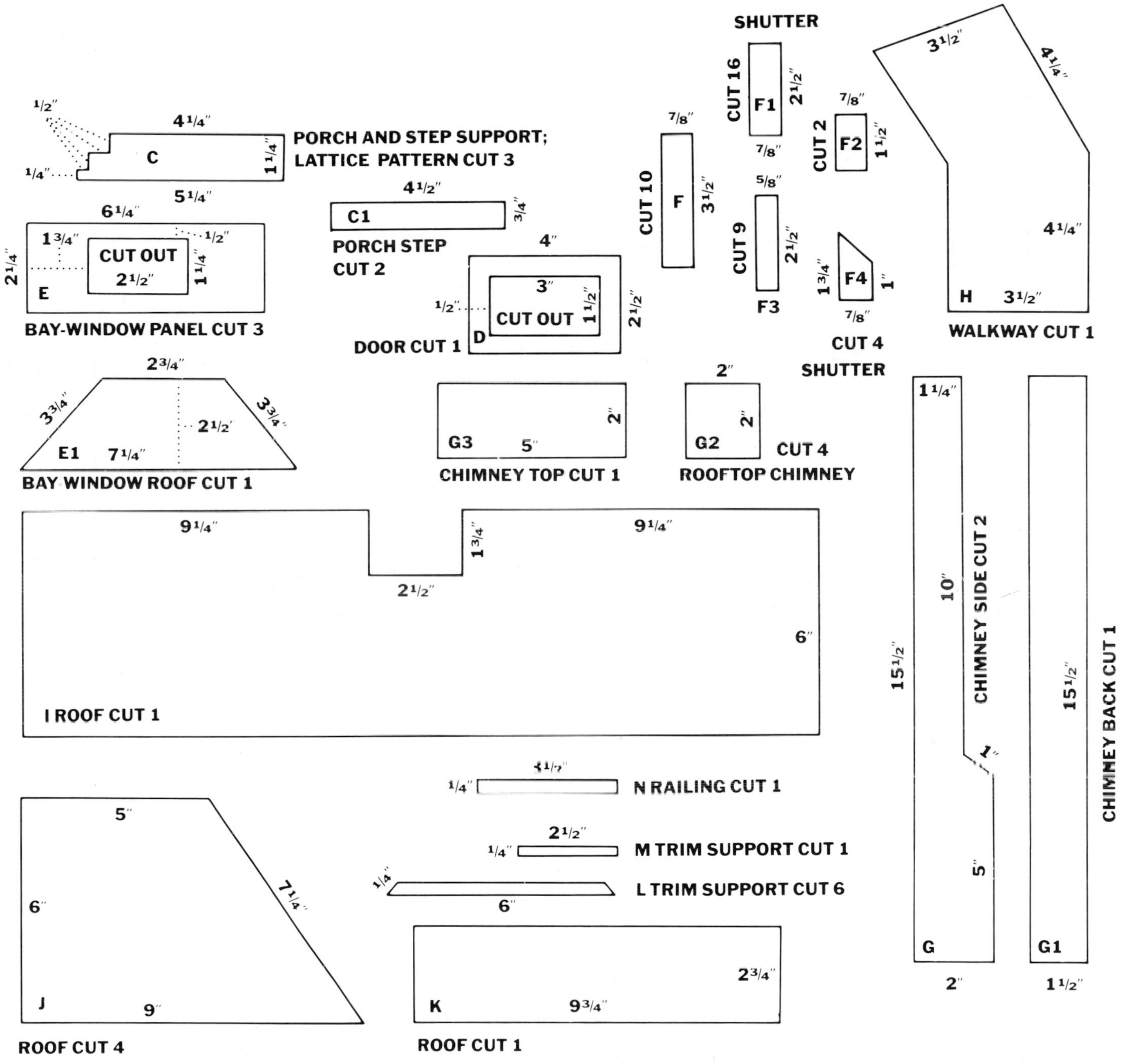
SHUTTER
CUT 16
F1
CUT 2
F2
CUT 10
F
CUT 9
F3
F4
CUT 4
SHUTTER
WALKWAY CUT 1
H
C
PORCH AND STEP SUPPORT;
LATTICE PATTERN CUT 3
C1
PORCH STEP
CUT 2
CUT OUT
E
BAY-WINDOW PANEL CUT 3
CUT OUT
D
DOOR CUT 1
E1
BAY WINDOW ROOF CUT 1
G3
CHIMNEY TOP CUT 1
G2
CUT 4
ROOFTOP CHIMNEY
I ROOF CUT 1
CHIMNEY SIDE CUT 2
CHIMNEY BACK CUT 1
G
G1
N RAILING CUT 1
M TRIM SUPPORT CUT 1
L TRIM SUPPORT CUT 6
J
ROOF CUT 4
K
ROOF CUT 1

Santa's Dream House
Patterns are one-fourth actual size.
(Instructions begin on page 232.)

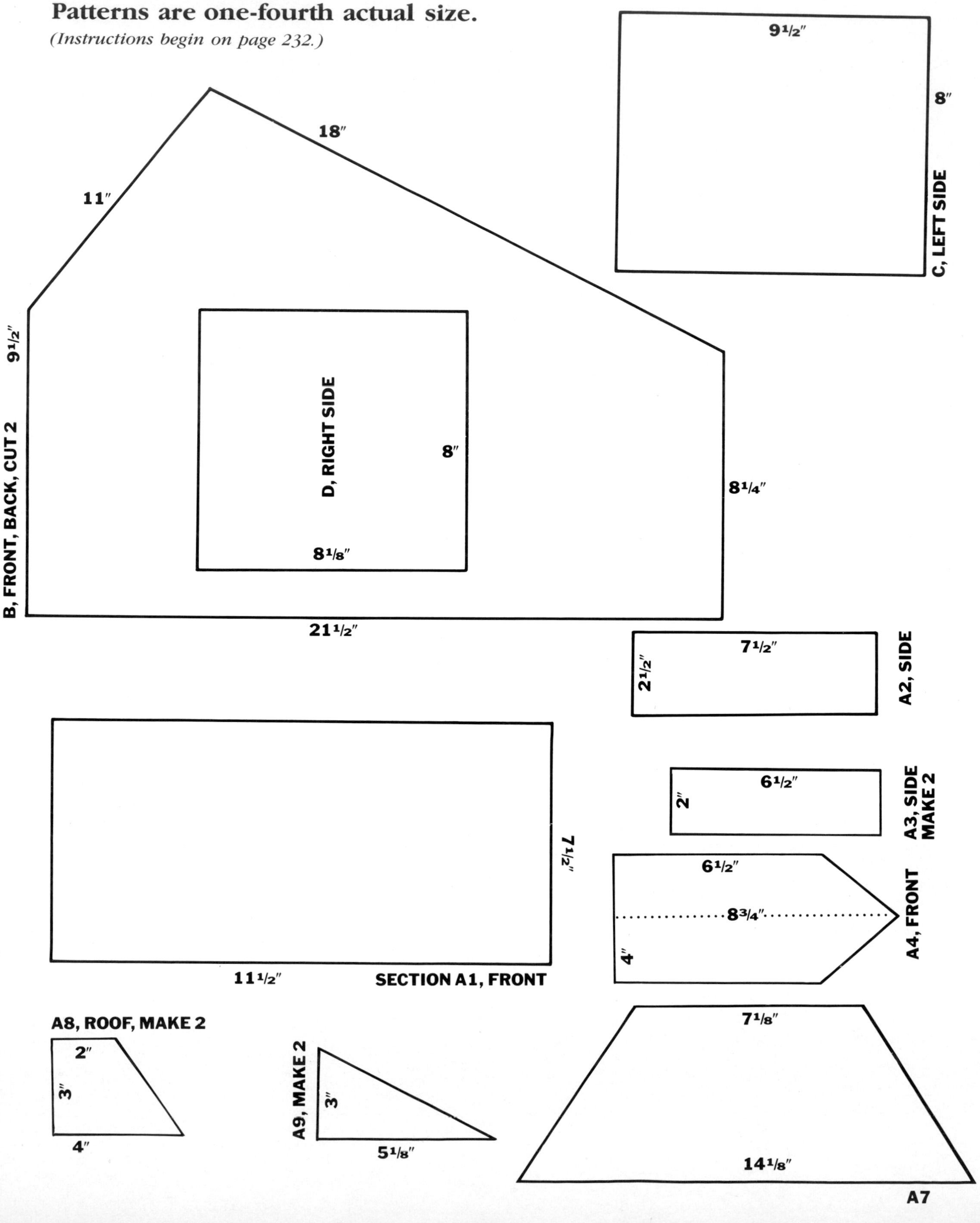

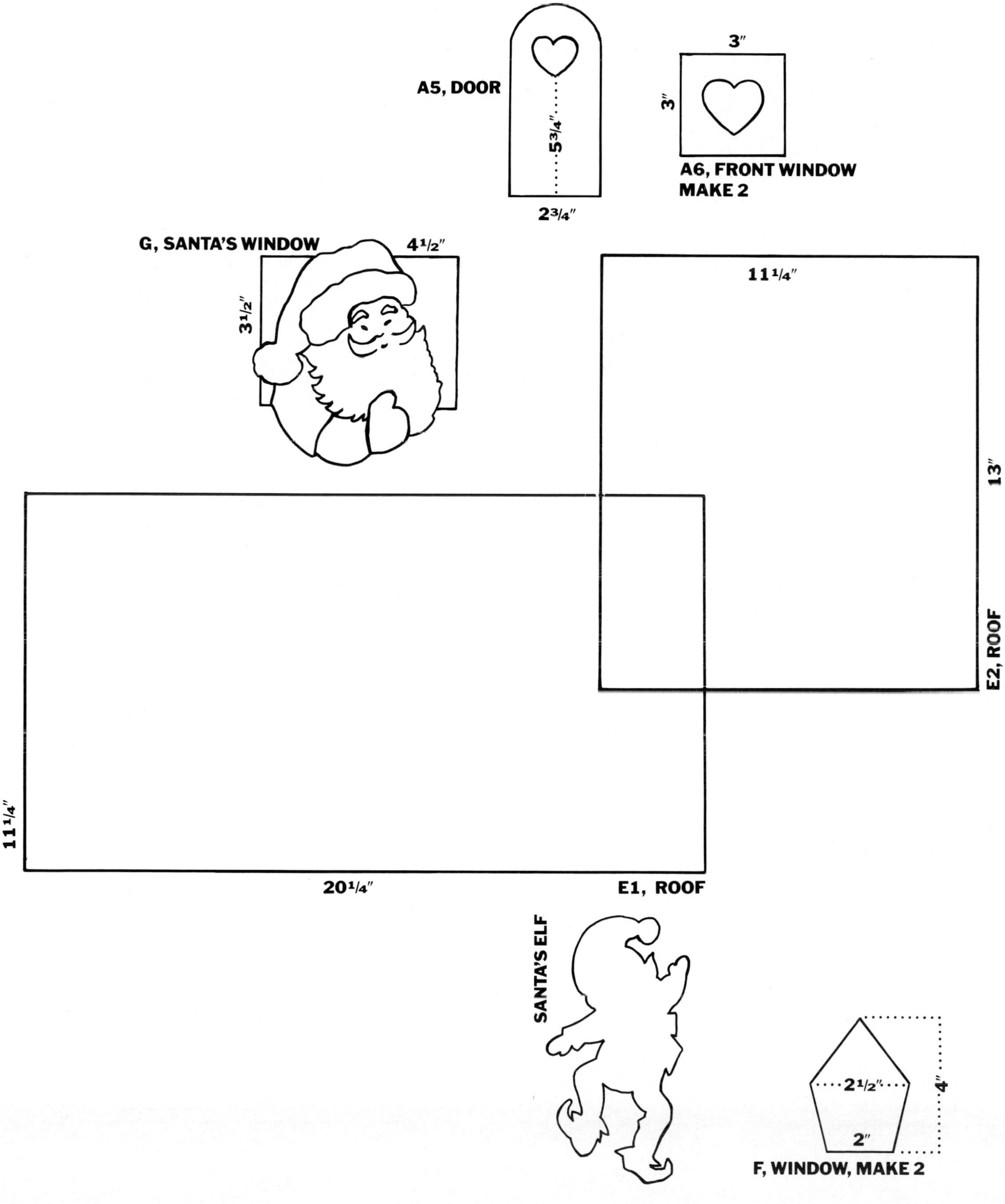
A5, DOOR
5¾″
2¾″
3″
3″
A6, FRONT WINDOW
MAKE 2
G, SANTA'S WINDOW
4½″
3½″
11¼″
13″
E2, ROOF
11¼″
20¼″
E1, ROOF
SANTA'S ELF
2½″
4″
2″
F, WINDOW, MAKE 2

General Recipe Index

Every recipe is listed by food category and/or major ingredient. Each microwave recipe page number is preceded by an "M."

Almonds
Marzipan Pinecones, 228
Spirals, Nut, 225
Twists, Almond, 39
Wreaths, Cherry-Almond, 230
Anchovy Crisps, 60
Appetizers
Antipasto Buffet, 54
Brie, Pepper-Baked, 17
Cheese-Filled Gouda, 198
Chicken, Lime, 76
Chicken Pinwheels, 76
Chutney Dipping Sauce, 76
Clams Casino, M206
Coconut Bites, 76
Dip, Zesty Avocado, 90
Flatbreads, Easy Chinese, 198
Pâté, Madeira, M207
Ribs With Two Sauces, Appetizer, 16
Salmon Mousse, Molded, 196
Teriyaki Wings, 198
Apples
Bars, Cranberry-Apple Streusel, 229
Pie, Deep-Dish Apple-Cider, 194
Pie, Sour-Cream Apple, 128
Sautéed Apples With Warm Custard, 93
Tart Deluxe, Apple, 204
Apricots
Nog, Apricot, M250
Pie, Pumpkin-Apricot Chiffon, 13
Sauce, Amaretto Apricot, 197
Soufflé, Berry-Topped Apricot, 40
Strudel, Warm Apricot-Cheese, 15
Artichokes
Cheesecake, Savory Artichoke, 194
Lamb-Stuffed Artichokes, 55
Savarin, Eggplant-Artichoke, 180
Asparagus
Platter, Leek-and-Asparagus, 25
Sesame Asparagus, 129
Avocado Dip, Zesty, 90

Bacon
Canadian Bacon, Champagne-Glazed, 15
Dumplings, Bacon, 179

Bananas
Bread, Kiwi-Banana, 128
Cake Kids, Banana Cone-, 43
Pie, Banana-Coconut-Cream, 126
Pops, Frozen Banana, 146
Soufflé, Frozen Banana-Toffee, 197
Torte, Pineapple-Banana, 25

Barbecued and Grilled
Asparagus, Sesame, 129
Bean Bake, Three-, 111
Bean Bundles, Green-, 129
Beef, Barbecued, M115
Beef, Creole, 107
Beef Tenderloin, Spit-Roasted, 111
Bread on a Skewer, 113
Celery, Grilled Sweet-and-Sour, 110
Chicken, Maple-Smoked, 107
Chicken Turnovers, Stuffed, 109
Chili Dogs, All-American, 90
Coleslaw, Skillet, 129
Cornbread, Confetti, 113
Cornish Hens, Grilled Oriental, 111
Corn Pudding, Roasted, 107
Crabs With Garlic-Tomato Butter, Soft-Shell, 110
Ham Waikiki, 108
Hens, Plum-Glazed, M114
Hens, Raspberry-Grilled, 126
Ice Cream Butterflies, 108
Lamb Kebabs, Greek, 109
Lamb, Minted Leg of, M148
Onions, Italian Stuffed, 106
Parmesan Fingers, 113
Potato-and-Onion Fans, 110
Ribs, Pineapple-Honey-Glazed, M149
Ribs, Texas-Style, 109
Ribs With Two Sauces, Appetizer, 16
Sausage-Vegetable Medley, 106
Shrimp, Wrapped Grilled, 90
Snapper, Seafood-Stuffed Grilled, 110
Swordfish Salade Niçoise, Warm, 108
Tomatoes, Dill, 129
Tortilla Roll-Ups, 113

Beans
Bake, Three-Bean, 111
Green-Bean Bundles, 129
Sautéed Escarole and Beans, 59
Beef
Barbecued Beef, M115
Braciòla Torino, 56
Creole Beef, 107
Dinner in a Bag, Beef, 22
Minestrone, 160
Prime Rib à l'Orange, 216
Satays, Fresh Pea Salad With Beef, 139
Tenderloin, Spit-Roasted Beef, 111
Beef, Ground
Bake, Cottage Supper, 23
Braciòla Torino, 56
Chili Dogs, All-American, 90
Meat Loaf, Mouth-Watering, 158
Beverages
Alcoholic
Apricot Nog, M250
Bloody Mary Slushes, 16
Coffee Liqueur, 19
Hazelnut Mocha Café, M250
Mandarin-Berry Tea, 199
Orange-Prune Nog, 199
Punch, Berry Float, 146
Punch, Creamsicle, 199
Punch, Holiday Currant, M250
Punch, Party Cranberry, 183
Punch, Pineapple-Lemon, 199

Blackberries
Butter, Berry, 127
Preserves, Many-Berry, 127

Blueberries
Pie, Blueberry-Cassis, 124
Preserves, Many-Berry, 127

Breads. *See also* specific types.
Anchovy Crisps, 60
Biscotti, 57
Breadsticks, Seasoned, 60
Flatbreads, Easy Chinese, 198
Focaccia, Deluxe, 60
French-Bread Twists, 214
Garlic-Cheese Bread, 58
Kiwi-Banana Bread, 128
Mozzarella Bread, 60
Onion Bread, Crisp, 202
Parmesan Fingers, 113

Pudding With Orange Sauce,
Bread, 78
Scones, Mini Potato, 195
Skewer, Bread on a, 113
Broccoli
Pesto, Broccoli and Celery, 193
Pizza, Three-Cheese Broccoli, 63
Slaw, Hot Broccoli, 179
Tomatoes, Baked
Broccoli-Stuffed, 219
Brussels Sprouts
Bisque, Brussels Sprouts, 197
Stir-Fry, Brussels Sprouts, 180
Butter
Berry Butter, 127
Snaps, Coffee Butter, 230
Butterscotch-Cream Bells, 224

Cabbage
Coleslaw, Skillet, 129
German-Style Red Cabbage, 180
Soup, Cabbage, M168
Cakes. *See also* Breads, Cookies.
Banana Cone-Cake Kids, 43
Birthday Balloon Cake, 143
Cassata, Holiday, 18
Cheesecakes
Artichoke Cheesecake,
Savory, 194
Espresso Cheesecake, M46
Fruit Cheesecake, Summer-, 124
Ultimate Cheesecake, The, 157
Chocolate Cake, Perfect, 156
Chocolate Cake, Triple-, 36
Chocolate Temptation Cake, 16
Christmas Cloud Cake, 220
Cinnamon-Pumpkin Cake, 220
Fruitcake, Dark-Chocolate-
Covered, 201
Fruitcake, Silver and Gold, 221
Hazelnut Triangle Treat, 36
Kong Cake, 144
Lady Baltimore Cake, 159
Nectarine-Chocolate Angel
Cake, 147
Pear Kuchen, 19
Popcorn Cake, Party, 42
Pound Cake, Della Robbia, 12
Pumpkin Cakes, Witchy, 183
Torte, Pecan Meringue, 37
Torte, Pineapple-Banana, 25
Torte, Sacher, M45
Watermelon Cake, 144
Candies
Macadamia Brittle, 19
Capon
Chestnut Stuffing, Roasted Capon
With, 196
Fruited Rice, Roast Capon With, 72
Caramel
Acorns, Caramel, 226
Popcorn Balls, Caramel, 146
Snacks, Chewy Caramel, M130
Sundaes, Deluxe Caramel, 89
Carrots, Citrus-Glazed, 215
Casseroles
Chicken Casserole With Rice and
Vegetables, Quick, 23
Macaroni and Cheese, Creamy, 160
Salmon-Noodle Bake, M97
Caviar-Crème Fraîche Omelet
Filling, 14
Celery
Pesto, Broccoli and Celery, 193
Sweet-and-Sour Celery, Grilled, 110
Cereal
Cocoa Gorp, 146
Cones, Happy Cereal, 145
Muffins, Nectarine-Oat-Bran, 127
Cheese
Bread, Garlic-Cheese, 58
Bread, Mozzarella, 60
Chicken Parmigiana, 59
Crisps, Anchovy, 60
Crisps, Zippy Cheddar, 17
Filling, Double-Cheese Omelet, 14
Filling, Zucchini With
Veal-and-Cheese, 59
Fingers, Parmesan, 113
Gouda, Cheese-Filled, 198
Grilled Chicken 'n' Cheese, M80
Knots and Rings, Parmesan, 58
Lamb Chops, Cheese-Topped, 88
Lasagna, Three-Cheese, M65
Linguine Verdi Alfredo, 57
Macaroni and Cheese, Creamy, 160
Pepper-Baked Brie, 17
Pizza, Three-Cheese Broccoli, 63
Potatoes, Do-Ahead
Cheese-Stuffed, 181
Potato Skins, Parmesan, 194
Strudel, Warm Apricot-Cheese, 15
Tirami Su, 58
Tomatoes Fontina, 178
Veal Parmigiana, 158
Cheesecakes. *See* Cakes/Cheesecakes.
Cherry-Almond Wreaths, 230
Chestnut Stuffing, 196
Chicken
Beer-Batter Chicken and Onions
With Fennel Slaw, 73
Bisque, Chicken, 75
Casserole With Rice and Vegetables,
Quick Chicken, 23
Cinnamon Chicken With
Couscous, 74
Coconut Bites, 76
Coq au Vin Blanc, 75
Creole Chicken, 165
Fajitas, Chicken, 89
Filling, Chicken-Liver, 14
Fruited Chicken and Stuffing, 23
Grilled Chicken 'n' Cheese, M80
Lemon Chicken in a Basket, 74
Lime Chicken, 76
Livers Montrachet, Chicken, 218
Maple-Smoked Chicken, 107
Mold, Chicken-and-Basmati, 166
Paprika With Galuska, Chicken, 162
Parmigiana, Chicken, 59
Pesto, Chicken, 17
Pinwheels, Chicken, 76
Ratatouille Nests, Chicken, 76
Red-Glazed Chicken, 77
Rice, Chicken Fried, 165
Roulades, Chicken, 165
Salad, Cobb, 142
Salad Loaf, Tarragon Chicken-, M81
Salad, Warm Chicken, 77
Sloppy Joes, Chicken, M185
Stir-Fry With Pilaf, Chicken, 74
Strata Olé, Chicken, M184
Tacos, Quick Chicken, M130
Teriyaki Wings, 198
Turnovers, Stuffed Chicken, 109
Chili Potato Topper, Turkey-, M96
Chocolate
Brownies, Luscious, 161
Café, Hazelnut Mocha, M250
Cakes and Tortes
Cassata, Holiday, 18
Cheesecake, Espresso, M46
Fruitcake, Dark-Chocolate-
Covered, 201
Hazelnut Triangle Treat, 36

Chocolate
(continued)
Kong Cake, 144
Nectarine-Chocolate Angel Cake, 147
Perfect Chocolate Cake, 156
Sacher Torte, M45
Temptation Cake, Chocolate, 16
Triple-Chocolate Cake, 36
Watermelon Cake, 144
Cocoa Gorp, 146
Cookies, Marbled Spritz, 227
Cookies, Neapolitan, 163
Cookiewiches, 145
More-and-Mores, M131
Mousse, Layered Chocolate-Mint, M47
Mousse, Perfect Chocolate, 13
Parfaits, Black 'n' White, 79
Parfaits, White-Chocolate, M91
Pie, Brandy Alexander, M44
Pretzels, Chocolate-Covered, M146
Sugar Bears, Chocolate, 231
Tirami Su, 58
Wraparound, Orange Mousse With Chocolate, 38
Christmas Creations
Cookie Tree, Pirouette, 248
Covered Bridge, 242
Gingerbread House, Grandma's, 244
Pastillage, 242
Patterns, Cake and Cookie, 252-261
Santa's Dream House, 232
Sleigh Scene, 240
Sugar-Syrup Glass, 247
Town House, 236
Truffle Wreath, 249
Clams
Casino, Clams, M206
Cioppino With Garlic-Cheese Bread, 57
Coconut
Bites, Coconut, 76
Pie, Banana-Coconut-Cream, 126
Tarts, Coconut-Eggnog, 230
Coffee
Hazelnut Mocha Café, M250
Liqueur, Coffee, 19
Snaps, Coffee-Butter, 230
Coleslaw. *See* Cabbage or Salads.
Cookies
Bars and Squares
Brownies, Luscious, 161
Citrus Cookies, Holiday, 19
Cranberry-Apple Streusel Bars, 229
Fruitcake Diamonds, 227
Raspberry-Oatmeal Bars, M130
Butterscotch-Cream Bells, 224
Candy Canes, 225
Caramel Acorns, 226
Cherry-Almond Wreaths, 230
Chocolate Sugar Bears, 231
Coffee-Butter Snaps, 230
Cookiewiches, 145
Gingerbread Dough, 247
Jack-O'-Lantern Cookie, 182
Kourambiedes, 224
Lace Cups, Mini, 228
Lemon-Fig Bites, 228
Marzipan Pinecones, 228
Mincemeat Rugelach, 229
Neapolitan Cookies, 163
Nut Spirals, 225
Pfeffernuesse, 230
Pistachio Wreaths, 228
Pizzelles, Anise, 226
Poppy-Seed Thumbprints, 227
Shortbread, Marble-Topped Hazelnut, 226
Snowflakes, 226
Springerle, 231
Spritz Cookies, Marbled, 227
Corn
Fritters With Yellow-Pepper Salsa, Corn, 179
Pudding, Roasted Corn, 107
Salad, Fresh Corn, 142

Cornbreads
Confetti Cornbread, 113
Crisps, Zippy Cheddar, 17

Cornish Hens
Grilled Oriental Cornish Hens, 111
Honey-Roasted Cornish Hens, 73
Plum-Glazed Hens, M114
Raspberry-Grilled Hens, 126
Roasted Game Hens With Harvest Vegetables, 204

Couscous
Chicken With Couscous, Cinnamon, 74
Peppers, Couscous-Stuffed, 177

Crab
Creole, Cod-and-Crab-, M27
Garlic-Tomato Butter, Soft-Shell Crabs With, 110
Cranberries
Bars, Cranberry-Apple Streusel, 229
Conserve, Pear-Cranberry, 192
Punch, Party Cranberry, 183
Relish, Roasted Duck With Orange-Berry, 25
Tarts, Cranberry-Raisin, 229
Tea, Mandarin-Berry, 199
Cucumbers
Salmon, Cucumber-Sauced, 161
Toss, Warm Cucumber, 17
Custard, Sautéed Apples With Warm, 93

Desserts. *See also* specific types.
Almond Twists, 39
Apples With Warm Custard, Sautéed, 93
Baklava, Pistachio, 34
Bombe, Festive, 201
Bombe, Pineapple, 37
Caramel Sundaes, Deluxe, 89
Cassata, Holiday, 18
Citrus Jellied Wine, 195
Coeur à la Crème, Double-Sauced, 35
Floating Heart Ritz, 40
"Flowerpot" Dessert, 90
French Toast, Tipsy, 125
Fruit Crisp, Three-, 42
Fruit Delight, Royal, 92
Fruit-Filled Meringues, 147
Fruit Medley With Zabaglione, 55
Fruit Mélange, Yogurt-Topped, 94
Fruit Sorbet, Tropical-, 147
Happy Ghost Mold, 183
Ice Cream Butterflies, 108
Jam Packets, 40
More-and-Mores, M131
(Palmiers), Elephant Ears, 40
Parfaits, Black 'n' White, 79
Parfaits, Strawberry, 42
Parfaits, White-Chocolate, M91
Pear Kuchen, 19
Pears, Crimson, 34
Praline Cream-Puff Ring, 35
Sauce, Gingered Orange, 195
Strawberries en Chemise, M88
Strawberry-Pineapple Bavarian, 78

Tirami Su, 58
Torte, Pecan Meringue, 37
Torte, Pineapple-Banana, 25
Torte, Sacher, M45
Viennese Pouf, 39
Zuppa Inglese, 217
Duck With Orange-Berry Relish, Roasted, 25
Dumplings
Bacon Dumplings, 179
Gnocchi With Hazelnut Butter, 56

Eggplant
Pizza, Ratatouille, 63
Ratatouille Nests, Chicken, 76
Ratatouille Quiche, 163
Savarin, Eggplant-Artichoke, 180
Eggs
Cloud, Eggs in a, 14
Eggnog-Mousse Pie, 201
Eggnog Tarts, Coconut-, 230
Omelets on Demand, 14
Ring, Ham-and-Egg, 202
Scrambler, Corn-Muffin, 203
Escarole and Beans, Sautéed, 59

Fajitas, Chicken, 89
Fennel Slaw, 73
Fettuccine, Ham-and-Peppers, M64
Fig Bites, Lemon-, 228
Fish
Cod-and-Crab-Creole, M27
Pinwheels, Basil Fillet, 91
Salmon, Cucumber-Sauced, 161
Salmon Mousse, Molded, 196
Salmon-Noodle Bake, M97
Snapper, Seafood-Stuffed Grilled, 110
Swordfish Salade Niçoise, Warm, 108
Frankfurters
Chili Dogs, All-American, 90
Fritters With Yellow-Pepper Salsa, Corn, 179
Frostings, Fillings, and Toppings
Fruit Compote, Dried-, 12
Orange Peel, Sugared, 38
Royal Icing, 234, 247
White Icing Glaze, 12
Fruit. *See also* specific types.
Cake, Christmas Cloud, 220
Cheesecake, Summer-Fruit, 124
Chicken and Stuffing, Fruited, 23
Compote, Citrus, 202
Compote, Dried-Fruit, 12
Cookies, Holiday Citrus, 19
Crisp, Three-Fruit, 42
Delight, Royal Fruit, 92
Fruitcake Diamonds, 227
Fruitcake, Dark-Chocolate-Covered, 201
Fruitcake, Silver and Gold, 221
Gazpacho, Fruit, 122
Medley With Zabaglione, Fruit, 55
Mélange, Shrimp-and-Fruit, 127
Mélange, Yogurt-Topped Fruit, 94
Meringues, Fruit-Filled, 147
Muffins, Fruited French, 203
Rice, Roast Capon With Fruited, 72
Salad, Fruited Pork, 166
Sorbet, Tropical-Fruit, 147

Goose, Holiday Stuffed, 219

Ham. *See also* Pork.
Bake, Glazed Ham-and-Squash, 22
Fettuccine, Ham-and-Peppers, M64
Ring, Ham-and-Egg, 202
Waikiki, Ham, 108
Hazelnuts
Butter, Gnocchi With Hazelnut, 56
Café, Hazelnut Mocha, M250
Shortbread, Marble-Topped Hazelnut, 226
Treat, Hazelnut Triangle, 36
Honey
Cornish Hens, Honey-Roasted, 73
Ribs, Pineapple-Honey-Glazed, M149
Hors d'Oeuvres. *See* Appetizers.

Ice Creams and Sherbets
Bombe, Festive, 201
Butterflies, Ice Cream, 108
Cones, Happy Cereal, 145

Jams and Jellies
Berry Preserves, Many-, 127
Packets, Jam, 40

Kebabs, Greek Lamb, 109
Kiwi-Banana Bread, 128

Lamb
Artichokes, Lamb-Stuffed, 55
Chops, Cheese-Topped Lamb, 88
Kebabs, Greek Lamb, 109
Leg of Lamb, Herb-Crusted, 56
Leg of Lamb, Minted, M148
Medallions, Lentil Salad With Roasted Lamb, 141
Lasagna
Cheese Lasagna, Three-, M65
Lasagna, Quick, 23
Vegetable Lasagna, M98
Leeks
Platter, Leek-and-Asparagus, 25
Tarts, Shrimp and Leek, 218
Lemon
Bites, Lemon-Fig, 228
Chicken in a Basket, Lemon, 74
Punch, Pineapple-Lemon, 199
Lentil Salad With Roasted Lamb Medallions, 141
Lime
Chicken, Lime, 76
Spareribs, Lime-Marinated, 123
Linguine Verdi Alfredo, 57
Lite Eating
Asparagus, Sesame, 129
Bean Bundles, Green-, 129
Desserts
Apple Tart Deluxe, 204
Bread Pudding With Orange Sauce, 78
Cake, Nectarine-Chocolate Angel, 147
Cakes, Witchy Pumpkin, 183
Cookie, Jack-O'-Lantern, 182
Fruit Mélange, Yogurt-Topped, 94
Happy Ghost Mold, 183
Meringues, Fruit-Filled, 147
Parfaits, Black 'n' White, 79

Lite Eating, Desserts *(continued)*
Pineapple-Banana Torte, 25
Sorbet, Tropical-Fruit, 147
Strawberry-Pineapple Bavarian, 78
Entrées
Chicken, Creole, 165
Chicken Fried Rice, 165
Chicken Roulades, 165
Duck With Orange-Berry Relish, Roasted, 25
Game Hens With Harvest Vegetables, Roasted, 204
Pasta With Wild-Mushroom Sauce, 94
Leek-and-Asparagus Platter, 25
Pears, Broomstick, 183
Pizza Dough, Quick and Thin, 63
Pizza, Ratatouille, 63
Pizzas, Roasted-Pepper Mini-, 63
Pizza, Three-Cheese Broccoli, 63
Salads
Chicken-and-Basmati Mold, 166
Coleslaw, Skillet, 129
Green Salad, Mixed, 204
Pork Salad, Fruited, 166
Shrimp Salad, Warm, 94
Turkey Oriental, Warm, 166
Tomatoes, Dill, 129

Macaroni and Cheese, Creamy, 160
Mango Mousse Pie, 38
Marzipan Pinecones, 228
Microwave
Appetizers
Clams Casino, M206
Pâté, Madeira, M207
Beverages
Apricot Nog, M250
Café, Hazelnut Mocha, M250
Punch, Holiday Currant, M250
Desserts
Cheesecake, Espresso, M46
Cookies, Neapolitan, M163
Mousse, Layered Chocolate-Mint, M47
Parfaits, White-Chocolate, M91
Pie, Brandy Alexander, M44
Strawberries en Chemise, M88
Torte, Sacher, M45
Entrées
Beef, Barbecued, M115
Chicken Strata Olé, M184
Fettuccine, Ham-and-Peppers, M64
Hens, Plum-Glazed, M114
Lamb, Minted Leg of, M148
Lasagna, Three-Cheese, M65
Lasagna, Vegetable, M98
Ribs, Pineapple-Honey-Glazed, M149
Spaghetti Pie, M65
Timbales, Pasta, M64
Salmon-Noodle Bake, M97
Sandwiches
Chicken 'n' Cheese, Grilled, M80
Chicken-Salad Loaf, Tarragon, M81
Chicken Sloppy Joes, M185
Snacks
Caramel Snacks, Chewy, M130
Chicken Tacos, Quick, M130
More-and-Mores, M131
Raspberry-Oatmeal Bars, M130
Soups and Stews
Bisque, Sherried Zucchini, M207
Bisque, Squash, M26
Cabbage Soup, M168
Cod-and-Crab-Creole, M27
Hot-and-Sour Soup, M169
Turkey-Chili Potato Topper, M96
Wurst-and-Potato Supper, M99
Mousses
Chocolate-Mint Mousse, Layered, M47
Chocolate Mousse, Perfect, 13
Orange Mousse With Chocolate Wraparound, 38
Pie, Eggnog-Mousse, 201
Pie, Mango Mousse, 38
Salmon Mousse, Molded, 196
Muffins
Corn-Muffin Scrambler, 203
Fruited French Muffins, 203
Little-Man Muffins, 203
Mouse Muffins, 203
Nectarine-Oat-Bran Muffins, 127
Mushrooms
Risotto With Mushrooms, 91
Sauce, Pasta With Wild-Mushroom, 94
Scandia, Mushrooms, 181

Nectarines
Cake, Nectarine-Chocolate Angel, 147
Muffins, Nectarine-Oat-Bran, 127
Noodles
Bake, Salmon-Noodle, M97
Basket, Fried Noodle, 75
Toss, Szechwan Noodle, 142

Oatmeal Bars, Raspberry-, M130
Omelets
Demand, Omelets on, 14
Filling, Caviar-Crème Fraîche Omelet, 14
Filling, Chicken-Liver, 14
Filling, Double-Cheese Omelet, 14
Filling, Smoked-Oyster, 14
Onions
Bread, Crisp Onion, 202
Chicken and Onions With Fennel Slaw, Beer-Batter, 73
Fans, Potato-and-Onion, 110
Soup, Silver-Onion, 193
Stuffed Onions, Italian, 106
Oranges
Béarnaise, Orange, 216
Mousse With Chocolate Wraparound, Orange, 38
Nog, Orange-Prune, 199
Relish, Roasted Duck With Orange-Berry, 25
Sauce, Bread Pudding With Orange, 78
Sauce, Gingered Orange, 195
Sugared Orange Peel, 38
Tea, Mandarin-Berry, 199
Oyster Filling, Smoked-, 14

Papaya Cups, Calypso, 140
Pasta. *See also* specific types.
Fried Pasta With Plum Sauce, 122
Noodle Toss, Szechwan, 142
Salad, Oriental Pasta, 125
Salad, Seaside Pasta, 111
Timbales, Pasta, M64
Tortellini in Brodo, 58
Tortellini Primavera, 140

Wild-Mushroom Sauce, Pasta With, 94
Ziti-Zucchini Timbale, 176
Peach Tart, Glazed, 123
Peanuts
Sauce, Peanut, 77
Sauce, Pork Satay With Spicy Peanut Dipping, 93
Pears
Broomstick Pears, 183
Conserve, Pear-Cranberry, 192
Crimson Pears, 34
Kuchen, Pear, 19
Pork, Pear-Stuffed Roast, 18
Tarts, Pear-Raspberry, 92
Peas
Hostess Peas, 195
Salad With Beef Satays, Fresh Pea, 139
Pecan Meringue Torte, 37
Peppers
Brie, Pepper-Baked, 17
Fettuccine, Ham-and-Peppers, M64
Pizzas, Roasted-Pepper Mini-, 63
Salsa, Corn Fritters With Yellow Pepper, 179
Sauce, Three-Vegetable Terrine With Roasted-Pepper, 176
Stuffed Peppers, Conscous-, 177
Pickles and Relishes
Conserve, Pear-Cranberry, 192
Orange-Berry Relish, Roasted Duck With, 25
Pies and Pastries
Apple-Cider Pie, Deep-Dish, 194
Apple Pie, Sour-Cream, 128
Banana-Coconut-Cream Pie, 126
Blueberry-Cassis Pie, 124
Boston Cream Pie, 162
Brandy Alexander Pie, M44
Eggnog-Mousse Pie, 201
Mango Mousse Pie, 38
Meringue Pie, Mile-High, 158
Pastries and Crusts
Almond Twists, 39
Chicken Livers Montrachet, 218
Jam Packets, 40
(Palmiers), Elephant Ears, 40
Pie Shell, 194
Puff Pastry, Quick, 40
Pumpkin-Apricot Chiffon Pie, 13
Spaghetti Pie, M65
Strudel, Warm Apricot-Cheese, 15
Tarts
Apple Tart Deluxe, 204
Coconut-Eggnog Tarts, 230
Cranberry-Raisin Tarts, 229
Peach Tart, Glazed, 123
Pear-Raspberry Tarts, 92
Raspberry Tarts, 126
Shrimp and Leek Tarts, 218
Pineapple
Bavarian, Strawberry-Pineapple, 78
Bombe, Pineapple, 37
Punch, Pineapple-Lemon, 199
Ribs, Pineapple-Honey-Glazed, M149
Torte, Pineapple-Banana, 25
Pizza
Cheese Broccoli Pizza, Three-, 63
Dough, Quick and Thin Pizza, 63
Pepper Mini Pizzas, Roasted-, 63
Ratatouille Pizza, 63
Upside-Down Pizza, 22
Plums
Hens, Plum-Glazed, M114
Sauce, Fried Pasta With Plum, 122
Popcorn
Balls, Caramel Popcorn, 146
Cake, Party Popcorn, 42
Pork, *See also* Bacon, Ham, Sausage.
Ribs, Pineapple-Honey-Glazed, M149
Ribs, Texas-Style, 109
Ribs With Two Sauces, Appetizer, 16
Roast Pork, Pear-Stuffed, 18
Salad, Fruited Pork, 166
Satay With Spicy Peanut Dipping Sauce, Pork, 93
Spareribs, Lime-Marinated, 123
Potatoes
Bake, Cottage Supper, 23
Cheese-Stuffed Potatoes, Do-Ahead, 181
Fans, Potato-and-Onion, 110
Gnocchi With Hazelnut Butter, 56
Italiano, Potatoes, 178
Rolls, Refrigerator Potato, 160
Salad, Russian Potato, 138
Scones, Mini Potato, 195
Skins, Parmesan Potato, 194
Supper, Wurst-and-Potato, M99
Turkey-Chili Potato Topper, M96
Potatoes, Sweet
Praline-Topped Sweet Potatoes, 192
Salad, Savory Sweet-Potato, 140
Praline Cream-Puff Ring, 35
Pretzels, Chocolate-Covered, M146
Prune Nog, Orange-, 199
Puddings
Bread Pudding With Orange Sauce, 78
Corn Pudding, Roasted, 107
Wild-Rice Yorkshire Pudding, 217
Pumpkin
Cake, Cinnamon-Pumpkin, 220
Cakes, Witchy Pumpkin, 183
Pie, Pumpkin-Apricot Chiffon, 13

Quiche, Ratatouille, 163

Raisin Tarts, Cranberry-, 229
Raspberries
Bars, Raspberry-Oatmeal, M130
Butter, Berry, 127
Hens, Raspberry-Grilled, 126
Preserves, Many-Berry, 127
Soufflé, Berry-Topped Apricot, 40
Tarts, Pear-Raspberry, 92
Tarts, Raspberry, 126
Ratatouille
Chicken Ratatouille Nests, 76
Pizza, Ratatouille, 63
Quiche, Ratatouille, 163
Relishes. *See* Pickles and Relishes.
Rice
Capon With Fruited Rice, Roast, 72
Chicken Casserole With Rice and Vegetables, Quick, 23
Chicken Fried Rice, 165
Patchwork-Quilt Rice, 177
Pilaf, Chicken Stir-Fry With, 74
Pudding, Wild-Rice Yorkshire, 217
Risotto With Mushrooms, 91
Pudding, Wild-Rice Yorkshire, 217 Salad, Cold Brown-Rice, 93
Zucchini 'n' Rice, Creamy, 91
Rolls and Buns. *See also* Breads.
Parmesan Knots and Rings, 58
Potato Rolls, Refrigerator, 160

Salad Dressings
Antipasto Dressing, 54
Vinaigrette, Special, 142
Salads
Basque Salad, 141
Chicken-and-Basmati Mold, 166
Chicken-Salad Loaf, Tarragon, M81
Chicken Salad, Warm, 77
Cobb Salad, 142
Coleslaw, Skillet, 129
Corn Salad, Fresh, 142
Green Salad, Mixed, 204
Lentil Salad With Roasted Lamb Medallions, 141
Mexican Salad Bowl, 89
Noodle Toss, Szechwan, 142
Papaya Cups, Calypso, 140
Pasta Salad, Oriental, 125
Pasta Salad, Seaside, 111
Pea Salad With Beef Satays, Fresh, 139
Pork Salad, Fruited, 166
Potato Salad, Russian, 138
Rice Salad, Cold Brown-, 93
Shrimp-and-Fruit Mélange, 127
Shrimp Salad, Warm, 94
Slaw, Fennel, 73
Spinach Salad, Tangy, 88
Sweet-Potato Salad, Savory, 140
Swordfish Salade Niçoise, Warm, 108
Taco Salad in Tortilla Baskets, 139
Tomatoes, Tonnato-Stuffed, 138
Tortellini Primavera, 140
Turkey Oriental, Warm, 166

Salmon
Bake, Salmon-Noodle, M97
Cucumber-Sauced Salmon, 161
Mousse, Molded Salmon, 196

Sandwiches
Chicken 'n' Cheese, Grilled, M80
Chicken-Salad Loaf, Tarragon, M81
Chicken Sloppy Joes, M185

Sauces
Apricot Sauce, Amaretto, 197
Chutney Dipping Sauce, 76
Orange Béarnaise, 216
Orange Sauce, Gingered, 195
Peanut Sauce, 77
Tomato Sauce, 158

Sausage
Medley, Sausage-Vegetable, 106
Pizza, Upside-Down, 22
Wurst-and-Potato Supper, M99

Seafood. *See also* specific types.
Bouillabaisse With French-Bread Twists, 214
Dutch Babies, Seafood-Filled, 15
Salad, Basque, 141
Snapper, Seafood-Stuffed Grilled, 110
Soufflé, Never-Fail Seafood, 20

Shrimp
Grilled Shrimp, Wrapped, 90
Mélange, Shrimp-and-Fruit, 127
Salad, Warm Shrimp, 94
Seafood-Filled Dutch Babies, 15
Sweet 'n' Sour Shrimp, 20
Tarts, Shrimp and Leek, 218

Soufflés
Apricot Soufflé, Berry-Topped, 40
Banana-Toffee Soufflé, Frozen, 197
Seafood Soufflé, Never-Fail, 20

Soups and Stews
Bisque, Brussels Sprouts, 197
Bisque, Chicken, 75
Bisque, Sherried Zucchini, M207
Bisque, Squash, M26
Bouillabaisse With French-Bread Twists, 214
Cabbage Soup, M168
Cioppino With Garlic-Cheese Bread, 57
Cod-and-Crab-Creole, M27
Consommé Bellevue, 218
Fruit Gazpacho, 122
Hot-and-Sour Soup, M169
Minestrone, 160
Onion Soup, Silver-, 193
Tortellini in Brodo, 58

Spaghetti Pie, M65

Spinach
Salad, Tangy Spinach, 88
Timbales, Pasta, M64

Spreads and Fillings
Caviar-Crème Fraîche Omelet Filling, 14
Cheese Omelet Filling, Double-, 14
Chicken-Liver Filling, 14
Oyster Filling, Smoked-, 14
Veal-and-Cheese Filling, Zucchini With, 59

Squash. *See also* Zucchini.
Acorn Squash Rings, 217
Bake, Glazed Ham-and-Squash, 22
Bisque, Squash, M26
Lo Mein, Vegetable Stir-Fry on Squash, 181
Stir-Fried Squash, 92

Stir-Fry
Brussels Sprouts Stir-Fry, 180
Chicken Stir-Fry With Pilaf, 74
Squash, Stir-Fried, 92
Vegetable Stir-Fry on Squash Lo Mein, 181

Strawberries
Bavarian, Strawberry-Pineapple, 78
Butter, Berry, 127
Chemise, Strawberries en, M88
Parfaits, Strawberry, 42
Preserves, Many-Berry, 127
Punch, Berry Float, 146

Stuffings and Dressings
Bread Stuffing, Roast Turkey With Three-, 192
Chestnut Stuffing, 196
Chicken and Stuffing, Fruited, 23

Sweet-and-Sour
Celery, Grilled Sweet-and-Sour, 110
Shrimp, Sweet 'n' Sour, 20

Tacos
Chicken Tacos, Quick, M130
Salad in Tortilla Baskets, Taco, 139

Toast
French Toast, Tipsy, 125
Tomato-Basil Toasts, 55

Tomatoes
Butter, Soft-Shell Crabs With Garlic-Tomato, 110
Dill Tomatoes, 129
Fontina, Tomatoes, 178
Sauce, Tomato, 158

Stuffed Tomatoes, Baked Broccoli-, 219
Stuffed Tomatoes, Tonnato-, 138
Toasts, Tomato-Basil, 55
Tortillas
Baskets, Taco Salad in Tortilla, 139
Roll-Ups, Tortilla, 113
Turkey
Florentine With Citrus-Glazed Carrots, Turkey Breast, 215
Oriental, Warm Turkey, 166
Potato Topper, Turkey-Chili, M96
Roast Turkey With Three-Bread Stuffing, 192

Veal
Filling, Zucchini With Veal-and-Cheese, 59
Parmigiana, Veal, 158
Piccata, Veal, 92

Vegetables. *See also* specific types.
Bake, Creamy Vegetable, 178
Chicken Casserole With Rice and Vegetables, Quick, 23
Dinner in a Bag, Beef, 22
Game Hens With Harvest Vegetables, Roasted, 204
Lasagna, Vegetable, M98
Medley, Sausage-Vegetable, 106
Stir-Fry on Squash Lo Mein, Vegetable, 181
Terrine With Roasted-Pepper Sauce, Three-Vegetable, 176

Yogurt-Topped Fruit Mélange, 94

Zucchini
Bisque, Sherried Zucchini, M207
Rice, Creamy Zucchini 'n', 91
Stir-Fried Squash, 92
Timbale, Ziti-Zucchini, 176
Veal-and-Cheese Filling, Zucchini With, 59

Recipe Title Index

Acorn Squash Rings, 217
All-American Chili Dogs, 90
Almond Twists, 39
Amaretto Apricot Sauce, 197
Anchovy Crisps, 60
Anise Pizzelles, 226
Antipasto Buffet, 54
Antipasto Dressing, 54
Appetizer Ribs With Two Sauces, 16
Apple Tart Deluxe, 204
Apricot Nog, M250

Bacon Dumplings, 179
Baked Broccoli-Stuffed Tomatoes, 219
Banana-Coconut-Cream Pie, 126
Banana Cone-Cake Kids, 43
Barbecued Beef, M115
Basil Fillet Pinwheels, 91
Basque Salad, 141
Beef Dinner in a Bag, 22
Beer-Batter Chicken and Onions With Fennel Slaw, 73
Berry Butter, 127
Berry Float Punch, 146
Berry-Topped Apricot Soufflé, 40
Birthday Balloon Cake, 143
Biscotti, 57
Black 'n' White Parfaits, 79
Bloody Mary Slushes, 16
Blueberry-Cassis Pie, 124
Boston Cream Pie, 162
Bouillabaisse With French-Bread Twists, 214
Braciòla Torino, 56
Brandy Alexander Pie, M44
Bread on a Skewer, 113
Bread Pudding With Orange Sauce, 78
Broccoli and Celery Pesto, 193
Broomstick Pears, 183
Brussels Sprouts Bisque, 197
Brussels Sprouts Stir-Fry, 180
Butterscotch-Cream Bells, 224

Cabbage Soup, M168
Calypso Papaya Cups, 140
Candy Canes, 225
Caramel Acorns, 226
Caramel Popcorn Balls, 146
Caviar-Crème Fraîche Omelet Filling, 14
Champagne-Glazed Canadian Bacon, 15
Cheese-Filled Gouda, 198
Cheese-Topped Lamb Chops, 88
Cherry-Almond Wreaths, 230
Chestnut Stuffing, 196
Chewy Caramel Snacks, M130
Chicken-and-Basmati Mold, 166
Chicken Bisque, 75
Chicken Fajitas, 89
Chicken Fried Rice, 165
Chicken-Liver Filling, 14
Chicken Livers Montrachet, 218
Chicken Paprika With Galuska, 162
Chicken Parmigiana, 59
Chicken Pesto, 17
Chicken Pinwheels, 76
Chicken Ratatouille Nests, 76
Chicken Roulades, 165
Chicken Sloppy Joes, M185
Chicken Stir-Fry With Pilaf, 74
Chicken Strata Olé, M184
Chocolate-Covered Pretzels, M146
Chocolate Sugar Bears, 231
Chocolate Temptation Cake, 16
Christmas Cloud Cake, 220
Chutney Dipping Sauce, 76
Cinnamon Chicken With Couscous, 74
Cinnamon-Pumpkin Cake, 220
Cioppino With Garlic-Cheese Bread, 57
Citrus Compote, 202
Citrus-Glazed Carrots, 215
Citrus Jellied Wine, 195
Clams Casino, M206
Cobb Salad, 142
Cocoa Gorp, 146
Coconut Bites, 76
Coconut-Eggnog Tarts, 230
Cod-and-Crab-Creole, M27
Coffee-Butter Snaps, 230
Coffee Liqueur, 19
Cold Brown-Rice Salad, 93
Confetti Cornbread, 113
Consommé Bellevue, 218
Cookiewiches, 145
Coq au Vin Blanc, 75
Corn Fritters With Yellow-Pepper Salsa, 179
Corn-Muffin Scrambler, 203
Cottage Supper Bake, 23
Couscous-Stuffed Peppers, 177
Covered Bridge, 242
Cranberry-Apple Streusel Bars, 229
Cranberry-Raisin Tarts, 229
Creamsicle Punch, 199
Creamy Macaroni and Cheese, 160
Creamy Vegetable Bake, 178
Creamy Zucchini 'n' Rice, 91
Creole Beef, 107
Creole Chicken, 165
Crimson Pears, 34
Crisp Onion Bread, 202
Cucumber-Sauced Salmon, 161

Dark-Chocolate-Covered Fruitcake, 201
Deep-Dish Apple-Cider Pie, 194
Della Robbia Pound Cake, 12
Deluxe Caramel Sundaes, 89
Deluxe Focaccia, 60
Dill Tomatoes, 129
Do-Ahead Cheese-Stuffed Potatoes, 181
Double-Cheese Omelet Filling, 14
Double-Sauced Coeur à la Crème, 35
Dried-Fruit Compote, 12

Easy Chinese Flatbreads, 198
Eggnog-Mousse Pie, 201
Eggplant-Artichoke Savarin, 180
Eggs in a Cloud, 14
Elephant Ears (Palmiers), 40
Espresso Cheesecake, M46

Fennel Slaw, 73
Festive Bombe, 201
Floating Heart Ritz, 40
"Flowerpot" Dessert, 90
French-Bread Twists, 214

Fresh Corn Salad, 142
Fresh Pea Salad With Beef Satays, 139
Fried Noodle Basket, 75
Fried Pasta With Plum Sauce, 122
Frozen Banana Pops, 146
Frozen Banana-Toffee Soufflé, 197
Fruitcake Diamonds, 227
Fruited Chicken and Stuffing, 23
Fruited French Muffins, 203
Fruited Pork Salad, 166
Fruit-Filled Meringues, 147
Fruit Gazpacho, 122
Fruit Medley With Zabaglione, 55

Garlic-Cheese Bread, 58
German-Style Red Cabbage, 180
Gingerbread Dough, 247
Gingered Orange Sauce, 195
Glazed Ham-and-Squash Bake, 22
Glazed Peach Tart, 123
Gnocchi With Hazelnut Butter, 56
Grandma's Gingerbread House, 244
Greek Lamb Kebabs, 109
Green-Bean Bundles, 129
Grilled Chicken 'n' Cheese, M80
Grilled Oriental Cornish Hens, 111
Grilled Sweet-and-Sour Celery, 110

Ham-and-Egg Ring, 202
Ham-and-Peppers Fettuccine, M64
Ham Waikiki, 108
Happy Cereal Cones, 145
Happy Ghost Mold, 183
Hazelnut Mocha Café, M250
Hazelnut Triangle Treat, 36
Herb-Crusted Leg of Lamb, 56
Holiday Cassata, 18
Holiday Citrus Cookies, 19
Holiday Currant Punch, M250
Holiday Stuffed Goose, 219
Honey-Roasted Cornish Hens, 73
Hostess Peas, 195
Hot-and-Sour Soup, M169
Hot Broccoli Slaw, 179

Ice Cream Butterflies, 108
Italian Stuffed Onions, 106

Jack-O'-Lantern Cookie, 182
Jam Packets, 40

Kiwi-Banana Bread, 128
Kong Cake, 144
Kourambiedes, 224

Lady Baltimore Cake, 159
Lamb-Stuffed Artichokes, 55
Layered Chocolate-Mint Mousse, M47
Leek-and-Asparagus Platter, 25
Lemon Chicken in a Basket, 74
Lemon-Fig Bites, 228
Lentil Salad With Roasted Lamb Medallions, 141
Lime Chicken, 76
Lime-Marinated Spareribs, 123
Linguine Verdi Alfredo, 57
Little Man Muffins, 203
Luscious Brownies, 161

Macadamia Brittle, 19
Madeira Pâté, M207
Mandarin-Berry Tea, 199
Mango Mousse Pie, 38
Many-Berry Preserves, 127
Maple-Smoked Chicken, 107
Marbled Spritz Cookies, 227
Marble-Topped Hazelnut Shortbread, 226
Marzipan Pinecones, 228
Mexican Salad Bowl, 89
Mile-High Meringue Pie, 158
Mincemeat Rugelach, 229
Minestrone, 160
Mini Lace Cups, 228
Mini Potato Scones, 195
Minted Leg of Lamb, M148
Mixed Green Salad, 204
Molded Salmon Mousse, 196
More-and-Mores, M131
Mouse Muffins, 203
Mouth-Watering Meat Loaf, 158
Mozzarella Bread, 60
Mushrooms Scandia, 181

Neapolitan Cookies, M163
Nectarine-Chocolate Angel Cake, 147
Nectarine-Oat-Bran Muffins, 127
Never-Fail Seafood Soufflé, 20
Nut Spirals, 225

Omelets on Demand, 14
Orange Béarnaise, 216
Orange Mousse With Chocolate Wraparound, 38
Orange-Prune Nog, 199
Oriental Pasta Salad, 125

Parmesan Fingers, 113
Parmesan Knots and Rings, 58
Parmesan Potato Skins, 194
Party Cranberry Punch, 183
Party Popcorn Cake, 42
Pasta Timbales, M64
Pasta With Wild-Mushroom Sauce, 94
Pastillage, 242
Patchwork-Quilt Rice, 177
Peanut Sauce, 77
Pear-Cranberry Conserve, 192
Pear Kuchen, 19
Pear-Raspberry Tarts, 92
Pear-Stuffed Roast Pork, 18
Pecan Meringue Torte, 37
Pepper-Baked Brie, 17
Perfect Chocolate Cake, 156
Perfect Chocolate Mousse, 13
Pfeffernuesse, 230
Pie Shell, 194

Pineapple-Banana Torte, 25
Pineapple Bombe, 37
Pineapple-Honey-Glazed Ribs, M149
Pineapple-Lemon Punch, 199
Pirouette Cookie Tree, 248
Pistachio Baklava, 34
Pistachio Wreaths, 228
Plum-Glazed Hens, M114
Poppy-Seed Thumbprints, 227
Pork Satay With Spicy Peanut Dipping Sauce, 93
Potato-and-Onion Fans, 110
Potatoes Italiano, 178
Praline Cream-Puff Ring, 35
Praline-Topped Sweet Potatoes, 192
Prime Rib à l'Orange, 216
Pumpkin-Apricot Chiffon Pie, 13

Quick and Thin Pizza Dough, 63
Quick Chicken Casserole With Rice and Vegetables, 23
Quick Chicken Tacos, M130
Quick Lasagna, 23
Quick Puff Pastry, 40

Raspberry-Grilled Hens, 126
Raspberry-Oatmeal Bars, M130
Raspberry Tarts, 126
Ratatouille Pizza, 63
Ratatouille Quiche, 163
Red-Glazed Chicken, 77
Refrigerator Potato Rolls, 160
Risotto With Mushrooms, 91
Roast Capon With Fruited Rice, 72
Roasted Capon With Chestnut Stuffing, 196
Roasted Corn Pudding, 107
Roasted Duck With Orange-Berry Relish, 25
Roasted Game Hens With Harvest Vegetables, 204
Roasted-Pepper Mini-Pizzas, 63
Roast Turkey With Three-Bread Stuffing, 192
Royal Fruit Delight, 92
Royal Icing, 234, 247
Russian Potato Salad, 138

Sacher Torte, M45
Salmon-Noodle Bake, M97
Santa's Dream House, 232
Sausage-Vegetable Medley, 106
Sautéed Apples With Warm Custard, 93
Sautéed Escarole and Beans, 59
Savory Artichoke Cheesecake, 194
Savory Sweet-Potato Salad, 140
Seafood-Filled Dutch Babies, 15
Seafood-Stuffed Grilled Snapper, 110
Seaside Pasta Salad, 111
Seasoned Breadsticks, 60
Sesame Asparagus, 129
Sherried Zucchini Bisque, M207
Shrimp-and-Fruit Mélange, 127
Shrimp and Leek Tarts, 218
Silver and Gold Fruitcake, 221
Silver-Onion Soup, 193
Skillet Coleslaw, 129
Sleigh Scene, 240
Smoked-Oyster Filling, 14
Snowflakes, 226
Soft-Shell Crabs With Garlic-Tomato Butter, 110
Sour-Cream Apple Pie, 128
Spaghetti Pie, M65
Special Vinaigrette, 142
Spit-Roasted Beef Tenderloin, 111
Springerle, 231
Squash Bisque, M26
Stir-Fried Squash, 92
Strawberries en Chemise, M88
Strawberry Parfaits, 42
Strawberry-Pineapple Bavarian, 78
Stuffed Chicken Turnovers, 109
Sugared Orange Peel, 38
Sugar-Syrup Glass, 247
Summer-Fruit Cheesecake, 124
Sweet 'n' Sour Shrimp, 20
Szechwan Noodle Toss, 142

Taco Salad in Tortilla Baskets, 139
Tangy Spinach Salad, 88
Tarragon Chicken-Salad Loaf, M81
Teriyaki Wings, 198
Texas-Style Ribs, 109
Three-Bean Bake, 111
Three-Cheese Broccoli Pizza, 63
Three-Cheese Lasagna, M65
Three-Fruit Crisp, 42
Three-Vegetable Terrine With Roasted-Pepper Sauce, 176
Tipsy French Toast, 125
Tirami Su, 58
Tomato-Basil Toasts, 55
Tomatoes Fontina, 178
Tomato Sauce, 158
Tonnato-Stuffed Tomatoes, 138
Tortellini in Brodo, 58
Tortellini Primavera, 140
Tortilla Roll-Ups, 113
Town House, 236
Triple-Chocolate Cake, 36
Tropical-Fruit Sorbet, 147
Truffle Wreath, 249
Turkey Breast Florentine With Citrus-Glazed Carrots, 215
Turkey-Chili Potato Topper, M96

Ultimate Cheesecake, The, 157
Upside-Down Pizza, 22

Veal Parmigiana, 158
Veal Piccata, 92
Vegetable Lasagna, M98
Vegetable Stir-Fry on Squash Lo Mein, 181
Viennese Pouf, 39

Warm Apricot-Cheese Strudel, 15
Warm Chicken Salad, 77
Warm Cucumber Toss, 17
Warm Shrimp Salad, 94
Warm Swordfish Salade Niçoise, 108
Warm Turkey Oriental, 166
Watermelon Cake, 144
White-Chocolate Parfaits, M91
White Icing Glaze, 12
Wild-Rice Yorkshire Pudding, 217
Witchy Pumpkin Cakes, 183
Wrapped Grilled Shrimp, 90
Wurst-and-Potato Supper, M99

Yogurt-Topped Fruit Mélange, 94

Zesty Avocado Dip, 90
Zippy Cheddar Crisps, 17
Ziti-Zucchini Timbale, 176
Zucchini With Veal-and-Cheese Filling, 59
Zuppa Inglese, 217